Causing A Stir

fabulous food to get people talking

Cover and section pages designed by
duo communication design, inc.

Junior League of Dayton, Ohio, Inc.
26 Brown Street
Dayton, Ohio 45402
Phone: (937)222-5541
Fax: (937)222-8646
E-mail: jldohio@earthlink.net
Website: jldohio.com

First Printing   November 2000   10,000 copies
Second Printing   October 2001   10,000 copies

ISBN 0-9603082-2-9

Mission Statement

The Junior League of Dayton, Ohio, Inc. is an organization of women committed to promoting voluntarism, developing the potential of women, and improving communities through the effective action and leadership of trained volunteers. Its purpose is exclusively educational and charitable.

Printed in the USA by

The Wimmer Companies
Memphis
1-800-548-2537

Table of Contents

Symbols by recipe titles represent:

☆ Celebrity Recipe

❄ Freezes Well

✒ Light & Healthy

 "Discover Dayton" Favorite Recipe

Foreword

A lot has changed since 1979, when the Junior League of Dayton, Ohio, Inc. published their cookbook, *Discover Dayton*—cooking styles, food trends, the Junior League's community projects, and Dayton itself.

But a lot has remained the same. Much of what was important to us then is just as important now—the Junior League's commitment to the community, Dayton's reputation as the City of Neighbors, and celebrating with family and friends!

Causing A Stir… Fabulous Food to Get People Talking! seeks to complement the cooking style of today with an emphasis on simple, yet elegant, food. Our thoughts are with the busy person whose lifestyle reflects graceful living, stylish entertaining and family focus, but who cannot afford to spend all day in the kitchen. *Causing A Stir's* unique offering of recipes, menu suggestions and tips will become a staple on your kitchen counter. You'll wonder how you ever lived without it.

The recipes represent a tempting array of flavors and styles… from comfort food like *Discover Dayton's* tried and true Egg, Sausage and Cheese Casserole or Caramel Apple Bread Pudding, to fresh new favorites like Black Bean & Mango Salsa, Sweet Potato Salad with Rosemary-Honey Vinaigrette or Thai Lemon Beef.

A Reason to Celebrate, our menus and ideas section, will ease your way, whether you're trying to make dinner in 30 minutes or less, or produce an elegant affair. Expand your entertainment options with our seasonal menus, accompanying wine selections and party planning hints.

Loads of helpful tips will allow you to make the most of the time you have. The Working Ahead comments for the recipe will enable you to better manage your timetable. Our selection of Special Deliveries and Food Gift Items provide a quick, delicious reference for that special friend or neighbor. Our Family Mealtime ideas will make memorable meals an everyday pleasure. We have dedicated a whole section to our Kids, featuring lots of fun food and creative party plans, from the first activity to the party favors!

The recipes only tell part of the story of what makes *Causing A Stir* so special. Each recipe section is highlighted by original artwork reflective of Dayton's history and character. The accompanying stories and notes on each page throughout the cookbook share the spirit of the place we call home, and the people who make it special.

The proceeds realized from the sale of *Causing A Stir* will be returned to the community through projects of the Junior League of Dayton, Ohio, Inc.

Mix it all together…we are definitely *Causing A Stir* in Dayton!

RECIPE SECTION CHAIRS
Carrie Craig
Kristin Evans
Jennifer Kane
Carrie McHenry
Kellie Rhodes
Margot Varley
Jane Winch

♦ ♦ ♦

TESTING COMMITTEE
Carla McKelvey, Assistant Chair
Kim Allen
Anita Brothers
Lynn Collins
Jennifer Kane
Amy Miller
Teri Macaulay
Carole Schram
Laura Scofield
Nancy Taylor
Julie Teeters

♦ ♦ ♦

EDITORIAL AND
PROOFREADING COMMITTEE
Angela Cothren
Kelly Huntington
Jan Kurdin
Cammi Mulligan
Jennifer Pickard
Kristin Woodward

♦ ♦ ♦

PUBLIC RELATIONS/
MARKETING COMMITTEE
Melissa Armstrong
Patti Blessing
Darla Flanders
Kelly Huntington
Terri Jacks
Clara Legeay
Teri Macaulay
Laura Scofield
Irene Wong

Herb and Spice Substitutions

Herbs and spices each have their own flavor and aroma. The following substitutions are recommended only for emergencies, as they may slightly affect the flavor of the recipe.

1 tablespoon fresh herbs	=	1 teaspoon dried herbs
1 teaspoon allspice	=	1 teaspoon equal parts cinnamon, nutmeg and cloves
1 teaspoon basil	=	1 teaspoon oregano
1 teaspoon caraway	=	1 teaspoon anise
1 teaspoon cayenne	=	1 teaspoon chili peppers
1 teaspoon chervil	=	1 teaspoon parsley or tarragon
1 teaspoon fennel	=	1 teaspoon anise or tarragon
1 tablespoon mustard	=	1 teaspoon dried mustard
1 teaspoon nutmeg	=	1 teaspoon mace
1 small fresh onion	=	1 tablespoon dehydrated minced onion
1 medium fresh onion	=	1 tablespoon onion powder
1 teaspoon oregano	=	1 teaspoon marjoram
1 teaspoon sage	=	1 teaspoon thyme
dash cayenne or red pepper	=	few drops hot pepper sauce

Measurement Equivalents

Liquid Measures

1 gallon	=		= 8 pints	=	16 cups	=	128 fluid ounces
½ gallon	=		= 4 pints	=	8 cups	=	64 fluid ounces
¼ gallon	=		= 2 pints	=	4 cups	=	32 fluid ounces
		½ quart = 1 pint		=	2 cups	=	16 fluid ounces
		¼ quart = ½ pint		=	1 cup	=	8 fluid ounces

Dry Measures

1 cup	=	8 fluid ounces	=	16 tablespoons	=	48 teaspoons
¾ cup	=	6 fluid ounces	=	12 tablespoons	=	36 teaspoons
⅔ cup	=	5⅓ fluid ounces	=	10⅔ tablespoons	=	32 teaspoons
½ cup	=	4 fluid ounces	=	8 tablespoons	=	24 teaspoons
⅓ cup	=	2⅔ fluid ounces	=	5⅓ tablespoons	=	16 teaspoons
¼ cup	=	2 fluid ounces	=	4 tablespoons	=	12 teaspoons
⅛ cup	=	1 fluid ounce	=	2 tablespoons	=	6 teaspoons
				1 tablespoon	=	3 teaspoons

A Reason to Celebrate

MENUS & IDEAS

Welcome To
Dayton, Ohio

City of Neighbors

DAYTON COMMUNITY

A REASON TO CELEBRATE

Creative, inventive and innovative are words that have described Dayton since the days of Orville and Wilbur Wright. One need only glance through the list of patents issued here, from the airplane and movie projector to the pop-top can and ink jet printer, to understand why we once held the nickname, "Tinkertown." This inspirational past has fostered today's multidimensional, thriving business community, boasting high-tech, manufacturing and service activity.

Dayton's renowned arts community continues to flourish, reflecting the vitality and diversity of its citizens. Whether they prefer classical ballet or cutting-edge modern dance, Dayton locals rejoice in their options. They may enjoy a vintage work of art, or delight in the creations of schoolchildren. From opera to folk music, comedy to Shakespearean tragedy, Dayton has something for everyone.

While Dayton celebrates its wondrously inventive past, it anticipates a bright future. As downtown Dayton continues to evolve, Dragons baseball at beautiful Fifth Third field, the RiverScape Project, and the development of the Schuster Performing Arts Center offer us more opportunities to celebrate together.

Dayton abounds in amenities often enjoyed only in larger cities, yet its strength is found in the collective gifts of its citizens. It is people that make this "City of Neighbors" a special place to work and live.

DALE HUFFMAN celebrates his hometown in his 1998 book, *Dayton: The Cradle of Creativity:* "Dayton is known for a great deal more than its patents. The community's 'winning spirit' has generated innumerable accolades for local performing arts groups and has nurtured countless celebrities in the entertainment, literary, and sports worlds. It even earned the city the chance to host the momentous Dayton Peace Accords, as well as three consecutive National Folk Festivals."

January

⁙

NEW YEAR'S EVE MARTINI PARTY

"A festive cocktail party to ring in the new year."

Metropolitan Martinis (p. 70)

Cocktails from the Open Bar (see guidelines)

Divine Caviar (p. 53) with Crostini Crackers

Chicken Satay with Spicy Peanut Sauce (p. 38)

Phyllo with Crab and Brie (p. 37)

Spinach Bites (p. 49) with Liz's Hot Mustard Sauce (p. 97)

Mixed Nuts and Olives

Baby BLTs (p. 44)

Meatballs with Sweet and Sour Sauce (p. 40)

Mushroom Tarts (p. 45)

Tasha's Dip (p. 62) with Baby Carrots and Asparagus

Chocolate Almond Toffee Bark (p. 285)

OPEN BAR FOR 30 TO 40 PEOPLE

1 Bottle Scotch	3 Quarts Club Soda
2 Bottles Gin	3 Quarts Tonic
3 Bottles Vodka	1 Quart Ginger Ale
1 Bottle Light Rum	1 Quart Cola
1 Bottle Bourbon	3 Quarts Sparking Water
1 Bottle Vermouth	5 Bags Ice
2 Quarts Orange Juice	6 Limes and 3 Lemons
1 Quart Cranberry Juice	2 Jars Olives
6 Bottles Chardonnay; 4 Bottles Cabernet Sauvignon Wine	1-2 Cases Beer
10 Bottles Champagne	
Cocktail Napkins	1 Corkscrew/Bottle Opener
1 Stirrer	Containers for Holding Ice
1 Paring Knife	1 Jigger
1 Cocktail Shaker	1 Bartender

CHINESE NEW YEAR CELEBRATION

"A beautiful and unique way to celebrate the new year."

Celebration Punch (p. 63)

Shrimp Curry Dip (p. 53) with Rice Crackers

Almond Orange Garden Salad (p. 130)

Sesame-Garlic Grilled Pork Tenderloin (p. 241)

Noodles with Curried Stir-Fried Vegetables (p. 186)

Gingersnaps (p. 277) with Mango Sorbet

1997 Kunde Estate Winery Red Zinfandel

1996-97 Au Bon Climat 'Isabelle' Pinot Noir

1993 Shafer Vineyards Merlot

SUPER BOWL PARTY WITH FRIENDS

*"Even the hostess will have time to enjoy
the game with this crowd-pleasing menu."*

Lager Beer

Sweet and Sour Chicken Wings (p. 39)

Asiago Cheese Dip (p. 51) with Crackers

Assorted Crudités

BBQ Beef Sandwiches (p. 250)

Cilantro Cole Slaw (p. 126)

Grandma Mo's Amazing Almond Sheet Cake (p. 266)
with Chocolate Ice Cream

1997 Ravenswood Sonoma Valley Cooke Red Zinfandel

1996 Sterling Vineyards Merlot

February

✿ ✿ ✿

BE MY VALENTINE DINNER FOR TWO

"A romantic palate pleaser."

Frozen Baci (p. 66)

French Mushroom Soup (p. 105)

Dried Cherries and Gorgonzola Salad (p. 125)

Green Beans with Shallot Butter (p. 155)

Saucy Sole (p. 194)

Wild Rice Pilaf

Brownie Torte (p. 265) with Raspberry Sorbet
(use heart-shaped cookie cutter for the brownies)

1996-98 Grgich Hills Chardonnay

1997-98 Kenwood Vineyards Sauvignon Blanc

MARDI GRAS MIDWESTERN STYLE DINNER

"Bring out your beads and enjoy this festive meal with friends."

Pale Shrimp Zinged with Lemon and Capers (p. 54)

Mixed Greens with Francesca's Salad Dressing (p. 97)

Green Beans with Toasted Pecans and Blue Cheese (p. 156)

Blackened Rib-Eye Steaks

Baked Bread Casserole with Wild Mushrooms and Onions (p. 159)

Rum Cake (p. 263) or Purchased King Cake

1996 Turley Wine Cellars Hayne Vineyard Red Zinfandel

1997 Rosenblum Cellars Samsel Vineyard Red Zinfandel

COME IN FROM THE COLD DINNER

"An elegant and delicious escape from winter's cold grasp."

Swiss Fondue (p. 50) with Baguette Pieces

Mixed Greens with Balsamic Vinaigrette

Provençal Roasted Tomatoes (p. 166)

Poulet Sauté Provençal (p. 211)

Potato Polpettes (p. 161)

Warm Chocolate Tarts (p. 260)

Decaffeinated Cappuccinos

1996 Ridge Vineyards Geyserville Red Zinfandel

1995-96 Chateau Du Tertre Red Bordeaux

1997-98 Bandol Rose

March

❦ ❦ ❦

FLYER FEVER FEAST WITH FRIENDS

*"Bring together University of Dayton fans to share in
March Madness and munchies."*

Pilsner Beer

Baby Carrots, Cucumbers and Cherry Tomatoes with Your Favorite Dip

Make-Ahead Caesar Salad (p. 125)

Ohio-Style Chili and Spaghetti (p. 117)

Heavenly Cornbread (p. 82)

Best Easy Chocolate Bundt Cake (p. 269) with Vanilla Ice Cream

COME SEE THE DAFFODILS DINNER

*"Invite your friends over to enjoy your newest
blooms and a spring-fresh meal."*

"That Junior League Pesto Mold" (p. 60) with Crackers

Here Comes the Sun Salad (p. 127)

Zucchini Imperial (p. 165)

Rosemary Pork Tenderloin (p. 242)

Roasted New Potatoes

Shortcakes with Strawberries and Whipped Cream (p. 264)

1995 Cline Cellars Big Break Red Zinfandel

1993 Stag's Leap Vineyards SLV Cabernet Sauvignon

1995 Martinelli Vineyard Russian River Valley Pinot Noir

Saint Patty's Day Supper with Family

"Ey, your families will love this!"

Code Blue Dip (p. 51) with Crackers

Pot O' Gold Dinner (p. 232)

Steamed Broccoli

Crusty Peasant Bread

Moist Oatmeal Cookies (p. 276) with "End of the Rainbow" Sherbet

Pinky's Homemade Irish Cream (p. 67) and Coffee

1993, 1996 Dunn Vineyards Cabernet Sauvignon

1997 Forman Vineyard Merlot

1996 Storybrook Mountain Vineyards Red Zinfandel

April

❧ ❧ ❧

EASTER EGG HUNT AND BUFFET

"Enjoy all of the fun of the hunt with a delightful meal to follow."

Mimi's Bloody Mary Mix (p. 69)

Frozen Cappuccinos (p. 68)

Orange Juice

Mushroom Tarts (p. 45)

Lemon Rice with Pine Nuts (p. 162)

Easter Lamb (p. 247)

Buttermint Carrots (p. 151)

Elsie's Biscuits (p. 82) with Spiral Sliced Baked Ham

Mango Chutney and Honey Mustard

Mimi's Carrot Cake (p. 268)

1995 Chateau Pichon Longueville Comtesse De Lalande

1996 Chateau Ducru Beaucaillou

1993 Caymus Vineyards Cabernet Sauvignon

Inaugurate the Grill Cookout

*"Make sure you fill the propane tank before your
guests arrive for this mouth-watering meal."*

Grilled Shrimp Skewers (p. 205)

Mixed Greens with Nana's French Dressing (p. 98)

Sicilian Carrots (p. 152)

Grilled Swordfish with Tomato Feta Relish (p. 191)

Couscous topped with Olive Oil and Fresh Herbs

Grilled Garlic Bread

Mocha Latte Decadence (p. 257)

1996 Beaulieu Vineyards Signet Collection Red Zinfandel

1995 Louis Jadot Montrachet

Town Hall Tea Party Luncheon

*"Enjoy the Junior League of Dayton's current trend-setting
speaker followed by a ladies luncheon to share what you learned."*

Lemon Shandies (p. 67)

Mint Tea Punch (p. 64)

Mixed Fresh Fruit Salad

Jane's Famous Gazpacho (p. 107)

Seafood Quiche (p. 77)

Tarragon Egg Salad (p. 145) Sandwich Fingers

Blackberry Mini-Tarts (p. 271)

Brown Sugar Pecan Shortbread Cookies (p. 276)

1998 Alderbrook Cellars Chardonnay Dorothy's Vineyard

1997 Domaine Leflaive Puligny Montrachet Les Pucelles

May

❦ ❦ ❦

CINQO DE MAYO SUPPER

"A festive feast from South of the Border."

White Sangría (p. 65)

Black Bean and Mango Salsa (p. 100) with Tortilla Chips

Fajitas filled with Pollo Asado (p. 215)

Mexicana Rice (p. 161)

Vanilla Ice Cream with Rich Caramel Sauce (p. 282) and Fresh Blackberries

1997 Howell Mountain Vineyards Red Zinfandel

1994 Ch. Montelena Cabernet Sauvignon

BABIES TO BRIDES SHOWER LUNCHEON

"Here's the menu you've been in search of for baby and wedding showers!"

Mint Tea Punch (p. 64)

Parmesan Bread Twists (p. 52)

Grilled Chicken with Lemon Chicken Marinade (p. 99) served over
Asparagus, Spinach, Pasta, and Cashew Salad (p. 133)

Zillions of Zucchini Bread (p. 85)

Poppyseed Muffins

Mrs. Huffman's Legendary Lemon Soufflé (p. 255)

1997-98 Cakebread Cellars Chardonnay

1997 Landmark Vineyards Damaris Reserve Chardonnay

Special Occasion Spring Brunch

"This menu is terrific for any special family event
— christenings, engagements, the day-after-the-wedding brunch, etc."

Mimosas

Zippy Punch (p. 63)

Fresh Roasted Coffee

Hot Curried Fruit (p. 154) with Spiral Sliced Baked Ham

Easy Baked Spinach, Eggs and Cheese (p. 73)

Mary's Strawberry and Poppyseed Salad (p. 131)

Braided Breakfast Danish (p. 88)

Caramelized Coconut Coffee Cake (p. 86)

1995 Roederer Estate Brut Champagne

June

❦ ❦ ❦

GRADUATION PARTY ON THE DECK

"Graduates and their friends of all ages will love this meal!"

Celebration Punch (p. 63)
Spicy Black Bean and Corn Salsa (p. 100) with Blue Corn Tortilla Chips
Blueberry, Orange and Cherry Salad (p. 132)
Sliced Pollo Asado (p. 215) served over Mexican Pasta (p. 180)
Century-Style Chocolate Sheet Cake (p. 267) and Butterscotch Ice Cream
1995 Hidden Cellars Winery Old Vine Red Zinfandel

CARIBBEAN COOKOUT

"Add some salsa music to enjoy an unforgettable evening, island style."

Mango Daiquiris (p. 66)
Tomato, Garlic, Cilantro Salsa (p. 99) and
Guadalajara Guacamole (p. 58) with Tortilla Chips
Brazilian Black Beans (p. 150)
Jerk Chicken (p. 213)
Long Grain White Rice Steamed with Pinch of Saffron and Turmeric
Bananas Caribbean (p. 260)
1997 Gallo Sonoma Red Zinfandel Barelli Creek

FATHER'S DAY BREAKFAST IN BED

"Make Dad's day with this tasty breakfast menu."

Fresh-Squeezed Orange Juice
Dad's Favorite Waffles (p. 73) with Warm Maple Syrup
Sara Jane's Baked Apples (p. 147)
Country Sausage Links
Coffee
Veuve Clicquot Brut Champagne Non Vintage

July

❀ ❀ ❀

CITY OF NEIGHBORS COOKOUT

"Invite some neighbors over for burgers and all the fixings!"

Pale Ale Beer and Soft Drinks
Sun-Dried Tomato and Herbed Goat Cheese Spread (p. 57) with Crackers
Grandma Ruby's Garlic Sweet Pickles (p. 101)
Southwestern Baked Beans (p. 149)
Cajun Hamburgers (p. 249)
Zesty Corn and Red Pepper Salad (p. 142)
Crunch Crowned Brownies (p. 300)

DOWN HOME COUNTRY SUPPER

"Y'all come for a great get-together!"

Raspberry Beer
Warm Vidalia Onion Dip (p. 50) with Pita Chips
Heavenly Cornbread (p. 82)
Zucchini Casserole (p. 168)
Devin's Best Baby Back Ribs (p. 246)
Sweet Potato Salad with Rosemary-Honey Vinaigrette (p. 141)
Fresh Peach Crisp (p. 275)
1998 Ridge Vineyards Lytton Springs Red Zinfandel

STAR-SPANGLED PICNIC SPREAD

"An all-American spread for your favorite Doodle Dandies."

Fresh-Squeezed Lemonade
Pretzel Sticks with Liz's Hot Mustard Sauce (p. 97)
Fried or Roasted Chicken
Marinated New Red Potato Salad (p. 140)
Fruit Salad
Lemon Blueberry Pie (p. 272)
1997 Chalone Vineyard Chalone Chardonnay
1996 Volker Eisele Cabernet Sauvignon

August

☾ ☾ ☾

WEGERZYN FARMERS' MARKET FEAST

"Have fun devouring your morning's purchases with this vegetarian meal."

Bellini (p. 64)

"That Junior League Pesto Mold" (p. 60) with Crackers

Stuffed Red Peppers (p. 160)

Vivid Summer Vegetables (p. 167)

Leafy Green Salad with Red Wine Vinaigrette (p. 98)

60-Minute Pesto Bread (p. 79)

Mixed Berry Crumble (p. 274)

1997 Kistler Vineyards Hudson Vineyard Chardonnay

HAPPY HOUR FIESTA BEFORE
THE FRAZE PAVILION CONCERT

"Your guests will love these cocktail hour goodies before the show."

Fru-Fru Swirlies (p. 69)

Mexican Beer with Fresh Lime

Spicy Peel and Eat Shrimp (p. 204)

Black Bean and Goat Cheese Quesadillas with Peach Mango Salsa (p. 48)

Guadalajara Guacamole (p. 58) with Blue Corn Tortilla Chips

1997 Chateau St. Jean Robert Young Vineyard Chardonnay

Sunset Picnic at Carillon Park

"A gorgeous meal for a gorgeous venue."

Southern Sweet Tea with a Twist (p. 69)

Croutons à la Tapenade (p. 55)

Dilly Bean Salad (p. 144)

Fresh Tomato Tart (p. 56)

Spring Island Couscous Salad (p. 136)

K's Crab Cakes with Homemade Tartar Sauce (p. 201)

Hawthorn Hill Coconut Macaroons (p. 275)

1997 Domaine Zind Humbrecht Gewurztraminer Goldert
(Alsatian White Wine)

1997 Domaine Bernard Moreau Chassagne Montrachet

1997 Ferrari-Carano Winery Chardonnay

September

❦ ❦ ❦

1ST DAY OF SCHOOL CELEBRATION LUNCH FOR MOMS

*"Moms will love this excuse to celebrate having a bit of free time
for themselves after a hectic summer schedule."*

Champagne Americana (p. 65)

Spicy Cheese Crisps (p. 44)

Lemon Tarragon Chicken Salad with Grapes (p. 137)
served over a bed of Leafy Greens

Almond Crescent Rolls (p. 89)

Raspberry Pear Tart (p. 271)

1997 Long Vineyards Chardonnay

1997 Franciscan Oakville Estate Cuvee Sauvage

HOMECOMING TAILGATE

"Root for the home team and enjoy this fall feast at half time."

Hot Spiced Cider (p. 68)

Apple and Gruyère Spread (p. 58) with Sliced Granny Smiths
and Wheat Crackers

Ham and Cheese Tailgate Sandwiches (p. 254)

Dilly Bean Salad (p. 144)

Chips and Pretzels

Grandma Ruby's Garlic Sweet Pickles (p. 101)

Classic Pumpkin Bars (p. 283)

Ohio Buckeyes (p. 285)

1998 Renwood Chardonnay

AFTER THE HIKE OUTDOOR LUNCH

"Please your weary troops with this mouth-watering picnic."

Soft Drinks and Bottled Waters

Pita Chips and Hummus Dip

Greek Peasant Salad (p. 124)

Warm Pastrami Panino (p. 251)

Lemon Pasta Salad (p. 135)

Walnut Butter Cookies (p. 277)

1995 Pahlmeyer Merlot

1996-97 Badia de Coltibuono Chianti Reserve

October

❦ ❦ ❦

Halloween Hayride and Home Cookin'

"Ghosts and goblins of all ages will howl with delight."

Apple Cider

Monster Mouths (p. 303)

Carrot Sticks with Dip

Tin Foil Hamburgers (p. 292)

Hash Brown Potato Casserole (p. 292)

Caramel Popcorn (p. 294)

Spooky Ghost Cookies (p. 303)

Oktoberfest Gathering

"Just add some accordions for authenticity!"

German Lager Beer

Reuben Dip (p. 39) on Party Rye Slices

Brockman's Brew Brats (p. 253) on Bakery Fresh Buns

Braised Red Cabbage and Apples (p. 151)

German-Style Potato Salad

Apple Pie with Walnut Streusel (p. 273)

Any of many 1997 Rieslings that are dry, too many to list

Pasta and Wine Festival

"A sampling menu for your pasta-loving friends."

Croutons à la Tapenade (p. 55)

Cheese Platter with Artisan Breads

Spinach Salad with Basil Dressing (p. 123)

Penne with Gorgonzola and Tomatoes (p. 176)

Fettuccine with Wild Mushrooms (p. 183)

Gemelli with Chicken and White Wine Cream Sauce (p. 173)

Tiramisu

1995 Tignanello

1995 Ruffino Chianti Classico Riserva

1996 Clos Du Val Semillon or Chardonnay

November

666

AUTUMN AT TABLE

"An elegant meal for the fall season."

Prosciutto Pinwheels (p. 42)

Harvest Squash Soup (p. 103)

Watercress Salad with Cranberries and Pecans (p. 128)

Stuffed Pork Tenderloin with Shallots (p. 240)

Southern Sweet Potato Soufflé (p. 165)

Green Beans with Shallot Butter (p. 155)

Baked Bread Casserole with Wild Mushrooms and Onions (p. 159)

Caramel Apple Bread Pudding (p. 256)

1996 Rabbit Ridge Red Zinfandel

1997 Sokol Blesser Pinot Noir

RUSTIC ITALIAN DINNER

"A taste of the Tuscan countryside."

Tomato, Bacon and Basil Crostini (p. 43)

Baby Greens tossed with Francesca's Salad Dressing (p. 97)

Escarole, Sausage and White Bean Stew (p. 115)

Overnight Focaccia (p. 80)

Double Chocolate Walnut Biscotti (p. 280)

Cappuccinos

1997 Banfi Brunello Di Montalcino

1997 Amadore Pinot Grigio

Mediterranean Tasting Menu

*"Tasting menus are appearing in restaurants around the country~
try this trend at home! This menu is designed for a crowd: guests have little
tastes of each course for a truly memorable evening. It's also fun
to try different wines with each course."*

Ciabatta Napoli (p. 47)

Herbed Mussels Normande (p. 35)

1997 Pouilly Fuisse Louis Latour

Tomato and Orzo Fennel Soup (p. 108)

Mediterranean Lentils and Roasted Red Peppers
with Lemon Vinaigrette (p. 157)

Gnocchi with Spinach (p. 181)

1997-98 Far Niente Chardonnay

Grilled Lamb Chops

1995 Solaia

Spanakopeta (p. 164)

Peperonata (p. 158)

Almond Fruit Tart (p. 270) in Miniature

Walnut Butter Cookies (p. 277)

1995 Elk Cove Late Harvest Riesling

1991 Fonseca Guimareans Port or LBV

**NOTE: You may want to have guests bring a dish with them, or host the
party with some friends to cut down on the work. Remember to make the
portions such that each guest eats about one-fourth the amount of a serving
for each dish.*

December

❦ ❦ ❦

COCKTAILS AND CAROLING

*"Warm up with these holiday hors d'ouevres
before spreading good cheer from door to door."*

Classic Eggnog (p. 70)

Smoked Salmon on Baguette Toasts (p. 35)

English Cucumber Slices and Red Bell Pepper Strips with Tasha's Dip (p. 62)

Creamed Cheeses with Brandied Cranberries (p. 61)

Mushroom Tarts (p. 45)

Sliced Smoked Turkey on Stephanie's Sweet Potato Biscuits (p. 83)
with Cranberry Sauce, Mustards and Herbed Mayonnaise

Peppermint Crunch Bark (p. 286)

1996 Kenwood Merlot

1997 Cakebread Chardonnay

HOLIDAY MAGIC DESSERT BUFFET

"Visions of sugarplums will dance in your head!"

Pinky's Homemade Irish Cream (p. 67)

Raspberry Pear Tart (p. 271)

Pecan Torte (p. 263)

Amaretto Irish Cream Cheesecake (p. 262)

Fruit Platter with Hot Fudge Sauce (p. 286) for Dipping

Mocha Truffles (p. 281) or Chocolate-Covered Caramels (p. 284)

1995 Ch. Suidaraut (Sauternes) White Wine

1993 Grgich Hills Late Harvest Riesling

Any 1985 or older vintage Port

1983 Graham's, Dow's or Warre's

Graham's LBV Late Bottle Vintage

YULETIDE BRUNCH

"A bountiful spread for the crowd on Christmas morn."

Juices, Coffee, Mimi's Bloody Mary Mix (p. 69)

Smoked Salmon Platter with Tomatoes, Capers, Red Onions,
Cream Cheese, and Bagels

Egg, Sausage and Cheese Casserole (p. 71)

Fresh Fruit Platter

Comfort Corn Pudding (p. 152)

Roasted Beet and Walnut Salad (p. 145)

Banana Cream Chocolate Chip Muffins (p. 94)

Chocolate Caramel Pecan Cheesecake (p. 261)

1990 Laurent Perrier Champagne

1985 Krug Brut Champagne

Choosing a Wine and Different Grapes

— Keith Browning, Vins Extraordinaire

Choosing wines is not difficult, but many people struggle because of common misperceptions about how to pair wine with food. Added to this dilemma is the fact that some meals are simply difficult to pair with a wine because of the taste, texture and resulting flavors from a specific food.

When preparing a dish that calls for wine, use the wine you are planning to drink with the meal. It is sure to go well. When wine has been opened and then re-corked or closed for a couple of days, don't use it in your recipe. The change in the wine will be noticeable and can affect the flavor of the dish.

Throughout this book, I have selected many different types of white and red wines to go with the various meals. Grapes used to make white wines are Chardonnay, Pinot Blanc, Pinot Gris, Riesling, Muscat, Chenin Blanc, Muscadet, Semillon, Pinot Grigio, and Sauvignon Blanc. When I list Chardonnay, I am speaking specifically of California Chardonnay, although the Chardonnay grape is also the predominant grape used to make White Burgundy and Bordeaux wines. California and Washington have produced several excellent vintages, and you can easily locate a wide variety of wines to try.

Likewise, the Cabernet Sauvignon, Pinot Noir and Merlot grapes I've listed refer to U.S. wine producers. Red Bordeaux wines are made with 100 percent Cabernet Sauvignon or Merlot, or a blend of these grapes with touches of Cabernet Franc. Red Burgundy wines are almost exclusively made with the Pinot Noir grape. You can insert either the Bordeaux or Burgundy in place of these grape varieties.

Pinot Noir wines tend to go with a wide variety of foods, although the consistency is not as good as the other grapes. I find Pinot Noir wines to be lighter, with good fruit. Merlot wines tend to be fuller wines with lots of fruit, the very best showing depth, some body structure and lighter tannins. Red Zinfandel wines are an interesting mix between a Merlot and Cabernet Sauvignon. They have plenty of fruit and almost all have some spiciness that make them perfect with everything from chicken to beef to hearty fish, like salmon or swordfish. The boldest and heartiest red wines are Cabernet Sauvignon. They tend to be more tannic (drier, thicker) and aged longer than other wines.

A White Zinfandel is a blending of white wine grapes, such as Chardonnay, with the skins and stems of a red wine grape, most predominantly the Red Zinfandel grape. Many people like White Zinfandel or blush wines. I didn't select any for these meals, primarily because I think they are a better apéritif.

The most important fact to remember about wines is to try many, and then drink what you like. There are no rules. Some people like white wines; some prefer reds. And a selected wine will taste different from one palette to the next. Don't be afraid to try new wines with these dishes. It's just like cooking. Sometimes you have to try different ingredients, and when you find the right combination it really can make a great meal. Bon Appetit!

Wine and Pasta

Pastas with light sauces and cream sauces typically go best with white wines, such as Sauvignon Blanc, Pinot Grigio, Alsatian, Chablis, or Chardonnay (lightest to heaviest). As I mentioned earlier, if your recipe calls for wine, use the wine you are planning to serve with the meal.

Many people prefer red wines with heartier or tomato-based sauces, although many light pastas will also stand up to a red wine. Try a Red Zinfandel, a Merlot, or possibly a Chardonnay or a bolder white wine, such as a White Burgundy.

Italian red wines, such as Chianti, Barolo and Brunello, will certainly go well with the pasta and meat dishes. I also believe Red Zinfandel, Pinot Noir and Merlot will add nicely to any of the pasta and meat dishes.

Wine and Chicken

I don't buy into the white meat-white wines combination. I think chicken can easily stand up to red wine, and have listed both a white and red to give an option for each of the recipes. Red wines can give a great balance to a meal, particularly if the dish is prepared in a tomato sauce or has many spices.

Remember to search out Chianti Classico Riserva for the highest quality Chiantis. They really do make a difference. Add a highlight to your menu by working with your wine shop to find wines that are aged properly.

Wine and Meats

I think all red wines go better with meat dishes, although you could pair a hearty White Burgundy with the pork dishes, and even with the veal dishes that feature light sauces. The most popular are Cabernet Sauvignon, Merlot, Red Zinfandel, Pinot Noir and blended red wines, called meritage in the U.S.

Wine and Fish

Fish has always created a dilemma for wine lovers. Many believe fish should be served with white wines, although I have found many fish dishes that stand up very well to a red, such as a Red Zinfandel or Merlot. A grilled salmon, tuna, swordfish, or thicker fish can be delightful when paired with a red wine, because the meat is more substantial than a flakier filet. Lighter fish dishes, such as white fishes, sole, grouper or steamed fish, should really be paired with whites, because the heavier red wines can overpower the delicate flavors of the fish. I find that shellfish are better with a heavier white wine, like an oaky-tasting Chardonnay. The white wines of Burgundy and Bordeaux also make an excellent choice, as the depth and flavor of these wines greatly enhances the richness of shellfish.

Keith Browning

For nearly two decades, Keith has been collecting and experiencing the great wines of the world. He has an extraordinary personal collection of more than 3,500 bottles, featuring unique and rare Red Bordeaux and vintage Port. Keith has toured vineyards and tasted wines from Napa Valley to Bordeaux.

He has participated in many tasting dinners led by world-renowned wine experts, including Hugh Johnson, Serena Sutcliffe, Jean-Bernard Delmas, and Terry Matthews. These tasting dinners, and the wonderful combinations of gourmet foods and wine, have greatly influenced the selections chosen for this book. Keith regularly shares his knowledge, expertise, and wine with friends and family.

Special Deliveries

Many newcomers to Dayton remark on the community spirit that exists in this "City of Neighbors." There is no better illustration of this phenomenon than when a family brings home a new baby. In many neighborhoods, for days and even weeks, meals appear at the door, one after another, home-cooked and delivered by some of the most kind-hearted people you'll ever know. The same goes for any circumstance that makes it difficult to get food on the table. Think of a family member or elderly neighbor who would appreciate a hot casserole, a pot of soup, or a basket of muffins on their doorstep this week. You may even want to host a baby shower for an expectant mom and ask guests to bring a frozen meal for when baby arrives. Here are some recipe suggestions for food that is easy to make, portable, and sure to bring a smile to someone in need.

Amy's Amazing Lemon Bread
Award-Winning Spaghetti with
    Meat Sauce
Banana Cream Chocolate Chip
    Muffins
BBQ Beef Sandwiches
Best Chocolate Chip Cookies
Best Easy Chocolate Bundt Cake
Brownie Torte
Buttermilk Scones
Buttermint Carrots
Caramel Apple Bread Pudding
Century-Style Chocolate Sheet
    Cake
Chicken Chili Bianco
Cinnamon Apple Cake
Classic Pumpkin Bars
Comfort Corn Pudding
Delicious Pumpkin Bread
Egg, Sausage and Cheese
    Casserole

Fresh Seafood Bake
Gingersnaps
Great-Grandmother's Pound Cake
Holly's Chicken Enchiladas
Julie's Very Berry Muffins
Lemon Pasta Salad
Marinated New Red Potato Salad
Mexicana Rice
Mexican Chicken Kiev
Moist Oatmeal Cookies
Old Faithful Pork Chop Casserole
Pasta Salad with Grilled Zucchini
    and Olives
Phyl's Layered Salad
Presidential Meatloaf
Provisions' Peanut Butter Cookies
Ridgewood Avenue Brisket
Rike's Famous Sloppy Joes
Rosa's Stuffed Peppers
Sara Jane's Apples

Sausage Fettuccine Torte
Sour Cream Coffee Cake
Spinach Mushroom Lasagna
Spring Island Couscous Salad
Sweet Potato Soufflé
Tex Mex Lasagna
Thai Pasta Salad
The Best Chicken Parmesan
The Ultimate Quiche
Tomato and Orzo Fennel Soup
Tomato Lentil Soup
Too Good Tortellini Soup
Turkey and Wild Rice Casserole
Vivid Summer Vegetables
Westerly Pot Roast
Whipped Potatoes Paprika
Zillions of Zucchini Bread
Ziti with Baked Tomato Sauce
Zucchini Casserole

The Gift of Food

These recipes make great gifts for a teacher, new neighbor, friend's birthday.... you name it!

Amy's Amazing Lemon Bread
Caramel Popcorn
Chocolate Almond Toffee Bark
Chocolate-Covered Caramels
Double Chocolate Walnut Biscotti
Easy Fresh Fruit Jam
Frosted Pecans

Gingerbread Cookies
Gingersnaps
Grandma Ruby's Garlic Sweet
    Pickles
Homemade Hot Fudge Sauce
Liz's Hot Mustard Sauce
Mocha Truffles

Ohio Buckeyes
Rich Caramel Sauce
Spicy Cheese Crisps
Sun-Dried Tomato and Herbed
    Goat Cheese Spread
Unscientific Pickled Peppers
Zillions of Zucchini Bread

Speed Scratch...
30 Weeknight Wonders

What on earth is Speed Scratch? It is a solution for those of us who just can't find the time to make dinner. Quite simply, Speed Scratch involves two components: "speed", ready-to-eat purchased food item(s); and "scratch", easy-to-prepare homemade item(s). Put them together for easy weeknight meals. Here are some ideas, but the possibilities are endless, depending on what's available in your area.

NOTE: Items in bold print are recipes featured in this cookbook. See index for our Quick & Easy Recipes!

Ridgewood Avenue Brisket, Purchased Twice-Baked Potatoes, Steamed Brussels Sprouts

Purchased Meatloaf, **Whipped Potatoes Paprika,** Steamed Broccoli

Purchased Cooked Pork Tenderloin Slices, **Sara Jane's Apples,** Hash Browns, Purchased Broccoli Raisin Salad

Pan-Fried Pork Chops, Purchased Macaroni and Cheese, **Dilly Bean Salad**

Purchased Pre-Marinated Pork Tenderloin (Teriyaki flavor), **Silky Asian Noodles,** Steamed Asparagus or Sautéed Snow Peas

Purchased Baked Ham Slices with Tangy Mustard, Steamed Green Beans, **Heavenly Corn Bread**

Pan-Fried Sliced Kielbasa Sausage, Pierogies (frozen food case) topped with Sour Cream, **Liliana's Fried Cabbage**

Purchased Thick-Sliced Smoked Turkey, Baked Sweet Potatoes, **Braised Red Cabbage and Apples,** Bakery Dinner Rolls

Cajun Hamburgers, Purchased Cole Slaw, Corn on the Cob

Rike's Famous Sloppy Joes, Purchased Bean Salad, Chips

Purchased Rotisserie Chicken, **Artichoke-Spinach Casserole,** White Rice, Sliced Raw Red Peppers

Purchased Rotisserie Chicken, **Buttermint Carrots,** Pan-Fried Potatoes, Bagged Garden Salad

Purchased Fried Chicken, **Southwest Baked Beans,** Baked Potatoes, Bagged Garden Salad

Purchased Grilled Chicken Breasts topped with **Spicy Black Bean and Corn Salsa,** Chopped Cucumber and Tomato Salad, White Rice

Purchased Grilled Chicken Breasts, **Lemon Pasta Salad,** Steamed Asparagus, Fruit Salad from Salad Bar

Purchased Chicken Enchiladas, **Mexicana Rice,** Sliced Cucumbers

Tangy Salmon Steaks, Corn on the Cob, Purchased Pasta Salad from the Deli

Saucy Sole, Orzo tossed with Butter and Fresh Herbs, Purchased Cooked Mixed Vegetables

Cooked Shrimp (seafood counter) served on Rice tossed with Kalamata Olives, Chopped Tomatoes, Feta Cheese, Parsley and Olive Oil, Lemon Sorbet, **Walnut Butter Cookies**

Pasta Salad with Grilled Zucchini and Olives, Purchased Rotisserie Chicken Breasts, Corn on the Cob

Ziti with Baked Tomato Sauce, Salad Bar Greek Salad, Crusty Bread

Award-Winning Spaghetti with Meat Sauce, Bagged Garden Salad, Garlic Bread

Pasta tossed with Purchased Pesto Sauce, **Greek Peasant Salad,** Crusty Bread

Cavatappi with Spinach, Garbanzo Beans and Feta, Purchased Grilled Chicken, Fruit Salad from the Salad Bar

Black Bean Chili, White Rice, Tomato and Avocado Slices

Bagged Garden Salad, **Tomato Lentil Soup,** Crusty Bread

Soup from the Salad Bar, **Warm Pastrami Panino,** Ice Cream Sundaes

Purchased Tortellini (refrigerated section) cooked in chicken broth (canned) and topped with Fresh Parmesan, Crusty Bread, **Stuffed Red Peppers**

Omelet with Thinly Sliced Sautéed Zucchini and Onions, **Dayton Steakhouse-Style Stewed Tomatoes,** Bagged Spinach Salad

Baked Potato Loaded with Toppings from the Salad Bar, **Make-Ahead Caesar Salad** topped with Sliced Purchased Grilled Chicken

Table Talk for Family Mealtime

Give your children warm family memories they can pass on to their own children. Here are some suggestions!

❦ ❦ ❦

CONVERSATION STARTERS

Try some of these topics to get everyone talking and sharing:

❦ Describe your idea of a dream vacation.

❦ If you could be anyone else for a day, who would it be and why?

❦ Name one new thing you learned today.

❦ If you won $100,000 tomorrow, what would you do with it? (What would you buy for yourself and for others? Would you save some for a future occasion?)

❦ What's your favorite book that you've read this week/month?

❦ Tell everyone the menu for your favorite meal.

❦ What can you do tomorrow/next week to help someone else or make this world a better place to live?

❦ What would you put in a time capsule for your family?

WONDERFUL THINGS ARE HAPPENING

On Mondays, chase away the gloom of a new work and school week by asking family members at breakfast to watch out for wonderful things that may happen during the day. Then ask everyone to share their findings at dinner. This helps everyone to focus on positive events during the day, not bad happenings.

PRACTICE MAKES PERFECT

Place a "word of the day" calendar on the breakfast table. Make it a daily practice to read the word and its definition and see who can use it in a sentence. At dinner, see who still remembers the word and can use it correctly. Did anyone have a chance to use the word that day?

LUNCH BOX MESSAGES

Surprise your young ones with a little love note from Dad, a news clipping, a cartoon, or an inspiring message in their lunch boxes. You'll be pleasantly surprised to hear them report back on their findings.

CHANGE OF PACE

Enliven your family mealtimes with some of these fun alternative traditions:

❦ On weekends, use plain paper place mats and leave crayons on the table for creative expression - doodles, art, etc. - before and after the meal.

❦ Assign each family member a day to be in charge of the centerpiece for the table. Let imaginations run wild and you may end up with a favorite toy, art projects, a pretty picture book...anything goes!

❦ Any night of the year, invite ghosts and goblins to dress up and come to the dinner table.

- At dinner one night, switch places at the table by swapping seats with another family member. Then, assume the identity of the family member that normally sits there, even parents. It's very enlightening to see the impressionists come to life.
- At lunch one day, have everyone switch hands - right handers eat with your left hand and vice versa.

HEAD HONCHO'S CHAIR

Bring a large armchair to the table, find a fancy hat or Indian headdress, or use a fancy place mat to denote the head honcho's spot at the table. Let family members sit in this spot in honor of a special occasion, like giving a book report at school, winning a swim meet or a soccer game, getting a good report card, or cleaning a room without being asked.

BAD MANNERS NIGHT

Cut up a piece of paper and write a bad table manner (such as talking with your mouth full, helping yourself first before passing food, reaching across the table, taking more than your share, not saying please and thank-you, etc.) on each piece of paper. Have family members pull their bad manner out of a hat before dinner and then see if you can get away with your selected bad manner without anyone noticing. Whoever catches the most "violations" wins a prize (maybe the first or biggest piece of dessert, a night off from clearing the table or doing the dishes, etc.).

THEME NIGHTS

Some of these family activities are so enjoyable, they might become part of your family's traditions:

- Have your family's helping hands work together to make a meal for a homeless shelter or a community center. (A quick call ahead can help with logistics and menu selection.)
- During the November election season, talk about the candidates and local ballot issues. On election night, take your children with you to the polls and home to dinner. Later, watch the results come in on the TV news.
- Once a year in the summer, plan ahead for nice weather, put the kids to bed early with their clothes on and get up before dawn to watch the sun rise together. Pack breakfast the night before and award a snack prize to the first person to see the sun peaking over the horizon. Have another prize for the person who correctly guesses how long it will take before the whole sun appears in the sky.

DESSERT WITH MOM OR DAD

If Mom or Dad often works late in the evenings, let him or her spend some one-on-one time over dessert with each child. Rotate this special privilege with all your children.

BIRTHDAY CUPCAKE

Give your birthday girls and boys a jump start to their special day. While they are sleeping the night before, tie a bunch of balloons to the end of their bed. Then, bring a cupcake with a candle shining on top to their beds when they first get up. (Use the extra batter when baking his or her birthday cake to make the extra cupcake.)

CANDLELIGHT CAN DO

During those dark winter months, candlelight can make even leftovers look great. Try something different and place a candle on the table for each family member. Once a week, before dinner begins, let family members (with help if needed) light their candles and share something that makes them happy. This can also be a good way to use up old candle stubs.

Opening Night

APPETIZERS

VICTORIA THEATRE

OPENING NIGHT

You don't have to visit 42nd street in New York City or the Kennedy Center in Washington, D. C., to pursue culture. Dayton's arts scene offers everything from weekend festivals to nationally recognized talent in music, theater, and the visual and performing arts. More than 220 arts and cultural organizations combine to offer one of Dayton's finest amenities.

FEEL LIKE LISTENING TO MUSIC? More than 60 organizations, ranging from the Dayton Philharmonic Orchestra and the Dayton Opera to the Dayton Bach Society and the CityFolk Festival, are ready to bring pleasure to your ears. YEARNING FOR AN EVENING OF DANCE? The Dayton Ballet, the second oldest regional ballet in the U.S., tap masters Rhythm in Shoes, and the Dayton Contemporary Dance Company will show you some of the best dance anywhere. STILL SEARCHING FOR SOMETHING TO DO? Dayton stages can magically transport you to any time or place you wish to go, courtesy of the Human Race Theatre Company, the Dayton Playhouse, W. Shakespeare & Co., La Comedia Dinner Theatre, or Kettering's Theatre Under the Stars.

One of the most revered cultural institutions in Dayton is the beautiful Victoria Theatre. Opened in 1866, the Victoria has triumphed over fire, flood, and economic downturns to become one of America's premiere show houses. Listed on the National Register of Historic Places, the Victoria provides the ideal backdrop for local dance and theater companies, and traveling productions.

"What we have is incredible creative ingenuity, and Dayton produces probably more new work than any city of comparable size and even some of the larger cities. We have dance companies producing more new work, ballet and contemporary dance at levels that are unheard of in other cities. The ballet alone does three to four new shows a year."
JIM CLARK, CULTUREWORKS

Smoked Salmon on Baguette Toasts

Easy, elegant and delicious

Yield: 30 slices

3	tablespoons olive oil	2	(4 ounce) packages pre-sliced
1	clove garlic, minced		smoked salmon
1-2	baguettes, thinly sliced	3	tablespoons capers, drained
3-4	tablespoons honey mustard	3	tablespoons diced red onion
		1	bunch fresh dill, chopped

🕐 *Have the bakery slice baguettes for you.*

❍ Preheat broiler.

❍ Whisk oil and garlic together. Brush each bread slice with oil mixture.

❍ Broil until bread just begins to brown.

❍ Spread each bread slice with a small dollop of mustard. Top with half of a slice of salmon.

❍ Garnish with capers, onion and dill.

Menu: *Offer these with Mushroom Tarts (page 45) and Tasha's Dip (page 62) with crudités for a simple cocktail party.*

Herbed Mussels Normande

"Viva la France"

Yield: 3 servings

4	pounds mussels	3	tablespoons minced fresh garlic
1	large red onion, chopped	2	tablespoons balsamic vinegar
1	cup white wine	1	teaspoon dried tarragon

❍ Scrub mussels well with a rough brush under running water. Remove beard with a knife. Discard any open mussels.

❍ Combine onion, wine, garlic, vinegar, and tarragon in a large skillet. Bring to a boil. Boil gently, uncovered, for 5 minutes.

❍ Add mussels. Cover; cook over medium heat, stirring once or twice, for 8 to 10 minutes, or until mussels open.

❍ Place opened mussels into a heated bowl; pour any remaining broth over top. Serve immediately.

Note: *Try pouring over pasta for a tasty entrée. Serve with fresh French bread for "dipping."*

- Smoked salmon should be sliced paper-thin, on the diagonal, immediately before serving.

- Be sure the salmon is cold.

- A squirt of fresh lemon juice is delicious; offer generous lemon wedges.

- Pass a pepper mill.

- Danish Pumpernickel is a natural accompaniment.

- Other embellishments include a dab of caviar, a dollop of sour cream or a sprinkling of chopped fresh dill.

- Champagne or chilled vodka, neat, are the approved libations.

The Dayton Ballet Company is the second oldest regional ballet in the United States. With more than 200 premieres in its history, it is often called "The Company of Premieres."

Shell Creek Lemon Scallops

An impressive first course

Yield: 6 servings

3	large lemons	2	sticks butter or margarine
¼	cup dry white wine	1	small clove garlic, crushed
1	pound sea scallops, quartered	1	tablespoon minced fresh parsley

🕐 *Lemon shells may be prepared 1 day ahead and refrigerated.*

6 Halve lemons and squeeze juice to measure ½ cup. Scoop out all pulp from lemon halves. Cut a thin slice from bottom of each lemon shell to make shell stand level. Set aside.

6 In a heavy enamel or stainless steel saucepan, blend ¼ cup lemon juice and wine. Add scallops; simmer, covered, for 5 minutes, or until tender. Drain scallops, discarding liquid.

6 Preheat broiler.

6 In same saucepan, melt butter. Add remaining ¼ cup lemon juice and garlic. Heat gently to blend flavors. Remove from heat and add scallops. Toss carefully.

6 Spoon scallops and lemon butter sauce into lemon shells. Broil 2 minutes to brown edges of scallops.

6 Remove from broiler and sprinkle with parsley. Serve immediately.

Menu: *This appetizer is a lovely table starter to an elegant dinner including beef tenderloin, Rice Pilaf (page 162) and Provençal Roasted Tomatoes (page 166).*

Dayton's Memorial Hall was dedicated in 1910 as a memorial to veterans and to serve as an exhibition/entertainment center. Entertainment included jazz, country, rock, gospel, and Broadway shows. It also served as a home to the Dayton Philharmonic Orchestra and the Dayton Opera. The cost of the original building was $250,000.

Phyllo with Crab and Brie ❄

A new filling for those yummy triangles that everyone loves!

Yield: 25 to 30 triangles

1	tablespoon butter		Tabasco sauce to taste (optional)
2	tablespoons minced shallots	8	ounces Brie cheese, cut into thin
8	ounces crabmeat, picked over		slices
¼	teaspoon salt	15	sheets phyllo dough
¼	teaspoon freshly ground black		(about 8 ounces)
	pepper	1½	sticks butter, melted
2	teaspoons minced fresh parsley		

🕐 *Triangles may be assembled, tightly covered and refrigerated up to 1 day ahead. To freeze, arrange unbaked triangles on plastic wrap lined baking sheets. Brush with butter, wrap tightly and freeze. When frozen, repackage more conveniently in layers (with plastic wrap between the layers) and return to freezer. To bake, arrange triangles on baking sheets and bake at 375 degrees until crisp and golden.*

🌀 Melt 1 tablespoon butter in a skillet. Add shallots; sauté until golden. Add crab and cook until heated through. Season with salt, pepper, parsley, and Tabasco sauce.

🌀 Lay cheese slices over crab mixture. Cook over low heat without stirring, until cheese softens enough to be stirred in without breaking up lumps of crab. When fairly combined, set aside to cool slightly.

🌀 Preheat oven to 375 degrees.

🌀 Place phyllo sheets in a stack. Cover stack with plastic wrap and top with a damp dish towel to prevent drying.

🌀 Remove covering and carefully cut the stack in half lengthwise using a very sharp knife. Recover.

🌀 For each packet, lay out 1 strip of phyllo with the short end toward you and brush lightly with melted butter. Fold in half lengthwise and butter again. Place about 1½ teaspoons of crab filling at the bottom of the strip, off to 1 corner. Fold up the strip in triangles as you would a flag so that you end up with a neat little triangular packet. Place packet on a greased baking sheet and brush with butter. Repeat with remaining strips of phyllo, laying out 2 or 3 at a time and keeping the rest covered.

🌀 Bake 20 to 25 minutes, or until crisp and golden. Serve hot.

Note: *Use the crab and Brie mixture in other ways, too… as a filling for omelets, quiche or stuffed mushrooms; or spread it while still warm on crackers, black bread or toast points.*

Crabmeat is sold frozen, pasteurized and vacuum-packed, or plain cooked. The plain cooked type is available in several grades, including lump, backfin or flake, and claw. Crabmeat should be used or frozen within 2 to 3 days of purchase. Defrost frozen crabmeat slowly, always in the refrigerator.

Chicken Satay with Spicy Peanut Sauce

Sophisticated outlet for peanut lovers

Yield: 50 pieces

Chicken

1¼	pounds boneless, skinless chicken breast, cut into ½x3-inch strips
2	tablespoons sesame oil
2	tablespoons corn oil
¼	cup dry sherry
¼	cup soy sauce
2	tablespoons lemon juice
1½	teaspoons minced garlic
1½	teaspoons minced ginger
¼	teaspoon salt
¼	teaspoon freshly ground black pepper
	Dash of Tabasco sauce

Spicy Peanut Sauce

4	teaspoons corn oil
2	teaspoons sesame oil
½	cup minced red onion
2	tablespoons minced garlic
1	teaspoon minced fresh ginger
1	tablespoon red wine vinegar
1	tablespoon brown sugar
⅓	cup peanut butter, smooth or chunky
½	teaspoon ground coriander
3	tablespoons ketchup
3	tablespoons soy sauce
1	tablespoon lime or lemon juice
½	teaspoon freshly ground black pepper
	Dash of Tabasco sauce
⅓-½	cup hot water
½	teaspoon turmeric for color (optional)
2-3	green onions, chopped, for garnish

Spicy Peanut Sauce can be made in advance. If it thickens or separates, simply whisk in a little hot water until desired consistency is achieved. Chicken must be prepared at least 1 hour in advance to allow for proper marinating.

⏰ Combine all chicken ingredients. Marinate in refrigerator 1 to 12 hours.

⏰ To make sauce, heat oils in a small saucepan. Add onion, garlic and ginger; sauté over medium heat until softened. Add vinegar and sugar; cook until sugar dissolves. Remove from heat.

⏰ Stir in peanut butter, coriander, ketchup, soy sauce, juice, black pepper, Tabasco sauce, hot water, and turmeric. Adjust seasonings to taste. If a smoother sauce is desired, blend in a food processor.

⏰ When ready to serve, preheat oven to 375 degrees.

⏰ Thread each piece of chicken onto a wooden toothpick or small skewer, and arrange on baking sheets.

⏰ Bake 5 to 10 minutes, or until just cooked.

⏰ Serve chicken hot with a bowl of room-temperature sauce for dipping. Sprinkle green onion over sauce to garnish.

Note: *May substitute beef, lamb or pork for chicken.*

Menu: *Can serve as a main course by grilling or sautéing chicken breast, then serving over noodles or rice. Top with Spicy Peanut Sauce and green onions.*

Sweet and Sour Chicken Wings

Keeps a crowd happy

Yield: 10 to 12 servings

3-5	pounds chicken wings	¼	cup brown sugar
½	cup orange juice	½	cup cranberry sauce, whole or
½	cup soy sauce		jellied

🕐 *Wings must marinate at least 8 hours.*

- Rinse and dry chicken wings. Separate drumettes. Clip away wing tips.
- Combine juice, soy sauce, sugar, and cranberry sauce. Reserve ½ cup marinade for later use. Add chicken to remaining marinade and marinate in refrigerator overnight.
- When ready to bake, preheat oven to 350 degrees. Place chicken in a 9x13-inch dish with enough marinade to cover the bottom.
- Bake 1 hour, basting frequently with the reserved marinade.

Note: *Hot chili sauce is a great accompaniment for spice lovers. Serve with a variety of colorful cocktail napkins.*

Reuben Dip

Excellent tailgate or Super Bowl appetizer

Yield: 6 to 8 servings

1	(16 ounce) jar sauerkraut, drained	1	(6 ounce) package corned beef,
8	ounces Swiss cheese, shredded		chopped
8	ounces cheddar cheese, shredded	1	cup mayonnaise

🕐 *Can be baked up to 8 hours ahead, covered and refrigerated. Reheat before serving.*

- Preheat oven to 350 degrees.
- Combine all ingredients and spread evenly in a square baking dish.
- Bake, uncovered, 35 to 40 minutes. Serve warm with bread pieces or Melba toast.

Note: *Try serving in a hollowed out round of rye or pumpernickel bread. We recommend Silver Fleece brand sauerkraut and Carl Buddig corned beef.*

Unlike many museum groups, the founders of the Dayton Art Institute wanted something more than a mere repository for works of art and antiquity. From the beginning, the DAI was thought of as "Dayton's Friendly Living Room" — a place where Daytonians of all ages could browse among the art treasures, listen to good music, or just relax and chat with friends.

When the Dayton Contemporary Dance Company performed in Moscow for sellout audiences in 1992, Russian capitalists scalped tickets outside the theater for two to three times the face value. In Germany, an audience gave the company a 10-minute standing ovation!

—Terry Morris,
Theater Critic
Dayton Daily News

Meatballs in Sweet and Sour Sauce

A classic favorite

Yield: 30 servings

Meatballs

2	pounds ground beef		2	eggs
1	cup homemade bread crumbs		½	teaspoon freshly ground black pepper
2	tablespoons soy sauce			
⅓	cup fresh parsley		⅓	cup ketchup
½	teaspoon garlic salt		½	medium onion, finely chopped

Sauce

2	tablespoons brown sugar		1	(16 ounce) can jellied cranberry sauce
1	tablespoon lemon juice			
1	(12 ounce) bottle chili sauce			

🕐 *Meatballs can be made ahead and frozen up to 3 months. Sauce should always be made and served fresh.*

- Preheat oven to 350 degrees.
- Combine all meatball ingredients. Form into bite-sized balls.
- Bake 30 minutes.
- Meanwhile, combine all sauce ingredients in a saucepan. Cook until heated through; add meatballs. Serve warm in a chafing dish.

Menu: *Serve these with Sweet and Sour Chicken Wings (page 39) and Reuben Dip (page 39) for your next football party.*

For many who attend the Dayton Art Institute's annual fundraiser, the Art Ball, it is an elegant rite of summer. That wasn't always the case. The Art Ball actually came into being on a cold December evening in 1957. It was a holiday dance staged by the Junior League of Dayton on behalf of the museum. In 1964, the Junior League turned the project over to the museum's newly organized associate board. What has made the Art Ball special for the past 37 years isn't the food, the orchestra or the clothes. It's the setting. In addition to wandering the wonderful galleries and enjoying the food, attendees may overlook the city from the vantage point of the balcony in the Sculpture Court, which is open only during the Ball.

Sensational Steak Strips
with Creamy Garlic Sauce

Yield: 8 servings

Beef

1	tablespoon Cajun blackening seasoning (we prefer Chef Paul Prudhomme's Meat Magic)	1	egg
		1	cup milk
		2	cups vegetable oil
		2	cups all-purpose flour
1	pound beef tenderloin, cut into narrow strips	2	teaspoons Cajun blackening seasoning

Creamy Garlic Sauce

2	teaspoons minced fresh garlic	1	tablespoon cider vinegar
2	teaspoons Cajun blackening seasoning	1	cup mayonnaise

- Combine 1 tablespoon Cajun seasoning and beef strips in a medium bowl. Mix well with hands to evenly distribute seasoning.

- In a separate bowl, beat egg and milk together.

- Pour oil into a 10-inch skillet. Heat on high for 8 to 9 minutes, or until oil reaches 350 degrees.

- While heating, combine flour and 2 teaspoons Cajun seasoning.

- Add beef to egg mixture. Remove about one-third of beef from egg mixture and drop into flour mixture. Mix until thoroughly coated. Shake off excess flour.

- Drop coated beef into hot oil in a single layer. Cook 4 to 5 minutes, or until golden brown and crisp, turning to brown evenly.

- Remove beef from oil with a slotted spoon. Drain on paper towels. Repeat with remaining strips.

- Serve immediately with sauce.

- To make sauce, mash garlic and Cajun seasoning together to form a paste. Stir in vinegar until blended. Mix in mayonnaise. Cover and refrigerate until ready to use.

Note: *Best when served hot right after preparation. Prepare Creamy Garlic Sauce in advance to enhance flavor.*

Did you know that you could toast nuts in the microwave? Place nuts on a microwave-safe plate. Microwave on high for 2 to 4 minutes per half-cup of nuts. Stir every 2 minutes. Toasting enhances and intensifies the flavor of nuts.

Prosciutto Pinwheels ❄

People will think you spent all day in the kitchen — but you didn't!

Yield: 60 pieces (30 pieces per log)

1	(17¼ ounce) package frozen puff pastry
10-12	ounces soft herb-garlic cheese (we prefer Alouette brand)
7	ounces lean prosciutto, sliced paper thin

🕐 *The pinwheel logs can be refrigerated for up to 2 days, or frozen for 3 weeks. To freeze, cover the plastic-wrapped logs with foil. Defrost prior to baking.*

⬬ Defrost puff pastry according to package directions. Roll each pastry sheet out on a lightly floured work surface to a 12x14-inch rectangle.

⬬ Spread cheese over pastry sheets, leaving a ½-inch border on one of the long sides of each sheet. Arrange prosciutto evenly over cheese.

⬬ Roll up pastry, starting with the long side without the border, into a tight coil. Moisten ½-inch border lightly with water and press to seal the end. Wrap rolls in plastic and freeze 45 minutes, or until firm.

⬬ Preheat oven to 450 degrees.

⬬ Cut logs into ¼-inch slices. Arrange pinwheels on baking sheets lined with lightly greased foil. If preparing in advance, cover baking sheets with plastic wrap and refrigerate up to 6 hours.

⬬ Bake 12 to 14 minutes. Flip pinwheels and bake 5 to 8 minutes, or until golden and crisp. Watch carefully to avoid burning. Serve hot.

Note: *Frozen pinwheel logs are great to have on hand for drop-in guests or last-minute gatherings.*

Phyllo freezes very well. To defrost, leave unopened package in refrigerator overnight so it thaws slowly and evenly. Fresh or defrosted phyllo keeps about five days in the refrigerator. When working with phyllo, keep the leaves you aren't currently using covered with a sheet of plastic wrap topped with a damp dishtowel to prevent the phyllo from drying out and becoming brittle.

Tomato, Bacon and Basil Crostini

Yield: 24 pieces

Topping

3	tablespoons olive oil
⅓	cup chopped shallots
2	teaspoons finely chopped garlic
1½	cups peeled, seeded and coarsely chopped tomato
¼	teaspoon salt, or to taste

¼	teaspoon dried red pepper flakes
¼	cup chicken broth
	Pinch of sugar (optional)
6	strips bacon, cooked crisp and crumbled
¼	cup julienned fresh basil leaves

Toasts

3	tablespoons butter
3	tablespoons olive oil

24	(⅜ inch thick) slices French bread

🕐 *Tomato topping can be prepared and refrigerated up to 1 day ahead. Toasts can be made several hours ahead and kept at room temperature loosely covered in foil.*

- ⊚ To make topping, heat olive oil in a skillet. Add shallots; sauté 2 minutes. Add garlic and sauté 1 minute. Add tomato, salt, pepper flakes, broth, and sugar. Cook and stir about 15 minutes, or until all liquid evaporates, and mixture is thick and chunky. Cool and cover.

- ⊚ To make toasts, preheat oven to 300 degrees.

- ⊚ Combine butter and oil; heat until melted. Brush mixture over both sides of bread.

- ⊚ Bake 10 to 12 minutes, or until golden and slightly crisp.

- ⊚ When ready to serve, spread each bread slice generously with warm topping. Sprinkle with bacon and bake 6 to 8 minutes.

- ⊚ Garnish with basil and serve.

Note: *Always use fresh basil and tomatoes. Try cherry or grape tomatoes if it's not tomato season. Try lightly topping crostini with high-quality shaved Parmesan cheese.*

Crostini, Italian for "little crusts," originated as a clever way of using the very last bit of bread from yesterday's loaf. These small toasts are traditionally grilled over an open wood fire or under the broiler, drizzled with good olive oil, and topped with various mixtures. Crostini will stand up to almost anything you want to put on them. Possibilities include coarsely chopped olives, anchovy paste, caper butter, and chopped fresh herbs with capers.

Baby BLTs

A bite-sized version of an old favorite

Yield: 8 to 10 servings

1	cup shredded Swiss cheese	¼	teaspoon seasoned salt
¼	cup Parmesan cheese	8	ounces bacon, cooked and crumbled
⅔	cup mayonnaise plus extra for spreading	1	loaf party rye or pumpernickel bread
½	cup finely minced green onion	1	pint cherry tomatoes, sliced
⅛	teaspoon garlic powder		
⅛	teaspoon cayenne pepper		

🕐 *Bacon and cheese mixture can be made up to 1 day ahead and refrigerated. Toasting and assembly can be done up to 4 hours ahead and refrigerated.*

⚬ Preheat oven to 350 degrees.

⚬ Combine cheeses, mayonnaise, onion, garlic powder, cayenne pepper, seasoned salt, and bacon.

⚬ Toast bread slices on 1 side by placing slices on an ungreased baking sheet; bake for 3 to 5 minutes.

⚬ Spread untoasted side of bread with a thin layer of mayonnaise. Place a dollop of cheese mixture on each bread slice. Top with a slice of tomato.

⚬ Bake 5 to 10 minutes, or until bubbly and brown.

Spicy Cheese Crisps ❄

A savory cocktail biscuit

Yield: 6 dozen

2	sticks margarine	¼	teaspoon cayenne pepper
2	cups shredded sharp cheddar cheese		Dash of Worcestershire sauce
2	cups flour	2	cups Rice Krispies cereal

🕐 *Crisps can be made ahead and frozen up to 3 months.*

⚬ Preheat oven to 350 degrees.

⚬ Combine all ingredients except cereal in a bowl. Blend well. Knead in cereal.

⚬ Form mixture into small balls, the size of large marbles. Place on a baking sheet and firmly flatten with the bottom of a glass. Flour glass as needed to prevent sticking.

⚬ Bake 15 to 20 minutes, or until light brown.

Note: *Be sure to press firmly to ensure crisps are thin and crunchy.*

🍷 *Excellent with Chardonnay or beer.*

Quick hors d'oeuvres:

• Wrap cubes of melon with strips of thinly sliced prosciutto, top with mint leaves and skewer with toothpicks.

• Fill miniature biscuits with Black Forest ham, cheddar cheese and fruit chutney.

• Spread thin slices of French bread with olive oil and pesto, top with slivers of sun-dried tomatoes and mozzarella, and broil briefly.

• Brush mushroom caps with olive oil; fill with pieces of Brie cheese, top each with a partially cooked piece of bacon and bake for 10 minutes at 350°.

When preparing the hors d'oeuvres for your party, plan on serving four bites per person if dinner will follow, or 10 bites for a cocktail party. If it's a grand affair, such as a wedding reception with no dinner following, allow 10 to 15.

Mushroom Tarts ❄

Store in freezer for unexpected guests

Yield: 45 tarts

4	tablespoons butter	½	teaspoon salt
3	tablespoons finely chopped shallots	⅛	teaspoon cayenne pepper
8	ounces mushrooms, finely chopped	½	teaspoon lemon juice
2	tablespoons flour	45	purchased frozen mini-phyllo tart shells (we prefer Athens brand)
1	cup heavy cream		Parsley sprigs for garnish
1	tablespoon finely chopped chives		

🕐 *Filling can be made up to 1 day ahead and refrigerated. Bring to room temperature before filling tart shells. Also, filled tarts may be frozen up to 3 months. To serve, do not thaw; bake at 400 degrees for 12 minutes.*

☙ Preheat oven to 350 degrees.

☙ Melt butter in a heavy skillet. Add shallots and sauté 4 minutes, or until softened but not browned. Add mushrooms; cook 10 to 15 minutes, or until all moisture evaporates. Sprinkle flour over top; mix well.

☙ Stirring constantly, add cream to mixture and bring to a boil. When thickened, reduce heat and simmer 1 to 2 minutes. Remove from heat. Stir in chives, salt, cayenne pepper, and lemon juice. Cool.

☙ Fill each tart shell with mushroom mixture.

☙ Bake 10 minutes. Garnish with parsley sprigs and serve immediately.

Victoria Theatre chronology

1866 Opened as Turner Opera House

1869 Destroyed by fire

1871 Rebuilt and reopened

1899 Renamed Victoria Opera House

1913 Destroyed by Dayton Flood—quickly rebuilt

1918 Destroyed by fire, again

1919 Rebuilt and reopened as Victory Theatre

1972 Marked for demolition, but saved by registration on National Register of Historic Places

1975 Tremendous community effort staves off wrecking ball, again

1976 Victoria Theatre Association volunteers begin restoration work

1977 Dayton Ballet makes theater its permanent home

1978 Victoria Theatre Association purchases building and continues restoration

1988 Arts Center Foundation acquires theater, begins $17.5-million renovation

1990 Re-opens as the Victoria Theatre

Zucchini Cakes with a Spring Vegetable Relish and Red Pepper Vinaigrette ⭐

Yield: 8 to 10 servings

Red Pepper Vinaigrette

1	large red bell pepper, roasted, peeled and seeded, juices reserved	1	tablespoon rice vinegar
		1	teaspoon honey
	Juice of 1 lemon	1	teaspoon sambal chili paste
1	teaspoon chopped shallots	½	teaspoon kosher salt
1	clove garlic, smashed	⅓	cup peanut oil
1	tablespoon Dijon mustard	⅓	cup light olive oil

Spring Vegetable Relish

⅔	cup shelled spring peas	1	tablespoon chopped fresh chives
⅔	cup 1-inch diagonal cut asparagus pieces	1	tablespoon chopped fresh thyme
8	ounces shiitake mushroom caps, thinly sliced	1	tablespoon chopped fresh chervil
			Juice of 1 lemon
1	cup thinly sliced leeks, white part only	¼	cup olive oil, or to taste
			Salt and white pepper to taste
	Olive oil	⅔	cup very small, firm cherry tomatoes

Zucchini Cakes

2	eggs, beaten	1½-2	teaspoons baking powder
½	cup club soda	¾-1	pound zucchini
1½	teaspoons olive oil		Salt and white pepper to taste
2	ounces Parmesan cheese		Vegetable oil for cooking
1	cup all-purpose flour		Parmesan cheese for garnish

6   To make vinaigrette, place all ingredients except oils in a blender. Puree on high until very smooth.

6   With machine running, slowly drizzle in oils. Run blender for 1 minute after all oil is added to ensure emulsion. Adjust seasoning and refrigerate until needed.

6   To make relish, blanch peas and asparagus separately. Plunge into cold water to stop cooking; drain.

6   Brush mushroom slices with olive oil. Season and roast until golden and crispy; cool.

6   Lightly sauté leeks in olive oil until very tender; cool.

6   Combine peas, asparagus, mushroom slices, leeks, chives, thyme, chervil, lemon juice, ¼ cup olive oil, salt, and pepper.

6   Halve tomatoes and add to mixture just before serving.

6   To make zucchini cakes, combine egg, club soda and oil in a large bowl with a fork until thoroughly mixed.

6   In a small bowl, combine cheese, flour and baking powder.

Most of the memories of my upbringing in Dayton revolve around food. Mom always prepared our favorites on our birthdays. Because I was a June baby I always had Silver Queen corn and sliced tomato salad. Strawberry shortcake with warm milk often took the place of a birthday cake.

We had a backyard garden with several vegetables, two fruit trees and a small grape arbor. The neighborhood kids always joked about the killer zucchini that would appear during our long summer vacation. We had our share of zucchini bread, and I have made my living for the last 14 years creating unique dishes with indigenous ingredients. In New Orleans, my home now, I have demonstrated this recipe many times at the local farmers' market.

—Anne Kearney Sand, Owner

Peristyle Restaurant, New Orleans

Zucchini Cakes continued

6 Coarsely grate zucchini onto a kitchen towel. Squeeze out excess water. Add 2½ to 3 cups of grated, dry squash and the flour mixture to the egg mixture. Mix until blended. Season batter generously.

6 Heat about 1 tablespoon oil in a large nonstick skillet. Add ¼ cup of the batter at once, forming a 4-inch circle. Cook over medium heat like a pancake, cooking until golden and crispy; wait until air bubbles rise before turning. Brown 2 minutes on other side. Blot off excess oil and hold in a warm oven. Repeat with remaining batter.

6 To serve, make a small pool of vinaigrette on a warm serving plate. Rest a cake on top. Repeat with other cakes. Top cakes generously with relish. Drizzle with olive oil, and garnish with Parmesan cheese and a basil blossom.

Ciabatta Napoli

Fresh and simple

Yield: 12 to 15 pieces

1	loaf ciabatta bread, sliced ½-inch thick (we prefer Orlando brand)	4-6	fresh ripe tomatoes, chopped
		¼	cup chopped fresh basil
1	tablespoon garlic salt		Freshly ground black pepper to taste
½	cup olive oil	½	cup Parmesan cheese

6 Preheat broiler or grill.

6 Place bread slices on a baking sheet.

6 Mix garlic salt and olive oil; brush over both sides of bread.

6 Broil or grill bread 4 minutes on each side, or until golden brown.

6 Use remaining oil mixture to sauté tomatoes and basil over medium heat for 10 to 12 minutes. Season with pepper.

6 Spoon tomato mixture onto each slice of bread. Sprinkle with cheese.

Note: *Using fresh tomatoes and basil transforms this appetizer. Try using Parmigiano-Reggiano for amazing Parmesan flavor.*

Menu: *Excellent with a mixed green salad with Francesca's Salad Dressing (page 97) followed by Fettuccine with Wild Mushrooms (page 183).*

In Italy, bruschetta is thickly sliced country bread grilled over an open fire, then rubbed while warm with a clove of garlic, drizzled with fruity green olive oil, and sprinkled sea salt. Embellishments may include tomato, fresh basil, cheese, and black pepper. Make up your own variations!

Black Bean and Goat Cheese Quesadillas with Peach Mango Salsa

Salsa makes this unique

Yield: 36 wedges

Quesadillas

12	large flour tortillas	6-8	ounces goat cheese
2	(16 ounce) cans refried black beans	¼	cup chopped fresh cilantro Butter for sautéing

Peach Mango Salsa

1½	cups coarsely chopped fresh mango	3	tablespoons chopped fresh cilantro
1	peach, peeled and coarsely chopped	3	tablespoons chopped fresh parsley
2	jalapeño peppers, chopped	3-4	tablespoons fresh lemon juice
1	clove garlic, minced	2	tablespoons olive oil
3	tablespoons finely chopped red onion		Salt and freshly ground black pepper to taste

⚬ Spread 6 tortillas with black beans. Divide goat cheese and cilantro over the top. Cover with remaining tortillas.

⚬ Melt ½ tablespoon butter in a 10-inch skillet over low heat, tilting to coat bottom. Sauté quesadillas, one at a time, over medium heat for 1 to 2 minutes per side, or until golden brown and cheese has melted. Add butter as needed.

⚬ Transfer sautéed quesadillas to warm baking sheets. Place in a 200 degree oven to keep warm until all quesadillas are cooked.

⚬ Cut each quesadilla into 6 wedges. Top with salsa.

⚬ To make salsa, combine all ingredients.

Note: *You may substitute your favorite cheese for goat cheese.*

Menu: *Try serving quesadillas with Guadalajara Guacamole (page 58). Great summer entertaining — serve with frozen margaritas!*

Spinach Bites
with Hot Mustard Sauce ❄

A vegetarian treat

Yield: 6 dozen (1 inch) balls

Hot Mustard Sauce

½	cup dry mustard	¼	cup sugar
½	cup white vinegar	1	egg yolk

Spinach Bites

2   (10 ounce) packages frozen chopped spinach, thawed and well-drained

2   cups seasoned bread crumbs or stuffing mix

1   cup firmly packed shredded Parmesan cheese

1   stick butter, melted

4   small green onions, finely chopped

3   eggs
    Dash of nutmeg

🕐 *Plan to begin recipe at least 4 hours ahead. Make sauce 1 day ahead and store, covered, in refrigerator. Spinach balls can be made and frozen up to 2 months, defrosted when needed and served at room temperature.*

6   To make sauce, combine mustard and vinegar. Cover and let stand at room temperature for 4 hours.

6   In a small saucepan, mix sugar and egg yolk. Add mustard mixture. Cook and stir over low heat until thick. Cover and chill. Bring to room temperature before serving.

6   To make spinach bites, preheat oven to 350 degrees.

6   Combine all spinach bite ingredients. Form into 1-inch balls.

6   Bake 10 to 15 minutes on an ungreased baking sheet. Serve with sauce.

Note: *This mustard sauce is very hot. You may wish to start with ¼ cup dry mustard and add more to suit your taste, or use your own mustard (we like Boar's Head Honey Mustard). Mustard sauce also is excellent with egg rolls.*

Founded in 1919, the Dayton Art Institute is the Miami Valley's only fine art museum and one of the nation's best. Renovated and expanded during 1996-97, the DAI's historical landmark facility houses a 12,000-object permanent collection rated as "superb in quality" by the American Association of Museums. The beautifully redesigned galleries feature art from around the world, highlighted by Asian, Renaissance, Baroque, American, and Contemporary works. The DAI hosts world-class special exhibitions, concerts, family and youth programs, social events and more. The DAI Experiencenter—the first gallery of its kind in the country—offers a fun, hands-on space for young people to learn about art and its many components.

Swiss Fondue

Great party food

Yield: 6 to 8 servings

2-3	cloves garlic, peeled		Freshly ground black pepper
⅔	cup dry white wine		Freshly grated nutmeg
8	ounces Gruyère cheese, cubed or shredded	¼	cup kirsch (cherry brandy)
8	ounces Emmentaler cheese, cubed or shredded	1	teaspoon cornstarch French bread, cut into 1-inch cubes

Cheese can be cubed or shredded up to 2 days ahead.

6 Rub garlic cloves over the inside of a fondue pot or a heavy pot. Discard cloves. Add wine to pot; bring to a boil over medium heat.

6 Add cheeses; cook and stir until cheese is melted and smooth. Season with pepper and nutmeg.

6 Combine kirsch and cornstarch in a small bowl. Add to cheese mixture. Cook, stirring constantly, until smooth and thickened.

6 Serve in pot over a heat source, with bread cubes and dipping forks on the side.

Note: *If fondue does not thicken, slowly stir in more cornstarch. Try using tart Granny Smith apples for dipping, or add a dash of dry mustard for a different flavor.*

Menu: *Pair with a fresh green salad and you have a great entrée for two.*

Warm Vidalia Onion Dip

There will be no leftovers

Yield: 6 to 8 servings

1	cup mayonnaise	Juice of ½ lemon (1 tablespoon)
1	cup shredded Swiss cheese	Salt to taste
1	cup grated Vidalia or sweet onion	A few drops Tabasco sauce

Dip can be prepared up to 8 hours ahead and stored in the refrigerator until ready to bake.

6 Preheat oven to 325 degrees.

6 Combine all ingredients and place in a small oven-safe serving dish.

6 Bake 20 to 30 minutes, or until bubbly. Transfer to broiler and cook 2 minutes, watching carefully. Serve with pita chips or crackers.

Note: *Do not substitute reduced-fat mayonnaise.*

According to legend, fondue was invented in the 16th Century when Zurich was under siege and the only available foods were bread, cheese and wine. Serendipity!

Quick Appetizers:

• Spread a mild creamy cheese on crackers or slices of whole-grain bread, then garnish with slivers of sun-dried tomatoes.

• Brush mushroom caps with olive oil, fill each with mozzarella and a dab of pesto, and bake at 350° for 10 minutes.

• Serve a large platter of blanched asparagus spears surrounded by bowls of several different dipping sauces.

Asiago Cheese Dip

Creamy and decadent

Yield: 8 to 10 servings

1	cup mayonnaise	⅓	cup chopped sun-dried tomatoes
1	cup sour cream		marinated in olive oil
⅓	cup sliced fresh mushrooms	1	cup shredded Asiago cheese
⅓	cup chopped green onion		

🕐 *Dip can be refrigerated up to 24 hours before baking.*

◑ Preheat oven to 350 degrees.

◑ Combine all ingredients in a large mixing bowl. Transfer to a 2-quart baking dish.

◑ Bake 15 minutes, or until warmed through.

Note: *Serve with crackers or crusty French bread slices. For a different appetizer, try spreading dip on bread slices, topping with additional cheese and broiling until just brown.*

Code Blue Dip

Disappears quickly — absolutely addictive!

Yield: 8 to 10 servings

2	(8 ounce) packages cream cheese, softened	1	pound bacon, cooked and crumbled
1½	cups finely chopped green onion	½	cup Parmesan cheese, or to taste
		1	cup sour cream

🕐 *Dip can be prepared up to 8 hours ahead and stored in refrigerator until ready to bake.*

◑ Preheat oven to 350 degrees.

◑ Mix all ingredients. Pour into an oven-safe serving dish.

◑ Bake 20 to 30 minutes. Serve with Triscuits or other cocktail crackers.

Note: *Can be served warm, at room temperature or cold. Can substitute light sour cream and cream cheese.*

A cheese tray is a beautiful and delicious addition to an hors d'oeuvre selection. Try a themed tasting, such as French or farmhouse cheeses. Select three to six cheeses, depending upon the number of guests. Vary the flavors, textures and shapes. Cheeses are generally categorized by texture: fresh, soft ripened, semi-soft, semi-firm, and hard. Flavors vary depending upon the milk used and the aging process. Serve with thin slices of French bread or whole-grain crackers. Fruit adds color, and complements the cheeses' flavors. Arrange cheeses and fruit on a tray lined with paper or fresh lemon leaves. Some suggestions: Chevré, Coulommiers, Havarti and Roquefort, Cheddar, St. Andre, Bucheron and Manchego.

◑ ◑ ◑

The start of Dayton's rich cultural climate can be traced back to April 22, 1816. The first theatrical performance in Dayton, titled "Matrimony", was given in the home of William Huffman on St. Clair Street.

Blue Cheese Bites

A blue cheese lover's dream

Yield: 40 pieces

1	(7½ ounce) container refrigerated biscuits	3	tablespoons crumbled blue cheese
4	tablespoons butter		

- ๑ Preheat oven to 400 degrees.
- ๑ Quarter biscuits and arrange in two 8- or 9-inch round baking dishes.
- ๑ Melt butter and blue cheese in a microwave. Drizzle over biscuits.
- ๑ Bake 12 to 15 minutes, or until brown. Serve warm.

Note: *Bites are best when served warm. Pie plates and quiche dishes work well for baking these bites.*

Parmesan Bread Twists

Great for company

Yield: 32 twists

1	(12 ounce) bag frozen roll dough (8 rolls)	¼	cup freshly grated Parmesan cheese
¼	cup extra virgin olive oil		Olive oil spray

🕐 *Can be made 6 to 12 hours ahead, covered and refrigerated. Bring to room temperature before baking.*

- ๑ Coat rolls lightly with oil and thaw at room temperature according to package directions. Let stand until dough is no longer chilled.
- ๑ Pinch each roll into 4 pieces. Flatten each piece to make a strip about ½-inch wide and 6 inches long. Let rest 15 minutes.
- ๑ Preheat oven to 400 degrees.
- ๑ Lightly coat top of strips with olive oil. Sprinkle lightly with cheese. Twist strips in tight spirals, cheese side in, and place on lightly greased baking sheets. Spray dough with olive oil spray.
- ๑ Bake 10 minutes, or until golden.

Note: *Variations: Brush strips of dough with butter and sprinkle with cinnamon sugar before twisting. Coat strips of dough with olive oil and sprinkle lightly with rosemary and finely chopped kalamata olives before twisting.*

For the best flavor, buy Parmigiano-Reggiano, the real Parmesan cheese. Never buy grated Parmigiano-Reggiano—it loses its flavor. To store cheese: remove the plastic wrap and let the cheese sit at room temperature briefly; rewrap it with plastic; and cover with aluminum foil. Change the wrap every time the cheese is used, or at least once a week. Store in the refrigerator.

Divine Caviar

Sheer elegance

Yield: 8 to 10 servings

6-8	hard-cooked eggs, chopped
1	stick butter, melted
2	green onions, minced
	Freshly ground black pepper to taste

1	(3½ ounce) jar black lumpfish caviar
	Sour cream to taste
	Capers, parsley and lemon slices for garnish

🕐 *Plan to begin recipe at least 1½ hours ahead. Can prepare butter mixture up to 1 day ahead.*

𝕆 Mix together egg, butter, onion, and pepper.

𝕆 Line a shallow round dish or pan with plastic wrap. Press egg mixture into dish. Fold plastic wrap over top; refrigerate until butter hardens and a mold is formed. This takes about 1 hour, or you may refrigerate overnight.

𝕆 Drain caviar in a fine mesh strainer for at least 20 to 30 minutes, removing as much oil as possible. Caviar should be as dry as possible.

𝕆 Remove mold from refrigerator and invert onto a serving platter. Spread sour cream on top. Gently place caviar on sour cream.

𝕆 Garnish as desired. Serve with crackers or toasted baguette slices.

Note: *Try serving with thin slices of cooked red skin potatoes.*

> Purists take their caviar straight on a spoon. Other serving options include toast or sliced black bread, a dab of sour cream, minced hard-cooked egg, finely chopped red onion, and chopped parsley. Iced vodka (store bottle overnight in freezer) or Champagne are the recommended accompanying beverages.

Shrimp Curry Dip

Yield: 10 to 15 servings

1	pound medium shrimp
1	(8 ounce) package cream cheese
¼	cup chutney (we prefer Major Grey's brand)
1	tablespoon curry

1	clove garlic, minced
½	cup sour cream
2	tablespoons milk
¼	teaspoon salt

🕐 *Dip must be refrigerated at least 3 hours before serving. Shrimp can be prepared ahead and stored in refrigerator.*

𝕆 Cook shrimp in boiling water; peel and devein. Chop shrimp into thirds.

𝕆 Use an electric mixer to blend cream cheese, chutney, curry, garlic, sour cream, milk, and salt. Mix in shrimp.

𝕆 Refrigerate at least 3 hours.

Note: *Excellent with wafer crackers. May substitute light cream cheese and light sour cream. While fresh shrimp are more flavorful, frozen shrimp may also be used to prepare this dip.*

> By June 30, 1933, the Chamber Orchestra, now known as the Dayton Philharmonic, was incorporated. It started business with nothing more than a rented phone, a filing cabinet and $100 in cash. It is the oldest and largest performing arts group in the Miami Valley.

Pale Shrimp Zinged with Lemon and Capers

A low-country favorite

Yield: 10 to 12 servings

Marinade

¼ cup fresh lemon juice
1½ teaspoons salt
    Hot pepper sauce to taste
1 teaspoon sugar
¾ cup olive oil

¾ cup red wine vinegar
¾ cup water
2 bay leaves
2½ teaspoons celery seeds

Shrimp

2 pounds shrimp, peeled, deveined and cooked
2 cups sliced onion

1 (2 ounce) bottle capers, undrained

🕐 *Must prepare at least 6 hours ahead.*

🌀 Combine all marinade ingredients in a bowl. Mix well.

🌀 To prepare shrimp, layer shrimp, onion and undrained capers in a large bowl.

🌀 Pour marinade over the layers. Cover and refrigerate 6 hours or longer. Drain, discarding marinade and bay leaves.

🌀 Serve mixture with wooden toothpicks.

Note: *Try including lemon slices in the dish to enhance color and flavor. Serve in a glass bowl to display colors. A refreshing, chilled summer appetizer. May increase salt and lemon juice in the marinade to suit taste.*

The National Afro-American Museum and Cultural Center is the only national black heritage museum chartered by Congress. More than 30,000 artifacts, photographs, and exhibits on art and music are on display. Library materials reflecting the traditions and social customs of African Americans also are housed at this complex.

Croutons à la Tapenade

Sophisticated but so simple

Yield: 2 cups

Tapenade

2	large cloves garlic	2	teaspoons chopped fresh rosemary
3½	cups pitted kalamata olives		
5	anchovy fillets	¼	cup fresh lemon juice
1	tablespoon drained capers	½	cup olive oil
2	teaspoons chopped fresh thyme		Freshly ground black pepper to taste

Croutons

2	French bread baguettes, sliced into rounds	4	large cloves garlic
		¼	cup olive oil

🕐 *Can be prepared up to 3 days ahead. Cover tapenade and refrigerate. Cool croutons completely and store in an airtight container at room temperature.*

- To make tapenade, finely chop garlic in a food processor. Add olives, anchovies, capers, thyme, and rosemary. Process until almost smooth. Add lemon juice.

- With machine running, gradually add olive oil. Blend until smooth. Season with pepper. Transfer to a small bowl.

- To make croutons, preheat oven to 350 degrees.

- Arrange bread slices on 2 baking sheets.

- Bake 15 minutes, or until crisp and golden brown.

- Rub garlic cloves over 1 side of each slice and drizzle with olive oil. Serve warm or at room temperature with tapenade.

Note: *Also goes great with stone wheat crackers.*

Crudités refers to an assortment of raw vegetables. Use the freshest available.
Some to try:
Radishes
Cucumber spears
Snow peas
Fennel strips
Blanched green beans
Jicama
Romaine lettuce hearts
Blanched asparagus
Strips of cooked beets

Fresh Tomato Tart

A great way to use summer tomatoes

Yield: 10 to 12 servings

1	refrigerated pie pastry dough (we prefer Pillsbury brand)	2	large tomatoes, sliced
3	tablespoons grated Parmesan cheese	2	tablespoons olive oil
2	egg whites	2	teaspoons fresh chopped thyme or ½ teaspoon dried
1	cup lowfat ricotta cheese	2	teaspoons fresh chopped basil or ½ teaspoon dried
2	cloves garlic, minced	3	tablespoons grated Parmesan cheese
1	tablespoon fresh chopped basil		
1	tablespoon fresh chopped thyme or lemon thyme		

❧ Preheat oven to 450 degrees.

❧ Fit dough into a 10-inch tart pan or pie plate. Trim dough even with rim of pan. Line with double thickness of foil.

❧ Bake 5 minutes. Remove foil and bake 5 to 7 minutes, or until done.

❧ Reduce oven temperature to 325 degrees.

❧ Sprinkle pastry with 3 tablespoons Parmesan cheese.

❧ Beat egg whites slightly in a mixing bowl. Stir in ricotta cheese, garlic, 1 tablespoon basil, and 1 tablespoon thyme. Spread mixture over pastry. Overlap tomato slices in a circle around edge. Arrange a second circle of tomato slices inside the first.

❧ Stir together olive oil, 2 teaspoons thyme and 2 teaspoons basil; brush over tomato slices. Sprinkle with 3 tablespoons Parmesan cheese.

❧ Bake 25 to 30 minutes, or until heated through and nearly set. Serve warm or at room temperature.

Note: *Try using several different colors and shapes of tomatoes for a beautiful presentation. Use high-quality fresh Parmesan cheese.*

Menu: *Add a leafy green salad and couscous for a fabulous luncheon.*

Sun-Dried Tomato and Herbed Goat Cheese Spread

Yield: 6 to 8 servings

1	(5 to 7 ounce) package high-quality goat cheese	1	tablespoon fresh chopped thyme
½	cup olive oil	2	large cloves garlic, minced
2	bay leaves		Sun-dried tomatoes packed in oil, chopped for garnish
½	tablespoon mixed peppercorns		Fresh basil for garnish

🕐 *Can season cheese up to 2 weeks ahead.*

🌀 Place cheese in a plastic or glass container with a lid.

🌀 Combine oil, bay leaves, peppercorns, thyme, and garlic in a saucepan. Simmer on high heat until mixture pops and sizzles. Pour over cheese and cover tightly.

🌀 Refrigerate up to 2 weeks.

🌀 To serve, bring cheese to room temperature and place on a serving platter.

🌀 Remove bay leaves. Use a slotted spoon to spoon marinade toppings over cheese, leaving oil in container.

🌀 Sprinkle cheese with sun-dried tomato and basil to garnish. Serve with crackers, toast points or baguette slices.

Note: *Decorate the goat cheese with fresh thyme sprigs or flowers. Makes a lovely food gift.*

When I was a member of the Dayton Ballet, we usually performed during the holidays and only had Christmas Day off. The Company dancers would gather at Stuart Sebastian's house for a big meal and a gift exchange. It was as close to family as we could get, and a lot of fun. One year I drew Stuart's name and was at a loss as to what to give to the man-who-had-everything, and on top of that was my boss! After Stuart dropped a hint, I decided on a waffle iron. One cold January afternoon, Stuart invited a small group of us to his house for breakfast to use his new waffle iron. It was very special. First because he cooked everything, and also because it was such a small, intimate group. I can still see him standing in the kitchen with a white apron on making waffles!

—Laura Frock Hinders, former member

Dayton Ballet Company

Guadalajara Guacamole

Guacamole with a kick

Yield: 1 to 2 cups

3	large cloves garlic	2	green onions, white plus 3 inches of green, chopped
1	jalapeño pepper, seeded and chopped	1	teaspoon Tabasco sauce
3	ripe avocados, peeled and halved	½	teaspoon salt
3	tablespoons fresh lemon juice	1	teaspoon freshly ground black pepper
2	plum tomatoes, seeded and chopped	2	tablespoons chopped fresh cilantro

Must be served within 2 hours to maintain fresh color.

⊙ Drop garlic and jalapeño into a food processor with the motor running. Process until finely chopped. Add half the avocado and the lemon juice. Process until smooth. Transfer to a mixing bowl and add remaining avocado. Mash with a spoon.

⊙ Add tomato, onion, Tabasco sauce, salt, pepper, and cilantro. Mix thoroughly with a fork.

⊙ Serve at room temperature within 1 to 2 hours.

Note: *Serve with multicolored tortilla chips. Try using a hollowed-out avocado shell as a serving dish.*

Apple and Gruyère Spread

Yield: 2 cups

4	ounces Gruyère cheese, shredded	½	teaspoon Dijon mustard
1	(8 ounce) package cream cheese, softened	1	large Granny Smith apple, unpeeled and shredded
½	tablespoon milk	¼	cup finely chopped pecans
1	teaspoon prepared yellow mustard (we prefer French's brand)	2	tablespoons chopped fresh chives

⊙ Blend cheeses, milk and mustards in a food processor until smooth.

⊙ Stir apple, pecans and chives into mixture.

⊙ Chill. Serve with crackers.

Note: *Try a hearty wheat cracker with this flavorful spread. May substitute light cream cheese.*

If you are using half an avocado, leave the pit in the unused half, cover it with plastic wrap and refrigerate. This will retard discoloration. If the avocado's cut surface should turn brown, gently scrape off the discoloration. The avocado should be fine underneath.

Gruyère cheese originates from Switzerland, where it has been made since the 12th Century. It is a great cooking cheese, and works beautifully in fondue.

Fiesta Black Bean Dip
with Flour Tortilla Chips

The life of the party

Yield: 8 to 10 servings

1	(16 ounce) can black beans, drained	½	teaspoon ground cumin
1	teaspoon vegetable oil	½	teaspoon chili powder
½	cup chopped onion	¼	cup shredded reduced-fat Monterey Jack cheese
2	cloves garlic, minced	¼	cup chopped fresh cilantro
½	cup diced tomato	1	tablespoon fresh lime juice
⅓	cup mild picante sauce		Flour burrito-size tortillas

Chips can be made up to 4 hours ahead. Let cool and seal in a zip-top bag.

- Place beans in a bowl and partially mash until chunky. Set aside.
- Heat oil in a medium nonstick skillet over medium heat. Add onion and garlic; sauté 4 minutes, or until tender.
- Mix in beans, tomato, picante sauce, cumin, and chili powder. Cook and stir 5 minutes, or until thickened. Remove from heat. Add cheese, cilantro and lime juice. Stir until cheese melts.
- Serve warm or at room temperature with flour tortilla chips.
- To make tortilla chips, preheat oven to 350 degrees.
- Cut tortillas into wedges and place on a greased baking sheet. The chips may overlap slightly.
- Bake 10 to 12 minutes or until cooked to desired crispness. The chips will become crisper after they are removed from oven.

Note: *Try a layer of cheese on top prior to baking. May substitute cheddar or "Mexican blend" cheese for different flavor. Excellent filling for enchiladas, tacos, burritos, or quesadillas.*

Try using these two recipes to create a fabulous three-layer Mexican dip:

1½ cups Fiesta Black Bean Dip

1½ cups Guadalajara Guacamole (page 58)

1½ cups sour cream seasoned with garlic powder, chili powder, ground cumin, salt, and freshly ground pepper. Spread bean dip over the bottom of a 10-inch round glass baking dish. Cover with the guacamole. Spread seasoned sour cream over guacamole layer. Sprinkle the top with ½ cup grated cheddar cheese, finely diced plum tomato, chopped black olives and sliced scallions. Chill or bake 15 minutes in 425° oven. Serve with taco chips.

"That Junior League Pesto Mold"

One of our favorites!

Yield: 24 to 30 servings

¼	cup pine nuts	½	cup olive oil
2-3	cloves garlic	3	cups Parmesan cheese
1	cup tightly packed fresh spinach	3	tablespoons butter, softened
1	cup tightly packed fresh basil	2	(8 ounce) packages cream cheese
½	cup fresh parsley	4	sticks unsalted butter, softened
½	teaspoon salt		Fresh parsley sprigs for garnish

Must be made at least 6 hours ahead.

- Preheat oven to 325 degrees.
- Roast pine nuts in oven on a baking sheet for 10 minutes.
- To make pesto, puree nuts, garlic, spinach, basil, parsley, and salt in a food processor. Add oil and blend. Add cheese and 3 tablespoons butter; mix, being careful to not over-blend.
- Beat cream cheese and 4 sticks unsalted butter together until smooth.
- To assemble mold, moisten and wring out an 18-inch piece of cheesecloth. Line a 6-cup mold with the cheesecloth, smoothing any wrinkles. (A dome shaped bowl works great and has a nice finished look.) Use a spatula to layer a quarter of cream cheese mixture into mold. Top with a quarter of the pesto mixture. Repeat layers until both mixtures are used up. Fold cheesecloth over and pack down lightly. Chill at least 6 hours or overnight for best results.
- Unfold cheesecloth and invert bowl onto a serving plate. Pull up bowl while holding cheesecloth down. Carefully remove cheesecloth. Garnish with fresh parsley. Serve with crackers or baguette slices.

Note: *For faster preparation, try using 2 cups prepared pesto. Try garnishing with sun-dried tomatoes for added color.*

My sister-in-law invited her Italian in-laws for dinner, and wanted to impress them by making pesto. Unfortunately, she did not have any fresh basil. The recipe called for 1 cup packed basil leaves, so she used 1 cup dried! It was a thick, bitter paste that turned out to be very unappealing, to say the least. No one could force down more than one bite, including my sister-in-law. We still tease her about it!

—Margot Varley

Creamed Cheeses
with Brandied Cranberries

Looks lovely, tastes great

Yield: 12 servings

1	(8 ounce) package cream cheese
¼	cup crumbled blue cheese
1	cup shredded white cheddar cheese
1	tablespoon finely chopped onion
1	cup fresh or frozen cranberries, thawed
¼	cup sugar
3	tablespoons frozen apple juice concentrate, thawed
3	tablespoons brandy

🕐 *Spread can be made several days ahead and stored, covered, in the refrigerator. Store cheese and sauce separately. Be sure to follow lead times for bringing cheese to room temperature.*

6 Line a flat, shallow 1½-cup dish with plastic wrap.

6 In a food processor with a metal blade, blend cheeses and onion. Spoon mixture into lined dish, smooth top, cover and refrigerate.

6 Combine cranberries, sugar and juice concentrate in a small saucepan. Cook over low heat, stirring frequently, until juices flow and cranberries pop. Cook 3 minutes longer or until slightly thickened. Remove from heat and cool 5 minutes. Stir in brandy, cover and refrigerate 30 minutes, or until cool.

6 About 30 minutes before serving, remove cover from cheese and invert onto a small serving plate. Remove plastic from cheese and let stand at room temperature for 30 minutes for best flavor.

6 Before serving, spoon cranberry mixture over cheese.

Note: *Serve with assorted crackers or crusty French bread.*

Toast nuts by spreading them in a single layer on a rimmed baking sheet and putting them in a preheated 350° oven for 5 minutes until they just begin to turn a pale golden brown. Check frequently to prevent burning.

Raspberry and Coconut Creamed Cheese Spread

This unusual combination will delight your guests

Yield: 8 to 10 servings

1	(8 ounce) package cream cheese, slightly softened	⅓	cup chopped cashews
3	green onions, green part only, thinly sliced	½-¾	cup raspberry jam
		½-1	cup shredded coconut, or to taste

◌ Roll cream cheese into a ball and then flatten into a 7-inch disc.

◌ Sprinkle onion over cheese, then cashews.

◌ Spread jam over the disc and top with coconut. Serve with a sturdy cracker.

Note: *If you can find it, frozen, shredded coconut has a wonderful, fresh flavor. Try serving with Triscuit crackers.*

More quick appetizers:
• Blend fresh goat cheese with minced fresh herbs, roll in more herbs or coarsely cracked peppercorns, drizzle with olive oil, and serve with a loaf of whole grain bread.
• Wrap stalks of blanched asparagus with thinly sliced prosciutto and pass an herb vinaigrette as a dipping sauce.
• Dip small chunks of vegetables in extra virgin olive oil; sprinkle with salt and pepper. Thread the vegetables on skewers and grill.

For a lovely, natural presentation, serve dips and sauces in hollowed-out vegetables, such as a purple cabbage or brightly colored bell peppers. Simply scoop out the core to hold the dip, and use the outer leaves to line the plate. Garnish with flowers or fresh herbs.

Tasha's Dip

Perfect crudités dip

Yield: 3 cups

2	cups mayonnaise	¾	teaspoon paprika
1	cup ketchup	¾	teaspoon salt
¼	medium onion, finely chopped	⅛	teaspoon freshly ground black pepper
	Juice of 1 lemon		
2	tablespoons honey	½	teaspoon Worcestershire sauce
1	tablespoon horseradish	8	drops Tabasco sauce
½	teaspoon curry powder	¼	cup chopped fresh parsley

⏰ *Must make 2 days ahead.*

◌ Combine all ingredients. Refrigerate 2 days to allow flavors to blend.

Note: *Especially nice with red peppers, cucumbers, tomatoes, and carrots. Try serving in a hollowed-out pepper or head of red cabbage.*

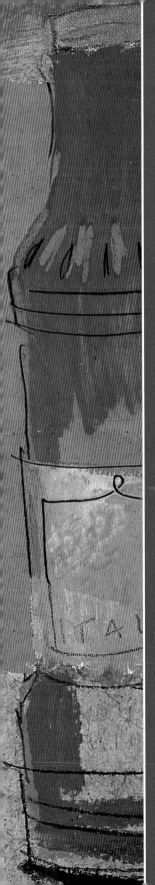

Let the Good Times Flow

BEVERAGES

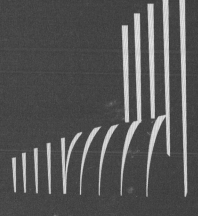

SCHUSTER PERFORMING ARTS CENTER

LET THE GOOD TIMES FLOW

The Benjamin and Marian Schuster Performing Arts Center will be a lively centerpiece for the Miami Valley's thriving arts community. World-renowned architect Cesar Pelli designed the state-of-the art facility, incorporating amenities for patrons of the arts, businesses and residents.

Dayton's Philharmonic Orchestra and the Dayton Opera will make the 2,300-seat performing hall their home, rejoicing in the grand acoustics and patron comforts. The Victoria Theatre Association also will use the hall to present large Broadway productions, as well as a portion of its regular season offerings. This frees up the popular Victoria stage for more mid-sized, nontraditional concerts, dances and community events.

The elegant Wintergarden will become Dayton's indoor gathering place. The space is perfect for events ranging from ballroom dancing to lunchtime concerts. And the residential and commercial tower will complete the structure that allows Dayton residents to work, live and play downtown!

The Schuster Performing Arts Center is certain to enhance Dayton's well-known reputation as a rich theater and arts community.

DR. BENJAMIN AND MARIAN SCHUSTER's gift was the largest private donation to the downtown Dayton performing arts center. Dr. Schuster explains their motivation: "We decided it was the time of my life to give something back to the community. Words cannot describe how thrilled we are to help make the performing arts center a reality. It makes the statement that Dayton will not settle for mediocrity. I think the building of the performing arts center will have a ripple effect and I think it will really enhance the city. I think the focus of activity is shifting back to downtown."

Celebration Punch

A tasty, yet sophisticated punch

Yield: 8 servings

1	quart ginger ale	1	quart pineapple juice
1	quart apple cider		Ice
1	quart white grape juice		

🕐 *If desired, an ice ring may be prepared in advance. For decoration, add maraschino cherries to ring before freezing.*

6 Mix all ingredients in a punch bowl.

6 Serve over ice.

Zippy Punch

A great punch for parties and celebrations

Yield: 9 servings

1	(10 ounce) container frozen sliced strawberries, thawed	1½	cups water
1	(6 ounce) can frozen lemonade concentrate, thawed	1	quart ginger ale, chilled
			Ice

🕐 *If serving in a punch bowl, prepare a frozen ice ring filled with fresh fruit.*

6 Mix all ingredients. Add ice and serve.

The Junior League of Dayton's first social event was held on April 5, 1920 at the Dayton Country Club. To attend this festive ball, you had to pay $3. JLD President Katherine Kennedy (Brown) wore "a smart frock of turquoise silk with overdrape of self-colored maline cream panels, and side streamers with rosettes of pink roses. She carried a turquoise feather fan and pink sweet peas." Festivities aside, it was soon down to business, as the first Provisional class was elected to membership on May 4, 1920. They had to "hit the books" right away for a tough course in Parliamentary law!

6 6 6

In 1921, a pound of coffee cost 25¢, pork chops cost 22¢ per pound, a pound of bacon was 24¢, and chuck roast was a mere 10¢ per pound!

Mint Tea Punch

Serve at your next shower or luncheon, and you'll get raves!

Yield: 16 to 20 servings

4	heaping tablespoons instant tea mix	2	(12 ounce) cans frozen lemonade concentrate, prepared
4	cups boiling water		Ice
2	cups sugar		Fresh mint and lemon slices for garnish
12	sprigs fresh mint		
2	(12 ounce) cans frozen orange juice concentrate, prepared		

⦿ Mix tea with boiling water. Stir in sugar and mint sprigs. Cool.

⦿ Add prepared orange juice and lemonade to cooled tea.

⦿ Serve chilled over ice garnished with mint and lemon.

Bellini

A peach of a refreshment!

Yield: 10 servings

2½	cups peach nectar	1	(750 ml) bottle champagne (dry or Asti Spumante)
3	tablespoons fresh lemon juice		Crushed ice
1¼	cups peach schnapps		
5	medium peaches, sliced		

⦿ Combine nectar, lemon juice and schnapps in a large pitcher. Stir in peaches.

⦿ Just before serving, add a bit of crushed ice and stir. Pour in champagne and serve.

Note: *"Prosecco" is an inexpensive Italian champagne that works well in this recipe. If fresh peaches aren't available, try frozen sliced peaches.*

When planning a wine tasting, here are a few tips to keep in mind.

• Consider having each person you invite bring a wine of their choosing.

• A blind test is fun, and you might be surprised what you like. Just mark each label with a letter or number and put the same number or letter on a cover around the bottle. Don't reveal the identity of the wines until everyone has tasted each wine.

• Have some bread or light crackers, and water on hand. Mints and strongly flavored foods should be avoided. Save the chocolate for dessert.

• Avoid smoking and strong perfumes. They affect how well guests can smell and taste wines.

• A fun way to have a tasting is to make it a part of a dinner you're hosting. It's an optimum time of day for a tasting and you'll have plenty of wine left over to enjoy with the meal.

Champagne Americana

This combination of brandy and bubbly gives you another reason to celebrate

Yield: 12 servings

1	pint brandy	1	(750 ml) bottle champagne
2	(28 ounce) bottles or 1 (2 liter) bottle ginger ale	1	(750 ml) bottle sparkling grape juice

🕐 *All bottles should be chilled prior to mixing. If desired, prepare an ice ring with raspberries or cranberries, depending on the season.*

🌀 Combine all ingredients. Serve immediately.

Note: *Do not make in advance… you don't want to lose the sparkle.*

At the end of a meal, pour leftover wine into an ice-cube tray and freeze it. Store cubes in well-sealed freezer bags, and you'll always have a bit of wine when the recipe calls for ¼ or ½ cup. You wouldn't want to thaw and drink the wine, but it's fine for cooking. Remember, because of the alcohol content, wine doesn't freeze hard like water.

White Sangria

A cool and crisp summertime drink

Yield: 16 to 20 servings

½	cup Grand Marnier	2	mangoes, peeled and thinly sliced
½	cup cognac	4	bottles dry white wine, such as White Bordeaux or Rioja
¼	cup sugar		
4	oranges, thinly sliced	1	quart ginger ale

🕐 *Initial ingredients must be mixed 1 hour prior to serving.*

🌀 Combine Grand Marnier, cognac, sugar, orange, and mango slices in a pitcher. Let stand for at least 1 hour.

🌀 Pour into a large bowl. Stir in wine.

🌀 Add ginger ale just before serving.

So what kind of wine do you use in cooking? First off, never use anything labeled "cooking wine." Take one sip of that and you'll spit it out. Conventional wisdom is to use the same wine you'll be serving with dinner. If you are not serving wine with dinner try these options: ¼ cup of dry vermouth will substitute for white wine; Marsala, either dry or sweet; or a nutty Madeira. The high alcohol content allows for on-the-shelf storage for any of these options.

Frozen Baci

"Baci" means "kisses" in Italian

Yield: 2 servings

½ cup vanilla ice cream
2 tablespoons hazelnut liqueur (such as Frangelico or Capella)

1 teaspoon unsweetened nonalkalized cocoa powder
Perugina Baci chocolates (optional)

- Combine all ingredients except chocolates in a blender. Process about 1 minute or until smooth.
- Pour mixture into 2 glasses. Serve with chocolates.

Note: *Any fine chocolate with hazelnuts may be substituted for Perugina Baci chocolates.*

George Newcom built Newcom Tavern in 1796. The two-room tavern is known to be one of Dayton's first permanent structures. It was used as many things, such as the town's first store, church, post office, courthouse, and jail.

Montgomery County and the county's Historical Society have twin projects in the works that complement other downtown projects. They are the restoration of the Old Courthouse to its 1860 grandeur, and the renovation of Memorial Hall into a first-class museum of local history. The museum will highlight the NCR Archive, which contains more than 3 million artifacts collected by John Patterson and his successors over the last 100-plus years. The museum will become an integral part of the RiverScape project.

Mango Daiquiris

The best frozen drink…ever!

Yield: 10 servings

1 (26 ounce) jar sliced mangoes (we prefer Sunfresh brand)
Colored decorator sugar
1 (6 ounce) can frozen limeade concentrate, thawed and undiluted

1 cup rum
½ cup Triple Sec
¼ cup Grand Marnier (optional)
Ice

- Spoon 3 tablespoons of mango liquid into a saucer. Place decorator sugar in a separate saucer. Dip rims of serving glasses in mango liquid and then in sugar. Set aside.
- Pour mangoes and remaining liquid into a blender. Add limeade, rum, Triple Sec and Grand Marnier. Process until smooth, scraping down sides once.
- Pour half of mixture into a small pitcher. Set aside.
- Add enough ice to remaining mixture in blender to bring it to the 5 cup level. Process until slushy. Scrape down sides.
- Pour mixture into prepared glasses. Repeat with remaining mango mixture and ice. Serve immediately.

Pinky's Homemade Irish Cream

Sweet and refreshing

Yield: 5 servings

1¾ cups Irish whiskey, or less as desired	4 eggs or egg substitute equivalent
1 (14 ounce) can sweetened condensed milk	2 tablespoons chocolate syrup
1 cup light cream	2 teaspoons instant coffee
	1 teaspoon vanilla extract
	½ teaspoon almond extract

🕐 *May prepare and store (tightly sealed) in the refrigerator for up to 1 month.*

🌀 Combine all ingredients in a blender. Process until mixed.

Note: *Serve as an apéritif for unexpected guests at holiday time, or with your favorite brewed coffee as an after-dinner treat.*

Lemon Shandies

A truly refreshing summer drink

Yield: 10 to 16 servings

1 cup sugar	1 cup fresh lemon juice
1 cup water	2 sprigs fresh mint
4 (3 inch) strips lemon zest	Chilled beer, such as pale ale
2 cups water	

🕐 *Lemonade portion may be made in advance.*

🌀 Combine sugar and 1 cup water in a small saucepan. Bring to a boil, stirring until sugar dissolves. Stir in zest. Cool sugar syrup to room temperature.

🌀 Transfer syrup to a small pitcher. Stir in 2 cups water, lemon juice and mint. Chill until cold.

🌀 Pour ¼ cup lemonade, or to taste, into chilled beer glasses. Top off with beer.

For a festive Halloween libation, serve a Black and Tan, the two-tone drink that layers light and dark beers. Pour Guinness Stout into a chilled beer mug until half-full. Carefully pour Bass Ale on top of the stout, letting a good head of foam rise just above the rim.

Beginning in 1853, the Rike's department store was known as a place where people wanted to be, so it is not a surprise that people mourned its passing when the building was torn down. Rising from the rubble, the Schuster Performing Arts Center will continue the tradition of Second and Main being a place where people want to gather!

Hot Spiced Cider 🚲

Great for fall harvest parties

Yield: 8 servings

2	quarts cider	1	teaspoon ground cinnamon
½	cup brown sugar	3	(3 inch) sticks cinnamon
1	teaspoon whole cloves	⅛	teaspoon nutmeg
1	teaspoon allspice		

❻ Place cider in a 2-quart capacity electric percolator.

❻ Place sugar, cloves, allspice, ground cinnamon, cinnamon sticks, and nutmeg in percolator basket.

❻ Perk 7 minutes. Serve hot in mugs.

Frozen Cappuccinos

A great variation of an old favorite

Yield: 2 servings

1	cup freshly brewed espresso, cooled to room temperature	¼	teaspoon cinnamon, plus extra for garnish
2	cups ice cubes	¼	cup Kahlúa or other coffee-flavored liqueur (optional)
¼	cup half-and-half or whole milk		
3	tablespoons superfine sugar, or to taste		

❻ Combine all ingredients in a blender. Process until smooth but still thick.

❻ Divide mixture between 2 tall glasses. Sprinkle with extra cinnamon to garnish.

Here is a drink to warm you up. Mix equal amounts of apple schnapps and cinnamon schnapps in shot glasses. Drop in a Red-Hot for panache!

An 8-ounce cup of coffee has 135 milligrams of caffeine. An 8-ounce cup of steeped tea has 50 milligrams of caffeine.

Southern Sweet Tea with a Twist

Perfect for a summer luncheon

Yield: 10 servings

2	cups boiling water
4	regular-size tea bags
1¼	cups sugar
⅓	cup lemon juice
1	teaspoon almond extract

1	teaspoon vanilla extract
2	quarts cold water
	Ice
	Lemon wedges and sprigs of mint for garnish

- Pour boiling water over tea bags. Steep 5 minutes. Discard tea bags.
- Add sugar, juice, extracts, and cold water. Mix well until sugar dissolves.
- Serve over ice. Garnish with lemon wedges and mint sprigs.

Beverages

Bring lemons to room temperature (or microwave on HIGH for 15 seconds), then roll them on the counter before squeezing to extract the most juice.

Mimi's Bloody Mary Mix

Beef bouillon gives this mix a robust taste

Yield: 4 servings

1	(10 ounce) can sauerkraut juice
6	tablespoons lemon juice
5	dashes Worcestershire sauce
3	dashes Tabasco sauce
1	heaping teaspoon instant beef bouillon dissolved in ¼ cup warm water

1	tablespoon prepared horseradish
2	cups V-8 juice
	Vodka

- Combine all ingredients except vodka. Shake well and add vodka, as desired.

Fru-Fru Swirlies

Bring the beach to your backyard

Yield: 8 servings

	Ice
1	(12 ounce) can frozen margarita mix

¾-1	cup tequila
¼	cup rum

- Fill a blender halfway with ice. Add margarita mix and tequila. Blend until smooth.
- Add more ice to fill blender. Add rum. Blend until smooth; serve.

Note: *This drink may be made with only rum by substituting 6 to 8 ounces rum for the tequila and using frozen limeade concentrate instead of the margarita mix.*

"Cheers!"

Yum sen—Chinese

Skål—Danish, Norwegian and Swedish

Proost—Dutch

A votre santé—French

Prosit—German

Eis Igian—Greek

L'Chaim—Hebrew

Cin cin—Italian

Kampai—Japanese

Na zdrowie—Polish

A sua saúde—Portuguese

Na zdorovia—Russian

Salud—Spanish

Classic Eggnog

Yield: 6 to 8 servings

⅓	cup sugar	1	teaspoon vanilla
2	eggs, separated		Brandy or rum flavoring to taste
¼	teaspoon salt	½	cup heavy cream, whipped
4	cups milk		Nutmeg for garnish
3	tablespoons sugar		

🕐 *Eggnog will need to chill up to 4 hours before serving.*

◟ In a medium saucepan, whisk ⅓ cup sugar into egg yolks. Stir in salt and milk.

◟ Cook over medium heat, stirring constantly, for 20 to 25 minutes, or until mixture coats a wooden spoon. Cool.

◟ Beat egg whites until foamy. Gradually add 3 tablespoons sugar, beating until soft peaks form.

◟ Add whites to custard and mix thoroughly. Stir in vanilla and brandy flavoring. Chill 3 to 4 hours.

◟ Pour into a punch bowl or individual serving cups. Dot with "islands" of whipped cream. Sprinkle with nutmeg and serve.

Metropolitan Martini

The ultimate cocktail

Yield: 1 serving

	Ice	1	tablespoon fresh lime juice
1½	ounces gin		Lemon slice for garnish
1½	ounces chilled cranberry juice cocktail		

◟ Fill a cocktail shaker halfway with ice. Add all ingredients, except lemon slice, and shake well.

◟ Strain into a chilled stemmed cocktail glass. Garnish with lemon and serve.

Note: *Vodka may be substituted for gin.*

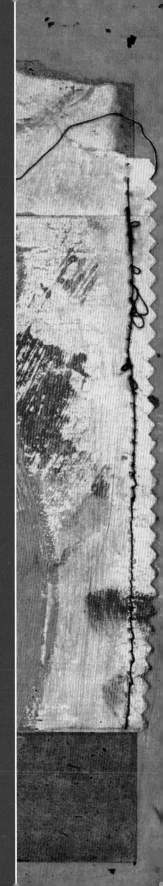

Born 'n Bread

BREAKFAST
BREADS & MUFFINS

DAYTON CELEBRITIES

BORN 'N BREAD

Many celebrities have called Dayton "home." One best-loved local celebrity was Erma Bombeck, who achieved international success by celebrating the humor in everyday life. An exuberant spirit, Bombeck worked as syndicated columnist of "The Wit's End" and authored 14 bestselling books.

Former Daytonian Jonathan Winters was honored with the 1999 Mark Twain Prize for humor! Always interested in making people laugh, Winters studied cartooning at the Dayton Art Institute. He went on to become one of the great improvisational geniuses of our time, thanks to his wide array of characters, sound effects and voices.

Ramón Estevez, who changed his name to Martin Sheen to avoid ethnic typecasting, began acting at Chaminade High School. Sheen has become almost as famous for his social activism as for his big screen roles. One of Sheen's most popular characters is President Bartlett on T.V.'s "The West Wing," where he is joined by fellow Dayton-born actors Rob Lowe and Allison Janney.

Phil Donahue realized from the beginning that the audience asked better questions than he did, so he left his chair and started roaming the aisles. For 30 years, the creator of the modern T.V. talk show gave viewers a forum for commenting on the controversial subjects of the day—and they loved it!

Humorist ERMA BOMBECK was quick to admit that her talents lay with the typewriter, not the Cuisinart. In a July 1970 column, Bombeck lets us glimpse into her kitchen: "As a cook, I am uninspired. I have one child who considers catsup a beverage, another who approaches the table with all the enthusiasm of discovering a suicide ring, and a third who would miss a meal to watch his bicycle rust."

Egg, Sausage and Cheese Casserole ❄ 🚲

An excellent casserole for a large gathering

Yield: 10 servings

8	slices thin white bread, crusts discarded, cubed
1	pound pork sausage, cooked, crumbled and drained
1½	cups fresh mushrooms, chopped and sautéed (optional)
2	cups shredded cheddar cheese
4	eggs

2½	cups milk
¼	teaspoon dry mustard
1	(10¾ ounce) can condensed cream of mushroom soup
½	soup can milk
2-3	tablespoons butter
1-2	cups plain stuffing mix (we prefer Pepperidge Farm)

🕐 *Initial ingredients must be assembled and refrigerated at least 12 hours ahead. Sausage may be cooked, crumbled and drained up to 4 hours ahead. Bread slices may be cubed up to 4 hours ahead.*

6 Place bread cubes in bottom of a greased, 8x12-inch baking dish. Add sausage, mushrooms and cheese.

6 In a separate bowl, mix eggs, 2½ cups milk and dry mustard. Pour over bread cube mixture. Refrigerate overnight.

6 Bring casserole to room temperature (allow 2 hours for this). When ready to bake, preheat oven to 325 degrees.

6 Mix soup and ½ can of milk together; pour over casserole.

6 In a saucepan, melt butter over low heat. Add stuffing. Spread mixture over casserole.

6 Bake 1 hour, 15 minutes.

Note: *If you wish to freeze casserole, remove from oven after 45 minutes of baking. Let casserole cool. Wrap tightly; freeze up to 3 months. To serve, thaw casserole and cook at 350 degrees for 30 minutes, or until cooked throughout.*

Menu: *Add Julie's Very Berry Muffins (page 92) and assorted sliced fruit for a special breakfast.*

I smile every time I even think of this recipe! It was heartily approved by about 50 of my son's Sigma Chi brothers, whom he invited to spend the weekend with us so they could attend a wedding. I went to Kroger's four times that night/early morning, and kept making and baking dish after dish. One of my favorite social events ever!! They presented me with a Sigma Chi pin before they left on Monday afternoon!!

—Pattie Edmonson

D.L.'s Tortilla de Patatas ⭐

Day-brightening food (and commentary) from Dayton humorist D.L. Stewart!

Yield: 4 adult servings (or 1 teenage serving!)

6-7	slices bacon, cut into 1-inch pieces	½	teaspoon freshly ground black pepper
1	medium onion, chopped		Ground cumin to taste (optional)
1	medium potato, cut into ½-inch cubes		Fresh parsley or cilantro for garnish
6	eggs, beaten		Your favorite Mexican salsa (optional)
¾	teaspoon salt		

◎ Cook bacon until crisp (or if you are a very good cook, sauté it). Remove and drain bacon, reserving 4 tablespoons fat in the pan (I usually try to do this part when my wife has her back turned).

◎ Add onion and potato to fat in pan; sauté 10 minutes or until tender but not brown. Add bacon, egg, salt, pepper, and cumin. Cover and cook 10 minutes, or until egg is firm on top and lightly browned on the bottom.

◎ Cut into wedges and garnish with parsley or cilantro (parsley and cilantro may be removed before eating, rinsed and saved for the next meal).

◎ Serve with lots of salsa on the side (the amount used will vary, depending on how badly burned the tortilla is).

Menu: *Serve with fruit for breakfast. Or, offer for dinner with Brazilian Black Beans (page 150) or Black Bean, Corn and Avocado Salad (page 143). Make Rum Cake (page 263) for dessert.*

This is one of my favorite recipes because it contains bacon and eggs, which are two things my wife won't let me eat because they are so bad for me, and I don't have a great deal of life insurance. But when I put them together, give them a foreign name, and garnish them with inedible things like parsley or cilantro, she doesn't mind. It's a big breakfast hit with my family, although I, personally, would rather go to the Golden Nugget pancake house.

—D. L. Stewart,
Columnist
Dayton Daily News

Easy Baked Spinach, Eggs and Cheese

Very tasty and easy to prepare

Yield: 6 to 8 servings

7-8	eggs, beaten	1	(24 ounce) container small-curd cottage cheese
1	(10 ounce) package frozen spinach, thawed and squeezed dry	7	tablespoons flour
1	stick butter, melted		Salt and freshly ground black pepper to taste
1	(12 ounce) package shredded cheddar cheese		

🕐 *Ingredients may be mixed and refrigerated 12 hours prior to baking.*

६ Preheat oven to 350 degrees.

६ Combine all ingredients and pour into a greased soufflé dish.

६ Bake 1 hour.

Menu: *For a simple brunch, add a smoked salmon plate with bagels, a fruit plate and Caramelized Coconut Coffee Cake (page 86).*

This recipe has become a tradition for my daughter's birthday brunch. It's so easy to throw this in the oven and enjoy your guests.

—Amy Skardon

Dad's Favorite Waffles ❄

These waffles have a wonderful texture…crispy on the outside and moist and rich on the inside

Yield: 6 to 8 servings

2	eggs	2	cups flour
2	cups buttermilk or sour milk	1	teaspoon baking soda
6	tablespoons shortening, softened	2	teaspoons baking powder
		½	teaspoon salt

६ Preheat waffle iron to "high" setting.

६ Beat eggs in a mixing bowl. Add milk and shortening. Mix well.

६ In a separate bowl, combine flour, baking soda, baking powder, and salt. Stir into egg mixture.

६ Pour batter into waffle iron and cook until steam stops escaping from iron.

Note: *Mix does not keep well in refrigerator. Excess mix should be made into waffles, which may be frozen for future use. Heat in toaster or microwave before serving.*

When I was a child, my Dad would wake up early on Sunday to make homemade waffles on an old waffle iron. Our favorite part was eating the run-off batter, after it had baked on the side of the waffle iron. We called these pieces "mellows." The taste of mellows, and the smell of fresh coffee and waffles—what a perfect Sunday.

—Heidi Donnelly

Crème Brûlée French Toast

An extraordinary interpretation of an old favorite

Yield: 6 servings

1 stick unsalted butter	5 eggs
1 cup brown sugar	1½ cups half-and-half
2 tablespoons corn syrup	1 teaspoon vanilla
1 (8 to 9 inch) round loaf country-style bread	1 teaspoon Grand Marnier
	¼ teaspoon salt

🕐 *Ingredients must be prepared and assembled at least 8 to 12 hours prior to baking.*

⚬ In a small heavy saucepan over medium heat, melt butter with sugar and corn syrup, stirring until smooth. Pour into a 9x13-inch baking dish.

⚬ Cut 6 (1-inch) slices from the center portion of the bread, reserving ends for another use. Trim crusts from slices. Arrange bread in a single layer in baking dish, squeezing them to fit.

⚬ In a bowl, whisk together eggs, half-and-half, vanilla, Grand Marnier, and salt until well-combined. Pour evenly over bread. Cover and refrigerate at least 8 hours and up to 1 day.

⚬ When ready to bake, preheat oven to 350 degrees. Bring bread mixture to room temperature.

⚬ Bake, uncovered, in middle of oven for 35 to 40 minutes, or until puffed and edges are pale golden. Serve immediately.

Note: *You may use a loaf of challah, or even a sliced baguette with the crust left on, as bread options.*

Mississippi Baked Grits 🚲

The family tradition for brunches, evening buffets and family meals

Yield: 4 to 6 servings

1 cup grits, not quick or instant	8 ounces sharp cheddar cheese, shredded
4 cups water	
½ teaspoon salt	4 tablespoons butter, melted
1 egg, beaten	1 teaspoon Worcestershire sauce
1 teaspoon freshly ground black pepper	½ cup milk
	⅛ teaspoon paprika

🕐 *Grits can be baked earlier in the day; keep covered at room temperature and reheat before serving.*

⚬ Preheat oven to 350 degrees.

⚬ Cook grits in 4 cups water and salt until just thickened. Remove from heat.

⚬ Add egg, pepper, cheese, butter, Worcestershire sauce, and milk. Mix well and pour into an ungreased, 1½-quart baking dish. Sprinkle with paprika.

⚬ Bake 1 hour.

Maple syrup has twice as much calcium as milk!

Since 1987, the voice of the animated television character, Bart Simpson, has been provided by Kettering native Nancy Cartwright. She never expected the 10-year-old smart aleck to become a cultural icon, leading to a Simpson family star on the Hollywood Walk of Fame!

Peter's Sunday Morning Pancakes ⭐

A home specialty from Peter Danis, owner of Figlio Restaurant

Yield: 16 medium-sized pancakes

1½	cups white flour	2	eggs
¼	cup whole wheat pastry flour	1½	cups lowfat buttermilk
¼	cup cornmeal	½	cup 2% milk
2	teaspoons baking powder	3	tablespoons unsalted butter, melted
1	teaspoon baking soda		Vegetable oil and butter for cooking
½	teaspoon salt		
2	tablespoons sugar		

🕐 *To save time in the morning, dry ingredients can be mixed together the night before. Keep covered.*

6 Heat a griddle to 375 degrees, or until a few drops of water sprinkled on the griddle bounces and splatters off the griddle.

6 Combine flours, cornmeal, baking powder, baking soda, salt, and sugar.

6 In a separate bowl, beat eggs. Stir in milks and butter. (Make sure butter is not too hot or else eggs will scramble!)

6 Stir dry ingredients into wet ingredients. Batter will be lumpy; do not overmix.

6 Brush a small amount of vegetable oil over griddle. Melt 1 teaspoon butter on griddle. Pour ⅓ cup batter per pancake onto griddle about 2 inches apart. Cook 2½ minutes, or until bubbles form on top of batter and edges are slightly dry. Flip and cook until golden on bottom. Repeat until batter is used up.

6 Serve with pure maple syrup or warm fruit compote.

When I was a young boy growing up in Dayton, I remember how special it was when I would wake up to the smell of pancakes on Sunday morning. My mother would occasionally cut up small chunks of apple and mix it into the pancake batter—she said it always reminded her of my grandfather, who sold shoes for many years at Rike's. Now that I do the cooking on Sunday mornings, I almost always make pancakes from a recipe that I have developed. Making pancakes represents a sense of warmth, security and good times for me. Hopefully, I am creating a wonderful memory for my three little girls that they will carry with them long after they have grown up and have families of their own. If you make these for your family, be sure to have your children help measure and mix—I'm convinced it enhances the flavor!

—Peter Danis, Owner
Figlio Restaurant

Cheese Soufflé

A simpler version of the classic

Yield: 4 to 6 servings

4 tablespoons butter or margarine	Dash of cayenne pepper
¼ cup flour	(we prefer ⅛ teaspoon for
1½ cups milk (we prefer 2% milk)	more flavor)
Salt to taste	8 ounces cheddar cheese,
2 tablespoons Worcestershire	shredded
sauce	4 eggs, separated

6 Preheat oven to 375 degrees.

6 In a medium saucepan, melt butter over low heat. Add flour and stir with a whisk until blended.

6 Meanwhile, bring milk to a boil. Add milk all at once to flour mixture. Stir vigorously with whisk. Season with salt, Worcestershire sauce and cayenne pepper. Turn off heat.

6 Stir in cheese. Beat in egg yolks, one at a time.

6 Beat egg whites in a bowl until stiff. Fold whites into soufflé mixture. Stir until smooth. Pour into a 2-quart soufflé dish.

6 Bake 30 to 45 minutes.

Note: *Not difficult and does not have to be served immediately. Soufflé can be held in oven; appearance may suffer but taste will still be wonderful.*

Menu: *Serve with sausage patties and sautéed apples for brunch, or asparagus and French bread for a light dinner.*

Reuben Brunch Casserole

A "meaty" alternative to a brunch casserole

Yield: 10 servings

10 slices rye bread, cut into ¾-inch cubes	6 eggs, lightly beaten
1½ pounds cooked corned beef, coarsely shredded	3 cups milk
2½ cups shredded Swiss cheese	¼ teaspoon freshly ground black pepper

Ingredients must be assembled and refrigerated 12 hours ahead.

6 Place bread cubes in a greased, 9x13-inch baking dish.

6 Layer beef over bread. Sprinkle with cheese.

6 Beat together egg, milk and pepper in a bowl until well-blended. Pour over bread mixture. Cover with foil and refrigerate overnight.

6 When ready to bake, preheat oven to 350 degrees.

6 Bake, covered, for 45 minutes. Uncover; bake 10 to 20 minutes longer, or until bubbly. Serve immediately.

After receiving the Democratic nomination for president in 1920, Daytonian James M. Cox selected Franklin Delano Roosevelt as his running mate without ever having met him.

My father's specialty was what he called "cheese eggs," which were simply scrambled eggs with melted American cheese. My brothers and I thought Dad had invented this recipe! As I was growing up I would tell Dad that I wanted him to make me "cheese eggs" on my wedding day. Sure enough, on the morning of my wedding, my dear father was in the kitchen making me "cheese eggs." The image of my father making me my "last" breakfast as his "little girl" will forever be in my heart.

—Cynthia Wagner

Seafood Quiche

Seafood lovers will enjoy this rich quiche dish!

Yield: 4 to 6 servings

2	tablespoons butter		Salt and freshly ground black pepper to taste
¼	cup minced onion		
1	tablespoon tomato paste	1	(9 inch) pie crust, baked
¼	cup Marsala wine	1¼	cups shredded Gruyère cheese
½	pound raw shrimp, peeled, deveined and cut into 1-inch pieces	¾	cup heavy cream
		¾	cup half-and-half
		5	eggs, lightly beaten
½	pound scallops, cut into ½-inch pieces	½	teaspoon dried basil, or 1½ teaspoons fresh
2	tablespoons minced fresh parsley	¼	teaspoon fennel seeds
2	tablespoons chopped fresh chives		Dash of cayenne pepper

⚭ Preheat oven to 375 degrees.

⚭ Melt butter in a large skillet over medium heat. Add onion and sauté until softened.

⚭ Stir in tomato paste and wine. Cook over high heat for 2 minutes, or until sauce is reduced to 2 tablespoons. Add shrimp; cook over medium heat until shrimp just turn pink.

⚭ Stir in scallops, parsley, chives, salt, and pepper. Cook 1 minute. Spoon into pie crust. Sprinkle with cheese.

⚭ Combine cream, half-and-half, egg, basil, fennel, and cayenne pepper. Pour over cheese.

⚭ Bake 35 to 40 minutes, or until well-puffed and set in the center. Cool on a rack for 10 minutes before serving.

Note: *"Jumbo" shrimp and small "bay" scallops work best.*

Menu: *Serve with Lemon Pasta Salad (page 135) and Spinach Salad with Basil Dressing (page 123).*

To determine whether an egg is fresh, immerse it in a pan of cool, salted water. If it sinks, it is fresh. If it rises to the surface, throw it away.

The Ultimate Quiche ❋

This flexible quiche forms its own crust, and can be adapted to satisfy the tastes of family members and friends

Yield: 4 to 6 servings

1-2	cups diced vegetables, such as onions, zucchini, yellow squash, broccoli, peppers, mushrooms, carrots, or spinach	6	eggs, beaten
		1	cup milk
		½	teaspoon herb salt (optional)
		¼	teaspoon dry parsley
4	tablespoons butter		Pinch of marjoram (optional)
¾	cup flour	1	cup shredded Monterey Jack or cheddar cheese

🕐 *Prepare vegetables up to 1 day ahead. Quiche also may be baked, cooled, wrapped well, and frozen up to 3 months. To serve, thaw; heat in oven or warm individual servings in microwave.*

- Preheat oven to 350 degrees.
- Sauté vegetables of choice for filling. Set aside.
- Melt butter. Add flour to make a roux. Slowly add egg, milk, herb salt, parsley, and marjoram, stirring constantly or using an electric mixer.
- Add sautéed vegetables and cheese to egg mixture. Pour into a greased, 9- or 10-inch pie plate.
- Bake 30 to 45 minutes, or until firm and golden.

Note: *Basil and garlic may be added to vary the seasonings. Cooked, crumbled bacon and Swiss cheese may be substituted to make a delicious quiche Lorraine.*

Menu: *A nice change of pace for dinner with a Make-Ahead Caesar Salad (page 125) and Provisions Peanut Butter Cookies (page 281).*

In the 1960s, Centerville was home to two individuals who went on to achieve national celebrity status: author/humorist Erma Bombeck and TV interview/talk show host, Phil Donahue. For a time, they lived across the street from each other in the Zengel Plat.

60-Minute Pesto Bread

Great for a casual dinner with friends

Yield: 1 loaf

4	tablespoons butter, melted	1	clove garlic, minced
⅓	cup grated Parmesan cheese	2¾-3¼	cups all-purpose flour (may
2	tablespoons fresh chopped basil		substitute half bread flour)
		1	teaspoon salt
2	tablespoons fresh chopped thyme	1	package rapid rise yeast
		1	cup very warm (125-130 degrees) water
2	tablespoons fresh chopped parsley	1	tablespoon butter, melted
2	tablespoons fresh snipped chives		Boiling water

- Combine 4 tablespoons butter, cheese, herbs, and garlic. Set aside.

- Stir together 2 cups flour, salt and yeast. Add warm water and 1 table-spoon butter. Mix in enough of remaining flour to form a soft dough. Knead 6 to 10 minutes, or until smooth. Cover with a damp towel and let rest for 5 minutes.

- On a lightly floured surface, roll dough into a 12x15-inch rectangle. Spread herb mixture evenly onto dough to within ½ inch of edges. Roll tightly starting from the long end and taper the ends to seal.

- Place on a greased baking sheet, seam-side down. Use a sharp knife to make a ⅛-inch-deep cut lengthwise to within 1 inch of the ends. Cover with a damp cloth.

- Place a large, shallow pan on the counter, preferably in a warm, draft-free place. Fill pan halfway with boiling water. Place baking sheet on top; let bread rise for 10 minutes or until bread rises to a nice size loaf.

- When ready to bake, preheat oven to 400 degrees.

- Bake loaf for 25 minutes or until done. Cool on a wire rack.

In 1884, John Henry Patterson bought a major interest in the National Manufacturing Company, a purchase for which he was so ridiculed that he tried to buy his way out. When that failed, he renamed it the National Cash Register Company, and turned it into an international industry leader by improving its physical plant and product, and by an innovative advertising and education campaign to generate a market. Above all, he pioneered the modern sales force, inventing everything from sales conventions and exclusive sales territories, to required calisthenics and generous employee benefits.

Overnight Focaccia ❄

A tasty alternative to garlic bread

Yield: 2 (10 to 12 inch) round loaves

2¾	cups warm (110 to 115 degrees) water	6-7½	cups unbleached white flour
1	package yeast		Olive oil, cornmeal and coarse salt
2	tablespoons olive oil		Water in a spray bottle
1	tablespoon salt		

🕐 *Assembled and kneaded focaccia must be refrigerated 8 to 12 hours prior to baking.*

- Combine water, yeast, oil, salt, and 6 cups of the flour in a large plastic bowl. Add as much of remaining flour as needed to form a dough.

- Turn dough out onto a floured surface and divide into 2 mounds. Knead each mound for 5 minutes; shape into thick discs or rectangles.

- Brush extra olive oil over baking sheets and sprinkle with cornmeal. Place dough on baking sheets, pulling gently to fit dough onto sheets.

- Cover with plastic wrap and refrigerate overnight.

- When ready to bake, preheat oven to 475 degrees.

- Dimple dough with fingers. Brush with olive oil and sprinkle with coarse salt.

- Bake 21 to 25 minutes. Use a spray bottle to spray bread with water every 7 minutes while baking.

Note: *Spraying with water makes a crispy crust. May add fresh herbs, olives and/or caramelized onions prior to baking to vary flavor.*

Menu: *A wonderful accompaniment for Italian or Mediterranean meals. Slice focaccia horizontally for scrumptious sandwiches.*

Cooking should inspire the artist in you. Never fall into painting by numbers— be passionate! Dare to be spontaneous!

—Bill Castro, owner El Meson Restaurant

Mama's Rolls ❋

An outstanding dinner roll

Yield: 2 dozen

½	cup shortening	2	packages yeast
½	cup sugar	½	cup warm water
3½	teaspoons salt	1	teaspoon sugar
2	cups hot milk (scalded)	2½-3	cups flour
4	cups flour		Melted butter
2	eggs, beaten		

- Combine shortening, ½ cup sugar and salt in a large bowl. Pour hot milk over top and cool slightly.

- When warm, add 4 cups flour and mix well. Stir in egg.

- Dissolve yeast in warm water with 1 teaspoon sugar. Add to flour mixture and mix well.

- Blend in remaining 2½ to 3 cups flour. Cover and let rise 1 hour in a warm, draft-free place.

- Punch down dough and place on a floured board. Roll out to ¼-inch thick. Cut with a biscuit cutter, then dip in melted butter. Fold circles in half and place on baking sheets. Cover and let rise 1 hour longer.

- When ready to bake, preheat oven to 450 degrees.

- Bake 6 minutes, or until light golden brown.

Note: *If dough is a little sticky, add a bit more flour so the dough is smoother. If there is leftover dough, gather it a ball and punch it down. Let rise another hour. Place in a bread pan and let rise another hour. Bake at 400 degrees for 15 minutes, then reduce heat to 350 degrees and bake until golden brown.*

During World War II, Erma Bombeck worked for the *Dayton Journal-Herald* as a copy girl. A co-op student at Parker High School, Erma earned $20 per week collecting newspaper copy from reporters and far-flung correspondents of the Miami Valley.

Elsie's Biscuits ❄

A very flaky biscuit

Yield: 2½ dozen

3	cups all-purpose flour	½	cup buttermilk
2	tablespoons baking powder	⅓	cup sour cream
1	teaspoon salt	⅛	teaspoon sugar
1	stick butter or margarine	⅛	teaspoon vanilla
½	cup milk		

- Preheat oven to 450 degrees.
- Combine flour, baking powder and salt. Cut in butter with a pastry blender until mixture is crumbly.
- In a separate bowl, combine milks, sour cream, sugar, and vanilla. Pour into dry ingredients, stirring just until moistened.
- Turn dough out onto a lightly floured surface; knead 3 or 4 times. Roll to ½-inch thick. Cut with a 1½-inch round cutter and place on a lightly greased baking sheet.
- Bake 7 to 9 minutes.

Note: *If using a 2½-inch cutter, bake for 10 to 12 minutes. Yields 1 dozen. A healthy alternative…use skim milk, lowfat buttermilk and fat-free sour cream.*

Persistence paid off for Gordon Jump, former Centerville resident. His many credits include Maytag commercials, "Get Smart," and a starring role as Arthur Carlson in the situation comedy, "WKRP in Cincinnati." Growing up on McEwen Road, the Centerville High School graduate was involved in basketball, football, drama and band.

Heavenly Cornbread

This cornbread is a bit sweeter than traditional cornbread

Yield: 12 to 16 servings

1⅔	cups all-purpose flour	5	tablespoons unsalted butter, melted
⅔	cup cornmeal		
¾	cup sugar	1	egg, beaten
4	teaspoons baking powder	1	teaspoon bacon fat or lard, melted (optional)
½	teaspoon salt, Kosher preferred		
1⅓	cups milk		

- Preheat oven to 350 degrees.
- Combine flour, cornmeal, sugar, baking powder, and salt in a large bowl.
- In a separate bowl, mix milk, butter, egg, and bacon fat. Slowly pour into dry ingredients. Mix until batter is smooth. Pour into a greased, 8-inch square baking pan.
- Bake 50 to 60 minutes, or until golden brown.
- Cut into 2x2-inch or 2x3-inch pieces and serve.

Menu: *For an easy homestyle meal, add this to a menu with purchased honey ham and green beans.*

Stone-ground cornmeal has a higher fiber and mineral content than enriched de-germinated cornmeal, and must be refrigerated.

Stephanie's Sweet Potato Biscuits ❄

This will become one of your favorite holiday recipes

Yield: 12 servings

1	pound sweet potatoes	½	cup light brown sugar
2¼	cups buttermilk baking mix	3	tablespoons water

🕐 *Potatoes can be baked and mashed up to 2 days ahead.*

◐ Preheat oven to 350 degrees.

◐ Bake potatoes 45 minutes or until tender; cool and peel. Mash potatoes in a bowl with a potato masher. Stir in baking mix and sugar. Add enough water to form a soft dough.

◐ Turn dough onto a lightly floured surface and pat into a ½-inch thick round. Cut out biscuits using a 2½-inch round cutter. Gather scraps, pat to ½-inch thickness and cut out more biscuits. Place biscuits on a greased, large baking sheet.

◐ Bake about 18 minutes, or until golden brown. Biscuits will rise only slightly.

◐ Cool biscuits on wire racks. Serve warm or at room temperature.

Note: *May use decorative cutter (i.e. star) to make a fancier presentation. Be careful not to overcook, as the biscuits will be dry.*

Menu: *Serve sliced and filled with smoked turkey slices and cranberry sauce on a holiday buffet.*

According to *People Magazine*, approximately 6 percent of the world's most beautiful people are from Dayton, Ohio. The magazine's list of the 50 most beautiful people in the world in 2000 included two from Dayton—actor Rob Lowe and chef Ming Tsai; plus step-Daytonian Hillary Swank, who is married to Chad Lowe. Which suggests that Dayton may also be First in Beauty. Although some homely newspaper writer in North Carolina probably will attempt to prove that all three were conceived down there.

—D.L. Stewart,
Columnist
Dayton Daily News

Amy's Amazing Lemon Bread ❄

Heavenly and sweet

Yield: 1 loaf

1	stick butter, softened	¼	teaspoon salt
1	cup sugar	½	cup milk
2	eggs, lightly beaten		Zest of 1 lemon
1¼	cups flour	¼	cup sugar
1	teaspoon baking powder		Juice of 1 lemon, strained

⊙ Preheat oven to 350 degrees.

⊙ Cream butter and 1 cup sugar together in a mixing bowl. Beat in egg.

⊙ In a separate bowl, mix flour, baking powder and salt. Add dry ingredients to creamed mixture, alternating with milk. Stir in zest. Pour into a greased loaf pan.

⊙ Bake 1 hour.

⊙ Meanwhile, prepare a glaze by mixing together ¼ cup sugar and lemon juice.

⊙ When removed from oven, pierce loaf several times with a skewer. Pour glaze over bread while still hot. Cool, cover and refrigerate.

Sour Cream Coffee Cake ❄

This delicious cake has the fine texture of a pound cake

Yield: 12 servings

Cake

2	sticks margarine, softened	2	cups cake flour
2	cups sugar		(or 1¾ cups all-purpose flour)
2	eggs	1	teaspoon baking powder
1	cup sour cream	¼	teaspoon salt
½	teaspoon vanilla		

Topping

1	cup pecans, chopped	½	cup brown sugar
1	tablespoon cinnamon		

🕐 *May be made up to 1 day ahead and covered at room temperature. Or, wrap thoroughly and freeze up to 3 months.*

⊙ Preheat oven to 350 degrees.

⊙ Cream margarine, sugar and eggs together with an electric mixer. At low speed, add sour cream, vanilla, flour, baking powder, and salt.

⊙ Spoon half of batter into a greased and floured 10-inch tube or Bundt pan.

⊙ Combine all topping ingredients. Sprinkle half of topping over batter in pan. Spoon remaining batter into pan. Sprinkle with remaining topping.

⊙ Bake 1 hour.

Delicious Pumpkin Bread ❄

Perfect for gift giving

Yield: 4 small loaves

5	eggs	2	(3 ounce) packages cook-and-serve vanilla pudding mix
1¼	cups vegetable oil		
1	(15 ounce) can solid-pack pumpkin	1	teaspoon baking soda
		1	teaspoon cinnamon
2	cups all-purpose flour	½	teaspoon salt
2	cups sugar		

- ❍ Preheat oven to 325 degrees.
- ❍ Beat eggs in a mixing bowl. Add oil and pumpkin. Beat until smooth.
- ❍ In a separate bowl, combine flour, sugar, pudding mix, baking soda, cinnamon, and salt. Gradually beat into pumpkin mixture. Pour batter into 4 greased, 5x3-inch loaf pans.
- ❍ Bake 65 minutes, or until a toothpick inserted into the center comes out clean. Cool on wire racks.

Note: *May add ½ cup raisins, chopped dates and/or chopped nuts. Bread may be baked in 2 greased, 8x4-inch loaf pans for 75 to 80 minutes.*

Zillions of Zucchini Bread ❄

Something delicious to make with all those zucchini!

Yield: 2 loaves

3	eggs	2	cups shredded zucchini
1	cup oil	2	teaspoons vanilla
1	teaspoon cinnamon	3	cups flour
1½	cups sugar	¼	teaspoon baking powder
½	cup combination of nuts and raisins	1	teaspoon baking soda
		1	teaspoon salt

- ❍ Preheat oven to 325 degrees.
- ❍ Mix all ingredients together. Pour batter into 2 greased and floured loaf pans.
- ❍ Bake 1 hour.

Deborah...knows everything about fashion, but there's nothing 'surface' about her. In fashion, there are not a lot of real people.

—Douglas Hannant, fashion designer, speaking about Deborah Hughes

The things I like most about myself are things that came from Dayton. I'm fair and honest and compassionate towards people.

—Deborah Hughes, Owner

Deborah Hughes Inc., New York public relations firm

Paul Laurence Dunbar, Dayton's most noted poet, was born on Howard Street on June 27, 1872. The son of slaves, he is considered the first black American to make a living as a writer. He died of tuberculosis in 1906; he was 33 years old.

Caramelized Coconut Coffee Cake

A crisp caramelized glaze makes this coffee cake a true specialty!

Yield: 8 to 10 servings

Cake

1⅓	cups biscuit baking mix	1	egg
¾	cup sugar	1	teaspoon vanilla
3	tablespoons butter, softened	¾	cup milk

Topping

3	tablespoons butter, softened	2	teaspoons milk
⅓	cup brown sugar	½	cup coconut

🕐 *Cake may be made up to 2 days ahead up to point before the topping is added. Cover and keep at room temperature, then proceed with broiling.*

- Preheat oven to 350 degrees.
- Combine all cake ingredients and mix well. Pour into a greased and floured 9-inch pan.
- Bake 35 to 40 minutes.
- While baking, whisk together topping ingredients. Butter may appear lumpy after mixing.
- When done, remove cake from oven and spread topping over cake. Broil 3 to 5 minutes, or until crispy and light brown. Watch carefully to prevent burning. Cool.
- Invert onto foil, then invert again onto a serving plate.

Note: *May garnish perimeter of finished cake with fresh berries. This cake has been served many times for dessert!*

The first two women to practice medicine in Dayton were Gertrude Felker and Eleanora S. Everhard, who worked jointly for more than 40 years. They began their practice in 1903.

Cinnamon Apple Cake 🪶❄️

A moist and spongy cake that will surprise guests!

Yield: 12 servings

1½	cups sugar	1½	teaspoons baking powder
1	stick margarine, softened	¼	teaspoon salt
1	teaspoon vanilla	¼	cup sugar
2	(3 ounce) packages fat-free cream cheese, softened	2	teaspoons cinnamon
2	eggs	3	cups chopped and peeled Rome apples (about 2 large apples)
1½	cups all-purpose flour		

🕐 *Make up to 1 day ahead. Or, wrap well and freeze up to 3 months.*

◎ Preheat oven to 350 degrees.

◎ Using an electric mixer at medium speed, beat 1½ cups sugar, margarine, vanilla, and cream cheese for 4 minutes, or until well-blended. Add eggs, one at a time, beating well after each addition.

◎ In a separate bowl, combine flour, baking powder and salt. Add to creamed mixture, beating at low speed until blended.

◎ Combine ¼ cup sugar and cinnamon. Mix 2 tablespoons cinnamon sugar mixture with apple in a bowl. Stir apple mixture into batter.

◎ Pour batter into an 8-inch springform pan coated with cooking spray. Sprinkle remaining cinnamon sugar mixture on top.

◎ Bake 1 hour and 15 minutes, or until the cake pulls away from the sides of the pan. Cool completely on a wire rack. Cut with a serrated knife.

Note: *A 9-inch square cake pan or springform pan may be used. Reduce cooking time by about 5 minutes. May add walnuts or raisins for a varied taste.*

This cake is usually served at Hanukkah, also known as the Festival of Lights, which occurs in December. More than 2,000 years ago, the Maccabees defeated the Syrian army in Jerusalem. When the Temple was clean, the Jews wanted to rekindle the light in the Temple with oil. Although there was only enough oil for one day, the flame lasted for eight days. For this reason, Hanukkah lasts eight days, in celebration of religious freedom. Many traditional foods are cooked during Hanukkah: potato latkes, pot roast, applesauce, soofganiyot, and many kinds of cakes.

Braided Breakfast Danish

This sweet-tasting Danish makes a beautiful presentation

Yield: 10 to 12 servings

1	package active dry yeast	1	(8 ounce) package cream cheese, softened
½	cup warm (110 to 115 degrees) water	½	cup sugar
2½	cups biscuit baking mix	1	tablespoon lemon juice
1	egg, beaten	¼	cup jam or preserves of choice
1	tablespoon sugar		

⚅ In a mixing bowl, dissolve yeast in water. Stir in baking mix, egg and 1 tablespoon sugar. Mix well. Turn onto a surface dusted with additional baking mix. Knead gently for 20 strokes.

⚅ Place dough on center of a greased, 12x15½-inch baking sheet. Roll dough to 9x14-inches.

⚅ In a mixing bowl, combine cream cheese, ½ cup sugar and lemon juice. Spread mixture lengthwise down the center third of rectangle. Make 3-inch-long cuts at 1-inch intervals on long sides. Fold strips at an angle over filling. Cover and chill overnight.

⚅ When ready to bake, preheat oven to 350 degrees.

⚅ Bake bread for 20 minutes. Spoon jam down center of loaf. Bake 5 minutes longer. Cool 10 minutes before serving.

Note: *Dough is very sticky when kneading. Don't hesitate to sprinkle with additional baking mix to reduce stickiness.*

Menu: *Serve at a coffee with assorted fresh fruit and Dried Cherry and Almond Muffins (page 93).*

Growing up in Dayton, Ohio, Ramón Estevez wanted to be an actor so badly that he purposely flunked an entrance exam to the University of Dayton so he could start his career instead. With his father's disapproval, he borrowed cash from a local priest and moved to New York in 1959. While continually auditioning for shows, he worked at various odd jobs and changed his name to avoid being typecast in ethnic roles. "Martin" was the name of an agent and friend, while he chose "Sheen" to honor Bishop Fulton J. Sheen.

Almond Crescent Rolls ❄

These individual-serving rolls are sure to please a crowd

Yield: 32 servings

Rolls

1	**(8 ounce) can almond paste**
1	**stick butter, softened**
1	**tablespoon lemon zest**

2	**tablespoons lemon juice**
2	**(8 ounce) packages refrigerated crescent rolls**

Icing and Garnish

1	**cup powdered sugar**
2	**tablespoons butter, softened**
1	**tablespoon milk**

1	**(2½ ounce) package sliced almonds**

🕐 *Filling may be made ahead and frozen until ready to use.*

- ✆ Preheat oven to 350 degrees.
- ✆ Mix together almond paste, 1 stick butter, zest and juice with a fork or pastry blender. Mixture will be coarse.
- ✆ Roll out crescent rolls. Cut each in half to each make 2 smaller triangles.
- ✆ Roll up a small ball of almond filling and place on a small triangle. Roll up triangle as shown on crescent roll package label and place on a baking sheet. Repeat with remaining triangles.
- ✆ Bake 10 to 15 minutes.
- ✆ To make icing, combine powdered sugar, 2 tablespoons butter and milk in a small saucepan over medium-low heat.
- ✆ Drizzle icing over baked rolls. Sprinkle with almonds while icing is hot.

Note: *Filling that has been frozen and then thawed is easier to work with than freshly made filling.*

Jeraldyne Blunden began studying dance at age 7, when her mother and several other black women approached Dayton Ballet founder Josephine Schwarz about teaching their children. Several years later, the Schwarzes turned over their West Dayton program to their prize student, Jeraldyne, who founded her own program, Jeraldyne's School of the Dance, in 1961. She went on to establish the Dayton Contemporary Dance Company (DCDC) in 1968. Over the past several years, the company has performed in France, Russia, Germany and Korea, as well as New York and Washington.

Buttermilk Scones ❄

Great with coffee, tea or hot chocolate

Yield: 18 servings

Dough

3	cups flour
⅓	cup sugar
2½	teaspoons baking powder
½	teaspoon baking soda
¾	teaspoon salt

1½	sticks butter, cut into pieces
¾	cup raisins or dried fruit of choice (optional)
1	teaspoon orange zest
1	cup buttermilk

Topping

1	tablespoon cream
¼	teaspoon cinnamon

2	tablespoons sugar

🕐 *Scones may be made and frozen up to 2 weeks ahead. Thaw and warm in oven, if desired, before serving.*

6 Preheat oven to 425 degrees.

6 Sift together flour, sugar, baking powder, baking soda, and salt. Cut in butter until mixture resembles coarse cornmeal.

6 Stir in raisins and zest. Add buttermilk and stir until dough pulls away from the bowl. Turn dough onto a floured surface. Roll to ½-inch thickness. Cut into heart shapes. Place on greased baking sheets.

6 Combine all topping ingredients and brush over scones.

6 Bake 12 minutes or until browned.

Note: *Chopped dried fruit, such as tart cherries, cranberries or apricots may be substituted for raisins.*

Menu: *Have a tea party! Serve the scones with jams and butter. Offer Amy's Amazing Lemon Bread (page 84), mini crustless sandwiches with Tarragon Egg Salad (page 145) and fresh berries.*

Much has been made of the "Rich and Famous" entertaining styles, but it means nothing if one does not possess the inner qualities. I believe every person can be a wonderful host if they possess and express the following:

A genuine desire to delight and inspire people.

Lots (and I mean lots!) of attention to detail.

Creativity.

Abounding joy for life and letting it show!

Ability to be open, vulnerable and warm.

I keep these rules close to my heart every day as we open our doors to our restaurant, wistfully anticipating the golden shining faces of our patron friends, along with the new faces who will enter, that we will get to know and express our love and friendship to for years to come...

—Nanci Schaefer
Owner, Nanci's Porches

French Breakfast Puffs ❄

Perfect for an afternoon tea

Yield: 12 muffins

1½	cups all-purpose flour	5	tablespoons butter or margarine, melted
½	cup sugar	¼	cup sugar
1½	teaspoons baking powder	½	teaspoon cinnamon
¼	teaspoon nutmeg	4	tablespoons butter or margarine, melted
⅛	teaspoon salt		
1	egg		
½	cup milk		

🕐 *To save time in the morning, you may mix dry ingredients together 1 day ahead and cover.*

❧ Preheat oven to 350 degrees.

❧ Combine flour, ½ cup sugar, baking powder, nutmeg, and salt in a mixing bowl. Make a well in the center.

❧ In a separate bowl, beat egg lightly. Stir in milk and 5 tablespoons butter. Add to dry ingredients and mix until just moistened. Batter will be lumpy. Pour batter into greased muffin cups, filling each two-thirds full.

❧ Bake 20 to 25 minutes, or until golden.

❧ Meanwhile, combine ¼ cup sugar and cinnamon in a shallow dish. Place 4 tablespoons melted butter in another dish. Immediately after removing from oven, dip muffin tops in butter, then into cinnamon sugar mixture until coated. Serve warm.

Note: *Serve with honey or jam.*

Did you know that movie legend Tyrone Power, who starred in classics including *The Sun Also Rises*, *The Razor's Edge* and *The Mark of Zorro*, is a University of Dayton alumnus?

Julie's Very Berry Muffins ❄

A delicious berry muffin that cannot be missed!

Yield: 20 muffins

3	cups unbleached all-purpose flour	2	eggs
1	tablespoon baking powder	2	sticks unsalted butter or unsalted margarine, melted
½	teaspoon baking soda	1	cup blueberries
½	teaspoon salt	½	cup diced strawberries
4½	teaspoons cinnamon	½	cup raspberries
1¼	cups milk	1½	cups sugar

🕐 *You may mix dry ingredients together the night before and cover.*

6 Preheat oven to 375 degrees.

6 Stir flour, baking powder, baking soda, salt, and cinnamon together in a large bowl. Make a well in the center.

6 Add milk, eggs and butter to the well and stir quickly until just combined. Add berries and sugar; stir quickly again to just combine.

6 Spoon batter into paper-lined muffin cups, filling each almost to the top.

6 Bake about 20 minutes, or until brown and crusty.

Note: *May use all one type of berry as a variation.*

Dried Cherry and Almond Muffins ❄

The almond paste adds rich flavor and keeps the muffins moist

Yield: 12 large muffins or 48 mini-muffins

6	tablespoons orange juice	1	(7 ounce) package almond paste, crumbled
4	ounces dried tart cherries		
1	cup flour	6	tablespoons unsalted butter, melted
½	cup sugar		
1½	teaspoons baking powder	3	eggs
¼	teaspoon salt	1½	teaspoons orange zest

🕐 *May be prepared 2 days ahead. Store in foil at room temperature and rewarm for 5 minutes at 350 degrees. The night before making the muffins, you may mix dry ingredients together and cover.*

- Preheat oven to 375 degrees.
- Bring orange juice to a boil in a small saucepan. Remove from heat and add cherries. Let stand 10 minutes, or until softened.
- Combine flour, sugar, baking powder, and salt in a medium bowl.
- In a large bowl, beat almond paste and butter until well-blended but still slightly chunky. Add eggs, one at a time, beating well after each addition. Mix in cherry mixture and zest. Add dry ingredients and mix until just blended.
- Divide batter among 12 greased muffin cups.
- Bake about 20 minutes. Serve warm.

Note: *Makes approximately 4 dozen mini-muffins. Bake 8 to 12 minutes.*

At WHIO in Dayton, Phil Donahue started a radio talk show called *Conversation Piece*. A few years later, he tried out a new format–a television talk show aimed at "women who think." His idea was to let the audience interact in person, or via telephone, with his guests. The topics were relevant, informative, and somewhat controversially progressive. His first guest, in 1967, was the famous atheist, Madeleine Murray O'Hare, who spent an hour decrying the existence of God, angels and heaven. Not surprisingly, local viewers were outraged, and loved being able to call up and say so! His way of asking the probing questions, his limitless curiosity, and trademark enthusiastic bounding up and down the aisles of his studio in order to get as many audience comments as possible, is legendary. He won nine Daytime Emmys, and a Lifetime Achievement Emmy in 1996.

Banana Cream
and Chocolate Chip Muffins

A rich, yummy muffin your inner child will love!

Yield: 12 to 18 muffins

1	stick butter, softened
1	(3 ounce) package cream cheese, softened
1	cup brown sugar
2	ripe bananas, mashed
1	egg

¼	cup sour cream
1½	cups flour
¾	cup chocolate chips
1	teaspoon baking soda
1	teaspoon baking powder
½	teaspoon salt

🕐 *You may mix dry ingredients together the night before in a bowl and cover.*

⚙ Preheat oven to 325 degrees.

⚙ Cream butter, cream cheese and brown sugar together. Add banana, egg and sour cream; mix thoroughly.

⚙ Combine flour, chocolate chips, baking soda, baking powder, and salt in a bowl. Make a well in the center. Pour creamed mixture into well and mix until just blended.

⚙ Pour batter into greased muffin cups, filling two-thirds full.

⚙ Bake 20 to 25 minutes.

Note: *Do not fill muffin cups more than two-thirds full, or muffins will be too soft.*

Mark Comisar, owner of Cincinnati's Masionette Restaurant-the longest running 5 Star restaurant in the country-grew up on Oakwood Avenue in Dayton, Ohio.

Return the Flavor

CONDIMENTS

DAYTON ART INSTITUTE

RETURN THE FLAVOR

Mrs. Julia Shaw Carnell was one of the most dynamic and generous persons ever to inhabit the city of Dayton. She made her love for art a citywide project, donating five acres for the site of the Dayton Art Institute.

In 1928, Mrs. Carnell made a deal with the citizens of Dayton to match, dollar for dollar, anything they could raise to build the Art Institute. Pledges were taken from thousands of citizens. The project had hardly gotten under way when the Depression hit. When the stock market collapsed, people couldn't meet their debts, much less their pledges. Mrs. Carnell understood this, quietly picking up the tab for all unpaid pledges, and then matching that figure dollar for dollar. In all, this generous gesture cost her close to $2 million. Until she died in 1944, she also took care of all the operating deficits of the Institute.

Of course, Dayton has benefited from many wonderful philanthropists. One of the most outstanding is Virginia Kettering, who has lent her support to numerous projects through the years, including the United States Air Force Museum, the Victoria Theatre and the recent renovation of the Dayton Art Institute.

Each of us owes a debt to the numerous benefactors who have devoted their energies and assets to making Dayton a better place. Thank you all.

Upon the 1940 dedication of Mrs. Carnell's portrait, MISS BILLIE ALLEN spoke of the debt we owe Dayton's philanthropists: "Out of the silence of this handsome portrait of you, Mrs. Carnell, will come an eternal reminder that here in our blessed America, and here in our blessed Dayton, we boys and girls can grow to manhood and womanhood inoculated against prejudice and against hatred because you - and others

Flawless Hollandaise

Really…it's done at the last minute and can't be ruined

Yield: ¾ cup

4	egg yolks		Dash of Tabasco sauce
1-2	tablespoons lemon juice	1	stick butter, melted

- Combine egg yolks, juice and Tabasco sauce in a blender. Mix on low speed for a few seconds.
- Increase to high speed and slowly pour in hot butter. Mix until completely emulsified.

Note: *Try serving as a dip for steamed artichokes or over Eggs Benedict.*

Menu: *Serve over steamed asparagus with Flank Steak (page 228) and new potatoes.*

Tonnato Sauce

A sophisticated sauce from our Italian friends

Yield: 2 to 3 cups

3	tablespoons capers	1	cup mayonnaise
1	(6 to 7 ounce) can white tuna in water, drained	2	tablespoons lemon juice
1	flat tin anchovies, undrained	1	teaspoon lemon zest
½	cup olive oil		Salt and pepper to taste
½	cup vegetable oil		Whole capers for garnish

- Blend all ingredients in a blender or food processor.
- Garnish, if desired, with whole capers.

Note: *A distinctively love it or leave it taste; we love it! Can be used as a dip for appetizers.*

Menu: *Excellent over sliced turkey breast or boneless pork loin.*

Muse Machine founder, Suzy Bassani, received the 2000 Lewis Hine Award from the National Child Labor Committee at the Museum of Television and Radio in New York City. Bassani remains active in the Muse Machine's national programs, and directs the local Muse Machine's annual advanced teacher training seminar. In recent years, educators from the Miami Valley have traveled to New York, Los Angeles and Italy to explore arts and culture.

General Motors gave the city of Kettering Delco Park, a 66-acre property with five softball diamonds, three soccer fields, a BMX track, two picnic shelters, and a large pond.

Simple Tomato Sauce with Basil and Garlic

A cinch to make and the aroma…WOW!

Yield: 4 servings

2	medium cloves garlic, minced	½	teaspoon dried basil
¼	cup extra virgin olive oil	¼	teaspoon dried oregano
1	(28 ounce) can crushed tomatoes (we prefer Muir Glen Ground Peeled)	¼	teaspoon sugar
			Pinch of salt
			Freshly ground black pepper

⚅ In a large saucepan or Dutch oven, heat garlic and oil over medium-high heat until garlic starts to sizzle. Stir in tomatoes, basil, oregano, sugar, salt, and a couple grinds of pepper. Bring to a simmer.

⚅ Cook 10 to 12 minutes, or until sauce thickens a bit and flavors meld. Adjust seasoning as needed.

Note: *Great basic sauce! For a heartier sauce, try sautéing ½ cup chopped onion and/or ¼ cup olives in oil before adding the garlic.*

Kraus Haus Marinade

A delicious white-meat marinade with a hint of ginger

Yield: 4 servings

1	teaspoon ginger	2	tablespoons molasses or honey
1	teaspoon dry mustard	¼	cup salad oil
½	cup soy sauce	3	cloves garlic, minced

🕐 *Make this marinade at least 5 hours before you plan to cook the meat.*

⚅ Combine all ingredients.

Note: *Marinate at least 5 hours; overnight is even better.*

Menu: *Marinate pork chops, and serve with Roasted Beet and Walnut Salad (page 145).*

Liz's Hot Mustard Sauce

Wonderfully hot and tangy

Yield: 2 cups

1	(4 ounce) can dry mustard	1	stick butter
1	cup tarragon vinegar	6	eggs
½	cup sugar		Juice of 1 lemon
1	teaspoon salt		

🕐 *This recipe must be started the night before. Once made, it will keep in the refrigerator up to 2 weeks.*

⚬ Place mustard in a mixing bowl. Pour vinegar over mustard; do not mix. Cover and let stand overnight.

⚬ The next day, transfer mustard mixture to a double boiler. Heat over medium heat. Stir in sugar, salt and butter. Add eggs, one at a time, mixing well with a whisk after each addition.

⚬ Cook 5 minutes, being careful to not let the sauce curdle. Remove from heat and add lemon juice. Refrigerate until ready to use.

Note: *Great as a dip for pretzels, or with chicken, beef or fish.*

Francesca's Salad Dressing

Sensationally simple

Yield: 2 cups

½	pound Romano cheese, finely ground		Juice of 2 lemons
2	cups canola oil	3	cloves garlic, minced

🕐 *Keeps up to 1 month in the refrigerator.*

⚬ Combine all ingredients. Shake well before using.

Note: *Can be used as a marinade, or on pasta or tossed salad. The recipe is easily halved.*

Nana's French Dressing

Grandmother's best

Yield: 4 cups

1	cup ketchup	1	teaspoon salt
1	cup salad oil	1	teaspoon paprika
¾	cup cider vinegar	1	teaspoon dry mustard
1	large onion, diced	2	cups sugar

🕐 *Best if refrigerated 24 hours before using.*

6 Blend ketchup, oil, vinegar, and onion in a blender. Add salt, paprika and mustard.

6 With blender running, slowly add sugar. Blend until well mixed.

Note: *If dressing is thick when taken from refrigerator, let stand at room temperature before using.*

There was always a bottle of this homemade French (Catalina-style) dressing in our refrigerator when I was growing up. This was my grandmother's own recipe.

—Abby Wagner

Red Wine Vinaigrette

Salad dressing with a refreshing zing

Yield: 1½ cups

½	cup red wine vinegar		Dash of Worcestershire sauce
1	heaping teaspoon coarsely ground black pepper		(optional)
1	tablespoon Dijon mustard	¼	teaspoon sugar or to taste
1	heaping teaspoon horseradish (optional)		Pinch of salt
		½	teaspoon minced garlic
		1	cup extra virgin olive oil

6 Combine all ingredients except olive oil.

6 Whisk in olive oil in a slow, steady stream.

The Junior League of Dayton successfully implemented several "big money" projects during the 1960s. The JLD donated the Planetarium to the Dayton Museum of Natural History (at a cost of $56,000) with the help of several fundraisers, including Town Hall, Decorator Showhouses and Christmas Balls. The League also donated $27,000 to the Cox Arboretum, which continues to be an outstanding attraction in the community.

Tomato, Garlic, Cilantro Salsa

Excellent flavor, a family favorite

Yield: 4 to 6 cups, plenty to share!

1	(28 ounce) can tomatoes in juice	½	tablespoon salt
1	(10 ounce) can tomatoes and green chiles (we prefer Rotel)	1	tablespoon sugar
3	cloves garlic, chopped	1	cup finely chopped fresh cilantro
¼	cup chopped onion		Juice of ½ lime
3	tablespoons ground cumin		

🕐 *Can be made ahead and refrigerated up to 2 weeks.*

⊘ Combine all ingredients in a food processor. Blend to desired texture.

Note: *If you like a chunkier salsa, don't puree but do very finely chop the cilantro. Add jalapeños for more heat.*

Menu: *Try these variations: add to soup stock for seasoning; add to rice for Spanish rice; or serve on top of chicken or meat loaf.*

Lemon Chicken Marinade

The fresh lemon and kosher salt add a lot of flavor to this marinade

Yield: 4 to 6 servings

¾	cup freshly squeezed lemon juice (about 4 lemons)	1	teaspoon freshly ground black pepper
¾	cup virgin olive oil	1	tablespoon minced fresh thyme, or ½ teaspoon dried
1	teaspoon kosher salt		

🕐 *Marinate chicken the night before for best flavor.*

⊘ Whisk together lemon juice, oil, salt, pepper, and thyme. Pour marinade over chicken in a nonreactive bowl. Cover and marinate in the refrigerator for 6 hours or overnight.

⊘ Grill as desired.

Note: *Be sure to use kosher salt. Regular table salt will not add enough flavor.*

Menu: *Serve with Pasta Salad with Grilled Zucchini and Olives (page 134), and corn on the cob for a great summer meal.*

🍷 *Chardonnay, White Burgundy*

Instead of drinking water, drink milk or eat other cold dairy products to cool the fire from spicy foods.

In November 1999, the DaCapo (Dayton Arts Culture and Peace Organization) Foundation teamed with the United Nations' annual International Day of Tolerance celebration to honor eight leaders, including actor Arnold Schwarzenegger and former Soviet president Mikhail Gorbachev, for their efforts toward promoting tolerance. A black-tie affair at the Plaza Hotel in New York City kicked off the foundation's efforts to create a lasting cultural arts festival that will use tolerance as its theme, and capitalize on Dayton's newfound international identity as the home of the 1995 Peace Accords.

Spicy Black Bean and Corn Salsa

A deliciously light and colorful salsa

Yield: 4 to 6 cups

16	ounces cooked black beans	3	tablespoons vegetable oil
16	ounces fresh or frozen corn	1	tablespoon ground cumin
½	cup chopped fresh cilantro		Salt and freshly ground black
¼	cup chopped green onion		pepper, to taste
¼	cup chopped red onion	½	cup chopped ripe tomatoes,
⅓	cup fresh lime juice		drained

🕑 *All but the chopped tomatoes should be prepared ahead and stored in the refrigerator. Add tomatoes just before serving and toss.*

۵ Combine beans, corn, cilantro, onion, lime juice, oil, and cumin in a large bowl. Season with salt and pepper.

۵ Cover and chill at least 2 hours or overnight.

۵ Just before serving, stir in tomato. Serve with blue and white corn chips.

Note: *Frozen white shoepeg corn is best. If you must use canned diced tomatoes, choose a no-salt-added variety.*

Black Bean and Mango Salsa

Not your average salsa!

Yield: 4 to 6 cups

2	cups peeled and diced fresh mango or 1 (28 ounce) jar mangoes, diced	¾	cup diced red onion
		½	cup chopped cilantro
			Juice of 2 limes
1	(16 ounce) can black beans, drained and rinsed	1	teaspoon chile oil
¾	cup fresh or frozen corn	1	teaspoon sugar

🕑 *Salsa must be made 1 to 2 hours ahead of time.*

۵ Combine all ingredients and let stand for 1 to 2 hours.

Note: *Serve with chips, or as a topping for grilled chicken, pork or fish.*

Always wear disposable gloves when chopping hot peppers to avoid "burning" your hands.

One of the theories about Dayton's nickname, the Gem City, originated in 1845. A reporter, using the byline "T," wrote in the *Cincinnati Daily Chronicle* after visiting our town: "In a bend of the Great Miami river, with canals on the east and south, it can be fairly said, without infringing on the rights of others, that Dayton is the gem of all our interior towns. It possesses wealth, refinement, enterprise, and a beautiful country, beautifully developed." It is thought that this column may have inspired Major William D. Bickham, editor of the *Dayton Journal* in the late 1840s, to begin campaigning for the nickname in his column.

Raspberry Cranberry Relish

Easy and delicious

Yield: 6 cups

1	pound fresh cranberries, finely chopped	1	(10 ounce) package frozen raspberries, thawed and drained
2	tart apples, peeled and chopped	½	cup orange marmalade
1	cup sugar		
1	teaspoon fresh lemon juice		

🕐 *Make ahead and store in the refrigerator up to 2 days before serving.*

🌀 Combine all ingredients and mix well. Chill before serving.

Menu: *Try with Juicy Marinated Turkey Breast (page 223) and Old-Fashioned Scalloped Oyster Stuffing (page 153).*

Grandma Ruby's Garlic Sweet Pickles

Great for picnics!

Yield: 1 quart

1	(32 ounce) jar whole kosher dill pickles, drained	4-5	cloves garlic
		1½	cups sugar

🕐 *Plan to make these pickles 24 hours ahead.*

🌀 Slice each pickle twice lengthwise and return to jar.

🌀 Add garlic cloves and sugar; do not add any liquid. Recap jar and let stand about 24 hours or until sugar dissolves; turn and shake jar occasionally. Store in refrigerator.

Dayton's name dates back to General Jonathan Dayton, a soldier, lawyer and politician from Elizabethtown, New Jersey, who owned about 250,000 acres between the Great Miami and Little Miami rivers in 1797. Other area landowners, General Arthur St. Clair, General James Wilkinson, Judge John Cleves Symmes and Colonel Israel Ludlow, are said to have agreed that Dayton's name had the most pleasing sound. Dayton, at 27 the youngest man to sign the U.S. Constitution, died in 1824, and may never have seen this city that carries his name.

The people of Dayton, familiar with the pain of the Great 1913 Flood, donated more than $20,000 in 1927 for flood relief in Mississippi.

Roasted Red Pepper Relish

Terrific condiment for tenderloin or red snapper

Yield: 1 cup

2 large red bell peppers, roasted, or 8 ounces roasted red peppers (from a deli or jar - see note below)	2 tablespoons sugar
	½ teaspoon dry mustard
	⅛ teaspoon cayenne pepper
	1 teaspoon salt
2 tablespoons olive oil	3 tablespoons cider vinegar
1 cup chopped onion	Minced fresh parsley
2 teaspoons minced garlic	

🕐 *Can be made ahead (except for the parsley) and refrigerated overnight. Allow to return to room temperature and add parsley just before serving.*

🌀 Dice peppers into ¼-inch pieces. Heat oil in a medium saucepan over medium-high heat. Sauté peppers in oil for 1 to 2 minutes. Add onion and garlic, and cook until soft.

🌀 Combine sugar, mustard, cayenne pepper, and salt in a small bowl. Stir in vinegar until sugar dissolves. Add mixture to sautéed vegetables in saucepan. Cook, stirring frequently, until all liquid is evaporated. Sprinkle with parsley.

Note: *If using deli or jarred peppers, rinse to remove any salty brine and pat dry before dicing.*

Menu: *Serve at room temperature over red snapper. Sprinkle extra parsley on top for added color. Add Wild Rice with Carrots and Onions (page 163), and steamed green beans for a terrific meal.*

Unscientific Pickled Peppers

Peter Piper would be pleased with these!

Yield: 3 pints

6-8 light green Italian peppers (long, slender ones)	1 teaspoon sugar
	1 clove garlic, minced
2 cups very hot water	1-2 tablespoons pickling spice
1 cup vinegar	

🕐 *Plan to make these peppers 2 to 3 days ahead.*

🌀 Slice peppers as desired and place in a clean, medium to large jar with a lid. Add water, vinegar, sugar, garlic, and spice.

🌀 Cover with lid. Let stand at room temperature for 48 hours, then refrigerate. Keeps up to 3 weeks in refrigerator.

Note: *Wonderful sandwich condiment. If hotter peppers are desired, add some jalapeños to the jar.*

Because of their belief that nature should be shared with others, Marie and John Aull would invite the public to walk through their private gardens and enjoy nature. After Mr. Aull's death in 1955, Marie Aull donated 70 acres of land to the Audubon Society. The Aullwood Audubon Center now consists of 300 acres and includes one of the largest prairies in Ohio. More than 20,000 school students are involved with programs at the center.

❂ ❂ ❂

John K. "Jack" Matthews established the Dayton Cradle of Creativity Award to reward an outstanding individual for creative accomplishments in the arts or sciences. Says Matthews, "I felt Dayton had a unique characteristic in the creative entrepreneurship that emanated from this community." He's right, of course! Census data shows that Dayton has three patents per 100 residents, ranking it well above the largest cities in Ohio.

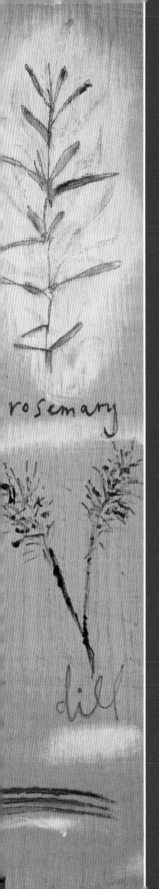

rosemary

dill

parsley

thyme

A Bowl Full of Fun

SOUPS & SALADS

FESTIVAL

MIAMI VALLEY FESTIVALS

A BOWL FULL OF FUN

Music, rides and crafts make for a fun festival, but the way to a festival fanatic's heart is through his stomach. From Troy's Strawberry Festival—the region's largest summer fest in terms of attendance—all the way through Lebanon's Blues & Barbecue Festival and Fairborn's Sweet Corn Festival, culinary priorities set the agenda. How do you feel about pickled cabbage? The Ohio Sauerkraut Festival in Waynesville is the second largest Miami Valley festival. Other favorite include the Beavercreek Popcorn Festival, the Germantown Pretzel Festival the Preble County Pork Festival, Apple Fest at Aullwood Audubon Farm Wilmington's Banana Split Festival, and the Spring Valley Potato Festival Are you hungry yet?

If you are interested in art with your festival fare, don't miss the Dayton Art Institute's Oktoberfest. The Victoria Children's Festival invites families for "Quality Play Time," combining theater, music and crafts. The famous CityFolk Festival features three days of music, dance, storytelling, crafts, and of course, food

Festivals also provide opportunities to learn about various cultures represented in the Miami Valley. Visit "A World A'Fair," which features global customs and traditions. At Kettering's Fraze Pavilion, the season is jam-packed with festive food, including Fiesta Latino-Americana's spicy fare; Spass Nacht's brats and brews; Caribbean Night's tropical delights; the jambalaya and étouffée of the Swamp Romp; and Venetian Night, with pastas and vino galore. Each year thousands of people visit the Sons of Italy Fall Festa, the Greek Festival, and the Dayton Black Cultural Festival. From the first hint of spring through the fall, there is always something to do (and EAT) in the Miami Valley.

TOM HOPKINS, writer for the *Dayton Daily News*, points out: "For many Miami Valley families, 'going out to dinner' on Saturday means finding the nearest festival"

Harvest Squash Soup

A beautiful soup rich in color and taste!

Yield: 12 servings

2	(2 pound) acorn squash	¾	teaspoon ground mace
2	(2 pound) butternut squash	¾	teaspoon ground ginger
1	stick unsalted butter		Pinch of cayenne pepper
8	teaspoons dark brown sugar		Salt to taste
3	carrots, halved	8	cups chicken broth
1	large onion, thinly sliced		Crème fraîche and chives for
2	cups chicken broth		garnish

🕐 *Squash may be baked, covered and refrigerated up to two days ahead. Soup may be made and refrigerated up to 4 days ahead.*

🌀 Preheat oven to 350 degrees.

🌀 Cut the 4 squash in half lengthwise. Scoop out and discard seeds. Place the halves, skin-side down, in a shallow roasting pan. Place 1 tablespoon of the butter and 1 teaspoon of the sugar in each half cavity. Arrange carrot and onion around the squash. Pour 2 cups broth in pan and cover tightly.

🌀 Bake 2 hours.

🌀 Remove vegetables from pan and cool slightly. Scoop out squash pulp and place in a soup pot. Add remaining vegetables and cooking liquid to pot.

🌀 Add mace, ginger, cayenne, salt, and 8 cups broth. Stir well; bring to a boil. Reduce heat and simmer, uncovered, for 10 minutes.

🌀 Puree soup, in batches, in a blender or food processor until smooth. Return to pot, adjust seasonings and heat through.

🌀 Garnish individual servings with a dollop of crème fraîche and a sprinkling of chives.

Note: *You may also use the hand-held "stick" blender to puree the soup in the pot to save time. Crème fraîche can be found in many dairy departments. Sour cream is an acceptable substitute.*

Menu: *Serve as a starter before Holiday Pork Roast (page 238) or present the soup as a main dish after Parigi Fall Salad (page 129). For dessert, try Classic Pumpkin Bars (page 283) and fresh pears.*

When a recipe calls for hot soup to be pureed in a blender, be certain to puree soup in small batches, approximately 1 cup at a time. Or, to save pureeing and clean-up time, use a hand-held stick blender in the soup pot.

Spicy Zucchini Soup

A unique and elegant first course

Yield: 8 servings

2	onions, coarsely chopped	1	teaspoon freshly ground black
5	tablespoons curry powder		pepper
4	tablespoons unsalted butter	5	zucchini, sliced
6	cups chicken broth	1½	cups heavy cream
2	potatoes, peeled and cubed	1	zucchini, julienned
1	teaspoon salt	1	tablespoon unsalted butter
			Snipped fresh chives for garnish

Onions and zucchini may be chopped/sliced and refrigerated up to 1 day ahead.

Sauté onion and curry powder in 4 tablespoons butter in a soup pot until wilted.

Add broth and potatoes; simmer 15 minutes. Season with salt and pepper. Add sliced zucchini and simmer 10 minutes longer.

Puree soup in small batches in a blender or food processor. While pureeing the soup, add cream slowly in small amounts. Strain soup through a food mill or a fine-mesh sieve; return to pot. Keep hot.

Sauté julienned zucchini in 1 tablespoon butter for about 1 minute. Stir into soup. Garnish with chives and serve.

Note: *If you enjoy making creamy soups, the purchase of a hand-held "stick" blender will save you lots of time.*

Menu: *This soup pairs wonderfully with Warm Chicken and Vegetables Wrapped in Flatbread (page 221). Also try as a prelude to Mango Lamb Chops (page 248).*

Area jazz fans have long recognized Cityfolk's Jazz Series as a local treasure. It received national recognition in 1993 when selected as one of 20 programs in the country to receive the Lila Wallace-Reader's Digest National Jazz Network Award. The grant allowed Cityfolk to develop artist-in-residency programs at area schools, coordinate senior citizen programs and co-sponsor the jazz stage at the 1994 Dayton Black Cultural Festival.

French Mushroom Soup

Rich flavor in no time!

Yield: 4 to 6 servings

2	tablespoons butter	1	clove garlic, minced
3	medium onions, chopped	¼	teaspoon freshly ground black
1	pound mushrooms, sliced		pepper
2	tablespoons chicken bouillon	½	cup dry white wine
	dissolved in 3 cups hot water	1	cup croutons for garnish
½	cup chopped fresh parsley	¼	cup freshly grated Parmesan
2	tablespoons tomato paste		cheese for garnish

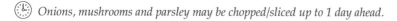

Onions, mushrooms and parsley may be chopped/sliced up to 1 day ahead.

6 Melt butter in a 3-quart saucepan over medium heat. Add onion and sauté until almost tender. Add mushrooms and sauté lightly.

6 Stir in bouillon mixture, parsley, tomato paste, garlic, and pepper. Bring soup to a boil, then reduce heat and add wine. Cover and simmer 5 minutes.

6 Garnish with croutons and cheese. Serve immediately.

Note: *Be sure to add the wine only 5 minutes before serving — it really enhances the flavor.*

Menu: *A beautiful beginning to a meal featuring Shadow Mountain Tenderloin (page 225). Chocolate Pâté (page 258) makes a fine ending.*

Amid the fun and festivity of the 1920s, the Junior League of Dayton still found time to dedicate its Membership to many community projects, including the Mary Garden Concert of 1923 and the Visiting Housekeepers project.

Cider Onion Soup

A fresh twist on an old stand-by

Yield: 4 to 6 servings

All-purpose yellow onions are the most common cooking onions. They are hot, and the most likely to make you cry while you cut them. Spanish onions are a large yellow onion that is milder and sweeter than most storage onions. Red onions are sharp and pungent, but also with a bit of sweetness to them. Their color fades when cooked unless lemon juice, wine or vinegar is added. White onions are hot, with a sharper flavor than yellows. They often are used in Mexican cuisine. Pearl onions are small, white, yellow or red onions, about 1 inch in diameter and mild in flavor.

Bread Rounds

1	French baguette, sliced into ½-inch rounds	4	tablespoons unsalted butter, melted

Soup

4	tablespoons unsalted butter	2½	cups shredded firm, smooth cheese, such as cheddar, Emmentaler or Gouda; or crumbled blue cheese, such as Stilton
5	cups thinly sliced yellow onion		
4	cups hard cider		
4	cups low-salt beef or chicken broth		
	Salt and freshly ground black pepper to taste		

🕐 *Baguette rounds may be prepared and stored in an airtight container up to 2 days ahead. Soup may be cooled, covered tightly and refrigerated for up to 2 days.*

6 Preheat oven to 325 degrees.

6 To make bread rounds, brush both sides of bread slices with butter. Arrange in a single layer on a baking sheet.

6 Bake about 25 minutes, or until crisp and golden.

6 To make soup, melt butter in a soup pot over low heat. Add onion. Cover and cook, stirring occasionally, for about 25 minutes, or until soft and just starting to color.

6 Increase heat to medium; cook, uncovered, for another 25 minutes, or until onion is deep golden brown and almost caramelized.

6 Add cider and broth; bring to a boil over medium-high heat. Season to taste with salt and pepper. Reduce heat to low. Simmer, uncovered, for about 30 minutes.

6 To serve, bring soup to a boil. Preheat broiler.

6 Place 3 bread rounds in the bottom of each individual, heat-resistant bowl. Ladle soup over breads and sprinkle with cheese.

6 Broil about 2 minutes, or until cheese is bubbly and just starting to brown. Serve hot.

Note: *Hard cider is an alcoholic beverage usually shelved alongside beer. When storing soups, refrigerate uncovered until cool, then cover tightly.*

Menu: *The Parigi Fall Salad (page 129) works well with the flavors of this soup. To follow with a main dish, try Stuffed Pork Tenderloin with Shallots (page 240).*

Jane's Famous Gazpacho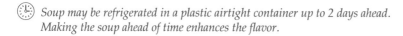

A great summer soup perfect for a Fourth of July picnic!

Yield: 6 servings

2	cups tomato juice	2	tablespoons olive oil
3	tomatoes, peeled and chopped	½	teaspoon dried basil
1-2	cucumbers, chopped	¾	teaspoon salt
1	yellow onion, chopped	½	teaspoon sugar
1	green bell pepper, chopped	¼	teaspoon freshly ground black
2	stalks celery, chopped		pepper
2	tablespoons chopped fresh parsley	½	teaspoon Worcestershire sauce
			Fresh basil to taste
1	clove garlic, minced		Sour cream for garnish
3	tablespoons red wine vinegar		

Soup may be refrigerated in a plastic airtight container up to 2 days ahead. Making the soup ahead of time enhances the flavor.

- Blend all ingredients except fresh basil and sour cream in a blender or food processor until mixture reaches desired consistency.
- Adjust seasonings. Add fresh basil and chill 2 hours.
- Serve in brightly colored summer mugs topped with sour cream.

Note: *For chunkier soup, reserve 1 to 2 cups of the chopped vegetables, then return to soup after processing.*

Menu: *Perfect prelude to Summer Lime Chicken Breasts (page 217). End the meal with Raspberry Coconut Squares (page 282).*

Nineteen years ago, Cityfolk's founders saw that there were very few opportunities in Dayton, Ohio for the general public to experience and come to learn about traditional arts. In addition, ethnic communities faced an ongoing and accelerated danger of losing elements of their cultural heritage if they allowed traditional artistic skills to fall by the wayside. The founders decided to do something about it. Today, concerts draw increasing audiences locally and from outside the Miami Valley. Cityfolk offers a tie to the varied cultures that keep the differences among us vibrant and exciting for all.

Tomato and Orzo Fennel Soup

A delicious way to introduce your family to fennel!

Yield: 6 servings

1	fennel bulb, coarsely chopped, top reserved	4	cups chicken broth
2	medium yellow onions, coarsely chopped	½	cup dry orzo pasta
3	cloves garlic, minced		Salt and freshly ground pepper to taste
6	tablespoons unsalted butter		Freshly grated Parmigiano-Reggiano cheese
1	(28 ounce) can peeled plum tomatoes with liquid		Chopped leafy fennel top for garnish

🕐 *Onions and fennel may be chopped and refrigerated up to 1 day ahead.*

⑥ Sauté fennel, onion and garlic in butter in a 2½-quart saucepan until transparent, but not brown. Add tomatoes and broth; simmer 30 minutes.

⑥ Carefully process small (1 cup or less) batches of mixture in a blender or food processor until only small pieces are visible. May use a hand-held "stick" blender.

⑥ Return mixture to saucepan and bring to a boil. Add orzo. Reduce heat to medium and cook until pasta is done. Season with salt and pepper.

⑥ Serve in bowls garnished with cheese and leafy fennel top.

Note: *If you are trying to eat light, butter may be reduced to 4 tablespoons.*

Menu: *Bake some Overnight Focaccia (page 80) to serve with this soup. Goes nicely with Artichoke and Hearts of Palm Salad (page 121).*

On St. Patrick's Day everybody is Irish, but in the Miami Valley, people have three days to be Greek. The Greek Festival at the Annunciation Greek Orthodox Church started in the 1950s as a congregational picnic, which grew as church members brought their friends. Sometime in the 1960s the festival was opened to the public, and since then has grown into a three-day event with 300,000 people. The festival features an assortment of Greek food and music, as well as tours of the church.

Cream of Leek and Potato Soup

A tasty, filling soup

Yield: 4 to 6 servings

4	tablespoons butter	4	large Yukon Gold or Yellow Finn potatoes, peeled and cubed
4	leeks, white part only, sliced and soaked in water		
1	small yellow onion, sliced	6	cups chicken broth
	Salt and freshly ground black pepper to taste	½	cup light cream
			Fresh chives

🕐 *Onion and leeks may be sliced and refrigerated the day before. Soup may be prepared up to 4 days ahead.*

᭲ Melt butter in a soup pot. Add leeks, onion, salt, and pepper; sauté about 15 minutes.

᭲ Add potato; cover and cook 5 minutes. Add broth and bring to a boil. Reduce heat, cover and cook 50 minutes.

᭲ Process 3 (1 cup) batches of the soup in a blender or food processor. Soup should be creamy, but still have some chunks of potato.

᭲ Stir in cream and serve hot.

Note: *Be certain to process batches of 1 cup or less at a time. Otherwise, the hot soup may explode the top off your blender!*

Menu: *Have as a main dish with crusty bread, or follow it with Strip Steak with Rosemary Red Wine Sauce (page 227).*

On April 12, 1850, the Montgomery County Courthouse was dedicated, three years after construction began. Today, Courthouse Square is a favorite outdoor gathering place, hosting several special events throughout the year.

thyme

Tomato Lentil Soup

Great for a cool fall evening — flavorful and versatile

Yield: 6 to 8 servings

4 tablespoons unsalted butter	½ cup dry red wine
2 cups chopped onion	4 cloves garlic, minced
2 cups chopped celery	½ teaspoon freshly ground black pepper
2 (35 ounce) cans chopped plum tomatoes with liquid	½ teaspoon salt
6 cups chicken broth	¼ teaspoon ground cloves
1 cup dried lentils	½ cup chopped fresh parsley
½ cup chopped fresh parsley	

🕐 *Onions and celery may be chopped, covered and refrigerated up to 1 day ahead. Soup can be made up to 3 days ahead, or frozen up to 3 months.*

⬡ Melt butter in a large soup pot. Add onion and celery; cook and stir over low heat for 10 minutes, or until vegetables are wilted.

⬡ Puree tomatoes with liquid in a blender; add to soup pot. Add broth and lentils and bring to a boil. Reduce heat. Simmer, uncovered, stirring occasionally, for 20 minutes.

⬡ Add ½ cup parsley, wine, garlic, pepper, salt, and cloves. Stir well and simmer 25 minutes longer.

⬡ Add ½ cup parsley and simmer 5 minutes. Serve immediately.

Note: *This soup is wonderful garnished with freshly grated Parmesan cheese!*

Menu: *A fine meal when served with bread and Spinach Salad with Basil Dressing (page 123).*

At the Ohio Renaissance festival in Warren County, you will find fighting nobles, singing peasant girls, strolling musicians, craft makers, and innkeepers slinging hearty turkey legs and ale. Add kings, queens, jesters and elephants, and you have the crowd-pleasing formula that brings about 200,000 people each year to the 30-acre permanent medieval village. Like most Miami Valley festivals, the Ohio Renaissance Festival offers food and entertainment for all ages.

Soup de Poisson (Fish Soup) ⭐

The "House Soup" of Victoria Theater!

Yield: 4 servings

Soup

3	tablespoons olive oil	⅓	pound potatoes, peeled and diced
¼	cup finely chopped onion		
1	teaspoon finely chopped garlic	1	cup water
½	cup chopped green bell pepper	1¼	pounds white-fleshed, non-oily fish fillets, such as cod, tilefish or a combination of 2 or more fish, cut into 1½-inch cubes
½	cup chopped leeks (optional)		
½	cup finely chopped carrot		
1	hot red pepper, crumbled		
1	bay leaf	½	pint bay scallops
2	teaspoons fresh thyme or ½ teaspoon dried	1	cup heavy cream
		¼	cup finely chopped fresh parsley
1	cup dry white wine		Salt and freshly ground black pepper to taste
1	cup chopped fresh or canned tomatoes		
		16	toasted croutons

Croutons

½	loaf French bread	¼	cup olive oil
1	clove garlic, peeled		

- To make soup, heat oil in a soup pot. Add onion, garlic, bell pepper, leeks, and carrot. Cook, stirring often, until onion wilts. Add red pepper, bay leaf, thyme, wine, and tomato. Bring to a boil.

- Soak potatoes in water briefly, then drain and add to soup pot. Cover and cook 10 minutes. Add 1 cup water and cook, uncovered, 5 minutes.

- Stir in fish and scallops; simmer 2 to 3 minutes. Do not overcook or fish will fall apart. Add cream and bring to a boil.

- Gently stir in parsley and season with salt and pepper. Float 1 or 2 croutons on each individual bowl and serve remaining croutons on the side. Serve piping hot.

- To make croutons, rub outside crust of bread all over with garlic.

- Cut bread into 16 thin slices. Arrange slices on a baking sheet and sprinkle with oil.

- Broil until golden on one side. Turn and brown lightly on the other side.

Menu: *Sliced French bread and a mesclun salad with Red Wine Vinaigrette (page 98) are excellent with this soup.*

"Master Class", starring Faye Dunaway, played the Victoria in January 1998. Scheduled for 16 performances, Ms. Dunaway took ill and cancelled five of the shows…one show at a time. She always waited until late in the afternoon to cancel, and then we would frantically call 1,139 people to tell them the show was off. It was a time of high stress, to say the least! That's when we fell in love with this delicious fish soup. Simple, hearty, fast to make, it is the perfect meal to chase away the winter blues and those little bitty setbacks of life.

—Mark Light, President Victoria Theatre Association

Chicken Lime Soup

A light, nutritious soup

Yield: 6 servings

1	tablespoon olive oil	¼	teaspoon ground cumin
	Juice of 1 lime	6	cups chicken broth
1¼	pounds boneless, skinless chicken breast	1	cup diced red bell pepper
		1	cup frozen corn
	Salt and freshly ground black pepper to taste	1	(14½ ounce) can Mexican-style diced tomatoes
½	tablespoon olive oil	1	cup diced zucchini
½	cup diced celery	¼	cup minced cilantro
1	cup diced carrot	⅓	cup fresh lime juice
2	cloves garlic, minced	1	bag blue tortilla chips
1	teaspoon chili powder		

🕐 *Pepper, celery, carrot, and zucchini may be diced and refrigerated 1 day ahead.*

🌀 Combine 1 tablespoon olive oil with juice of 1 lime. Brush onto both sides of chicken breasts. Season with salt and pepper. Grill or broil 5 minutes on each side. Cool, then shred chicken into bite-sized chunks; set aside.

🌀 Heat ½ tablespoon olive oil in a soup pot. Add celery, carrot, garlic, chili powder, and cumin. Sauté 3 minutes.

🌀 Add chicken broth and bring to a boil. Add bell pepper and corn. Simmer, partially covered, for 15 minutes. Add chicken, tomato and zucchini. Simmer 5 minutes longer.

🌀 Remove from heat. Stir in cilantro and ⅓ cup lime juice.

🌀 Serve with tortilla chips on the side or crumbled in the soup.

Note: *Can serve 3 to 4 as a main course.*

Menu: *Our Cilantro Cole Slaw (page 126) with this soup makes a great light meal.*

Try these simple tips to control your sodium intake:

Dietitians teach that if a food has twice as much sodium as it does calories, then it's probably too much sodium.

Do not trust your taste buds. Many foods with a high sodium content do not taste salty.

Take a break from the salt shaker. Just ¼ teaspoon of salt contains a whopping 600 milligrams of sodium.

Rinse off canned vegetables before eating them, cutting sodium intake by 40 percent; or buy items with "no salt added."

Jambalaya ❉

For those of us with a little Cajun spice in our blood!

Yield: 8 servings

1 pound smoked sausage, sliced	2 teaspoons thyme
1 pound ham, cubed	2 teaspoons salt
⅓ cup vegetable oil	1 teaspoon freshly ground black pepper
2 cups chopped onion	½ teaspoon cayenne pepper
2 cups chopped bell pepper	2 cups converted rice
2 cups chopped celery	3 tablespoons Worcestershire sauce
2 cups chopped green onion	2 pounds shrimp, peeled and deveined
4 cloves garlic, minced	Hot pepper sauce to taste
2 (14½ ounce) cans diced tomatoes, drained, liquid reserved	

🕐 *Onions, peppers and celery may be chopped and stored separately the day before. Ham and smoked sausage may be browned and refrigerated 1 day ahead. Shrimp may be peeled and refrigerated 1 day ahead.*

6 Brown sausage and ham in a large soup pot or Dutch oven over medium heat for about 30 minutes. Remove meat from pot. Add oil, onion, bell pepper, celery, green onion, and garlic to pot; sauté until soft, but not clear. Add tomatoes, thyme, salt, and peppers. Stir in rice.

6 Add enough water to reserved tomato liquid and Worcestershire sauce to make 6 cups of liquid. Pour into pot. Bring to a boil. Add ham and sausage; reduce heat to a simmer. Cover and cook 20 minutes, stirring occasionally.

6 Add shrimp and cook 3 to 5 minutes. Serve in bowls with hot sauce on the side.

Note: *If you are concerned about fat content, you may use light smoked sausage and reduced-fat ham.*

Menu: *For special dinners, top off this meal with Bananas Caribbean (page 260).*

Soups

Each December, I move from the museum's Board Room and art galleries to my kitchen at home. There, I prepare dinner for more than 100 of our best friends, colleagues and acquaintances. I brought the theme and tradition with me when I moved to Dayton from Mississippi in 1992.

Our annual Jambalaya Holiday Party features chicken and sausage Jambalaya, okra Jambalaya, slow-cooked collard greens, hot boiled peanuts, spicy boiled crawfish, and French bread. The dinner is topped off with Orange/Bourbon Sweet Potato pie. I make sure I've charred the bottom side of the potato skins, a key element in the flavor of really good sweet 'tater pie. Add to this eclectic menu icy cold Dixie beer and authentic Mint Juleps, and you have the perfect holiday celebration.

The Jambalaya Party is a great way to gather and eat some down-home cooking. Best of all, it is a way to give back and say thanks for a year of friendship.

—Alex Nyerges, Director Dayton Art Institute

"Too Good" Tortellini Soup

A hearty soup for fall or winter

Yield: 6 servings

1	pound bulk Italian sausage
1	cup chopped onion
2	cloves garlic, sliced
5	cups beef broth
½	cup water
½	cup red wine
2	cups canned diced tomatoes
1	cup sliced carrot
½	teaspoon basil
½	teaspoon oregano
1	(8 ounce) can tomato sauce
8	ounces fresh tortellini
1½	cups sliced zucchini
3	tablespoons chopped fresh parsley
1	medium green bell pepper, cut into ½-inch pieces
	Parmesan cheese

Onions, carrots, zucchini, and bell pepper may be chopped and refrigerated separately the day before. Sausage may be browned and refrigerated up to 2 days ahead.

Brown sausage in a soup pot. Remove sausage from pot. Discard all but 1 teaspoon of fat from pot. Add onion and garlic to pot; sauté until tender. Add cooked sausage, broth, water, wine, tomatoes, carrot, basil, oregano, and tomato sauce. Bring to a boil. Reduce heat and simmer, uncovered, for 30 minutes.

Skim fat from soup. Stir in tortellini, zucchini, parsley, and bell pepper. Simmer, covered, for 20 minutes.

Sprinkle individual servings with Parmesan cheese.

Menu: *This one-dish meal works well with a simple green salad and good bread. Sorbet is a light ending to the meal.*

The World A'Fair at the Dayton Convention Center is the place to find 32 countries coexisting peacefully under one roof. The festival is a unique opportunity to sample cultures from all over the globe, and features various ethnic dances, gifts, music, costumes, cultural displays, and of course, food!

Escarole, Sausage and White Bean Stew

A hearty Italian stew

Yield: 4 to 6 servings

1	teaspoon olive oil	4	tablespoons unsalted butter
8	ounces bulk Italian sausage, broken into 1-inch chunks	½	cup freshly grated Parmesan cheese, or combination of Parmesan and Romano cheeses
5	large cloves garlic, minced		
½	teaspoon dried red pepper flakes	2	plum tomatoes, diced
1	head escarole, leaves washed, dried and chopped into 2-inch pieces	2	tablespoons chopped fresh parsley
			Salt and freshly ground black pepper
3	cups canned white beans		Extra virgin olive oil
3	cups chicken stock or low-sodium canned chicken broth		Parmesan cheese for topping

🕐 *Escarole, tomatoes and parsley may be chopped and refrigerated 1 day ahead.*

⚙ Heat 1 teaspoon olive oil in a large soup pot. Add sausage and cook over medium-high heat for 10 minutes, or until starting to brown.

⚙ Add garlic and pepper flakes; sauté 2 minutes. Add escarole; cook and stir about 2 minutes or until wilted.

⚙ Add the beans; cook and stir 1 minute. Add the stock and bring to a gentle boil. Add butter, cheese, tomato, and half the parsley. Mix to combine. Cook until butter melts and mixture is heated through. Add salt and pepper to taste.

⚙ Serve in heated bowls, sprinkled with remaining parsley and drizzled with olive oil. Use a vegetable peeler to shave curls of Parmesan cheese over each bowl, or sprinkle with grated cheese.

Menu: *Offer this stew as a one-dish main course, served with Overnight Focaccia (page 80), and a dessert of Double Chocolate Walnut Biscotti (page 280).*

If you consider the connection between a monk in 610 A.D. and the late Lester Peck of Germantown, you will be surprised at the familiar twist in the story-pretzels. It was a monk in either southern France or northern Italy-the exact location is unknown-who took leftover bread dough, formed it into the shape of a child's arms folded in prayer, and gave it away as a reward. In 1980 when Germantown was looking for a German theme for a festival, it was Peck who came up with the idea of soft pretzels. Now, when it comes to fall events in the Miami Valley, the Germantown Pretzel Festival is a household word.

Chicken Chili Bianco

A unique chili that's sure to warm you up!

Yield: 6 to 8 servings

1	pound dry white beans	¼	teaspoon ground cloves
6	cups chicken broth	¼	teaspoon cayenne pepper
2	cloves garlic, minced	4	cups diced cooked chicken
2	medium onions, chopped	3	cups shredded Monterey Jack
1	tablespoon vegetable oil		cheese
2	(4 ounce) cans chopped green		Diced tomato, sour cream, diced
	chiles		onion, and tortilla chips for
2	teaspoons ground cumin		toppings
½	teaspoon dried oregano		

🕐 *Beans must be soaked overnight. Chili may be prepared up to 2 days ahead.*

⊙ Cover beans with about 2 inches of water in a saucepan. Cover and soak overnight. The next day, drain and return to pan. Add broth, garlic and half the onion. Bring to a boil. Reduce heat and simmer for 3 or more hours.

⊙ Sauté remaining onion in oil until tender. Add chiles, cumin, oregano, cloves, and cayenne pepper. Mix together; add to bean mixture.

⊙ If a thinner soup is desired, add more broth.

⊙ Stir in chicken and simmer 1 hour.

⊙ Just prior to serving, add 1 cup Monterey Jack cheese. Stir to melt.

⊙ Serve with remaining cheese, diced tomato, sour cream, diced onion, and tortilla chips.

Note: *A 2½-pound jar of precooked white beans, drained, may be substituted for the 1 pound of white beans.*

Menu: *A simple salad with Francesca's Salad Dressing (page 97) is excellent with the chili. Finish with fruit and Moist Oatmeal Cookies (page 276).*

In 1994, the National Council for the Traditional Arts selected Cityfolk to co-produce the National Folk Festival for 1996-1998. The Festival was a grand success, and drew larger crowds to downtown Dayton each consecutive year. The festival was so popular, it has continued as the annual Cityfolk Festival. It features top-quality performers and artists from throughout the nation in a fun, safe downtown setting.

Ohio-Style Chili and Spaghetti ❄

This chili originated just south of Dayton; we enjoy this version!

Yield: 8 to 10 servings

Soup

4	cups cold water
2½	pounds ground beef
1	(6 ounce) can tomato paste
2	medium onions, chopped (about 1½ cups)
1½	tablespoons vinegar
1	teaspoon Worcestershire sauce
1	clove garlic, minced
2	tablespoons chili powder
5	bay leaves

2	teaspoons cinnamon
1	teaspoon allspice
2	cayenne peppers or ½ teaspoon ground cayenne pepper
1½	teaspoons unsweetened cocoa
	Salt and freshly ground black pepper to taste
1½	pounds dry spaghetti, cooked and drained

Garnishes

1	pound cheddar cheese, finely shredded
1	(16 ounce) bag oyster crackers

1	(16 ounce) can kidney beans, drained
1	onion, finely chopped

🕐 *The chili may be prepared up to 2 days ahead, then refrigerated or frozen; spaghetti and toppings should be prepared the day of serving.*

6 Place water in a large soup pot. Crumble raw beef into water. Add remaining soup ingredients.

6 Bring to a boil. Stir frequently to break up meat as it cooks. Cover and simmer 2 or more hours, stirring occasionally.

6 To serve, place spaghetti in individual serving bowls. Pour chili on top. Add remaining garnishes as desired.

Note: *If you find the chili is too thick for your personal taste, an additional cup of water may be added. Chili also may be used to make coney dogs.*

Menu: *A green salad with Nana's French Dressing (page 98) works well with this dish. For dessert, try our Best Chocolate Chip Cookies (page 279).*

🍷 *Beer!*

The proper way to serve this chili is over spaghetti on an oval dish. For a "3-Way" top it off with a pile of shredded cheese and a dish of oyster crackers. For a "4-Way" add a spoonful of onions before putting cheese on top. For a "5-Way" add beans in addition to the onions and cheese.

Margarita di Dayo Chili ❄

A thick, hearty chili packed with flavor

Yield: 4 servings

Soup

¾	pound ground beef	2-3	teaspoons chili powder
1	cup chopped onion	½	teaspoon dried basil, crushed
½	cup chopped red bell pepper	¼	teaspoon salt
2	cloves garlic, minced	¼	teaspoon freshly ground black pepper
1	(16 ounce) can diced tomatoes with liquid	3	cups hot cooked rice
1	(16 ounce) can dark red kidney beans, drained		Chopped fresh tomatoes, sour cream, shredded cheddar cheese, and chopped green onion for garnish
1	(16 ounce) can black beans, drained		
2	(8 ounce) cans tomato sauce		

🕐 *Chili may be prepared up to 2 days ahead; or, freeze up to 3 months (without rice or garnishes).*

6 In a soup pot, cook beef, onion, bell pepper, and garlic until meat is brown. Drain and return to pot.

6 Add undrained tomatoes, kidney and black beans, tomato sauce, chili powder, basil, salt, and black pepper. Bring to a boil. Reduce heat and simmer 30 minutes, or longer if desired.

6 Serve over rice. Top with garnishes.

Note: *Try this variation we call "Chili, Cheese n' Chips" — serve chili in bowls, top with shredded cheddar and Fritos corn chips.*

Menu: *Rum Pie (page 274) or Rum Cake (page 263) makes a fine finish to this hearty one-dish meal.*

Black Bean Chili

A fresh version — the lime juice gives it a wonderful, bright taste

Yield: 4 servings

1	medium onion, diced	1	(14½ ounce) can diced tomatoes
1	red bell pepper, seeded and diced	1	teaspoon dried oregano, crumbled
1½	teaspoons ground cumin, toasted	1½	teaspoons salt or to taste
2	tablespoons olive oil	2	(16 ounce) cans black beans
2	jalapeño peppers, stemmed, seeded and diced	2	tablespoons chopped fresh cilantro
4	large cloves garlic, minced	1	teaspoon fresh lime juice, or more to taste

🕐 *Onions and peppers may be chopped and refrigerated separately 1 day ahead.*

◔ Sauté onion, bell pepper and cumin in olive oil for about 5 minutes. Add jalapeño pepper and garlic; cook 1 minute. Add tomatoes, oregano, and salt. Cook over medium-low heat for about 20 minutes.

◔ Add beans; cover and cook 20 to 30 minutes. Add 1 to 2 cups water if a thinner soup is desired.

◔ Add cilantro and cook 5 minutes. Season to taste with lime juice and salt. Serve hot.

Note: *This is fabulous served over white rice. To toast cumin, cook in a dry pan over medium-low heat for 3 to 5 minutes.*

Menu: *A Raspberry Pear Tart (page 271) makes a delicious ending to this vegetarian one-dish meal.*

The Storytelling Festival, which regularly draws crowds up to 600 people, is now formally known as the "Annual Storytelling Festival, Terrifying Tales & Tall Tales at Carriage Hill MetroPark Farm." The lengthy title signifies the fact that the festival has grown into a three-part event, including a story swap, tall tales and terrifying tales.

Parigi Spring Salad

Beautiful and delicious!

Yield: 4 to 6 servings

4	large handfuls mesclun	1	yellow bell pepper, roasted, peeled and julienned
16	spears asparagus, lightly blanched, cut into 2-inch pieces	½	ounce fresh basil, chopped
		½	cup balsamic vinaigrette
1	red bell pepper, roasted, peeled and julienned	4	ounces goat cheese, crumbled
		2	tablespoons pine nuts, toasted

🕑 *Salad may be prepared up to the point of adding the dressing earlier in the day. Just prior to serving, toss with dressing, top with goat cheese and pine nuts, and serve.*

🌀 Toss mesclun, asparagus, bell peppers, basil, and vinaigrette together.

🌀 Top individual servings with about ¾ to 1 ounce cheese each. Sprinkle top with pine nuts.

Note: *To roast peppers, slice in half; remove stems and seeds. Place, skin-side up, on a broiler pan. Broil 10 to 15 minutes on highest rack in oven or until slightly charred and almost weepy. Place peppers in a brown paper bag and close bag. Allow to stand for 10 minutes. Peel and slice peppers.*

Menu: *Serve this salad at a spring luncheon with crusty bread and sliced grilled chicken. Serve Lemon Blueberry Pie (page 272) for dessert.*

For a fresh, unique flavor, try adding fresh herbs to basic, mixed green salads. It is simple to grow your own herbs; however, Italian parsley, chives, dill, or cilantro are readily available at most supermarkets.

Artichoke and Hearts of Palm Salad

This salad goes well with Italian entrées

Yield: 6 to 8 servings

1	head romaine lettuce	1	red onion, thinly sliced
1	head iceberg lettuce	½	cup grated Parmesan cheese
1	(10 ounce) can hearts of palm, drained and sliced into ¼-inch pieces	½	cup olive oil
		⅓	cup red wine vinegar
1	(14½ ounce) can artichoke hearts, drained and quartered	1	tablespoon sugar
			Salt and freshly ground pepper to taste
1	(4 ounce) jar diced pimientos, drained		

🕐 *To prepare 1 day ahead, clean, dry and tear lettuce; store in plastic zip-top bags. Combine all other ingredients and refrigerate. To serve, toss the lettuce with the dressing mixture, adjust seasonings and serve.*

6 Wash and dry romaine and iceberg lettuce; tear into small pieces.

6 Combine lettuce, hearts of palm, artichoke, pimiento, onion, and cheese.

6 Mix oil, vinegar and sugar; pour over salad. Season generously with salt and pepper. Add extra Parmesan cheese, if desired. Toss and serve.

Note: *It is important to use grated Parmesan cheese from a canister, not shredded. The grated Parmesan acts as a thickening agent for the vinegar and oil dressing.*

A state's signature dishes tell, in part, about its history and culture. To say that Ohio does not have one dish that outshines all others says much about the state's trademark diversity. In Ohio, hundreds of traditions have converged from foreign and regional cultures to create something that is truly unique. According to James Hope, co-author of *Bountiful Ohio*, "Ohio food is a mix of flavors and accents, not singular enough to gain a high-profile identity the way some places have for their cuisine. Ohio food is not pretentious. It is generous. It is comfortable. It is good food from home."

Salad with Warm Brie Dressing

A wonderful rich dressing

Yield: 8 servings

An easy way to get your salad greens ready for dressing, if you do not have a salad spinner, is to tear them into bite-sized pieces, wash well, shake a bit in a colander to drain, then spread out on a dry dish towel. Roll up in the towel, fold the roll in half and tuck it in the refrigerator. When you're ready to serve the salad, you will have dry, crisp, chilled greens to toss in the dressing.

3	heads lettuce, such as romaine, red or green leaf, or curly endive	½	cup sherry wine vinegar or red wine vinegar
6	tablespoons olive oil for sautéing	2	tablespoons lemon juice
1	medium shallot, minced	4	teaspoons Dijon mustard
4	medium cloves garlic, minced		Freshly ground black pepper to taste
		10	ounces Brie cheese, rind removed
		1	(5 ounce) bag garlic croutons

Lettuce may be washed, dried, torn, and stored in zip-top bags in the refrigerator 1 day ahead. Shallots and garlic may also be minced and stored in the refrigerator 1 day ahead.

- Wash, dry and tear lettuce; place in a salad bowl.

- To make dressing, heat olive oil in a medium skillet over low heat. Add shallots and garlic; sauté until tender. Add vinegar, lemon juice and mustard to skillet; mix thoroughly. Season with pepper. Break cheese into chunks and add to skillet. Stir dressing until smooth.

- Toss croutons with lettuce. Pour dressing over salad, toss and serve immediately.

Note: *Let the Brie stand at room temperature for 30 minutes before adding to dressing; it melts much easier this way.*

Menu: *A rich beginning to meals featuring beef and veal.*

Spinach Salad with Basil Dressing

Yield: 6 servings

Basil Dressing
½ cup olive oil
¼ cup red wine vinegar or
     balsamic vinegar
5 fresh basil leaves, julienned

2 teaspoons sugar
1 clove garlic, minced
    Salt and freshly ground black
     pepper to taste

Salad
1 pound fresh spinach
1 avocado, peeled and sliced
½ cup crumbled feta cheese

½ cup chopped walnuts or pine
     nuts, toasted
½ cup Greek olives, pitted

🕐 *Dressing must be made at least 1 hour ahead. Spinach leaves may be prepared and refrigerated in a zip-top bag 1 day ahead.*

6 To make dressing, combine oil, vinegar, basil, sugar, garlic, salt, and pepper in a blender. Blend well. Chill dressing 1 to 2 hours.

6 Wash and dry spinach. Remove stems and tear into small pieces.

6 Toss spinach with dressing, avocado, cheese, walnuts, and olives.

Note: *Try substituting toasted pine nuts for the walnuts — delicious!*

Menu: *Serve this salad with Mediterranean-flavored meals.*

To reduce the sodium content of feta cheese: drain; rinse cheese in fresh cold water; dry with paper towels; crumble into your dish!

Spinach Chutney Salad 🚲

Very different and tasty

Yield: 6 to 8 servings

¼ cup white wine vinegar
¼ cup vegetable oil
2 heaping tablespoons chutney
2 teaspoons sugar
½ teaspoon salt
2 teaspoons curry powder
1 teaspoon dry mustard

1 pound fresh spinach, torn into
     bite-sized pieces
1½ cups chopped, unpeeled apple
½ cup golden raisins
¾ cup almondized peanuts
     (we prefer Jump's)
3 tablespoons sliced green onion

🕐 *Dressing may be made up to 2 days ahead.*

6 Combine vinegar, oil, chutney, sugar, salt, curry powder, and mustard in a blender or food processor. Blend well. Cover and chill well before serving.

6 Mix spinach, apple, raisins, peanuts, and onion in a large salad bowl. Add dressing and toss.

Miami Valley's largest festivals:

Troy Strawberry Festival, Troy

Ohio Sauerkraut Festival, Waynesville

Ohio Renaissance Festival, Harveysburg

Kettering Holiday at Home, Kettering

Miami County Fair, Troy

Greek Peasant Salad

A fresh, savory salad

Yield: 6 servings

A caper is not a fruit, vegetable or legume. Capers are pickles created by plucking the unopened flower buds of a trailing shrub that thrives in the climate of the Mediterranean shores.

Salad

6	Italian plum tomatoes, diced	½	cup sliced kalamata olives
1	medium Vidalia onion, chopped	1	large English cucumber, unpeeled and chopped
8	ounces feta cheese	3	tablespoons chopped fresh basil

Dressing

⅓	cup olive oil	1	teaspoon dried oregano
⅓	cup canola oil		Kosher salt
⅓	cup red wine vinegar		Freshly ground black pepper
1	clove garlic, minced		Pinch of sugar

🕐 *Tomatoes, onion, cucumber, and herbs may be chopped and stored separately in the refrigerator 1 day ahead. Dressing can be made up to 2 days ahead and refrigerated.*

⊘ Combine tomato, onion, cheese, olives, cucumber, and basil in a large bowl.

⊘ Prepare dressing in a separate bowl by mixing oils, vinegar, garlic, oregano, salt, pepper, and sugar. Shake and lightly pour over salad.

Note: *This recipe serves 6 as a side dish.*

Menu: *Offer this salad with a pasta salad and a green salad for a "salad sampler" plate.*

Make-Ahead Caesar Salad

Easy and delicious

Yield: 4 to 6 servings

1	head romaine lettuce	¼	teaspoon salt
1	teaspoon dry mustard	1	tablespoon lemon juice
1-2	cloves garlic, minced	¼	cup vegetable oil
⅛	teaspoon freshly ground black pepper	2	tablespoons Parmesan cheese, plus extra for topping

🕐 *The entire salad may be assembled and refrigerated, covered tightly, 1 day ahead.*

❀ Wash, dry and tear lettuce.

❀ Mash mustard into garlic. Mix in pepper, salt, lemon juice, oil, and cheese. Place dressing mixture in the bottom of a salad bowl.

❀ Place lettuce on top of dressing, cover tightly and refrigerate up to 24 hours.

❀ When ready to serve, toss lettuce with dressing. Sprinkle with extra cheese to taste.

Note: *Croutons and/or anchovies as garnish make this salad especially good.*

Dried Cherries and Gorgonzola Salad

Yield: 6 to 8 servings

Dressing

2	tablespoons white wine vinegar	½	cup olive oil
1	tablespoon plus 1 teaspoon Dijon mustard		Freshly ground black pepper

Salad

1	head red leaf lettuce	5	ounces Gorgonzola cheese, crumbled
2	ounces dried cherries		
4	ounces whole walnuts, toasted		

🕐 *Lettuce can be prepared and stored in a zip-top bag in refrigerator up to 1 day ahead. Dressing can be made and refrigerated up to 3 days ahead.*

❀ Combine dressing ingredients in order listed and beat until thick.

❀ Wash, dry and tear lettuce. Combine lettuce with cherries and walnuts in a salad bowl.

❀ Pour dressing over salad and toss. Add cheese and toss lightly; serve.

Note: *Walnuts may be toasted in the microwave: spread nuts on a microwave-safe dish and cook on high for 3 to 4 minutes, stirring after each minute.*

Menu: *This salad works well with fall and winter meals that feature pork.*

Eat your greens! Romaine lettuce has twice the potassium and folic acid, and eight times as much beta-carotene as iceberg lettuce.

In 1981, the first Dayton Black Cultural Festival was held at River's Edge park in downtown Dayton. It was called Kuzli Wa, which means "rebirth" in Kishwahili. It showed how cultural aspects of the Black American experience related to African roots. The current festival tackles that goal on a larger scale, incorporating as many cultural aspects as possible–from art, to music, dance and speakers.

Cilantro Cole Slaw

The most beautiful cole slaw you've ever seen!

Yield: 18 servings

Fresh herbs will stay fresh longer if they are stored in the refrigerator with stems in a glass of water.

Dressing

½	cup canola oil		Juice of 3 limes
4	cloves garlic, minced		Salt to taste
¼	bunch fresh cilantro, finely chopped		

Salad

2	large Granny Smith apples, julienned	1	small head green cabbage, julienned
1	large red bell pepper, julienned	1	small head red cabbage, julienned
1	large green bell pepper, julienned	1	cup fresh cilantro leaves
1	large yellow bell pepper, julienned	1	cup lightly crushed blue or yellow corn tortilla chips for garnish

🕐 *Peppers and cabbage may be prepared and stored separately in zip-top bags 1 day ahead. The dressing may also be made and refrigerated 1 day ahead.*

6 To make dressing, mix oil, garlic, cilantro, lime juice, and salt. Blend thoroughly.

6 For salad, combine apple, bell peppers, cabbage, and cilantro leaves in a salad bowl. Mix well.

6 Pour dressing over salad mixture. Toss well. Garnish with tortilla chips and serve immediately.

Note: *This recipe makes lots of slaw; you may want to halve the recipe.*

Menu: *A great side dish with Pollo Asado (page 215) or other Latin American-flavored dishes.*

Here Comes the Sun Salad

Make this salad to celebrate the first juicy red strawberries of spring

Yield: 8 to 10 servings

Dressing

½	cup dried cranberries	1	tablespoon minced garlic
¼	cup red wine vinegar	1¼	teaspoons salt
¼	cup balsamic vinegar	1	cup extra virgin olive oil

Salad

1	(10 ounce) bag fresh spinach, stems removed	1½	cups sliced strawberries
½	cup raisins	1	(11 ounce) can Mandarin oranges, drained
½	cup very thinly sliced red onion	1	cup walnut pieces, toasted

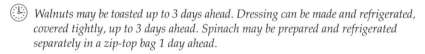 Walnuts may be toasted up to 3 days ahead. Dressing can be made and refrigerated, covered tightly, up to 3 days ahead. Spinach may be prepared and refrigerated separately in a zip-top bag 1 day ahead.

- To make dressing, combine cranberries, vinegars, garlic, and salt. Whisk in oil; allow to stand for at least 20 minutes.

- For salad, wash and dry spinach leaves. Combine spinach, raisins, onion, strawberries, and oranges in a salad bowl.

- Drizzle dressing over salad a small amount at a time, tossing between additions, until desired consistency is reached. Some dressing will be left over. Sprinkle salad with walnuts and serve.

Note: *To toast walnuts, spread on a baking sheet and bake at 400 degrees for 5 minutes, stirring twice; cool.*

Menu: *Serve with Julie's Very Berry Muffins (page 92) for a festive luncheon.*

The FDA recommends that you wash your fruits and vegetables with warm water to dislodge any dirt and disease-causing bacteria from the surface or in the cracks. To further ensure your safety, remove the outer leaves of leafy vegetables and use a smooth, non-absorbent cutting board. Scrub your cutting board with hot, soapy water after each use, and sanitize it with a bleach solution or by running it through the dishwasher.

Watercress Salad with Cranberries and Pecans

Perfect for winter holidays!

Yield: 16 to 20 servings

Dressing

½	cup chopped dried cranberries		1	tablespoon minced garlic
¼	cup red wine vinegar		1¼	teaspoons salt
¼	cup balsamic vinegar		1	cup extra virgin olive oil

Salad

6	bunches watercress (about 12 cups)		3	small heads radicchio
3	bulbs fennel		1	cup pecan halves

🕐 *Dressing must be prepared 20 minutes ahead. May be refrigerated, covered tightly, up to 3 days ahead.*

❻ To make dressing, combine cranberries, vinegars, garlic, and salt in a small bowl. Whisk in olive oil. Let stand for at least 20 minutes.

❻ Rinse, dry and tear watercress, removing large stems. Clean and trim fennel, then slice lengthwise into thin shreds. Clean and core radicchio; tear into bite-sized pieces. Combine watercress, fennel and radicchio in a large salad bowl. Refrigerate until ready to serve.

❻ When ready to serve, whisk dressing and pour over salad, a small amount at a time, until desired consistency is reached. Add pecans, toss and serve.

Note: *You may substitute red romaine or red leaf lettuce for all or part of the watercress.*

Menu: *Serve with Juicy Marinated Turkey Breast (page 223) and Southern Sweet Potato Soufflé (page 165) for a mini-Thanksgiving!*

Toast nuts by spreading them in a single layer on a rimmed baking sheet; put them in a preheated 350° oven for 5 minutes, or until they just begin to turn a pale golden brown. Check frequently to prevent burning.

rosemary

chives

Parigi Fall Salad

A truly unique salad!

Yield: 4 servings

Walnut Oil Vinaigrette

¼	cup red wine vinegar
1	tablespoon Dijon mustard

Salt and freshly ground black pepper
½ cup walnut oil

Salad

1 tablespoon unsalted butter
1 medium yellow onion, thinly sliced
½ cup dry white wine
4 large handfuls mesclun

1 ripe Bartlett pear, chopped
1 Granny Smith apple, chopped
¼ cup walnut pieces, toasted
6-8 ounces Gorgonzola cheese

⏱ *Dressing may be prepared and refrigerated, covered, up to 3 days ahead. Whisk dressing well before adding to salad.*

6 To make vinaigrette, whisk together vinegar, mustard, salt, and pepper in a mixing bowl. Slowly drizzle in oil, whisking constantly, until mixture is well-blended.

6 To make salad, melt butter in a small skillet. Add onion; sauté until golden brown. Add wine; simmer until all liquid evaporates.

6 Combine sautéed onion, mesclun, pear, and apple in a bowl. Add enough vinaigrette to coat; toss.

6 Place salad on serving plates. Top with walnuts and cheese.

Menu: *Pair this with Harvest Squash Soup (page 103) for a wonderful autumn lunch or light dinner.*

Originally, the main intention of the Dayton Art Institute's Oktoberfest was to draw people into the museum to see the collection of art works that are housed there. Now that people realize that the museum itself is a worthy destination any time of year, the goal of the Oktoberfest has changed. Over the years, the DAI Associate Board and more than 2,000 volunteers have raised well over $2.5 million for the Art Institute through the annual festival.

Almond Orange Garden Salad

You will make this salad again and again

Yield: 8 servings

Dressing

1	cup vegetable oil	1	teaspoon freshly ground black pepper
¼	cup white wine vinegar		
¼	cup sugar	1	tablespoon chopped fresh parsley
1	teaspoon salt		

Salad

1	cup sliced almonds	6	green onions, chopped
¼	cup sugar	1½	cups fresh orange sections, or 2 (11 ounce) cans Mandarin oranges, drained
½	head iceberg lettuce		
½	head romaine lettuce		

Almonds may be made up to 3 days ahead. Cool and store in a zip-top bag until ready to use.

- To make dressing, combine all dressing ingredients in a jar and shake until well-mixed.

- To make salad, combine almonds and sugar in a skillet. Cook over medium heat, stirring and watching closely, until almonds are browned. Transfer to foil to cool.

- Tear lettuce into bite-sized pieces; place in a salad bowl. Add onion and orange sections.

- Pour dressing over salad to taste and toss lightly. Top with almonds and serve.

Note: *You may not need all of the dressing, so add a little at a time.*

Menu: *This salad works well with Asian-flavored meals.*

To create perfect orange sections, start by slicing a bit off the top and bottom of an orange, enough to reveal the flesh of the fruit. Stand the orange on end, and cut away the peel and white pith by running a paring knife from top to bottom, following the curves of the orange. Hold the peeled orange over a bowl to catch the juice. Carefully work the knife in toward the center along one side of a segment as close to the membrane as possible, and then rotate the knife slightly so the blade lifts the section from the other membrane. Continue, working your way around the orange until all the sections have been removed. This method can be used for other citrus fruits, as well.

Mary's Strawberry and Poppyseed Salad

The perfect salad for your spring menus

Yield: 10 to 12 servings

Dressing
1	cup vegetable oil	1	teaspoon salt
½	cup red wine vinegar	1	clove garlic, minced
⅔	cup sugar	½	red onion, coarsely chopped
1	tablespoon poppyseeds		

Salad
3	large heads butter lettuce	½	red onion, thinly sliced
1	quart strawberries, thinly sliced	½	cup toasted walnuts (optional)

🕐 *Dressing may be prepared and refrigerated, covered tightly, up to 3 days ahead. Lettuce and sliced onion may be prepared and refrigerated in zip-top bags 1 day ahead.*

⚬ To make dressing, combine all dressing ingredients in a blender. Puree until smooth.

⚬ To make salad, clean, dry and tear lettuce. Combine lettuce, strawberries and onion in a salad bowl.

⚬ Pour dressing over salad, adding a small amount at a time, until reaching desired consistency. Toss and sprinkle with walnuts, if desired.

Note: *To toast walnuts, bake at 400 degrees on a baking sheet for 4 to 5 minutes.*

In 1980, the Troy Strawberry Festival earned a spot in the Guinness Book of World Records for the largest strawberry ice cream sundae. It weighed more than 11,000 pounds and was over 15 feet tall.

Blueberry, Orange and Cherry Salad

Colorful!

Yield: 12 servings

Dressing

½	cup olive oil	¼	teaspoon beef bouillon granules
3	tablespoons sugar	3	tablespoons white wine vinegar
½	teaspoon coarsely ground black pepper	¼	teaspoon dried basil
½	teaspoon salt	1	tablespoon reserved Mandarin orange juice (from salad)

Salad

¾	cup fresh blueberries	8	cups mixed salad greens
½	cup dried cherries or cranberries	1	(11 ounce) can Mandarin oranges, drained, juice reserved
⅓	cup chopped green onion		
⅓	cup slivered almonds, toasted		

🕐 *Dressing may be prepared and refrigerated up to 3 days ahead. Fruits and greens may be prepared up to 1 day ahead and refrigerated in separate containers.*

☙ Combine all dressing ingredients; shake well or mix in a blender.

☙ Combine all salad ingredients in a large salad bowl. Pour dressing over salad and toss.

Note: *To toast almonds, bake at 400 degrees on a baking sheet for 3 to 5 minutes. Check frequently to avoid burning.*

Menu: *Add Amy's Amazing Lemon Bread (page 84) or Zillions of Zucchini Bread (page 85) for a heavenly lunch.*

Orange Vinaigrette

3 tablespoons
Orange-Juice Reduction

2 tablespoons
white-wine vinegar

Salt and pepper

3 tablespoons
extra-virgin olive oil

In a bowl, whisk together the orange-juice reduction and vinegar. Season with salt and pepper. Whisking, slowly add oil. Store up to 5 days in refrigerator. To make orange-juice reduction: Place 3 cups freshly squeezed orange juice in small nonreactive saucepan over medium-high heat. Gently boil until liquid has reduced to ½ cup and is syrupy, about 1 hour.

Asparagus, Spinach, Pasta, and Cashew Salad

A one-dish salad perfect for summer guests

Yield: 6 to 8 servings

Dressing

½	cup olive oil	2	tablespoons soy sauce
1	cup sliced green onion	1	teaspoon sesame oil
6	tablespoons rice wine vinegar		

Salad

1	pound dry bow-tie pasta		Salt and freshly ground black pepper to taste
1	tablespoon olive oil		Dried red pepper flakes to taste
1	pound asparagus	1	cup cashew pieces, roasted and salted
1	cup cherry or grape tomatoes, halved	1½	pounds boneless, skinless chicken breasts, grilled and sliced on the diagonal
6	ounces baby spinach, cleaned and stemmed		

⏲ *Chicken may be grilled and refrigerated 1 day ahead. Dressing may also be prepared and refrigerated 1 day ahead.*

- Combine all dressing ingredients in a blender or food processor until smooth. Chill.

- To make salad, cook pasta according to package directions; drain and rinse. Add olive oil and stir with a wooden spoon. Cool.

- Blanch asparagus for about 3 minutes, or until crisp-tender. Diagonally slice into 1-inch pieces. Reserve some asparagus tops for garnish.

- Pour dressing over pasta and toss lightly. Add asparagus, tomatoes and spinach. Toss; season with salt, pepper and pepper flakes. Place salad on individual dinner plates and sprinkle with cashews.

- Arrange chicken on top of salad. Garnish with reserved asparagus tops. Serve at room temperature.

Note: *Buying grilled chicken breasts from the deli saves time.*

Menu: *Offer some Overnight Focaccia (page 80) with this salad to complete the meal. For dessert, serve Fresh Peach Crisp and Vanilla Crème Fraîche (page 275).*

Try these salad combinations:

Fresh spinach, cubes of feta cheese and cooked black beans in lemon-juice vinaigrette.

Chicken, new potatoes, blanched asparagus, and tomatoes in mayonnaise flavored with lemon juice.

Tortellini, black olives, celery, red onions, and cherry tomatoes in garlic vinaigrette.

Smoked turkey, brown and wild rice, celery, onions, blanched broccoli flowerets, and vinaigrette using sherry vinegar.

Pasta Salad with Grilled Zucchini and Olives

Bring this to your next potluck dinner

Yield: 6 to 8 servings

1½ pounds vine-ripened tomatoes, chopped	Salt and freshly ground black pepper to taste
½ cup finely chopped red onion	1 pound dry penne or other tubular pasta
2 cloves garlic, minced and mashed into a paste with 1 teaspoon salt	⅔ cup coarsely chopped kalamata or other brine-cured olives
2 tablespoons red wine vinegar	6 ounces ricotta salata or feta cheese, diced
¼ cup extra virgin olive oil, plus extra for brushing zucchini	1½ cups whole small (or torn large) fresh basil leaves
1½ pounds zucchini, diagonally cut into ⅓-inch slices	

🕐 *Pasta may be made up to 4 hours ahead and kept covered at room temperature.*

ⓖ In a large bowl, gently stir together tomato, onion, garlic paste, vinegar, and ¼ cup oil.

ⓖ Lightly brush 1 side of zucchini slices with extra olive oil; season with salt and pepper.

ⓖ Heat a well-seasoned ridged grill pan over medium heat until hot. Grill zucchini in batches, oiled-side down, brushing tops of slices with oil before turning. Grill 1 to 2 minutes on each side, or until just tender but not soft. Transfer grilled zucchini to a small bowl.

ⓖ Cook pasta in boiling salted water until just tender; drain well. Add hot pasta to tomato mixture and toss well. Cool slightly and stir in zucchini, olives, cheese, and basil. Season with salt and pepper to taste. Serve warm or at room temperature.

Note: *For a lighter olive flavor, regular black olives can be substituted. Zucchini can also be cooked on the grill.*

Menu: *Serve with grilled steak, chicken or burgers for a wonderful side dish.*

Thai Pasta Salad

Spicy and sweet

Yield: 4 servings

1	teaspoon dried red pepper flakes	8	ounces dry linguine or similar Asian noodles, cooked and drained
3	tablespoons canola oil		
3	tablespoons sesame oil	2	tablespoons chopped fresh cilantro
3	tablespoons honey		
2	tablespoons soy sauce, or more to taste	¼	cup chopped green onion
		¼	cup honey-roasted peanuts
		1	tablespoon sesame seeds, toasted

⏱ *Dressing and noodles must be prepared and combined at least 1 day ahead.*

6 Heat pepper flakes in oils over medium-high heat for 1 to 2 minutes. Remove from heat and stir in honey and soy sauce. Pour over noodles and chill overnight.

6 When ready to serve, add cilantro, onion, peanuts, and sesame seeds. Serve at room temperature.

Note: *To make this salad into a full meal, add 1 pound of diced skinless chicken breast. Brush chicken with soy sauce and sesame oil, if desired. Cover with foil and bake at 350 degrees for 20 to 25 minutes. Toss diced chicken with pasta and serve over field greens.*

Menu: *Try serving this with Szechwan Chicken Salad (page 138) and Almond Orange Garden Salad (page 130) for a "salad sampler" luncheon.*

Lemon Pasta Salad

The fresh taste of summer

Yield: 10 servings

	Juice and zest of 2 lemons	1	pound dry pasta, cooked al dente and drained
½	cup olive oil		
4	green onions, sliced diagonally	⅔	cup Parmesan cheese
1	teaspoon salt	½	cup chopped fresh parsley
	Freshly ground black pepper to taste	¼	cup pine nuts, toasted

6 Combine lemon juice and zest, oil, onion, salt, and pepper. Pour mixture over warm pasta.

6 Toss salad with cheese, parsley and pine nuts. Serve immediately.

Note: *It is essential to combine all ingredients, especially the fresh lemon zest, just prior to serving.*

Menu: *Accompany Grilled Swordfish with Tomato Feta Relish (page 191) with this salad and some sautéed zucchini.*

Wilmington's Banana Split Festival celebrates the birthplace of the Banana Split-Hazard's Restaurant. In 1907, there was a winter storm that trapped everyone in Wilmington, and Ernest Hazard was looking for a way to draw people to his drug store. He came up with the idea of topping ice cream and banana slices with nuts, whipped cream and a cherry.

The Victoria Children's Festival features a variety of musical and theatrical performances, as well as hands-on artistic activities for children. The Victoria modeled the festival after Toronto's, which also combines indoor and outdoor venues with an emphasis on the arts.

Spring Island Couscous Salad

Yield: 6 to 8 servings

2¼ cups water
1 (10 ounce) box couscous
    (about 1½ cups)
½ teaspoon salt
3 tablespoons fresh lemon juice,
    or to taste
¼ cup olive oil

Salt and freshly ground black
    pepper to taste
2 cups shredded fresh spinach
3 large green onions, thinly sliced
3 tablespoons finely chopped
    fresh dill, or to taste

🕐 *Must be made 2 hours, or up to 24 hours, ahead.*

❂ Bring 2¼ cups water to a boil in a saucepan. Stir in couscous and ½ teaspoon salt. Remove from heat and cover. Let stand 5 minutes. Fluff with a fork and transfer to a bowl.

❂ Stir in lemon juice, oil, salt, and pepper to taste. Cool couscous completely.

❂ Stir in spinach, onion and dill. Cover and chill at least 2 hours, or overnight.

Note: *Make sure couscous is completely cool or spinach and dill will turn brown.*

Menu: *Serve with a Fresh Tomato Tart (page 56) and Parmesan Bread Twists (page 52) for a gorgeous luncheon.*

Pack picnic salads in zip-top plastic bags. They will stay colder and fit better in the cooler. When it is time to eat, simply pour the salads into serving bowls.

Lemon Tarragon Chicken Salad with Grapes

Perfect for a shower or ladies' luncheon

Yield: 8 to 10 servings

Lemon Mayonnaise

1	cup mayonnaise	2	teaspoons dried tarragon
¼	cup lemon juice		White pepper to taste

Salad

3	large boneless, skinless chicken breasts	2	cups peeled, seeded and chopped cucumber
1	cup heavy cream		Zest of 1 lemon
2	cups cantaloupe chunks	¼	cup chopped fresh dill
2	cups whole seedless red grapes		Salt and freshly ground black pepper to taste
1	cup slivered almonds, toasted		

🕐 *Lemon Mayonnaise may be prepared up to 1 day ahead. Fruit and cucumber may be prepared and refrigerated 1 day ahead. Chicken can be cooked, shredded and refrigerated, tightly covered, up to 1 day ahead.*

- Combine all ingredients for the mayonnaise in a small bowl; set aside.
- To prepare the salad, preheat oven to 350 degrees.
- Place chicken in a baking dish. Pour cream over chicken. Bake 20 to 25 minutes; cool and shred.
- Combine chicken, cantaloupe, grapes, almonds, cucumber, zest, and dill in a salad bowl.
- Fold in lemon mayonnaise. Season with salt and pepper.

Note: *Add the lemon mayonnaise a little at a time until the salad reaches the desired consistency. You may not use all of it.*

Menu: *Serve with French Breakfast Puffs (page 91). Make Blackberry Mini-Tarts (page 271) for dessert.*

Troy senior citizens use an average of 1,300 quarts of strawberries to make their famous strawberry shortcakes to sell at the festival.

Szechwan Chicken Salad

Chicken salad with a kick!

Yield: 4 to 6 servings

2	whole chicken breasts
1	cup chopped green onion
2	(2 inch long) slices fresh ginger
2	tablespoons peanut oil
⅓	cup chopped green onion (white part and some green)
2	teaspoons minced fresh ginger
1	fresh jalapeño pepper, seeded, deveined and finely chopped
½	teaspoon ground Szechwan peppercorns
2	tablespoons soy sauce
1	tablespoon hoisin sauce
2	tablespoons fresh orange juice
1	teaspoon honey
2	cloves garlic, minced
1-2	teaspoons chili oil
4	cups shredded napa cabbage

The chicken may be prepared and refrigerated up to 1 day ahead. The cabbage may be shredded and refrigerated in zip-top bags 1 day ahead.

Bring 3 to 4 cups water to a boil in a 2-quart saucepan. Add chicken, 1 cup green onion and 2 slices ginger. Cover tightly; cook over high heat for 10 minutes. Remove from heat and cool in liquid 45 minutes. Remove chicken from liquid, discard skin, and refrigerate until well-chilled. Shred meat into coarse pieces and refrigerate until ready to assemble salad.

Combine peanut oil, ⅓ cup green onion, 2 teaspoons ginger, jalapeño and ground peppercorns in a small saucepan. In a small bowl, combine soy sauce, hoisin sauce, orange juice, honey, garlic, and chili oil. Bring peanut oil mixture to a boil and cook 1 minute over medium heat. Add soy sauce mixture and heat, but do not continue to boil.

Combine chicken and cabbage in a salad bowl. Pour sauce over top and toss gently. Serve on individual plates.

Tips for easy
main dish salads:

• Let one flavorful, hearty ingredient be the star of the salad.

• Use bags of prewashed greens.

• Limit the salad to five or six ingredients.

• Make sure that at least one ingredient does not require time-consuming peeling or chopping, such as canned beans, nuts, sunflower seeds or olives.

• Find a fabulous bottled dressing, or keep a homemade dressing on hand and ready to use.

Grilled Sirloin Salad

A salad for meat lovers

Yield: 4 servings

2	tablespoons reduced-sodium soy sauce	¾	pound beef sirloin, trimmed of visible fat
2	tablespoons balsamic vinegar		Salt to taste
2	teaspoons sesame oil	16	green onions, white part only
2	teaspoons brown sugar	1	red bell pepper, halved lengthwise
1	teaspoon finely chopped fresh ginger	12	cups washed, dried and torn salad greens, such as escarole, curly endive, radicchio or watercress
1	clove garlic, finely chopped		
2	teaspoons black peppercorns, crushed		

🕐 *Salad greens may be prepared and refrigerated in zip-top plastic bags 1 day ahead.*

6 Preheat grill.

6 To make dressing, combine soy sauce, vinegar, oil, sugar, ginger, and garlic in a blender or food processor; blend until smooth.

6 Press peppercorns into both sides of beef. Season lightly with salt.

6 Place beef, onions and pepper halves on the grill; cook 4 minutes. Turn beef and vegetables; cook 3 to 4 minutes longer, or until beef is medium-rare and vegetables are slightly charred. Remove from grill. Let meat stand 5 minutes before cutting against the grain into very thin slices. Cut green onions into 1-inch pieces. Slice pepper into long, thin strips.

6 Toss salad greens with dressing. Place greens on a serving platter, or divide among 4 individual plates. Arrange meat and vegetables on top; serve.

Note: *This salad serves 4 as an entrée.*

Menu: *Add Potato Polpettes (page 161) to round out the meal.*

For delicious fudge, combine sugar and cocoa. Add the sauerkraut.

Sauerkraut?

Sauerkraut—chopped cabbage fermented in its juice along with salt-doesn't seem the thing of which such foods are made. But in Waynesville, toss in the sauerkraut and you've got the makings for a festival. Every fall, the town is overflowing with visitors coming to sample sauerkraut fudge, sauerkraut pizza, sauerkraut cookies, and sauerkraut cream pie!

Marinated New Red Potato Salad

A delicious alternative to mayonnaise-based potato salads

Yield: 4 to 6 servings

Vinaigrette

½	cup olive oil	¼	teaspoon dry mustard
⅓	cup white wine vinegar	¼	teaspoon freshly ground black pepper
1	tablespoon sugar		
3	large cloves garlic, minced	½	teaspoon salt

Salad

1½	pound tiny new red potatoes	½	small red onion, thinly sliced and separated into rings
1	(13 ounce) can artichoke hearts, drained and halved	½	cup kalamata olives, pitted and halved
1	small green bell pepper, cut into strips	2	tablespoons snipped fresh parsley
8-10	cherry tomatoes, halved		

This salad must be made at least 4 hours, and up to 24 hours, ahead.

⚬ Combine all vinaigrette ingredients and shake well; set aside.

⚬ Cook potatoes in a covered saucepan of boiling salted water for 15 to 20 minutes, or until tender. Drain well.

⚬ Cut potatoes into quarters into a bowl. Add artichoke hearts, bell pepper, tomatoes, onion, olives, and parsley. Pour vinaigrette over mixture and toss gently.

⚬ Cover and chill 4 to 24 hours, stirring occasionally. Season with salt and pepper to taste. Serve cold or at room temperature.

Menu: *Pair this with Flank Steak (page 228) for an easy make-ahead meal.*

Think you know what a new potato is? What separates new potatoes from the rest is the skin—not the size. A new potato is a thin-skinned young potato of any variety, any color. True new potatoes are immature, so they always have a low-starch content and waxy texture. They hold a clean shape, even when cooked until very tender.

Sweet Potato Salad with Rosemary-Honey Vinaigrette

An interesting mix of flavors

Yield: 6 servings

4½ cups cubed, peeled sweet potato	2 tablespoons chopped fresh rosemary
1 tablespoon olive oil	2 cloves garlic, minced
¼ cup honey	½ teaspoon salt
3 tablespoons white wine vinegar	½ teaspoon freshly ground black pepper
1 tablespoon olive oil	

Dressing can be prepared 1 day ahead.

- Preheat oven to 450 degrees.
- Toss together potato and 1 tablespoon oil on a 10x15-inch jelly-roll pan lined with foil and sprayed with cooking spray.
- Bake 35 minutes, or until tender.
- Meanwhile, whisk together honey, vinegar, 1 tablespoon oil, rosemary, garlic, salt, and pepper in a large bowl.
- Add potato and toss well. Cool.

Menu: *A special side dish for purchased rotisserie chicken. Add a green salad to round out the meal.*

Some quick salad combinations:

- Green leaf lettuce, watercress and sliced peaches with raspberry vinaigrette.

- Watercress, sliced crisp apples and chips of Cheddar cheese, with vinaigrette of walnut oil and sherry vinegar.

- Cooked shrimp with pasta shells, blanched broccoli flowerets, julienned red pepper, and herb vinaigrette.

- Cubed cooked new potatoes, peas, chopped fresh mint, equal parts sour cream and mayonnaise, and salt and pepper.

Zesty Corn and Red Pepper Salad

A crisp and colorful summertime dish

Yield: 6 servings

4	cups fresh corn (about 8 ears)	½	cup raspberry wine vinegar
1	cup water	¼	cup sugar
1⅓	cups chopped red bell pepper	1	tablespoon vegetable oil
1	cup sliced celery	½	teaspoon salt
½	cup sliced green onion	¼	teaspoon freshly ground black
½	cup chopped fresh parsley		pepper
½	cup chopped fresh basil		

Must be made at least 4 hours, and up to 8 hours, ahead. Keep refrigerated.

6 Combine corn and 1 cup water in a medium saucepan. Bring to a boil. Reduce heat; simmer, uncovered, for 15 minutes, or until tender. Drain well.

6 Combine corn, bell pepper, celery, onion, parsley, and basil in a large bowl.

6 Combine vinegar, sugar, oil, salt, and pepper. Pour mixture over vegetables and toss well. Cover and chill at least 4 hours, stirring occasionally. Toss gently before serving.

Note: *Can substitute frozen white shoepeg corn (thawed) if necessary.*

To cook an ear of corn in the microwave: shuck it, rinse it, wrap in plastic wrap, and cook on high for 3 to 5 minutes. Let rest for 2 more minutes.

rosemary

dill

Chives

Black Bean, Corn and Avocado Salad

A beautiful accompaniment to summer meals

Yield: 8 servings

3	ears white corn	1	cup chopped fresh cilantro
¾	cup water	⅓	cup fresh lime juice
3	medium tomatoes, peeled, seeded and chopped	¼	teaspoon salt
2	jalapeño peppers, seeded and minced	¼	teaspoon freshly ground black pepper
2	(16 ounce) cans black beans, rinsed and drained	2	avocados

🕐 *Can be made 1 day ahead (except avocados) and kept refrigerated. Add finely chopped avocados at the last minute, stir and serve.*

✿ Cut corn from cob into a saucepan. Add ¾ cup water and bring to a boil. Reduce heat, cover and simmer 6 to 7 minutes, or until tender. Drain and transfer to a large bowl.

✿ Add tomato, jalapeño, beans, cilantro, lime juice, salt, and pepper to corn. Stir gently and chill.

✿ When ready to serve, peel and finely chop avocados. Stir into salad and serve.

Menu: *Great with Summer Lime Chicken Breasts (page 217) and a salad.*

Place an avocado in a paper bag to speed ripening. Once softened, it can be refrigerated for up to 10 days before it is used.

Dilly Bean Salad

Crisp and delicious

Yield: 8 servings

Salad

2	pounds fresh green beans, cut into 3-inch lengths	1	dash Tabasco sauce
2	tablespoons chopped fresh parsley	¼	cup sliced green onion
3	tablespoons chopped fresh dill	¼	cup olive oil
1	clove garlic, minced		Salt and freshly ground black pepper to taste
1	teaspoon seasoning salt (we prefer Accent)		Cherry tomatoes and quartered hard-cooked eggs for garnish

Lemon Sauce

3	tablespoons fresh lemon juice		Salt and freshly ground black pepper to taste
1½	teaspoons lemon zest		
1½	teaspoons Dijon mustard	6	tablespoons olive oil
1½	teaspoons sugar		

🕐 *Salad must marinate at least 1 hour.*

6 Cook beans in boiling salted water for 3 to 5 minutes, or until crisp-tender. Drain and plunge into ice water to stop cooking. Drain, pat dry and place in a bowl.

6 Combine parsley, dill, garlic, seasoning salt, Tabasco sauce, onion, oil, salt, and pepper; pour over beans. Marinate at least 1 hour.

6 Meanwhile, mix all lemon sauce ingredients until well-blended.

6 When ready to serve, arrange beans in a serving dish. Garnish with tomatoes and egg quarters. Drizzle lemon sauce over the top; serve at room temperature or chilled.

Note: *Use fresh dill whenever available. If you must use dried herbs, halve or third the volume.*

Menu: *Bring along with Marinated New Red Potato Salad (page 140), purchased fried chicken, and The Best Chocolate Chip Cookies (page 279) for a delicious picnic.*

When the local tomatoes are perfectly ripe, be sure to enjoy this classic salad. Layer slices of tomatoes, fresh mozzarella and torn fresh basil on a platter, drizzle with vinegar and olive oil, sprinkle with salt and pepper.

rosemary

dill

Chives

Roasted Beet and Walnut Salad

A beautiful and flavorful addition to any plate

Yield: 8 servings

8-10	medium beets (about 2 pounds)		Salt and freshly ground black pepper to taste
2	tablespoons cider vinegar	¼	cup olive oil
1½	teaspoons Dijon mustard	½	cup coarsely chopped walnuts
½	teaspoon sugar	4	ounces blue cheese, coarsely crumbled

🕐 *Roast beets the night before and store wrapped in the refrigerator. Unwrap and cut when needed.*

◐ Preheat oven to 350 degrees.

◐ Wrap beets individually in foil. Place on a baking sheet and roast 1 to 1½ hours or until tender. Unwrap, cool and remove skin. Cut beets into ½-inch cubes.

◐ Make a dressing by whisking together vinegar, mustard, sugar, salt, and pepper. Whisking constantly, slowly drizzle in oil and whisk until thickened.

◐ Add dressing to beets and toss well. Just before serving, toss in walnuts and sprinkle with blue cheese.

Menu: *A lovely prelude to a meal featuring Stuffed Pork Tenderloin with Shallots (page 240).*

Roasting vegetables preserves the nutrients and intensifies natural flavors.

Tarragon Egg Salad

A delicious way to use up the Easter eggs!

Yield: 2 cups

6	hard-cooked eggs, diced	⅛	teaspoon salt, or to taste
½	stalk celery, diced	½	teaspoon Worcestershire sauce
2	scant teaspoons Dijon mustard	1	scant teaspoon celery seeds (optional)
2	tablespoons mayonnaise		Freshly ground black pepper to taste
1	tablespoon chopped fresh tarragon		
1	tablespoon chopped fresh parsley		

🕐 *This salad can be made 1 day ahead.*

◐ Combine eggs and celery in a bowl.

◐ Combine mustard, mayonnaise, tarragon, parsley, salt, Worcestershire sauce, celery seeds, and pepper in a separate bowl. Mix well and fold into egg mixture.

◐ Adjust seasonings as needed and serve.

Note: *Make sure to use fresh herbs. Dried herbs tend to make this salad bitter.*

To "chop" fresh herbs, place leaves in a short juice glass and snip them several times with kitchen scissors.

145

Phyl's Layered Salad

This salad is great for summer gatherings!

Yield: 8 servings

Dressing

1	cup mayonnaise	½	teaspoon salt
½	cup sour cream	½	teaspoon freshly ground black
2	teaspoons Dijon mustard		pepper
¼	cup chopped green onion		

Salad

1½ cups dry macaroni, cooked, drained and rinsed
1   tablespoon vegetable oil
2   cups shredded iceberg lettuce
3   hard-cooked eggs, sliced
¾   pound boiled ham, cubed

1   (10 ounce) package frozen baby peas
1   cup shredded Monterey Jack cheese
    Freshly ground black pepper to taste

🕐 *The salad must be prepared 1 day prior to serving.*

6   Combine all dressing ingredients; set aside.

6   Toss together cooked macaroni and oil.

6   In a large bowl, layer lettuce, macaroni, egg, ham, peas, cheese, and pepper. Spread dressing evenly on top. Cover and refrigerate 24 hours before serving.

Note: *For added presentation, serve in a glass bowl and/or top with sliced hard-cooked eggs and chopped green onion!*

If you enjoy cooked fennel, be sure to try it raw as part of your crudités selection, or instead of celery in a salad. In Italy, a bulb is served simply with salt and a bowl of extra virgin olive oil for dipping—delicious! Or, for an unusual salad, combine sliced fennel, peeled orange sections, greens, and a dressing of olive oil, orange juice and red wine vinegar.

On the Sidelines

SIDE DISHES

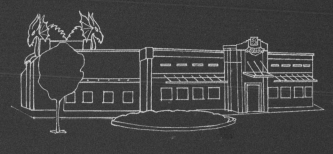

FIFTH THIRD FIELD

Although no one from Dayton ever invented a major sport, Dayton's sports history is replete with notable accomplishments.

West Milton native Carl M. Brumbaugh became the first T-formation quarterback in the National Football League when he played for the Chicago Bears in the 1930s.

Fairview High School graduate Mike Schmidt began his Hall-of-Fame career in 1972. After winning 10 Gold Gloves, hitting 548 home runs, and being named National League MVP three times, Schmidt is considered by many to be the greatest third baseman ever to play Major League Baseball.

Edwin C. Moses, another Fairview High School graduate, captured two Olympic gold medals for the 400-meter hurdles. During The Streak, he won an incredible 122 consecutive races. ESPN named him one of the 50 greatest athletes of the 20th century.

And if it weren't for Alter High School graduate and NBA Chicago Bulls star John Paxson, maybe Michael Jordan would have been just another bald 6-foot-6 shooting guard with a couple fewer rings.

From the Dayton Triangles, a founding team of the National Football League in 1920, to the Dayton Dragons, the single-A affiliate of Major League Baseball's Cincinnati Reds, Dayton continues to influence the world of sports.

RITTER COLLETT, Sports Editor Emeritus for the *Dayton Daily News*, states, "Dayton has a rich history in the athletic world. A community that produced the greatest hurdler in the world, Edwin C. Moses, and the greatest all-around third baseman in major league baseball, Mike Schmidt, has a lot to talk about. There is no way to pay tribute to

Sara Jane's Baked Apples

A wholly delicious version of a Midwest favorite

Yield: 6 servings

6	medium apples; red, yellow or combination	½	teaspoon cinnamon
½	cup sugar	3-4	tablespoons butter
		3	tablespoons water

- Preheat oven to 350 degrees.
- Score skin around center of apples, wash and core. Place apples in a shallow baking dish.
- Fill hollow apple centers with the following layers: half the sugar, all of the butter, all of the cinnamon, remaining sugar. Sprinkle water over the tops of the apples.
- Bake, uncovered, for 1 hour, basting every 10 to 15 minutes.

Menu: *Try with Holiday Pork Roast (page 238) and stuffing with raisins, or any roast pork, turkey or chicken as part of a "fall feast."*

Artichoke-Spinach Casserole

A double E rating: easy and elegant

Yield: 6 to 8 servings

2	(10 ounce) packages frozen chopped spinach	1	(8 ounce) package cream cheese
2	(14 ounce) cans artichoke hearts, drained and sliced	1	stick butter or margarine
		½	cup herb-seasoned bread crumbs
		½	cup Parmesan cheese

Can be made 1 day ahead and refrigerated. Reheat and serve.

- Preheat oven to 350 degrees.
- Cook spinach according to package directions, drain.
- Place spinach in the bottom of a 9x13-inch baking dish. Top with artichoke hearts.
- Melt cream cheese and butter; pour over vegetables. Sprinkle bread crumbs and cheese over the top.
- Bake for 20 to 25 minutes.

Note: *Try this on a brunch buffet, or for a ladies' luncheon.*

Menu: *Serve with Shadow Mountain Tenderloin (page 225), roasted potatoes, and Mary's Strawberry and Poppyseed Salad (page 131) for a truly elegant meal.*

The Dayton Dragons are the first team in the history of the National Association of Professional Baseball Organizations (NAPBO) ever to sell out all home games before the first pitch of the season is thrown.

—Kevin Rochlitz, V.P. Sales and Marketing Dayton Dragons

A surefire way to cook large amounts of asparagus, especially effective when they have thicker stems:

Preheat oven to 350°. Place 2 pounds of asparagus two layers deep in a casserole. Season with salt and pepper, and drizzle with olive oil. Add 2 tablespoons water and cover tightly. For medium-sized asparagus, bake for 14 minutes; thicker asparagus may take up to 17 minutes. Keep dish covered until it is served.

Asparagus and Portobello Mushrooms with Goat Cheese

High heat develops the rich, subtle flavors

Yield: 4 servings

1	teaspoon minced fresh rosemary		Salt and pepper to taste
2	medium cloves garlic, minced	1¼	pounds asparagus spears, tough ends snapped off
2	tablespoons lemon juice	2	large portobello mushroom caps
¼	cup extra-virgin olive oil	1	ounce goat cheese, crumbled

- Preheat broiler.
- Whisk together rosemary, garlic, lemon juice, and oil in a medium bowl. Season with salt and pepper.
- Brush asparagus and mushroom caps with about 2 tablespoons of dressing mixture to coat lightly.
- Place asparagus in a single layer on a heavy jelly-roll or rimmed baking sheet. Broil asparagus about 4 inches from heat source for 6 to 8 minutes, or until tender and browned in some spots, shaking baking sheet once halfway through cooking to rotate spears.
- Broil mushroom caps, top side facing heat source, for 8 to 10 minutes, or until tender and browned. Cool slightly and cut into thin slices.
- Toss together asparagus, mushroom slices and remaining dressing mixture. Transfer to a serving platter and adjust seasoning as needed. Sprinkle with goat cheese and serve immediately.

Note: *Be sure to use thin to medium spears (no larger than ⅝-inch thick). Thicker spears may surface burn before cooking through.*

Menu: *Add Flank Steak (page 228), crusty French bread and a salad, and you've got a delicious, easy meal.*

In 1991, I was in Moscow to recruit the son of Alexander and Natalia Petrov. Alexander was one of the great Soviet basketball players of all time. His son, Pavel, was 6'10" and 225 pounds, and they invited me over for dinner. Upon my arrival, Pavel showed me his father's Olympic silver medals from the 1960 and 1964 games. I was truly honored to hold these treasures and see the son's reverence for his father's accomplishments. Soon we were called for dinner.

As I sat down, in front of me was a shot glass about twice the size we use in the states and there were several bottles of Lemon Vodka ready for distribution. Once the glasses were filled, Alexander stood up and toasted, "To Mark!" Everyone raised their glasses and knocked it down! I sipped until Alexander looked at me and said, "Nyet!" I threw it down faster than you can say "borscht."

I noticed a gelatin mold staring at me, and entombed in the clear cube was a cow's tongue.

Southwestern Baked Beans

Different bean varieties add wonderful texture

Yield: 10 to 12 servings

1	tablespoon vegetable oil	½	teaspoon hot pepper sauce
5	ounces Canadian bacon, cut into ½-inch pieces	1	(16 ounce) can chickpeas, rinsed and drained
2	cups chopped onion	1	(16 ounce) can kidney beans, rinsed and drained
2	(8 ounce) cans tomato sauce		
1	cup brown sugar	1	(16 ounce) can black beans, rinsed and drained
6	tablespoons apple cider vinegar		
3	tablespoons molasses	1	(16 ounce) can butter beans, rinsed and drained
1	tablespoon Worcestershire sauce		
1	tablespoon chili powder		

🕐 *Can be prepared up to 1 day ahead. Cover and refrigerate; bake as directed the next day.*

⚙ Preheat oven to 375 degrees.

⚙ Heat oil in a large, heavy ovenproof pot over medium-high heat. Add bacon and onion; sauté about 10 minutes or until brown.

⚙ Mix in tomato sauce, sugar, vinegar, molasses, Worcestershire sauce, chili powder, and hot pepper sauce. Add all beans. Stir and cover.

⚙ Bake, stirring occasionally, about 1½ hours or until mixture thickens.

Note: *Adjust cooking time to 2 hours if cooking after refrigeration.*

Asparagus with Chinese Vinaigrette

Yield: 4 generous servings

1⅓	pounds fresh thin asparagus	1	clove garlic, minced
1	tablespoon rice vinegar	¼	teaspoon minced fresh ginger
1	teaspoon soy sauce		Dash of chili oil or hot pepper sauce
1	teaspoon sesame oil		

🕐 *Can be made the day before and refrigerated.*

⚙ Blanch asparagus 3 minutes in boiling water. Rinse in cold water; pat dry. Place in a serving dish.

⚙ Combine vinegar, soy sauce, sesame oil, garlic, ginger, and chili oil; pour over asparagus.

⚙ Chill at least 30 minutes.

Note: *If making ahead, turn asparagus occasionally to recoat with marinade. Also makes a beautiful salad over Bibb lettuce.*

Menu: *Grill a pre-purchased teriyaki-marinated pork tenderloin. Add Almond Orange Garden Salad (page 130) and rice for an easy, colorful meal.*

Then I saw orange fish eggs I normally use as bait, and some kind of red vegetable that looked like an Indiana Jones side dish. The only thing that saved me was the bread. Vodka shot after vodka shot chased the bread and the mystery meal I was eating. After a dozen shots Alexander stood and shouted, "Let's party!"

I jitterbugged with Natalia and the Petrov family until 2:00 am and Pavel signed a National Letter of Intent to play for me at Washington State. The next day, I could feel the cow tongue chewing its cud, the fish eggs hatching, and the mystery vegetable growing. It was a long day, but at least I got the player I came to sign!

—Mark Adams
Host of WHIO radio show "Flyer Feedback" and former Division I Head Coach

Brazilian Black Beans

A flavorful vegetarian dish

Yield: 6 to 8 servings

8	ounces dry black beans (1⅛ cups), rinsed	1	medium sweet potato, halved lengthwise and sliced ¼-inch thick
½	cup chopped onion	1	(14½ ounce) can diced tomatoes
2	cloves garlic, minced	½	teaspoon finely shredded orange zest
1	bay leaf	3	cups hot cooked rice
¼	cup snipped fresh parsley		Shredded kale, spinach or flat-leaf parsley for garnish
½	teaspoon salt		
½	teaspoon dried red pepper flakes		
3	cups water		

To save time: simmer, soak, drain, and rinse beans the night before.

⚬ In a large saucepan, combine beans with enough water to cover. Bring to a boil. Reduce heat and simmer 2 minutes. Remove from heat and cover. Let soak 1 hour. Drain and rinse in a colander.

⚬ Return beans to saucepan. Stir in onion, garlic, bay leaf, parsley, salt, and pepper flakes. Stir in 3 cups water and bring to a boil. Reduce heat and simmer, covered, about 1½ hours or until beans are tender. Add more water, if necessary, and stir occasionally while cooking.

⚬ Meanwhile, cook sweet potato in enough boiling salted water to cover for 15 to 20 minutes, or until tender; drain and set aside.

⚬ Remove bay leaf from beans and discard. Add tomatoes to bean mixture.

⚬ Simmer beans, uncovered and stirring occasionally, for 15 to 20 minutes, or until a thick gravy forms. Stir in orange zest.

⚬ To serve, spoon beans over hot rice. Serve sweet potato on the side. Garnish with kale, spinach or parsley.

Note: *Sliced sweet potato can be used as a companion item served on the side, or layered between the rice and beans. It's delicious either way! Can be served as a vegetarian main dish for four.*

Menu: *Try as an accompaniment to Mexican Chicken Kiev (page 214). It's also great with Jerk Chicken (page 213)!*

Ritter Collett's Memories of Downtown Dayton in the 1940s

When I took a job on the long-gone *Dayton Journal* fresh out of the Air Force in January, 1946, the working hours on the morning paper were mid-afternoon to midnight, and sometimes beyond. I was dependent on downtown eating facilities. The choices were many within blocks of the newspaper office at Fourth and Jefferson. On the east side of Main between Second and Fifth were three medium-priced, full-service restaurants. My favorite was the Green Mill operated by the Stephan family. There were two cafeterias—the Virginia on Third, east of Main and Culp's on Fourth, west of Main. The Virginia later was the scene of a major fire that took the fire department six or seven hours to control.

Braised Red Cabbage and Apples

A lovely side dish for fall menus

Yield: 8 servings

2	small heads red cabbage, quartered	½	cup brown sugar
1	onion, thinly sliced	1	tablespoon salt
6	McIntosh apples, peeled and thinly sliced		Black pepper to taste
		½	cup red wine vinegar
		2	cups chicken broth

6 Preheat oven to 350 degrees.

6 Place cabbage, onion and apple into a baking pan.

6 In a saucepan, combine sugar, salt, pepper, vinegar, and chicken broth. Heat until sugar dissolves. Pour over cabbage mixture.

6 Bake, covered, for 1 hour or until cabbage is soft.

Menu: *Offer this beautiful dish with Stuffed Pork Tenderloin with Shallots (page 240).*

A favorite of the newspaper gang was McShane's Bar and Grill in the Arcade Building. I remember a thin but tasty top steak for $1.25.

More upscale were the King Cole and Servis and Buhl restaurants. And who can ever forget the Van Cleve hotel dining room?

For late night snacks, the popular Purple Cow in the Miami Hotel at Second and Ludlow was always crowded!

—Ritter Collett, Sports Editor Emeritus

Dayton Daily News

Buttermint Carrots

Yield: 8 to 10 servings

2	pounds baby carrots	¼	teaspoon salt
3	tablespoons butter	¼	teaspoon freshly ground black pepper
2	tablespoons honey		
2	teaspoons white wine vinegar	3	tablespoons chopped fresh mint

🕐 *Carrots can be boiled and drained up to 2 days ahead. Cover and refrigerate until ready to use.*

6 Cook carrots in a large pan of boiling water for 5 to 7 minutes, or to desired tenderness. Drain and plunge into cold water until completely cooled. Drain again and set aside.

6 Melt butter in a large saucepan. Add honey, vinegar, salt, and pepper. Mix well.

6 Add carrots; cook and stir over medium heat until carrots are heated through, and thoroughly glazed. Reduce heat if necessary to prevent burning.

6 Stir in mint and serve.

Menu: *Fabulous with any roast lamb. We recommend Easter Lamb (page 247).*

Sicilian Carrots

A beautiful dish that's light and different

Yield: 6 to 8 servings

	Nonstick olive oil spray
2	pounds baby carrots or thinly sliced regular carrots
2	tablespoons extra virgin olive oil
¼	cup dried cranberries
3	tablespoons pine nuts
9	medium basil leaves, julienned
2	tablespoons extra virgin olive oil
	Salt and freshly ground pepper to taste

⏱ *This dish must be prepared at least 12 hours, or up to 2 days, ahead.*

❻ Preheat oven to 400 degrees.

❻ Spray 2 large roasting pans with nonstick olive oil spray. Divide carrots among pans and drizzle with 2 tablespoons oil. Mix to coat; arrange carrots in a single layer on the pans.

❻ Bake 30 to 40 minutes, or until carrots soften and start to brown, stirring occasionally to prevent burning. Remove from pan to cool.

❻ In a bowl, combine carrots, cranberries, pine nuts, basil, and 2 tablespoons oil. Cover and refrigerate overnight.

❻ Season with salt and pepper as desired. Serve at room temperature.

Note: *High-quality olive oil makes a tremendous difference in the flavor of this dish.*

Menu: *Offer alongside Veal Saltimbocca (page 236) for bright color and flavor.*

Comfort Corn Pudding

A Southern favorite

Yield: 6 to 8 servings

1	(8 ounce) box corn muffin mix	1	(16 ounce) can cream corn
1	(16 ounce) can whole corn, undrained	1	cup sour cream
		1	stick margarine, melted

❻ Preheat oven to 350 degrees.

❻ Combine all ingredients in a large mixing bowl. Mix until blended.

❻ Pour mixture into a shallow, 2-quart baking dish.

❻ Bake, uncovered, for 45 to 50 minutes. Serve immediately.

Note: *May substitute non-fat sour cream.*

Menu: *A perfect accompaniment to Devin's Best Baby Back Ribs (page 246).*

Thanks to the Five River MetroParks, the Miami Valley boasts an extensive system of beautiful bikeways. With new connections, it is now possible for anyone living between Springfield and Milford to ride a bike to downtown Dayton. And people in Miamisburg can pedal all the way to King's Island or to John Bryan State Park in Yellow Springs. You can even ride right to Young's Dairy, so you can feel like you earned that ice cream cone!

Virginia Hollinger was the first national women's tennis champion from Dayton. In 1935, when she was just 16, Hollinger won the highly prestigious girls indoor tournament. She is memorialized at the Virginia Hollinger Memorial Tennis Club of Dayton, in Oakwood.

Old-Fashioned Scalloped Oyster Stuffing

The "timeless" favorite

Yield: 10 servings

⅔	cup plain stuffing mix (we prefer Pepperidge Farm)
1	cup butter cracker crumbs, crushed fine
1	stick butter, melted
1½	pints fresh oysters, liquid reserved

	Freshly ground black pepper to taste
¾	teaspoon salt
3	tablespoons chopped fresh parsley
½	tablespoon Worcestershire sauce
3	tablespoons milk or cream

⏰ *Can prepare casserole in the morning up to the point where the liquid is added. In the evening, add liquid, bake and serve.*

6 Preheat oven to 350 degrees.

6 Mix together bread crumbs, cracker crumbs and butter; place in the bottom of a greased 1-quart casserole dish.

6 Add half of oysters. Sprinkle with pepper, half of salt and half of parsley. Add remaining oysters; sprinkle with pepper, remaining salt and remaining parsley.

6 Combine ⅓ cup oyster liquid with Worcestershire sauce and milk. Pour over oyster mixture.

6 Bake, uncovered, for 45 minutes.

Note: *If your oysters are large, chop them into halves or thirds for a richer taste in every bite.*

Menu: *Great with Juicy Marinated Turkey Breast (page 223), Raspberry Cranberry Relish (page 101) and a steamed green vegetable.*

This is a family favorite at Thanksgiving. My dad especially loves it because his mother used to make it for him. We now have potluck Thanksgiving dinners so Mom doesn't have to do all the work. This recipe is my "assignment," and I love it because it is so easy and deliciously different.

—Molly Treese

153

Hot Curried Fruit

Great side dish for brunch

Yield: 12 servings

1	stick butter, melted	1	(29 ounce) can sliced pears, drained
1	cup brown sugar		
1	teaspoon curry powder	2	(20 ounce) cans pineapple chunks, drained
1	tablespoon cornstarch		
½	cup white wine	1	(17 ounce) can tart red cherries, drained
1	(29 ounce) can sliced peaches, drained		
		1	(11 ounce) can Mandarin oranges, drained

🕐 *Can be prepared a day ahead, covered and stored in the refrigerator. Reheat in a 350 degree oven for about 30 minutes.*

❻ Preheat oven to 350 degrees.

❻ Combine butter, sugar and curry powder in a saucepan. Cook over medium heat until sugar dissolves.

❻ Spoon one-third of sugar sauce into a small bowl. Blend in cornstarch until well-mixed; return to saucepan. Add wine to saucepan and stir until smooth.

❻ Arrange fruit in a baking dish. Bake for 30 minutes.

❻ Pour hot sauce over warmed fruit and serve.

Menu: *Try serving with Easy Baked Spinach, Eggs and Cheese (page 73), Caramelized Coconut Coffee Cake (page 86) and sliced ham for an easy and elegant brunch.*

ESPN's Dan Patrick was named Sportscaster of the Year in 2000. He is a graduate of the University of Dayton.

Green Beans with Shallot Butter

Marvelous recipe for the holidays

Yield: 12 servings

4	tablespoons butter or margarine	½	teaspoon freshly ground black pepper
1	tablespoon olive oil		
⅔	cup thinly sliced shallots	3	pounds fresh green beans, trimmed
4	tablespoons butter or margarine		
½	teaspoon salt	1	cup toasted slivered almonds

Beans may be trimmed and stored in refrigerator up to 1 day ahead. Shallot butter can be made and stored in refrigerator up to 5 days ahead.

- To make shallot butter, melt 4 tablespoons butter with oil over medium heat in a small skillet. Reduce heat to low. Add shallots and cook 7 to 9 minutes; or until very tender. Stir in 4 tablespoons butter, salt and pepper. Remove from heat.
- Cook green beans in a large pot of boiling water until crisp-tender. Drain well and return to pot.
- Add shallot butter to beans and toss well. Add some almonds and toss. Transfer to a serving dish and sprinkle with remaining almonds.

Mushrooms with Basil Cream

Yield: 6 servings

3	tablespoons butter	¼	cup dry white wine (optional)
1	pound large mushrooms, sliced ¼-inch thick	½	cup heavy cream
		½	teaspoon salt
1	tablespoon chopped fresh basil or 1 teaspoon dried		Dash of freshly ground black pepper

Can be prepared up to 1 hour ahead and kept warm in a 300 degree oven. Cover loosely with foil.

- Melt butter in a nonaluminum skillet over medium-high heat. Add mushrooms and sauté about 5 minutes, or until mushrooms release some of their juices. Remove with a slotted spoon and set aside.
- Add basil, wine, cream, salt, and pepper to juices in skillet. Simmer over low heat for about 5 minutes, or until slightly thickened.
- Add mushrooms to skillet and toss to coat. Serve.

Menu: *A great topping for beef. Try with Flank Steak (page 228), Comfort Corn Pudding (page 152) and steamed broccoli for a tasty winter dinner.*

My best memories of Dayton are at the University of Dayton arena. Covering Flyer basketball as I do, I've seen first-hand what great fans the Flyer faithful are. To see and hear 13,500 screaming fans at the arena on any given night is truly a sight to behold in college basketball!

—Dax Dunbar, Former Voice of the UD Flyers

Dayton is home to the U.S. Air Force Marathon. This elite event attracts more than 2,800 runners from all around the world.

Green Beans with Toasted Pecans and Blue Cheese

Truly divine!

Yield: 2 to 3 servings

¼	teaspoon Dijon mustard
½	tablespoon olive oil
1	teaspoon cider vinegar
2	teaspoons finely chopped shallots
½	tablespoon olive oil

½	cup pecans
	Salt and pepper to taste
12	ounces green beans
1½	ounces blue cheese, such as Maytag

⚅ In a large bowl, whisk together mustard, ½ tablespoon oil, vinegar, and shallots to make a dressing.

⚅ In a small, heavy skillet, heat ½ tablespoon oil over medium-high heat, until hot but not smoking. Add pecans and salt; sauté about 1 minute, or until slightly darker. Transfer to paper towels. When cool, coarsely chop.

⚅ Blanch beans in a large saucepan of boiling salted water for about 3 minutes, or until crisp-tender. Drain and plunge beans into a bowl of ice water, stirring until just cool. Drain well.

⚅ Add beans to dressing. Crumble cheese and sprinkle half of pecans over top; toss. Season with salt and pepper.

⚅ Sprinkle with remaining pecans and serve at room temperature.

Note: *Frozen green beans cooked al dente will do, if necessary.*

Before retiring from his 13-year career in the NFL, Roth High School graduate, Keith Byars, set the league's reception record (610) for running backs. He is considered to be the best pro football player ever from Dayton. Along the way he built a reputation as a hard runner, feisty blocker and sure-handed receiver. Not to mention philanthropist, team leader, friend, Christian, and all-around good guy!

Mediterranean Lentils with Roasted Red Peppers and Lemon Vinaigrette

Yield: 8 servings

Lemon Vinaigrette

	Juice and zest of 1 lemon	1	clove garlic, minced
¼	teaspoon paprika	¼	teaspoon salt
	Pinch of cayenne pepper	6-8	tablespoons olive oil

Salad

1½	cups dry small lentils, rinsed	8	ounces roasted red peppers, chopped
5	cups water		
1	medium carrot, diced	3	tablespoons chopped fresh parsley
½	small onion, finely diced		
1	bay leaf	1	tablespoon chopped fresh thyme
1	clove garlic, finely chopped		Freshly ground black pepper
½	teaspoon salt		Red wine vinegar to taste
		8	ounces feta cheese

Vinaigrette can be prepared up to 2 days ahead and refrigerated.

- To make vinaigrette, combine juice, zest, paprika, cayenne pepper, garlic, and salt in a bowl. Whisk in oil. Adjust seasonings to taste.

- To make salad, combine lentils, water, carrot, onion, bay leaf, garlic, and salt in a pot; bring to a boil. Simmer about 20 to 25 minutes, or until tender but firm. Drain well.

- Fold vinaigrette into warm lentils. Add roasted pepper, parsley, thyme, and black pepper.

- Just before serving, taste and add vinegar as desired. Crumble cheese over top and gently stir into lentils.

Note: *Garnish with cooked eggs, olives and tomatoes for more color and texture.*

Menu: *Serve with The Ultimate Quiche (page 78) for an exotic luncheon.*

As part of the Dayton Pro/Am Cycling series, Five Rivers MetroParks helps bring together professional cyclists from around the country. Cyclists compete for more than $40,000 in prize money in the Saturn USPRO Tour Bike Races. Reaching speeds well over 40 mph, these pro cyclists provide thrills for young and old alike.

Baked Vidalias with Sage

Your new favorite side dish for steak!

Yield: 6 to 8 servings

2	pounds Vidalia onions, quartered	2	tablespoons olive oil
12	leaves fresh sage, torn into pieces	2	tablespoons balsamic vinegar
½	teaspoon salt	¼	cup chopped fresh flat-leaf parsley

- Preheat oven to 375 degrees.
- Slice onion quarters lengthwise, ¹⁄₁₆-inch thick.
- Combine onion slices, sage, salt, oil, and vinegar in a baking dish.
- Bake for 1 hour.
- Sprinkle with parsley and serve.

Menu: *This sweet onion dish goes nicely with any steak or roasted meat. Serve with Nancy's Green Pepper Steak (page 230), steamed carrots, and a tossed salad for family dinner with a new twist.*

I remember my parent's kitchen on Sundays. Every Sunday, everyone—family, neighbors, everyone—came over. The food was great; everybody filled their plates and walked away stuffed!

—Oliver Purnell,
Head Coach
University of Dayton
Men's Basketball

Peperonata

Good and good looking, this Dayton Daily News *recipe is a winner*

Yield: 4 servings

6	tablespoons olive oil	1½	cups skinned and chopped tomato
1	onion, sliced	1	tablespoon chopped fresh parsley
1	clove garlic, sliced		
4	large red and yellow bell peppers, sliced into strips		Pinch of crushed red pepper flakes (optional)
	Salt and freshly ground pepper to taste		

- *Slice peppers and onions up to 1 day ahead. Or, dish may be fully prepared up to 2 days ahead and reheated.*

- Heat oil in a heavy skillet. Add onion and garlic; cook 5 minutes.
- Add bell pepper, salt and pepper. Cook 5 minutes, stirring occasionally. Stir in tomato and parsley. Add red pepper flakes.
- Adjust seasonings. Cover and simmer 20 to 30 minutes, stirring frequently, until thickened. Serve hot or at room temperature.

Menu: *A beautiful accompaniment to Veal Saltimbocca (page 236).*

Johnny Bench, the great Cincinnati Reds catcher and a minor-league consultant for the team, was at Fifth Third Field, home of the Dayton Dragons, on the team's opening day. He gave the Dragons' catchers a hands-on demonstration before the game, then talked about Dayton as a sports town. "In the 1970s when we were doing so well, I think 50 percent of our crowd was from the Dayton area. This is a real sports town. That's why I think this team is going to do so well."

Baked Bread Casserole
with Wild Mushrooms and Onions

Great with poultry and game

Yield: 8 to 10 servings

¾	ounce dried wild mushrooms, such as chanterelles, morels or porcini
4	cups boiling water
1	large onion, sliced
2	tablespoons unsalted butter or olive oil
2	tablespoons dark brown sugar
½	teaspoon salt

½	loaf potato bread or other firm-textured bread
1	tablespoon snipped fresh sage
1	cup shredded Gruyère cheese
¼	teaspoon caraway seed
¼	cup grated sapsago or Parmesan cheese
	Fresh sage for garnish

◐ Preheat oven to 375 degrees.

◐ Place mushrooms in a large bowl. Add boiling water. Cover and let stand 30 minutes. Drain, reserving liquid. Coarsely chop mushrooms and set aside.

◐ In a large covered skillet, cook onion in butter over medium heat for 10 minutes, or until softened. Remove from heat; stir in sugar and salt. Set aside.

◐ Cut some of the bread into 1-inch slices. Line the bottom of a 2-quart rectangular baking dish with bread slices, cutting to fit. Top with sage, Gruyère cheese and mushrooms.

◐ Cut remaining bread into bite-sized pieces and sprinkle over mushrooms. Spoon onion mixture over bread. Pour reserved mushroom liquid over all. Sprinkle caraway seed and sapsago cheese over top.

◐ Bake 45 minutes or until heated through. Garnish with fresh sage.

Menu: *Try serving with purchased rotisserie chicken, Sara Jane's Baked Apples (page 147) and a mixed green salad for a winning combination.*

The Grand American Trapshoot Championships in Vandalia attracts more than 150,000 visitors from around the globe. It's the largest trapshoot in the world!

Stuffed Red Peppers

This meatless dish is rich and satisfying

Yield: 6 servings

1½ teaspoons olive oil	12 ounces cherry tomatoes, halved
1½ teaspoons balsamic vinegar	1 cup diced mozzarella cheese
1 clove garlic, minced	½ cup fresh basil, cut into strips
Salt and freshly ground black pepper to taste	3 red bell peppers, halved, cored and seeded

๑ Preheat oven to 375 degrees.

๑ Combine oil, vinegar, garlic, salt, and pepper. Add tomatoes, cheese and basil. Mix well.

๑ Fill each pepper half with cheese mixture.

๑ Bake 40 minutes or until tender.

Note: *You may also use half mozzarella and half Parmesan cheese for a stronger flavor.*

Menu: *Add Mexicana Rice (page 161) for a filling and delicious vegetarian meal.*

Whipped Potatoes Paprika

A tasty variation on mashed potatoes

Yield: 4 to 5 servings

8 small to medium boiling potatoes (we prefer Yukon Gold)	¼ teaspoon paprika
	½ cup sour cream
	1 teaspoon chopped fresh parsley
3 ounces cream cheese, softened	2 tablespoons butter, or more to taste
1 teaspoon garlic salt	Paprika for garnish
¼ teaspoon freshly ground black pepper	

๑ *Can be made up to 1 day ahead and reheated.*

๑ Preheat oven to 400 degrees.

๑ Boil potatoes and whip until smooth.

๑ Combine potatoes with cream cheese, garlic salt, pepper, paprika, sour cream, and parsley. Place in a casserole dish.

๑ Dot with butter. Sprinkle with paprika to garnish.

๑ Bake, covered, for 25 minutes. Uncover and bake 10 minutes longer.

Menu: *Great with Juicy Marinated Turkey Breast (page 223) and steamed broccoli.*

Dayton is the site of the Winter Guard International Sport of the Arts World Championships. This color guard and percussion competition features more than 400 units, 12,000 athletes, and spectators from throughout the world.

Place an apple in your bag of potatoes to keep the potatoes from sprouting.

Potato Polpettes

Guests will give rave reviews of these little beauties

Yield: 4 servings

1¼	pounds boiling potatoes (we prefer Yukon Gold)
4	ounces feta cheese
4	green onions, chopped
3	tablespoons chopped fresh dill
1	egg, beaten

1	tablespoon lemon juice
	Salt and freshly ground black pepper
	Flour for dredging
3	tablespoons olive oil

🕐 *Patties can be prepared, to the point before dredging, up to 1 day ahead.*

- Boil potatoes in lightly salted water until soft; drain. Peel while still warm. Place in a bowl and mash.
- Crumble cheese into potatoes. Add onion, dill, egg, and lemon juice. Season as desired with salt and pepper. Mix well. Cover and chill until firm.
- Form mixture into walnut-sized balls, then flatten slightly and dredge in flour.
- Heat oil in a skillet. Add potato patties and fry until golden brown on each side. Drain on paper towels and serve immediately.

Mexicana Rice

Muy bueno!

Yield: 6 servings

1	(16 ounce) can whole kernel corn, drained
1	(16 ounce) can black beans, rinsed and drained
1	(10 ounce) can tomatoes and green chiles
1	(8 ounce) container sour cream
1	(8 ounce) jar picante sauce
2	cups shredded cheddar cheese

2	cups cooked rice
¼	teaspoon freshly ground black pepper
1	bunch green onions, chopped
1	(2¼ ounce) can sliced black olives, drained
2	cups shredded Monterey Jack cheese

- Preheat oven to 350 degrees.
- Combine corn, beans, tomatoes and chiles, sour cream, picante sauce, cheddar cheese, rice, and pepper. Spoon into a lightly greased, 9x13-inch baking dish.
- Sprinkle with onions, olives and Monterey Jack cheese.
- Bake for 50 minutes.

When eating french fries, feel free to use your fingers if you are using them for the rest of your meal. For instance, if you're polishing off a hamburger or sandwich, utensils aren't required. But if the entrée is a steak or some other food that requires a knife and fork, then you should cut up the fries and eat them with a fork.

After graduating from Stebbins High School, Joe Green went on to win the Olympic bronze medal in long jump at Barcelona in 1992 and Atlanta in 1996. The latter gave the United States team a 1-2-3 sweep.

In 1964, West Milton's Bob Schul was the first and only American to win the Olympic 5,000-meter gold medal.

Lemon Rice with Pine Nuts

This wonderful recipe originally appeared in Ann Heller's "It's Simple" column in the Dayton Daily News

Yield: 4 to 6 servings

3	tablespoons butter	1½	teaspoons lemon zest
¾	cup chopped onion	¾	cup pine nuts, toasted
1½	cups dry long-grain rice	⅓	cup chopped fresh parsley,
2¼	cups hot chicken broth		chives or green onions

6 Melt butter in a heavy saucepan. Add onion; cook until softened, but not brown. Add rice and stir to coat. Cook and stir over medium heat for about 5 minutes.

6 Stir in chicken broth and zest. Cover and bring to a boil. Reduce heat; simmer 17 minutes, or until all liquid is absorbed. Remove from heat.

6 Stir in pine nuts; cover saucepan with a double layer of paper towels. Cover with lid and set aside for 10 minutes.

6 Just before serving, stir in herbs.

Menu: *Goes beautifully with any fish entrée. We recommend Carolina Trout with Dill Sauce (page 196) or Saucy Sole (page 194).*

Rice Pilaf ⭐

This James Beard classic comes to us via Allison Janney

Yield: 4 servings

Emmy Award-winning actress Allison Janney, of NBC's "The West Wing," fondly remembers her favorite birthday dinner from when she was a young girl. Allison's mother, Macy Janney, would prepare beef fondue with various sauces, asparagus, and this James Beard rice pilaf.

4	tablespoons butter	1	cup dry long-grain rice, rinsed
1	large onion, sliced	2	cups broth, boiling

6 Preheat oven to 350 degrees.

6 Melt butter in a saucepan. Add onion and cook until lightly browned.

6 Stir in rice; cook over low heat for 4 to 5 minutes, or until lightly browned, stirring often.

6 Pour boiling broth into saucepan, adding enough to cover rice by 1½ inches. Cover saucepan tightly.

6 Bake 25 to 30 minutes, or until liquid is absorbed; or cook on stovetop over very low heat. Serve with plenty of butter.

Variations:
Sauté 8 ounces sliced mushrooms with the onion.
Add a pinch of thyme or oregano to the broth.
Sauté slivered blanched almonds with the onion.
Add a pinch of saffron to the rice.

Wild Rice with Carrots and Onions

Yield: 2 servings

⅓	cup dry wild rice, rinsed and drained	2	tablespoons unsalted butter
½	teaspoon salt	⅓	cup chopped onion
1	cup cold water	1	teaspoon fresh lemon juice
⅓	cup finely diced carrot	2	tablespoons minced fresh parsley

🕐 *The rice may be made 1 day ahead and kept covered and refrigerated. Before serving, add 1 tablespoon water and reheat over medium-low heat, stirring until heated through.*

⑥ Combine rice, salt and cold water in a small saucepan. Bring to a boil. Reduce heat, cover and simmer 40 to 50 minutes, or until rice is tender. Drain.

⑥ Meanwhile, cook carrot in butter in a skillet over medium-low heat for 5 minutes. Add onion; cook and stir 5 minutes.

⑥ Remove skillet from heat. Stir in cooked rice, lemon juice and parsley.

Menu: *Try serving with K's Crab Cakes (page 201), steamed asparagus and Salad with Warm Brie Dressing (page 122) for an elegant meal.*

Liliana's Fried Cabbage

A tribute to Dayton's sizeable German population

Yield: 4 generous portions

4	strips bacon	¼	teaspoon sugar
1	head cabbage, quartered and sliced ¼- to ½-inch thick		Salt and pepper to taste

⑥ In a heavy skillet, fry bacon until crisp; remove bacon and set aside. Leave 1 to 2 teaspoons bacon fat in skillet; drain off excess.

⑥ Add cabbage to skillet and cook over medium heat. Add sugar, salt and pepper. Gently stir, allowing cabbage to wilt and brown.

⑥ Crumble bacon and sprinkle over cabbage.

Note: *Impossible to overcook, it just gets better.*

Menu: *Serve with Presidential Meatloaf (page 235) and mashed potatoes for a delicious home-style meal.*

Lucinda Williams Adams, a.k.a. Lady Dancer, ran the third leg of the 4x100-meter relay that won her team the gold medal at the 1960 Rome Olympics. At the 1958 Pan American Games, Williams won three gold medals and posted an American record for the women's 220-yard dash. In 1994, she was elected president of the National Association for Sports and Physical Education, and went on to work for the Dayton public school system.

Guy Trottier played on the first Dayton Gems hockey team before playing for the Toronto Maple Leafs. He now helps coach the Dayton Bombers. Another Dayton Gems player, Pat Rupp, played on the 1964 and 1968 Olympic teams. He later played with the Philadelphia Flyers.

Spanakopeta ❄

Much easier to make than the individual triangle version!

Yield: 10 to 12 servings

1	green onion, chopped	1	(1 pound) container dry cottage cheese
2	tablespoons butter		
2	(10 ounce) packages frozen chopped spinach, cooked and well-drained	8	ounces feta cheese
		6	eggs
1	(15 ounce) container ricotta cheese	1	(1 pound) package frozen phyllo dough
		2	sticks unsalted butter, melted

🕐 *Spinach may be cooked and drained up to 2 days ahead. Entire dish can be assembled up to 3 days ahead, covered and refrigerated, or frozen up to 2 months. Bake directly from freezer at 375 degrees until crisp and golden.*

6 Preheat oven to 350 degrees.

6 Sauté green onion in 2 tablespoons butter. Transfer to mixing bowl. Add spinach, all the cheeses and eggs. Beat until well-blended.

6 Layer 10 sheets of phyllo dough in a 9x13-inch baking pan, brushing each sheet of dough with melted butter. Add spinach mixture to top of dough layer. Top with 8 more buttered sheets of dough.

6 Bake for about 30 minutes, or until brown.

Menu: *This dish can stand as a vegetarian entrée when paired with Greek Peasant Salad (page 124) and some mixed olives.*

My mother-in-law is a wonderful Greek cook. She loves to make spanakopeta for every holiday, baby shower, birthday party, etc. Ever since I can remember, she has gathered my husband, his twin, and myself in her kitchen to make the triangles. It is tedious, but a lot of fun when done in a group. I always said that on my own, I would only make the casserole version.

—Vallery Tzagournis

Southern Sweet Potato Soufflé ❄

Better than your grandmother's

Yield: 8 servings

10	medium or 5 to 7 large sweet potatoes, peeled	4	tablespoons butter
6	eggs	½	cup chopped pecans
2	cups granulated sugar	¼	cup flour
½	cup milk	2½	tablespoons butter
3	tablespoons vanilla	½	cup brown sugar

🕐 *Can be prepared up to 8 hours ahead and refrigerated before baking; or bake and freeze up to 2 months. Potatoes may also be boiled up to 2 days ahead and kept refrigerated.*

ⓖ Preheat oven to 325 degrees.

ⓖ Place sweet potatoes in a large pot and cover with water. Bring to a boil and cook until tender; drain well.

ⓖ Transfer potatoes to a large mixing bowl; beat with an electric mixer. Add eggs, granulated sugar, milk, vanilla, and 4 tablespoons butter. Beat until smooth.

ⓖ Pour mixture into a 2-quart casserole dish that has been sprayed with nonstick cooking spray.

ⓖ In a small bowl, combine pecans, flour, 2½ tablespoons butter, and brown sugar to make a topping. Sprinkle evenly over potato mixture.

ⓖ Bake 30 to 45 minutes or until set.

When I left Georgia to go to college at Ohio State, the one recipe I took with me was my grandmother's Sweet Potato Soufflé. Even before I had an apartment at school, I would use my friend's kitchen to make it occasionally. I took this recipe with me not only because it's the most fabulous food I've ever eaten, but because it reminds me of my dear grandmother and my family I left behind. I get such a warm feeling inside when I eat it; it's almost like I'm back home again!

—Melanie Moore

Provençal Roasted Tomatoes

A great way to use your summer tomato bumper crop

Yield: 8 servings

¼	cup extra virgin olive oil	¼	cup best-quality red wine
12	firm tomatoes, halved		vinegar
	lengthwise	¼	cup snipped fresh mixed herbs,
	Sea salt to taste		such as parsley, tarragon, basil
			or rosemary

🕐 *If dish will be served at room temperature: prepare up to 8 hours ahead, let cool, then cover.*

⑥ Preheat oven to 400 degrees.

⑥ In a very large skillet, heat oil over medium-high heat. When hot, place a single layer (do not crowd) of tomatoes, cut-side down, in skillet. Sear, without moving the tomatoes, for 3 to 4 minutes, or until they are dark and almost caramelized. Transfer tomatoes, cooked-side up and overlapping slightly, to a large baking dish. Repeat until all tomatoes are seared. Season with salt.

⑥ Remove skillet from heat and deglaze with vinegar. Return skillet to high heat, scraping the bottom to loosen drippings. Pour liquid over tomatoes.

⑥ Sprinkle with fresh herbs. Bake 30 minutes, or until tomatoes are soft and shriveled. Serve hot, warm or at room temperature.

Menu: *Great with Chicken Alouette in Puff Pastry (page 207), Lemon Rice with Pine Nuts (page 162), and a mixed green salad with Red Wine Vinaigrette (page 98).*

Dayton native Edwin Moses was named No. 47 among ESPN's top 50 greatest athletes of the century. He will forever be known as an Olympic champion (he won gold medals in 1976 and 1984, and a bronze in 1988) and the greatest 400 intermediate hurdler in history. What you may not know is his degree in physics from Morehouse College and his master's degree from Pepperdine University have prepared him to serve on a White House commission, the National Science Foundation, and the board of directors at Springfield College in Massachusetts. As a financial consultant for Solomon Smith Barney, he's on the cutting edge of the hi-tech information superhighway.

Dayton Steakhouse-Style Stewed Tomatoes

Inspired by Dayton's favorite steakhouses

Yield: 4 servings

1	small onion, chopped	5	cups canned tomatoes
4	tablespoons butter	1	teaspoon salt or to taste
1½	cups dry plain bread cubes	½	teaspoon freshly ground
½	cup light brown sugar		black pepper or to taste

- Preheat oven to 350 degrees.
- Sauté onion in butter until soft, but not browned. Add bread cubes and brown sugar. Cook and stir over low heat for 3 to 5 minutes.
- Stir in tomatoes. Season with salt and pepper. Transfer to a greased shallow casserole dish.
- Bake 30 to 40 minutes or until bubbly.

Note: *If desired, top each serving with homemade croutons: drizzle plain bread cubes with melted butter, season as desired, and bake 5 to 10 minutes.*

Menu: *Terrific with Filet Mignon, baked potatoes and Salad with Warm Brie Dressing (page 122).*

Vivid Summer Vegetables

Unique and full of flavor

Yield: 6 servings

2	pounds sweet potatoes, peeled	½	pound asparagus, cut into 1-inch lengths
1	red bell pepper, cut into 1x2-inch wedges	8	cloves garlic, coarsely chopped
1	yellow bell pepper, cut into 1x2-inch wedges	1	tablespoon chopped fresh rosemary
1	red onion, cut into 1x2-inch wedges	2	tablespoons chopped fresh thyme
		2	tablespoons olive oil
		¼	teaspoon salt

- *Vegetables may be cut and cleaned up to 1 day ahead.*

- Preheat oven to 500 degrees.
- Cut potatoes in half lengthwise, then into ½-inch slices.
- Combine potato, bell peppers, onion, and asparagus in a bowl. Stir in garlic, rosemary, thyme, and oil.
- Spread mixture on a cookie sheet. Sprinkle with salt.
- Bake 10 minutes. Reduce heat to 400 degrees and bake 10 minutes longer, or until potatoes are tender.

Menu: *Try with pork chops marinated in Kraus Haus Marinade (page 96) and Whipped Potatoes Paprika (page 160).*

In August 1932, Dayton Ducks manager, "Ducky" Holmes, punched an umpire, was suspended and ordered to leave the park-so he climbed a nearby telephone pole and managed his team with exaggerated hand signals.

Did you know that Ron Harper, Jim Paxson and John Paxson, all of NBA fame, were Dayton-area natives?

Zucchini Casserole ☆

Yield: 8 servings

½	teaspoon salt	3	ripe tomatoes, sliced
½	teaspoon garlic powder	2	medium onions, sliced
½	teaspoon dried oregano	4	ounces sharp cheddar cheese, shredded
¼	teaspoon black pepper		
2	cups sliced zucchini	5	slices bacon, uncooked

🕐 *Can be assembled in the morning and refrigerated. Bake before serving.*

6 Preheat oven to 350 degrees.

6 Combine salt, garlic powder, oregano, and pepper.

6 Alternate layers of zucchini, tomato and onion in a greased casserole dish, sprinkling each layer with seasoning mixture.

6 Cover top layer with cheese. Top with bacon slices.

6 Bake 45 minutes.

Usually when an actor drinks a Manhattan or a glass of wine on stage, he is really ingesting tea; ice cream may be mashed potatoes (ugh!). For a production in July 1974, my wife concocted a zucchini recipe for a dinner scene, which she prepared for the run of the play.

At first dress rehearsal the actors turned up their noses at the casserole. However, as the smell wafted toward them, their noses changed position, their eyes lit up, and their tongues licked their lips. One bite later and they were confirmed lovers of zucchini!

Because the casserole was more than could be eaten in the stage time, the crew happily finished the meal. The play was a treat for me, and the food a treat for the cast and crew.

—Abe J. Bassett,
Professor
Emeritus of Theatre
Wright State University

Zucchini Imperial

Majestic treatment for a noble squash

Yield: 4 to 6 servings

2	eggs, lightly beaten		Salt and pepper to taste
1	cup mayonnaise	4	cups sliced zucchini
1	Vidalia onion, chopped	1	tablespoon butter
1	Anaheim chili pepper, chopped	3	tablespoons bread crumbs (we prefer Pepperidge Farm)
1	cup freshly grated Parmesan cheese		

6 Preheat oven to 350 degrees.

6 Combine egg, mayonnaise, onion, pepper, cheese, salt, and pepper. Stir in zucchini.

6 Pour mixture into a greased, shallow baking dish. Dot with butter and sprinkle with bread crumbs.

6 Bake 30 minutes.

Note: *Tastes just as delicious with reduced-fat mayonnaise.*

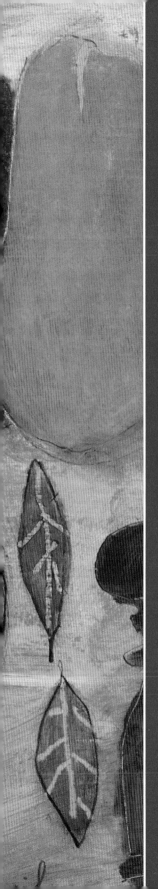
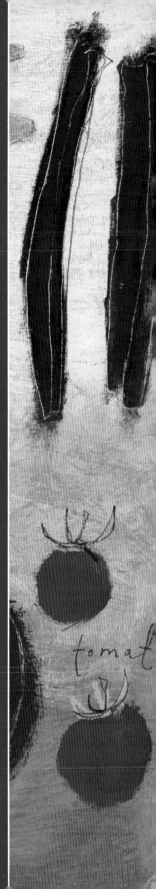

Using Our Noodles

PASTAS & PIZZA

.10

NATIONAL

DAYTON INVENTIONS

tomat

USING OUR NOODLES

Orville Wright, Charles "Boss" Kettering and Colonel Edward Deeds used to meet for lunch at the Engineers Club to discuss their latest ideas. There have been many other "pioneers" who used Dayton as their creative breeding ground. We all know about the Wright brothers and their fabulous flying machine, but did you know that the following items all got their start here in Dayton?

Automobile Self-Starter, Charles F. Kettering / Cash Register, James Ritty / Cellophane Tape, Dr. William Hale Church / Gas Mask, Daniel Webster Schaeffer / Human Heart-Lung Machine, Leland Clark / Ice Cube Tray, Arthur Frei / Liquid Crystal Alignment Methodology (Mood Ring, Digital Watches), John Janning / Microfiche, Carl Carlson / Modern Salesmanship (Trained Sales Force, Quotas, Territories, Conventions), John H. Patterson / Movie Projector, Movie Camera, Movie Film, and Movie Theater, C. Francis Jenkins / Parachute, Floyd Smith / Parking Meter, John Morton / Pull Tab and Poptop Beverage Cans, E. T. Fraze / Space Food, Maurice Krug / Step Ladder, John Balsley

Lest you think that Dayton's most creative days are behind us, consider this fact. In the past 20 years, Dayton inventors have been issued more than 8,000 patents, securing our reputation as a place where creativity is a way of life!

"I think it was the Brookings Institute that made a study that said the more education you had the less likely you were to become an inventor. The reason why is: from the time a kid starts kindergarten to the time he graduates from college, he will be examined two to three times a year, and if he flunks once, he's out. Now, an inventor fails 999 times, and if he succeeds once, he's in... It therefore seems that the factor which needs to be corrected is to teach the educated person that it is not a disgrace to fail, and that he must analyze each failure to find its cause. We paraphrase this by saying, 'You must learn how to fail intelligently.' Failing is one of the greatest arts in the world. One fails forward toward success." CHARLES F. KETTERING

Spinach-Mushroom Lasagna ❄

A delicious change from traditional lasagna

Yield: 8 to 10 servings

2 pounds fresh bulk spinach (about 10 ounces), stemmed	3 tablespoons chopped fresh basil
¼ cup vegetable oil	¼ teaspoon freshly ground black pepper
1 onion, chopped	8 ounces dry lasagna noodles, cooked and drained
3 cloves garlic, minced	
2 pounds fresh mushrooms, sliced	1¼ cups shredded extra-sharp cheddar cheese
¼ teaspoon dried red pepper flakes	4 cups shredded mozzarella cheese
2 cups ricotta cheese	1 (4 ounce) jar sliced pimientos, drained
1 cup Parmesan cheese	

🕐 *Can be assembled, covered and refrigerated up to 2 days before baking. Bring to room temperature and bake 20 to 25 minutes, or until top is golden brown and bubbling.*

🔥 Preheat oven to 350 degrees.

🔥 Discard stems from spinach. Wash leaves, drain and shake off excess water. Tear into 2-inch pieces.

🔥 Heat oil in a large skillet. Add onion and garlic; sauté until softened. Add mushrooms and pepper flakes. Cook, stirring over medium-high heat, until just tender. Pile spinach on top. Cook and stir until spinach wilts. Remove from heat.

🔥 In a medium bowl, stir together ricotta cheese, Parmesan cheese, basil, and black pepper.

🔥 To assemble, spread one-third of spinach mixture (along with some of its liquid) in the bottom of a 9x13-inch casserole. Top with half the lasagna noodles. Spoon half of remaining spinach mixture over noodles. Spread entire ricotta mixture over spinach and smooth as evenly as possible. Sprinkle with half the cheddar and half the mozzarella cheese. Place pimiento slices over cheese. Cover with remaining noodles, overlapping if necessary. Top with remaining spinach mixture, plus any liquid remaining from mixture.

🔥 Place dish on a baking sheet and bake 15 minutes. Sprinkle with remaining cheddar and mozzarella cheese and bake 15 to 20 minutes longer, or until golden brown and bubbly. Remove from oven and let stand 15 minutes before serving.

Menu: *Serve with tomato and cucumber salad for a splendid meatless meal.*

🍷 *Chianti*

> When making lasagna, it is not necessary to precook the pasta. Assemble lasagna as usual, but let it sit (refrigerated) overnight before baking.
> —Cheryl Brandewie Owner, Cafe Potage

Tex Mex Lasagna ❄

This will quickly become a family favorite

Yield: 8 to 10 servings

1	pound ground beef	1	teaspoon dried basil
½	cup chopped onion	1	cup ricotta or cottage cheese
1	cup tomato paste	¾	cup shredded colby-jack cheese
1	cup picante sauce (medium or mild)	8	ounces dry lasagna noodles
¾	cup water	1½	cups shredded colby-jack cheese
1	teaspoon dried cilantro		Sour cream and chopped fresh cilantro for garnish

🕐 *Must be assembled the night before.*

❻ Brown beef and onion; drain. Mix in tomato paste, picante sauce, water, cilantro, and basil.

❻ In a separate bowl, combine ricotta and ¾ cup colby-jack cheese.

❻ In a greased 9x13-inch baking pan, layer ⅓ cup of meat sauce, half the lasagna noodles and half the ricotta mixture. Repeat layers. Top with remaining meat sauce. Sprinkle with remaining 1½ cups colby-jack cheese.

❻ Cover and refrigerate overnight. When ready to bake, preheat oven to 350 degrees.

❻ Uncover and bake 1 hour. Garnish with sour cream and chopped fresh cilantro.

Menu: *Serve with Black Bean, Corn and Avocado Salad (page 143). For dessert, offer mango and kiwi fruit salad.*

🍷 *Spanish Red, Chianti*

The Wright brothers were interested in more than just airplanes—they were constantly inventing gadgets. Orville had a summer camp in Canada, which apparently was plagued by uneven bread... and he loved thin toast. So he invented a contraption to line up and hold the bread, making it possible to cut perfect, even slices.

Sausage Fettuccine Torte

A very attractive dish that travels well

Yield: 6 to 8 servings

1	pound dry fettuccine, cooked and drained	¼	cup finely chopped combination of fresh parsley and fresh basil
2	tablespoons butter	½	teaspoon black pepper
1	pound bulk Italian sausage (sweet, hot or combination)	3	eggs, beaten
1	tablespoon olive oil	3	tomatoes, thinly sliced
1	medium onion, finely chopped	½	cup shredded Gruyère cheese
1	large green bell pepper, finely chopped	½	cup shredded mozzarella cheese
½	cup sliced black olives	2	tablespoons Parmesan cheese, or more to taste

May be baked the night before and reheated.

- Preheat oven to 375 degrees.

- Toss hot fettuccine with butter and cover to keep warm.

- Brown sausage in olive oil; drain. Add onion and bell pepper and cook 5 minutes.

- Combine sausage mixture, olives, herbs, black pepper, and warm noodles. Stir in egg and toss to mix well.

- Press half of mixture into a greased springform pan. Layer half of tomato slices over noodles. Sprinkle with Gruyère and mozzarella cheeses. Repeat noodle and tomato layers. Sprinkle with Parmesan cheese.

- Cover with foil and bake 50 minutes or until set. Slice into wedges to serve.

Menu: *This hearty dish goes well with a green salad and 60-Minute Pesto Bread (page 79).*

Brunello, Barolo

It sounds strange, but I distinctly remember the first time that I ate pizza. I really couldn't imagine anything tasting worse! A friend's mother had made it for us when I was 12 years old...40 years ago.

—Mike Kelly,
Head Football Coach
University of Dayton

Award-Winning Spaghetti with Meat Sauce ❋

This sauce won a top prize out of 20 contenders at a local church's annual sauce cook-off

As newlyweds in far-away Ohio, when we couldn't get to Tennessee for Thanksgiving, this spaghetti dish would be the Thanksgiving dinner for this new cook!

—Jane Corbly

Yield: 12 servings

1½	pounds ground beef round	2	teaspoons basil
1	pound bulk Italian sausage	1	cup water
1	large sweet onion, such as Vidalia, chopped	2	teaspoons salt
4-6	cloves garlic, chopped	½	teaspoon freshly ground black pepper
4	(6 ounce) cans tomato paste	2	tablespoons sugar
2	(28 ounce) cans diced or crushed tomatoes	2	bay leaves
2½	teaspoons dried oregano	3	pounds dry spaghetti
			Freshly grated Parmesan cheese

🕐 *The sauce must be made 4 hours ahead. May be refrigerated up to 4 days or frozen.*

6 Brown beef and sausage with onion and garlic in a large pot; drain.

6 Add tomato paste, tomatoes, oregano, basil, water, salt, pepper, sugar, and bay leaves.

6 Bring to a boil. Stir and lower heat to a slow simmer. Cook 3 to 4 hours.

6 Cook spaghetti according to package directions.

6 Serve sauce over spaghetti. Sprinkle with Parmesan cheese.

Note: *Make sure you use a quality Italian sausage in the sauce — it's what makes it a real crowd pleaser. This dish is perfect for casual entertaining.*

Menu: *Add Artichoke and Hearts of Palm Salad (page 121), garlic bread and Best Easy Chocolate Bundt Cake (page 269) to make a terrific casual meal.*

🍷 *Chianti, Brunello, Barolo*

Gemelli with Chicken and White Wine Cream Sauce

Special enough to serve to guests

Yield: 4 servings

1	pound dry gemelli pasta	2	tablespoons chopped green onion
1	cup white wine	¼	red onion, thinly sliced
1	teaspoon thyme	¼	pound chopped prosciutto
2	tablespoons minced garlic	2	tablespoons chopped chives
2	tablespoons minced onion	2	tablespoons chopped fresh basil
2	bay leaves	3	tablespoons butter
3	tablespoons olive oil	1½	cups heavy cream
	Salt and pepper to taste	½	cup Parmesan cheese
3	boneless chicken breasts		
3	tablespoons minced garlic		

Chicken may be marinated in the refrigerator up to 8 hours before grilling.

- Cook pasta according to directions.
- Combine wine, thyme, 2 tablespoons garlic, onion, bay leaves, oil, salt, and pepper. Add chicken and marinate 2 hours.
- Remove chicken from marinade and grill until done. Slice very thin.
- Sauté 3 tablespoons garlic, green and red onion, prosciutto, chives, and basil in butter for about 5 minutes.
- Add sliced chicken and cream; simmer 15 minutes.
- Toss together pasta and chicken mixture. Add cheese and serve.

Menu: *Finish this rich dish with fresh fruit and sorbet.*

Red Zinfandel, Chardonnay

More Dayton inventions:
Glass photographic negatives
Instant blood-glucose level testing
Liberty engine
Computerized aircraft loading system
Fuzzbuster and radar detectors
Airplane supercharger
Portable breathing resuscitator
Artificial heart
Artificial kidney
Chrome plating

Pasta with Shrimp in Tomato Cream

Impressive enough for company, but not a lot of effort!

Yield: 4 servings

2	cloves garlic, minced	⅓	cup sun-dried tomatoes packed in oil, cut into slivers
2	tablespoons oil from sun-dried tomatoes packed in oil	¼	teaspoon ground white pepper
1	pound (31 to 35 count) shrimp, peeled and deveined	1	cup chicken broth
		¾	cup vermouth
¼	cup thinly sliced green onion	1	cup heavy cream
2	tablespoons chopped fresh basil, or 1 teaspoon dried	10	ounces dry linguine
			Freshly grated Parmesan cheese

ↂ Combine garlic and tomato oil in a large skillet over medium-high heat. Add shrimp and sauté 6 minutes, or until opaque in the center. Transfer shrimp mixture to a dish; set aside.

ↂ Add onion, basil, tomato, pepper, broth, vermouth, and cream to skillet. Boil, uncovered, over high heat until reduced to about 1½ cups. Add shrimp and stir until heated through.

ↂ Meanwhile, cook linguine in boiling water for 8 minutes or until tender to bite; drain well.

ↂ Add cooked pasta to shrimp sauce and toss to blend. Serve with cheese on the side.

Menu: *Chocolate Pâté (page 258) is a scrumptious ending to this special occasion entrée.*

🍷 *Chianti, Merlot*

Sun-dried tomatoes are a great addition to many pasta dishes, but beware of tomatoes not packed in oil and sold at a lower price. They often don't reconstitute well, remaining tough. Look for tomatoes that are packed in oil and are bright red, rather than brownish.

Cajun Shrimp and Angel Hair Pasta

A nice alternative to shrimp scampi

Yield: 4 servings

Angel Butter

4	tablespoons butter, softened	1	teaspoon freshly ground black pepper
1	(2 ounce) jar chopped pimientos, drained	1	teaspoon dried tarragon
1	tablespoon capers	1	teaspoon dried oregano
2	tablespoons chopped shallots	2	tablespoons Dijon mustard
2	tablespoons chopped garlic	¼	cup lemon juice

Cajun Shrimp

24	(16 to 20 count) shrimp, peeled and deveined	½	cup heavy cream
			Angel Butter
3	tablespoons butter	1	pound dry angel hair pasta
1	tablespoon Cajun spice mix, or to taste		Chopped fresh parsley for garnish
½	cup white wine		

🕐 *Angel butter may be made in advance and frozen until ready for use. Roll butter in wax paper and seal in a zip-top bag. Thaw completely before using.*

🌀 To make Angel Butter, cream butter with an electric mixer. Add pimientos and capers, and mix well. Mix in shallots, garlic, pepper, tarragon, oregano, mustard, and lemon juice until thoroughly blended; do not overmix.

🌀 Sauté shrimp in butter 1 to 2 minutes. Add Cajun spice and toss to mix. Remove shrimp and set aside. Add wine and deglaze pan. Add cream and cook over medium heat until slightly reduced. Stir in Angel Butter until melted and combined. Put shrimp back in pan; heat until opaque and warm.

🌀 Meanwhile, cook pasta according to package directions; drain and transfer to a serving dish. Pour shrimp and sauce over pasta. Garnish with parsley and serve immediately.

Menu: *Serve after Mushroom Tarts (page 45) and a mesclun salad with Francesca's Salad Dressing (page 97) for an elegant dinner. End the meal with Almond Fruit Tart (page 270).*

🍷 *Merlot, Red Zinfandel, Chardonnay*

Cook and drain fresh pasta, then toss with...

• Slivered black olives, feta cheese, tomatoes, sliced scallions, olive oil, and ground pepper.

• Chopped spinach sautéed in olive oil with minced garlic, ground pepper, slivers of roasted red peppers, and Parmesan cheese.

• Briefly sautéed bay scallops, pesto and Parmesan cheese.

• Lump crabmeat sautéed in butter with curry powder, cooked peas and melted butter.

• Slivered smoked salmon, warmed sour cream or Crème Fraîche, snipped fresh dill, or a garnish of caviar.

• Peeled shrimp sautéed briefly in butter with minced garlic, crushed red pepper flakes, reduced white wine, and minced parsley.

Be creative; invent your own combinations.

Penne with Gorgonzola and Tomatoes

Rich and worth every bite!

Yield: 4 servings

3	tablespoons olive oil	1	pound dry penne pasta
1	medium onion, chopped	½	cup chopped fresh basil, or
4	cloves garlic, minced		1 tablespoon dried
1	(14½ ounce) can diced tomatoes, drained		Salt and pepper
1	stick butter, softened		Freshly grated Romano cheese (optional)
6	ounces Gorgonzola cheese, softened		

◐ Heat oil in a large heavy skillet over medium heat. Add onion and garlic; sauté 4 minutes or until translucent. Stir in tomatoes and cook 10 minutes, stirring occasionally, or until mixture thickens.

◐ Meanwhile, use a spoon to blend butter and Gorgonzola cheese.

◐ Cook pasta in a large pot of boiling salted water, stirring occasionally, until just tender but still firm to bite; drain and return pasta to pot.

◐ Whisk butter mixture into tomato sauce. Stir in basil.

◐ Add sauce to pasta and toss to coat. Season with salt and pepper. Sprinkle with Romano cheese and serve.

Note: *If Gorgonzola is not soft or crumbly enough, soften in microwave.*

Menu: *Enjoy this pasta with a simple green salad and breadsticks.*

Tired of peeling garlic cloves? For every two cloves, microwave on high for seven seconds. Cloves will pop right out of their skins!

Pasta with Tomatoes, Bacon, Arugula, and Goat Cheese

Spicy crushed red pepper, rosemary and garlic enhance this main course

Yield: 6 servings

2½ pounds plum tomatoes, seeded and chopped (about 5 cups)	1 tablespoon chopped fresh rosemary
2 tablespoons balsamic vinegar	½ teaspoon dried red pepper flakes
Salt and pepper	5 cups coarsely chopped fresh arugula (about 6 ounces)
3 tablespoons olive oil	
6 thick slices bacon, cut into ½-inch pieces	2 (9 ounce) packages fresh fettuccine
2 medium leeks (white and pale green parts only), finely chopped	6 tablespoons freshly grated Parmesan cheese
	6 ounces soft goat cheese (such as Montrachet), crumbled
2 tablespoons finely chopped garlic	Additional grated Parmesan cheese

- Combine tomatoes and vinegar in a large bowl. Season with salt and pepper. Let stand about 15 minutes or until tomatoes release their juice.

- Heat oil in a large heavy skillet over medium-high heat. Add bacon and cook 5 minutes, or until crisp. Use a slotted spoon to transfer bacon to paper towels.

- Add leeks to bacon drippings; sauté 3 minutes or until tender. Add garlic, rosemary and pepper flakes; sauté 1 minute. Stir in tomato mixture and bacon. Simmer 4 minutes or until heated through. Add arugula and simmer 1 minute or until arugula is wilted.

- Meanwhile, cook fettuccine in a large pot of boiling salted water for 3 minutes or until tender but still firm to bite; drain.

- Transfer pasta to a large serving bowl. Add 6 tablespoons Parmesan cheese and tomato mixture. Toss to combine. Season with salt and pepper. Serve, passing goat cheese and additional Parmesan cheese on the side.

Note: *Make sure crumbled goat cheese is kept refrigerated prior to serving.*

Menu: *For dessert, serve blueberries and sliced nectarines with crème fraîche (available in many supermarkets' dairy case).*

Red Zinfandel, Chardonnay

Census data shows that Dayton has three patents for every 100 residents, ranking it above Akron, Cincinnati, Cleveland, Toledo, and Columbus!

Summer Pasta

A delicious warm weather meal

Yield: 6 to 8 servings

1	pound fresh mozzarella cheese, diced
8	medium tomatoes, diced
4	cloves garlic, finely chopped
1	cup olive oil
1	cup coarsely chopped fresh basil

1	tablespoon plus 1 teaspoon kosher salt
	Freshly ground black pepper
	Crushed red pepper flakes
1½	pounds dry linguine or penne

- Toss cheese, tomato, garlic, oil, basil, and kosher salt in a bowl. Season generously with black pepper and red pepper flakes. Let stand 30 minutes.

- Meanwhile, cook pasta in a large pot of boiling salted water until tender but firm to the bite; drain well and return to pot.

- Add tomato mixture to pasta and toss well. Serve hot or at room temperature.

Note: *Use only the best fresh tomatoes for this dish. If they are not in season, "on-the-vine" supermarket tomatoes may be substituted. Do not substitute regular mozzarella for the fresh variety.*

Menu: *Serve after a big bowl of Herbed Mussels Normande (page 35) or Grilled Shrimp Skewers (page 205).*

Pinot Grigio, Chianti

The next time you turn a key to start your car, stop and think for a moment...In 1912, Dayton resident Charles F. Kettering devised his greatest invention, the electric self-starter for the car. It debuted on the 1912 Cadillac, and meant no more cranking!

Ziti with Baked Tomato Sauce

A hearty flavor that makes a very satisfying meatless dish

Yield: 4 to 6 servings

½	cup olive oil	¼	cup Italian-seasoned bread crumbs
1	(28 ounce) can diced tomatoes		
2	cloves garlic, minced	¼	cup Parmesan cheese
½	teaspoon salt	1	pound dry ziti pasta
¼	teaspoon freshly ground black pepper		

❁ Preheat oven to 400 degrees.

❁ Pour half of the oil into the bottom of an 8-inch square baking dish. Tilt to spread evenly. Place tomatoes in dish. Add garlic, salt and pepper; mix lightly.

❁ Combine bread crumbs and cheese in a separate container. Sprinkle evenly over tomato mixture. Drizzle remaining oil over top.

❁ Bake 40 minutes.

❁ Meanwhile, cook ziti according to package directions; drain.

❁ Toss baked tomato sauce with cooked pasta and serve immediately.

Note: *For variety, you can add chopped roasted red peppers, artichokes or mushrooms to the sauce as it bakes; use your imagination!*

Menu: *Serve this hearty dish after a simple green salad with Francesca's Salad Dressing (page 97). Make Mocha Latte Decadence (page 257) for dessert.*

🍷 *Chianti*

Spray plastic containers with nonstick cooking spray before pouring in tomato-based sauces— no more stains!

Mexican Pasta

A fun dish for entertaining, which guests can individualize with their favorite toppings

Yield: 2 to 4 servings

4-5 tablespoons vegetable oil	1 pound ripe tomatoes, peeled, seeded and chopped, or 1 (28 ounce) can diced tomatoes, drained
8 ounces dry fideos or vermicelli pasta, broken into 2- to 3-inch pieces	
½ cup minced onion	1 teaspoon dried oregano, crumbled
1 fresh mild green chile (also called California or Anaheim chile), seeded and chopped, or ⅓ cup canned green chiles	1½ cups unsalted chicken broth Salt and freshly ground pepper to taste
2 medium cloves garlic, minced	5 tablespoons chopped fresh cilantro

Toppings (optional)

1 small avocado, peeled, and sliced or diced	Chopped fresh cilantro
Sour cream	Cherry tomatoes
Chopped green onions	Shredded Monterey Jack cheese

- Heat 4 tablespoons oil in a large skillet over medium heat. Add dry pasta and sauté 7 minutes, or until golden. Use a slotted spoon or tongs to transfer to a bowl.

- If skillet is dry, add another tablespoon oil and heat over low heat. Add onion and chile; sauté 5 minutes or until softened. Stir in garlic, tomato and oregano. Increase heat and bring to a boil. Add broth and a pinch of salt; return to a boil.

- Add pasta and stir. Reduce heat to low. Cover and simmer, stirring occasionally, for about 12 minutes, or until liquid is absorbed and pasta is tender. If skillet becomes dry before pasta is tender, add a few tablespoons extra broth or water.

- Meanwhile, prepare toppings, if desired.

- Add 4 tablespoons cilantro to pasta. Adjust seasoning as desired. Transfer to a heated serving bowl. Sprinkle with remaining tablespoon cilantro and serve with toppings on the side.

Note: *The thin Spanish noodles, called fideos, are available in many supermarkets, but regular vermicelli makes a fine substitute. For variety, experiment with different types of chile peppers. For extra spiciness, add 1 to 2 tablespoons chopped jalapeño pepper with the chopped chile.*

Menu: *The bright tastes of this dish work well with a salad of spinach, fresh orange segments, chopped mangoes and a lime-olive oil dressing.*

🍷 *Rioja, Red Zinfandel*

This is my favorite entertaining dish. It's beautiful and fun. It can be made slightly before company arrives and "dolled up" with toppings. My old college roommate and I discovered this recipe when we were first on our own out of school. We enjoyed sipping wine and making this together. Since then, we have both shared it with countless friends and family. It can be easily doubled (or tripled if you use two pans). It goes great with citrus salad and garlic bread, and makes great leftovers!

—Molly Treese

Gnocchi with Spinach

This wonderful recipe is from Dottie Overman of Dorothy Lane Market

Yield: 6 to 8 servings

¼	cup olive oil		Salt and freshly ground pepper
6	large cloves garlic, minced		to taste
1	pound fresh spinach, chopped	2	pounds gnocchi
¼	teaspoon dried red pepper flakes		Grated Romano cheese to taste

Spinach can be made a few hours ahead, then reheated.

◎ Heat oil in a skillet over low heat. Add garlic and sauté until softened. Add spinach and pepper flakes. Increase heat, cover and cook about 15 minutes or until tender, stirring occasionally. Season with salt and pepper; keep warm.

◎ Meanwhile, cook gnocchi according to package directions; drain.

◎ Add gnocchi to spinach. Serve immediately with Romano cheese on the side.

Note: *We recommend using vacuum-packed gnocchi (such as Bellino brand) instead of the frozen type. To save time, buy prewashed chopped spinach from your grocer's salad bar. This dish is excellent served as an appetizer in a large bowl with toothpicks on the side.*

Menu: *Serve Greek Peasant Salad (page 124) before the gnocchi for a nice meal, or serve the gnocchi as a side dish with beef or lamb.*

ⓥ *Chianti*

A Dayton motorist made history in April 1923 by purchasing the first tank of ethyl gasoline ever sold. Thomas Midgley, Jr. and Charles F. Kettering developed the gas at General Motors' labs.

Cavatappi with Spinach, Garbanzo Beans and Feta

A simple vegetarian supper

Yield: 6 to 8 servings

Confused about pairing pasta shapes and sauces? Try these!

Thin ribbons, like linguine—light vegetable or light cream sauce

Thick ribbons, like lasagna—meat, game, hearty vegetable, or heavy cream sauce

Thin strands, like capellini—light vegetable sauce, or use in soups

Thick strands, like spaghetti—seafood, hearty vegetable or heavy cream sauce

Small tubes, like penne—creamy cheese sauce, or use in soups or salads

Large tubes, like cannelloni—hearty vegetable, chunky meat or heavy cream sauce

Small shapes, like farfalle—light vegetable or light cream sauce, vinaigrette, or use in soups or salads

8	cups coarsely chopped spinach (8 ounces)
1	pound cavatappi pasta, cooked and hot
1	cup crumbled feta cheese
¼	cup olive oil
2	tablespoons fresh lemon juice
½	teaspoon salt
½	teaspoon freshly ground black pepper
2	(19 ounce) cans chickpeas or other white beans, drained
3	cloves garlic, minced
	Freshly ground black pepper
	Lemon wedges for garnish

🕐 *Clean and chop spinach earlier in the day or use prewashed bagged spinach as a timesaver.*

🌀 Combine spinach, pasta, feta cheese, oil, lemon juice, salt, pepper, chickpeas, and garlic in a bowl. Toss well.

🌀 Season to taste with freshly ground black pepper. Garnish with lemon wedges.

Menu: *This light main dish works well after Ciabatta Napoli (page 47) and some mixed olives. It is also good as a side dish to Grilled Swordfish with Tomato Feta Relish (page 191).*

🍷 *Chardonnay*

Fettuccine with Wild Mushrooms

Mushrooms are a standout in this recipe!

Yield: 2 to 4 servings

6	ounces fresh shiitake, chanterelle, oyster, cepes, or porcini mushrooms
2	tablespoons vegetable oil
4	tablespoons butter
	Salt and freshly ground black pepper to taste
2	tablespoons minced shallots

1½	teaspoons chopped fresh thyme, or ½ teaspoon dried and crumbled
1	(9 ounce) package fresh fettuccine, or 8 ounces dried
3	tablespoons butter
2	tablespoons chopped fresh parsley
	Freshly grated Parmesan cheese

🕐 *Mushrooms may be sautéed and kept covered at room temperature for up to 2 hours.*

✆ Gently rinse mushrooms and dry on paper towels. If using shiitake mushrooms, remove stems. Cut large mushrooms lengthwise into ½-inch-wide strips.

✆ In a large skillet, heat oil and 4 tablespoons butter over medium heat. Add mushrooms, salt and pepper. Sauté about 3 minutes. Add shallots and thyme; sauté over medium-high heat 3 minutes longer, or until mushrooms are browned and tender, and liquid has evaporated.

✆ Cook pasta in a large pot of boiling salted water over high heat, uncovered, until tender but firm to the bite. Drain well and transfer to a heated serving dish.

✆ Add 3 tablespoons butter and parsley to pasta. Season with salt and pepper; toss until coated. Spoon mushroom mixture on top. Offer Parmesan cheese on the side.

Menu: *Serve with a sourdough baguette, and Watercress Salad with Cranberries and Pecans (page 128).*

🍷 *Chardonnay, Chianti, Red Zinfandel*

With the microwave oven has come the possibility of successfully reheating pasta, with or without sauce. The microwaves affect only the water molecules, thereby warming the pasta without drying it. Microwave leftover pasta in a covered dish on high power for about a minute; if the pasta is still cold, stir and continue to microwave, checking at 15-second intervals. You can also wrap pasta in aluminum foil and reheat it in a 350° oven until hot, checking after 15 to 20 minutes.

Farfalle Milano

A tasty pasta dish that comes together in less than 15 minutes

Yield: 4 servings

1	pound dry farfalle (bowtie) pasta	1	cup frozen peas, thawed
4	tablespoons butter	2	tablespoons butter
12	ounces mushrooms, thinly sliced		Salt and pepper to taste
¼	pound ham or prosciutto, thinly sliced		Parmesan cheese

Buy pre-sliced mushrooms as a timesaver, or slice them in the morning and refrigerate until later.

6   Cook pasta according to package directions; drain.

6   Meanwhile, melt 4 tablespoons butter in a large skillet over medium heat. Add mushrooms and ham and sauté 5 minutes, or until mushrooms are tender.

6   Add peas to mushroom mixture and heat through. Add 2 tablespoons butter and stir until melted.

6   Toss hot pasta with mushroom mixture. Season with salt and pepper. Sprinkle with Parmesan cheese.

Note: *Using prosciutto and freshly grated Parmesan cheese makes this dish extra flavorful.*

Menu: *Enjoy this pasta with Dried Cherries and Gorgonzola Salad (page 125). Have ice cream and Rich Caramel Sauce (page 282) for dessert.*

Pinot Grigio, Sauvignon Blanc

World War I veterans had Daytonian Lizern Custer to thank for inventing an electric three-wheeled "invalid chair." The Custer chairs were also a hit at the 1939 New York World's Fair, where 110 of them were rented.

Penne Alla Carbonara ⭐

This pasta is a specialty in Rome

Yield: 6 servings

5	tablespoons virgin olive oil	1	cup freshly grated Parmesan cheese
1	clove garlic, lightly crushed	1	cup heavy cream
8	ounces thickly sliced bacon, cubed		Freshly ground black pepper
6	egg yolks	1	pound dry penne pasta

- Heat oil in a skillet. Add garlic and sauté until lightly browned. Discard garlic. Add bacon to skillet and cook over medium heat until well-cooked, but not crisp. Remove skillet from heat to cool.

- In a large mixing bowl, combine egg yolks, cheese and cream. Mix well to make a sauce. Add cooled bacon and oil. Season sauce with pepper.

- Cook pasta according to package directions until al dente. Drain and immediately toss with sauce. Mix well. If pasta is not creamy enough, add a small amount of half-and-half or chicken stock. Serve immediately.

Note: *For a healthier alternative, cut olive oil down to 1 tablespoon and use skim milk instead of cream. Also, for garnish, use chopped fresh Italian parsley.*

Menu: *Serve with Make-Ahead Caesar Salad (page 125), make Almond Fruit Tart (page 270) for dessert.*

🍷 *Pinot Grigio, Sauvignon Blanc, Chardonnay*

I really feel that this is the "Soul Food of The Muse Machine," and kept it going for many years. From the early days in my basement, it was always a favorite of the staff, the teachers and the Board members. The students at the cast parties of the musicals, those held in the Biltmore Space and the Learning Center Space, adored it! Naturally, I used to multiply this by 10, and sometimes 20. Maybe some even remember it today, even though it has been six years since I last made it!

—Suzy Bassani,
former director
The Muse Machine

Noodles with Curried Stir-Fried Vegetables

A great side dish for pork

Yield: 4 side dish servings

Sauce

½	cup chicken broth	1	tablespoon sugar
1	teaspoon cornstarch	1	teaspoon salt
¼	cup soy sauce	1	teaspoon Asian sesame oil
2	tablespoons Scotch		

Stir-Fry

1	bunch broccoli, cut into flowerets	1½	tablespoons minced ginger
3	medium carrots, julienned	1	tablespoon curry powder
1	medium leek, white and pale green parts, julienned	4	green onions, julienned
1	medium red onion, thinly sliced (about 2 cups)	8	ounces dry Asian noodles or linguine, cooked al dente and drained
2	teaspoons peanut oil	¼	cup chopped fresh cilantro
1½	tablespoons minced garlic		

Vegetables may be cooked earlier in the day and refrigerated until ready to use.

- To prepare sauce, combine sauce ingredients together in a bowl in order listed. Mix until cornstarch dissolves.

- Cook broccoli in boiling water, covered, for 1 to 2 minutes. Remove from water with a slotted spoon. Add carrot and leeks and cook 1 minute. Remove and add onion and cook 1 minute. Remove vegetables and set aside.

- Heat peanut oil in a large skillet over high heat. Add garlic and ginger; stir fry about 30 seconds or until fragrant. Add curry powder and stir fry about 30 seconds. Stir in sauce and bring to a boil, stirring constantly. Gently stir in cooked vegetables and green onion.

- Add pasta to stir-fry. Garnish with cilantro and serve immediately.

Menu: *These flavors work well with Sesame-Garlic Grilled Pork Tenderloin (page 241). Gingersnaps (page 277) with fresh pear slices and vanilla ice cream make a fine finish.*

Merlot, Chianti

Silky Asian Noodles

Authentic Asian flavors enhance this dish, the perfect complement to any Oriental pork or chicken entrée

Yield: 4 servings

2	(6 ounce) packages dry udon noodles	1	cup thinly sliced shiitake mushrooms
1½	tablespoons dashi soup stock	1	cup shredded savoy cabbage
¼	cup mirin	1	bunch green onions, sliced
2	tablespoons soy sauce		

۶ Cook noodles in 6 cups boiling water for 6 to 8 minutes. Remove noodles with a slotted spoon, reserving boiling water. Rinse noodles, drain and transfer to a shallow serving bowl.

۶ Add soup stock, mirin and soy sauce to boiling water. Reduce heat and simmer 5 minutes.

۶ Add mushrooms to simmering broth and cook 2 minutes. Add cabbage and cook 2 minutes longer.

۶ Spoon broth over the noodles and sprinkle with green onion.

Note: *Udon noodles are widely available in Asian supermarkets, but vermicelli or linguine may be substituted. Also, fish bouillon granules may be substituted for dashi. If desired, use 4 teaspoons sugar in place of the mirin.*

Menu: *Serve with Pork with Plum Sauce (page 239) and Asparagus with Chinese Vinaigrette (page 149).*

🍷 *Chardonnay, Red Zinfandel*

NCR invented carbonless copy paper in 1955.

Pops' Singapore Noodles ☆

East meets West in this recipe!

Yield: 4 servings

1	pound baby shrimp, peeled and deveined
1	boneless, skinless chicken breast, cut into ¼-inch-thick strips
¼	cup white wine
2	tablespoons thin soy sauce
1	tablespoon cornstarch
½	teaspoon white pepper
	Canola oil for cooking
1	tablespoon minced ginger
½	cup julienned green onion

1	tablespoon minced garlic
½	pound bean sprouts
1	red bell pepper, julienned
1	onion, julienned
	Salt and white pepper to taste
2	eggs, lightly beaten
1	pound dry thin rice noodles, soaked in cold water for 2 hours, then drained
2	tablespoons Madras curry powder

⏲ *Vegetables can be chopped earlier in the day and refrigerated. Noodles must soak for at least 2 hours; they may soak for up to 1 day ahead.*

6 Marinate shrimp and chicken in wine, soy sauce, cornstarch, and white pepper for 20 minutes.

6 In a hot wok coated well with canola oil, stir fry ginger, green onion and garlic. Add marinated shrimp and chicken; stir fry quickly for 30 to 60 seconds. Remove shrimp and chicken; set aside. Add bean sprouts, bell pepper and onion to oil in wok. Season with salt and pepper; cook 1 minute. Remove and set aside.

6 Wipe out wok and coat well with oil. Heat oil until smoking hot. Add egg and rotate the pan so as to quickly spread egg like a pancake. Before totally set, add rice noodles to egg. Stir and break up into small pieces. Add curry powder and adjust seasonings, continuing to stir to prevent noodles from sticking to pan. When steaming hot, add shrimp, chicken and vegetables to noodles. Continue to stir until entire dish is steaming hot.

Menu: *Start this meal with Almond Orange Garden Salad (page 130). Serve the noodles, then end with Gingersnaps (page 277) and a tropical fruit sorbet.*

🍷 *Chardonnay, Sauvignon Blanc*

Ming Tsai started cooking at his family's Chinese restaurant in Dayton while he was still a teenager. His hit television series, "East Meets West with Ming Tsai", debuted in September 1998 on the Food Network. In May 1999, he was awarded a Daytime Emmy for Outstanding Service Show Host. Ming also owns the Blue Ginger Restaurant in Wellesley, Massachusetts.

Pasta Spirals with Butter-Cooked Onions

A simple entrée, or a nice alternative to rice or potatoes

Yield: 4 side-dish servings

4	**tablespoons butter**
1	**pound onions, thinly sliced**
	Salt and freshly ground pepper to taste
2	**teaspoons fresh thyme, or ¾ teaspoon dried**
1	**bay leaf**
8	**ounces dry fusilli or other spiral pasta**
	Freshly grated Parmesan cheese (optional)

🕐 *The cooked onions may be kept in the refrigerator for up to 2 days — reheat in skillet over low heat before continuing.*

6 Heat butter in a large skillet over medium-low heat. Add onion, salt, pepper, thyme, and bay leaf. Sauté about 25 minutes or until onion is softened.

6 Increase heat to medium-high and sauté 5 minutes, or until onion is lightly browned. Discard bay leaf.

6 Cook pasta in a large pot of boiling salted water according to package directions; drain well. Mix pasta and onion. Serve with Parmesan cheese on the side.

Menu: *Offer this as a side with Poulet Sauté Provençal (page 211), and some steamed green beans drizzled with olive oil and balsamic vinegar.*

▼ *Depends on main dish*

More Dayton inventions:

Photoelectric cell - the black light

Collapsible portable crib

Price tag-affixing machines

Lighted score board

Solenoid

Incentive stamps

Automobile air bags

Frost-proof refrigerator

Laser weapons

Room air conditioner

Grilled Pizza with Sausage, Bell Peppers, Onions, and Cheese

A fun "assemble your own pizza" entertaining idea

Yield: 4 servings

4	(10 ounce) tubes refrigerated pizza dough, or equivalent amount of dough purchased from a pizzeria (in Dayton, try Milano's)	1	large red onion, cut into ½-inch wedges
			Salt and pepper
¾	cup olive oil	2	cups shredded mozzarella cheese
6	tablespoons balsamic vinegar	½	cup freshly grated Parmesan cheese
3	tablespoons minced garlic		
2	tablespoons chopped fresh rosemary	2	cups crumbled soft goat cheese (such as Montrachet), chilled
1	pound spicy Italian sausages	4	plum tomatoes, seeded and chopped
2	yellow or red bell peppers, quartered lengthwise	¾	cup chopped green onion tops

Vinaigrette, sausage and vegetables can be prepared up to 2 hours ahead.

- Whisk together olive oil, vinegar, garlic, and rosemary to make a vinaigrette. Let stand at room temperature for 15 minutes, or refrigerate up to 2 hours.

- Preheat grill.

- Arrange sausages, bell pepper and onion on a baking sheet. Brush with vinaigrette; season with salt and pepper. Grill sausages about 12 minutes, or until cooked through. Grill bell pepper and onion about 8 minutes, or until slightly charred and crisp-tender. Turn and baste occasionally while grilling. Remove from grill.

- Cut sausages into ½-inch pieces. Cut bell pepper into thin strips.

- Divide dough into 4 equal pieces. Using a floured surface, flatten each piece into a 9-inch circle.

- Place 2 dough circles on grill over low heat. Cook 3 minutes, or until dough puffs and is crisp on the bottom. Turn circles over and grill 1 minute longer. Transfer to a baking sheet with well-grilled side up. Repeat with remaining dough circles.

- Divide mozzarella and Parmesan cheeses among crusts. Top each with sausage, onion and bell pepper. Divide goat cheese among crusts, then top with tomato and green onion. Drizzle each pizza with 1½ tablespoons vinaigrette.

- Using a large metal spatula, return 2 pizzas to grill. Close grill or cover pizzas loosely with foil. Grill 5 minutes, rotating as needed for even cooking, or until cheese melts and crust is cooked through and browned. Repeat with remaining pizzas.

Menu: *Nibble on Croutons à la Tapenade (page 55) while assembling pizzas with your guests. Offer a big green salad with the pizzas. Finish the meal with Double Chocolate Walnut Biscotti (page 280) and ice cream.*

Ⓨ *Chianti*

Tired of the same old thing? Try these toppings on your pizza crust:

Tomato sauce, capers, Niçoise olives, tuna, fresh basil, drizzle of olive oil, and ground pepper.

Thinly sliced red onions, roasted garlic, toasted pine nuts, rosemary, and a dusting of light brown sugar.

Tomato sauce, red onions, chorizo or anchovy fillets, and rosemary.

Sliced mozzarella, roasted garlic cloves, fresh basil, and thinly sliced plum tomatoes.

Onion marmalade, wild mushrooms, fresh thyme, and grated Pecorino cheese.

Tomato sauce, roasted peppers, red onion, fresh basil, and shredded Romano cheese.

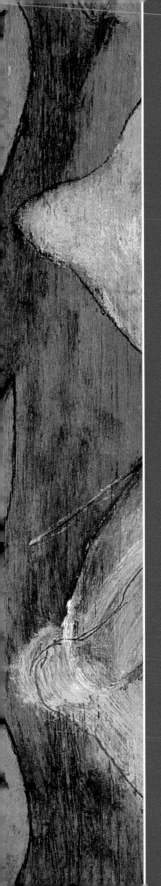

A River Runs Through It

SEAFOOD

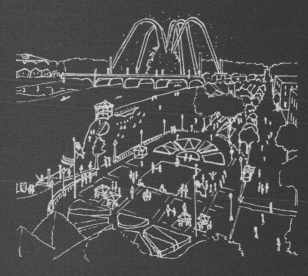

RIVERSCAPE

A RIVER RUNS THROUGH IT

Ever since Dayton's founders landed on its banks 200 years ago, the Great Miami River has played an important role in the region's history and character. Spreading devastation during the Great Flood of 1913, it now stands as the centerpiece of an exciting plan to revitalize our center city.

It took an awe-inspiring blend of teamwork, vision and determination to make the most of Dayton's assets. Five Rivers MetroParks hired Belgium garden designer Francois Goffinet to establish a new vision along the river, while the Downtown Dayton Partnership convened a broad-based group of community volunteers to develop a master plan for the riverfront. The result is the RiverScape Project. Phase One of the project features a laser-lit fountain at the Great Miami and Mad Rivers; a Festival Plaza with an interactive fountain; a Canal Walk honoring the city's history; and the Inventors' Riverwalk.

In collaboration with RiverScape, the Junior League of Dayton developed a children's program for the Inventor's Riverwalk. This interactive walkway is punctuated with Invention Stations, where children learn about a particular Dayton invention, along with its history and development process.

The RiverScape Project is a shining example of what can be accomplished with some determination. Together we've created something that will benefit all of us.

"Today, we celebrate not just the successful completion of the RiverScape fundraising campaign, but a milestone for our community. RiverScape, combined with the projects already underway downtown, will create a synergy of excitement and vibrancy that will make this a place people will want to live, work and do business. Our center city will be ready to shine when the world comes to visit in 2003 for the anniversary of powered

Grilled Swordfish
with Tomato Feta Relish

Great on a hot summer's night

Yield: 4 servings

Tomato Feta Relish

1	medium tomato	1	tablespoon lemon juice
1	small green onion, sliced	2	teaspoons chopped fresh dill
¼	cup crumbled feta cheese		Freshly ground black pepper to
¼	cup extra virgin olive oil		taste

Swordfish

¼	cup Dijon mustard	1	teaspoon oregano
2½	tablespoons red wine vinegar	½	teaspoon salt
¼	cup extra virgin olive oil	4	swordfish or salmon steaks
1	teaspoon garlic powder		

🕐 *The relish may be made and refrigerated up to 6 hours ahead.*

6 To prepare relish, core tomato and cut in half horizontally. Scoop out and discard pulp and seeds, leaving only outer shell. Dice outer shell. Combine tomato, onion, feta, oil, lemon juice, dill, and pepper. Set aside.

6 Preheat grill.

6 Combine mustard, vinegar, oil, garlic powder, oregano, and salt to make a glaze.

6 Brush 1 side of each steak with glaze. Grill steaks, glazed side down, for about 3 minutes. Brush top side of steaks with glaze. Turn steaks and grill an additional 2 to 3 minutes. Top steaks with relish before serving.

Note: *If your steaks are large, you may want to double the relish — it's delicious!*

Menu: *Serve the fish with Spring Island Couscous Salad (page 136), Peperonata (page 158) and a bowl of mixed Greek olives.*

🍷 *Red Zinfandel, White Burgundy*

> To test for a medium-hot grill, you should be able to hold your hand over the grill at food height for 3 seconds before having to pull your hand away.

Grouper with Fresh Salsa

Fresh fish at its best!

Yield: 6 servings

Salsa

1½	cups peeled, seeded and coarsely chopped tomato
½	cup peeled, seeded and coarsely chopped cucumber
¼	cup finely chopped green onion
1-2	jalapeño peppers, seeded and finely chopped

1½	tablespoons snipped fresh cilantro
1	tablespoon white wine vinegar
1	teaspoon lemon juice
½	teaspoon salt

Grouper

2	pounds Florida grouper fillets
	Salt and pepper to taste
¼	cup light olive oil

2	tablespoons lemon juice
1	tablespoon finely chopped garlic

🕐 *Salsa may be made up to 2 hours ahead.*

6 Combine all salsa ingredients and set aside.

6 To prepare grouper, rinse fillets and pat dry. Season with salt and pepper. Combine oil, lemon juice and garlic. Brush mixture over fillets and let stand at room temperature 15 minutes.

6 Preheat grill.

6 Grill fish, uncovered, over medium-high heat for 4 to 6 minutes per ½-inch fillet thickness, carefully turning once and brushing often with remaining lemon mixture.

6 Transfer grouper to a serving platter and top with fresh salsa.

Note: *May also use red snapper or black sea bass fillets.*

Menu: *Offer rice and Vivid Summer Vegetables (page 167) with the fish. The Brownie Torte (page 265) makes an excellent finish.*

🍷 *Chardonnay*

Baked Fish with Artichokes and Mushrooms

Colorful and flavorful

Yield: 4 servings

4	(8 to 10 ounce) fish fillets (mahi mahi, grouper, tilapia, or any thick, white-fleshed fish)	2	fresh tomatoes, diced
		1	(14 ounce) can artichoke hearts, drained and quartered
	Melted butter for basting	8	ounces fresh mushrooms, sliced
1	lemon, halved	¼	cup capers
	Old Bay seasoning to taste	2	tablespoons chopped fresh parsley
4	tablespoons butter		
2	teaspoons minced garlic	1	cup dry white wine

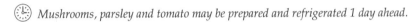

Mushrooms, parsley and tomato may be prepared and refrigerated 1 day ahead.

- Preheat oven to 450 degrees.

- Place fish on a baking sheet. Baste with melted butter. Squeeze lemon over fillets and sprinkle with Old Bay seasoning.

- Bake fish 10 to 15 minutes, or until firm to the touch.

- Meanwhile, melt 4 tablespoons butter in a sauté pan over high heat.

- Add garlic; sauté for 15 to 20 seconds. Add tomato, artichoke, mushrooms, capers, and parsley. Sauté until vegetables are heated through.

- Add wine to sauté pan and reduce until sauce is slightly thickened. Spoon sauce over baked fish and serve immediately.

Menu: *Begin the meal with Salad with Warm Brie Dressing (page 122). Then serve fish over rice, orzo or angel hair pasta.*

Chardonnay, Sauvignon Blanc

The first settlers arrived in Dayton on April 1, 1796. They were from Cincinnati, having traveled up the Miami River in several flatboats, and landed at the head of St. Clair Street.

Saucy Sole

Quick, easy and delicious!

Yield: 4 servings

6-8 sole fillets (about 1½ pounds)	5 tablespoons butter, softened
1½ tablespoons lemon juice	⅓ cup chopped green onion
¼ teaspoon garlic powder	½ cup sliced mushrooms
Salt and pepper to taste	(optional)
⅓ cup Parmesan cheese	Dash of hot pepper sauce
⅓ cup shredded mozzarella cheese	1-2 tablespoons mayonnaise

🜚 Rinse and pat dry fish. Place in a greased baking dish just large enough so fillets fit snuggly and overlap slightly. Brush with lemon juice and garlic powder. Season with salt and pepper.

🜚 Broil fillets 4 to 6 minutes, or until flaky. Remove dish from heat and set aside.

🜚 While fish cools, combine cheeses, butter, onion, mushrooms, pepper sauce, and mayonnaise.

🜚 Spread mixture evenly over fish. Broil 4 minutes, or until lightly browned. Serve immediately.

Note: *May use Parmesan only, instead of mozzarella and Parmesan. This recipe doubles easily.*

Menu: *A delightful dinner when served with rice and steamed broccoli. Walnut Butter Cookies (page 277) and ice cream round out the meal.*

🍷 *Chardonnay, Sauvignon Blanc*

Frozen fish tips from L'Auberge:

• Glazed, whole fish and frozen shrimp should be stored at -20° to 0°F until ready to thaw and cook.

• Do not accept any frozen fish with white frost on the edges. This is freezer burn caused by improper packaging, thawing or refreezing.

• Thaw fish in its original wrapping in the refrigerator. Place in a shallow container and allow to thaw as long as necessary.

Orange Soy Tuna

An elegant entrée!

Yield: 4 servings

½	cup vegetable oil	2	cloves garlic, minced
¼	cup orange juice		Lemon pepper to taste
3	tablespoons soy sauce	4	yellowfin tuna steaks
1	teaspoon orange zest		(about 1½ to 2 pounds)
1	teaspoon ground ginger		

Marinade can be prepared and steaks can be marinated up to 1 day ahead.

⚅ Combine oil, orange juice, soy sauce, zest, ginger, garlic, and lemon pepper for a marinade. Pour half the marinade over steaks in a glass baking dish. Refrigerate 45 minutes, then allow to stand at room temperature for 15 minutes prior to grilling.

⚅ Preheat grill to medium-high heat.

⚅ Grill steaks until done (see cook's note). The texture should be firm, yet tender to the bite.

⚅ Heat remaining marinade to a boil. Reduce slightly and serve over grilled fish.

Note: *Fish should generally be grilled or broiled 4 to 6 minutes for each ½-inch thickness of flesh.*

Menu: *Silky Asian Noodles (page 187), and steamed broccoli or Asparagus with Chinese Vinaigrette (page 149) are the perfect accompaniments to the tuna.*

🍷 *Pinot Noir, Merlot, Red Zinfandel*

I had tuna prepared this way for the first time when I was in college visiting Norfolk, Virginia. Before that, I thought tuna was only the stuff of "tuna fish" salad. Boy, what a pleasant surprise.

—Molly Treese

Carolina Trout with Dill Sauce

An authentic recipe handed down by a long-time trout farmer

Yield: 6 to 8 servings

Trout

6-8	trout fillets, boned	1	egg, lightly beaten
2	teaspoons salt	6	tablespoons fine dry white
	Freshly ground black pepper to		bread crumbs
	taste	4	tablespoons butter, melted
2	cups coarsely chopped fresh dill	1	lemon, cut into wedges

Dill Sauce

1	packet vegetable bouillon	2	teaspoons sugar
2	cups warm water	2	egg yolks
2	tablespoons butter	½	cup heavy cream
2	tablespoons flour	3-4	tablespoons finely chopped
1	tablespoon white wine vinegar		fresh dill
½	teaspoon lemon juice		

Fish can be prepared earlier in the day up to the point where the bread crumbs are sprinkled on top. Cover tightly and refrigerate until ready to bake.

- Preheat oven to 475 degrees.
- Rinse trout well and pat dry. Season both sides with salt and pepper.
- Spray a large ovenproof casserole dish with nonstick cooking spray. Cover bottom of dish with dill. Place fish, skin side up, on dill. Brush fish generously with egg and sprinkle bread crumbs on top.
- Just before baking, pour butter over fish. Bake 25 minutes. Serve with lemon wedges and Dill Sauce.
- To prepare Dill Sauce, dissolve bouillon in warm water.
- Melt butter in a skillet. Dust flour over butter and mix together. Blend in bouillon water. Bring to a boil; cook and stir 3 to 5 minutes. Add vinegar, lemon juice and sugar.
- In a heavy saucepan, cook egg yolks and cream over low heat until thickened, stirring almost constantly. Do not boil. Remove from heat.
- Blend bouillon mixture into yolk mixture. Stir in dill. Adjust to desired sourness or sweetness by adding extra vinegar or sugar.

Note: *This recipe was also tested with salmon fillets and was excellent.*

Menu: *Start with a salad of cucumbers, tomatoes and sweet onions. Offer steamed baby new potatoes and Buttermint Carrots (page 151) with the fish.*

Sauvignon Blanc, Chardonnay

Fresh fish tips from L'Auberge:

- Fish should have clean, fresh, "sea" aroma.
- Skin should feel slick and moist, with firmly attached scales.
- Fins and tail should be moist, fresh, flexible and full; they should not be ragged or dry.
- Flesh should feel firm and elastic, with no visible fingerprint after being pressed.
- Eyes should be clear and full, not sunken (walleye will have milky eyes).
- Gills should be red to maroon in color, with no traces of gray or brown.
- There should be no breaks or tears in the belly skin.

Tangy Salmon Steaks

Perfection on the grill

Yield: 4 servings

4	(1 inch thick) salmon steaks	¼	cup dark brown sugar
½	cup Dijon mustard	2	cloves garlic, minced
½	cup soy sauce		Pinch of ground cloves

Marinade may be prepared the day ahead and refrigerated. Steaks must be placed in marinade 1 hour prior to grilling.

- Pat steaks dry with paper towels and place in a nonreactive baking dish.

- Combine mustard, soy sauce, sugar, garlic, and cloves to make a marinade. Pour marinade over fish, coating both sides of steaks. Cover and refrigerate 45 minutes. Remove from refrigerator 15 minutes prior to grilling.

- Preheat grill to medium-high heat (see cook's note).

- Remove steaks from marinade and grill about 5 minutes on each side. Serve immediately.

Note: *To test a grill for medium-high heat, you should be able to hold your hand over the heat at food-grate height for 3 seconds before having to pull away.*

Menu: *The salmon is fabulous accompanied by Lemon Rice with Pine Nuts (page 162), a green salad and sliced ripe tomatoes. Make dessert Blackberry Mini-Tarts (page 271).*

The focal point of the RiverScape project is the laser-lit fountain, shooting water 180 to 200 feet in the air and 400 feet out over the river. It is designed to be one of the largest fountains in the country in terms of its water-throwing power.

Salmon and Rice Toss

A great summer entrée — fresh and colorful!

Yield: 4 to 6 servings

3 tablespoons fresh lemon juice	1 pound skin-on salmon fillets
1 teaspoon Dijon mustard	1 cup frozen corn
2 tablespoons olive oil	3 tablespoons finely chopped
½ teaspoon salt	fresh chives
Pinch of white pepper	3 tablespoons chopped fresh dill
1 (6 ounce) box long grain and wild rice mix	2 tablespoons finely chopped green onion

Dressing must be made 1 day ahead. Rice can be cooked and refrigerated separately up to 1 day ahead.

Combine lemon juice, mustard, oil, salt, and pepper to make a dressing. Refrigerate 24 hours.

Cook rice according to package directions.

Cook salmon by grilling or baking at 400 degrees for 12 to 15 minutes. Cool 15 minutes before removing skin and cutting salmon into bite size pieces.

Combine cooked rice, dressing, corn, chives, dill, and onion. Toss in salmon.

Note: *You may want to double the dressing if a more moist salad is preferred.*

Menu: *Serve fresh tomato slices alongside this dish. End the meal with Lemon Blueberry Pie (page 272).*

Red Zinfandel, Merlot, Chardonnay

The worst flood in Dayton history came in March 1913. Several days of heavy rain produced a raging torrent that claimed 300-400 lives, and caused $100 million in damage. Nearly 4 trillion gallons of rain, the amount of water that cascades over Niagara Falls in a month, fell on the Dayton area between March 23-27.

Tomato Caper Seafood Sauce

This is one of our favorites

Yield: 4 to 6 servings

6	tablespoons butter	1	(28 ounce) can crushed tomatoes
½	cup olive oil	3	cups raw shellfish of choice:
1	cup white wine		mussels, crabmeat, scallops,
6	large cloves garlic, minced		clams, shrimp, or combination
1	teaspoon crushed dried	½	cup minced fresh parsley
	rosemary	½	teaspoon sugar
	Pinch of dried oregano	1	(3½ ounce) jar capers, drained
1	large onion, chopped		Salt and pepper to taste

Onions can be chopped and refrigerated 1 day ahead. The sauce can be assembled, up to the point when the seafood is added, ahead of time. Allow sauce to cool and refrigerate up to 8 hours. To serve, reheat sauce, add seafood, heat through and serve over pasta.

- Heat butter and oil in a large skillet over medium-high heat until butter melts and mixture starts to bubble.

- Add wine, garlic, rosemary, oregano, and onion. Cook and stir until wine evaporates and butter is golden. Reduce heat and add tomatoes.

- Add shellfish, parsley, sugar, capers, salt, and pepper. Stir until seafood is done. Mussels and clams can be left in shells; shells will open when done.

Note: *Serve over pasta of your choice.*

Menu: *Salad with Warm Brie Dressing (page 122) is excellent as a prelude to this dish. Finish with Chocolate Caramel Pecan Cheesecake (page 261).*

White Burgundy, Bordeaux, Chardonnay

In 1882, James Jacob Ritty opened the Pony House Restaurant. He commissioned wood carvers from Barney and Smith Car Works to turn 5,400 pounds of Honduras Mahogany into a bar. The fruit of their labor is the bar you now see standing in Jay's Seafood Restaurant.

Fresh Seafood Bake

Yield: 4 to 6 servings

4	pounds fresh seafood of choice: scallops, haddock, raw shrimp, cooked lobster meat, or combination	20	butter crackers, crushed
1	teaspoon salt	6	tablespoons butter
1	tablespoon freshly ground black pepper	⅓	cup sherry
½	teaspoon onion powder	2	tablespoons lemon juice
3	tablespoons snipped fresh parsley	2	cloves garlic, minced
		1	teaspoon paprika
		1½	tablespoons snipped fresh parsley

This dish may be assembled, covered and refrigerated up to 6 hours before baking.

- Preheat oven to 400 degrees.

- Clean seafood and cut into bite-size pieces. Sprinkle with salt, pepper, onion powder, and 3 tablespoons parsley.

- Arrange seafood in a 2-quart casserole dish. Sprinkle with cracker crumbs.

- Melt butter in a saucepan. Add sherry, lemon juice and garlic. Cook 2 minutes. Pour mixture over cracker crumbs. Sprinkle with paprika and 1½ tablespoons parsley.

- Bake, uncovered, for 25 minutes.

Note: *This is wonderful served over rice. You may also sprinkle ½ cup shredded cheddar cheese over the top 10 minutes before baking is complete.*

Menu: *Make a complete meal out of this dish and Mary's Strawberry and Poppyseed Salad (page 131).*

White Burgundy or Bordeaux, Chardonnay

Born during the 1913 flood, Cash Durst was named for his birthplace, the National Cash Register factory. During the flood that inundated Dayton, NCR workers made boats from packing-crate lumber to rescue stranded people.

K's Crab Cakes

Try these with our tartar sauce!

Yield: 4 to 5 servings

2	pounds crabmeat, picked over	2	tablespoons minced fresh parsley
1	cup fine bread crumbs		
6	tablespoons regular or light mayonnaise	2	teaspoons Worcestershire sauce
		4	green onions, finely chopped
2	tablespoons Dijon mustard	2	tablespoons unsalted butter
2	eggs, lightly beaten		

🕐 *Crab cakes may be assembled, covered and refrigerated up to 8 hours ahead.*

❻ Lightly mix crabmeat and bread crumbs.

❻ In a separate bowl, combine mayonnaise, mustard, egg, parsley, Worcestershire sauce, and onion. Gently fold mixture into crabmeat so that chunks of crabmeat remain.

❻ Shape mixture into 10 crab cakes. Cover and refrigerate.

❻ When ready to serve, melt butter in a nonstick skillet. Add cakes and sauté on both sides for 4 minutes total, or until golden brown.

Note: *These are great as an appetizer or a main course.*

Menu: *Serve with asparagus and Fresh Tomato Tart (page 56). Offer Shortcakes with Strawberries and Whipped Cream (page 264) for dessert.*

> I remember sitting at the kitchen table, which was covered with the *New York Times,* with a huge pile of blue crabs that my grandmother and mom prepared. It was the best dinner, and it was not over until every bit of the crab was removed from the tiny hiding places!
>
> —Lisa Darnell

Homemade Tartar Sauce

This is great when made fresh!

Yield: 1½ cups

1	cup mayonnaise	2	tablespoons finely minced shallots
2	tablespoons fresh lemon juice		
1	teaspoon Worcestershire sauce	2	tablespoons tiny capers, drained
	Dash of Tabasco sauce		Salt and freshly ground black pepper to taste
¼	cup finely diced dill pickle		
¼	cup chopped fresh flat leaf (Italian) parsley		

🕐 *Plan to prepare at least 1 hour ahead.*

❻ Combine mayonnaise, lemon juice, Worcestershire sauce, and Tabasco sauce in a bowl. Fold in pickle, parsley, shallots, and capers. Season with salt and pepper. Refrigerate at least 1 hour before serving.

Note: *Refrigeration allows the flavors to blend.*

Thai Crab Cakes
with Cilantro-Peanut Sauce

A new twist on an old standby!

Yield: 4 servings

Crab Cakes

1¼	cups fresh bread crumbs	⅛	teaspoon cayenne pepper
1	cup chopped fresh bean sprouts	1	egg, lightly beaten
¼	cup finely chopped green onion	1	egg white, lightly beaten
¼	cup coarsely chopped fresh cilantro	1	pound lump crabmeat, picked over
2	tablespoons fresh lime juice	2	tablespoons olive oil, divided

Cilantro-Peanut Sauce

¼	cup balsamic vinegar	⅛	teaspoon salt
2½	tablespoons granulated sugar	1	clove garlic, minced
2	tablespoons brown sugar	2	tablespoons creamy peanut butter
2	tablespoons low-sodium soy sauce	½	cup chopped fresh cilantro
½	teaspoon dried red pepper flakes	2	tablespoons chopped fresh mint

🕐 *The sauce may be made up to 1 day ahead. The crab cakes may be assembled, covered tightly and refrigerated up to 8 hours ahead.*

6 Combine bread crumbs, bean sprouts, onion, cilantro, juice, cayenne pepper, egg, egg white, and crabmeat in a medium bowl. Cover and chill 1 hour. Divide mixture into 8 equal portions. Shape each portion into a ½-inch-thick patty.

6 Heat 1 tablespoon oil in a large nonstick skillet over medium heat. Add 4 patties and cook 3 minutes on each side or until lightly browned. Remove patties and keep warm. Wipe skillet clean with paper towels. Recoat skillet with remaining tablespoon oil and cook remaining 4 patties. Serve with Cilantro-Peanut Sauce.

6 To make sauce, combine vinegar, sugars, soy sauce, pepper flakes, salt, and garlic in a small saucepan. Bring to a boil, stirring frequently. Remove from heat.

6 Add peanut butter and stir with a whisk until smooth; cool. Stir in cilantro and mint.

Note: *Fresh bread crumbs make the difference in this recipe — don't use dried!*

Menu: *These are a marvelous beginning to an Asian-inspired menu. Try them before Pops' Singapore Noodles (page 188) or your favorite stir-fry.*

🍷 *Sancerre, Chardonnay*

Steamed Clams

This recipe may be served as an appetizer or an entrée

Yield: 4 to 6 servings

1	cup bottled clam juice	1	(28 ounce) can chopped tomatoes in juice
1	cup white wine	2	dozen little neck clams, scrubbed and rinsed
1	cup water	¼	cup chopped fresh flat leaf parsley for garnish
4	tablespoons butter		
4	cloves garlic, chopped		
2	tablespoons salt		
2	tablespoons freshly ground black pepper		

- Combine clam juice, wine, water, butter, garlic, salt, pepper, and tomatoes in a large pot. Bring to a boil.

- Add clams and steam about 5 minutes or until open.

- For an appetizer, divide clams among 4 to 6 large soup bowls. Ladle juice over clams and sprinkle with parsley.

- For an entrée, arrange clams on top of cooked hot pasta in a large serving bowl. Ladle juice over pasta and garnish with parsley. Serve hot.

Menu: *If made as an appetizer, serve with crusty French bread on the side, follow with Grilled Swordfish with Tomato Feta Relish (page 191). Or, make a supper out of the clams with pasta and Make-Ahead Caesar Salad (page 125).*

Pinot Grigio, Sauvignon Blanc, Chardonnay

I usually serve this recipe for first-time gatherings with new friends. This is not just to impress them, but more importantly, to be able to flash back to those special moments when I serve it again. It keeps the memory alive.

—Kim Donnelly

Spicy Peel and Eat Shrimp

Yield: 4 to 6 servings

2-3 **pounds large shrimp in the shell**	½ **cup Worcestershire sauce**
2 **lemons, thinly sliced**	2 **teaspoons salt**
4 **sticks butter**	3 **tablespoons freshly ground black pepper**
¾ **teaspoon dried rosemary**	¾ **teaspoon Tabasco sauce**
¾ **teaspoon dried basil**	3 **cloves garlic, crushed**

Marinade and shrimp/lemons may be prepared up to 1 day ahead. Warmed marinade and shrimp/lemons may be combined up to 4 hours prior to cooking.

In a large, shallow glass baking dish, place shrimp in a single layer. Cover with lemon slices.

In a saucepan, heat butter, rosemary, basil, Worcestershire sauce, salt, pepper, Tabasco sauce, and garlic. Bring to a boil. Pour mixture over shrimp and marinate up to 4 hours in refrigerator. Bring shrimp to room temperature before cooking.

When ready to cook, preheat oven to 450 degrees.

Bake shrimp for 15 to 20 minutes.

Note: *This tasty dish can be a bit messy; you may want to serve with extra napkins!*

Menu: *Try these festive shrimp with Zesty Corn and Red Pepper Salad (page 142), Zucchini Casserole (page 168) and cold beer.*

My favorite food is the Chilean Sea Bass from the Oakwood Club. When not in Dayton, I miss the old-fashioned steak houses with great service and top-notch food...such as the Oakwood Club and the Pine Club.

—Tim Davis, Chair Carillon Park Bell Board

Grilled Shrimp Skewers

This recipe comes from Kitty Sachs, former Dayton restaurateur

Yield: 4 to 6 servings

2	pounds (31 to 35 count) shrimp, peeled and deveined
3½	tablespoons extra virgin olive oil, or as needed
3½	tablespoons vegetable oil, or as needed

⅔	cup fine dry plain bread crumbs
½	teaspoon finely chopped garlic
2	teaspoons finely chopped fresh parsley
	Salt and freshly ground black pepper to taste

🕐 *Shrimp may be breaded and seasoned, covered with plastic wrap, and left at room temperature for up to 2 hours.*

- Rinse shrimp in cold water and pat dry thoroughly. Place shrimp in a large, shallow bowl.

- Add oils to shrimp, using as much as needed to coat shrimp. Add bread crumbs, using only as much as is needed to coat shrimp lightly and evenly. Add garlic, parsley, salt, and pepper. Toss to coat well. Let stand at least 20 minutes.

- Preheat boiler or grill.

- Skewer shrimp, tightly curling the tail end inward so skewer goes through shrimp 3 times to prevent slipping during cooking.

- Cook shrimp close to the heat source for about 2 minutes on first side and 1½ minutes on second side, or just until they form a thin, golden crust. Serve immediately.

Menu: *For a tasty summer meal, try pairing the shrimp with Lemon Pasta Salad (page 135) and grilled zucchini. For dessert, serve Mixed Berry Crumble (page 274) and vanilla ice cream.*

🍷 *White Burgundy or Bordeaux, Chardonnay*

Seafood storage tips from Jay's Restaurant:

- Seafood should be stored as close to 35°F as possible to maintain "fresh taste" quality. It is best to store fish in the back of the refrigerator where cool air is less likely to escape during opening and closing.

- When you arrive home, put your fish in the freezer for 20-30 minutes (this brings down the temperature for storage). Fish will not freeze until it reaches 27°F.

- To store shellfish in the shell: do not put in water; instead, cover with a damp cloth or damp paper towel.

- To store shucked shellfish: clams, oysters and mussels all need to be left covered in their own liquid, and wrapped well.

Shrimp Scampi with Red Bell Peppers and Zucchini

It tastes as good as it looks!

Yield: 4 to 6 servings

1½	sticks butter	¼	cup drained capers
2	red bell peppers, cut into ½x2-inch strips	2	pounds large raw shrimp, peeled and deveined
¾	pound zucchini, cut into ½-inch rounds	⅓	cup chopped fresh basil
¾	cup chopped shallot (about 4 shallots)	1-1½	pounds dry angel hair pasta, cooked and drained, or 3 to 4 cups hot cooked rice (optional)
¼	cup finely chopped garlic		

⏲ *Vegetables may be sautéed up to 4 hours ahead. After adding capers and transferring to a baking dish, allow vegetables to cool. Cover and let stand at room temperature.*

☙ Preheat oven to 450 degrees.

☙ Melt butter in a large heavy skillet over high heat. Add bell pepper, zucchini, shallot and garlic. Sauté 4 minutes or until shallot begins to soften. Stir in capers. Transfer mixture to a large baking dish.

☙ Mix shrimp into vegetables. Bake, stirring occasionally, about 10 minutes or until shrimp are cooked through. Sprinkle with basil.

☙ Serve immediately over pasta, if desired.

Note: *For added presentation, leave tails on shrimp when cleaning. This recipe will serve 6 to 8 if served over angel hair pasta or rice, and sprinkled with Parmesan or feta cheese.*

Menu: *Serve with Greek Peasant Salad (page 124), or Artichoke and Hearts of Palm Salad (page 121). Warm Chocolate Tarts (page 260) make a fine finish.*

🍷 *White Burgundy, Chardonnay*

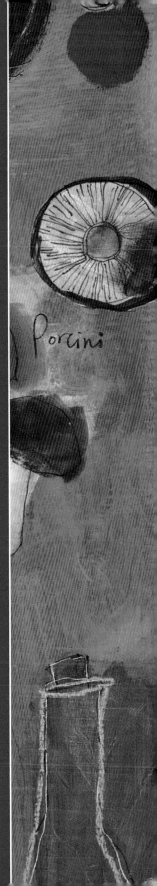

Flights of Fancy

POULTRY

HAWTHORNE HILL

FLIGHTS OF FANCY

As Dayton and the world celebrate 100 years of powered flight, we're inspired to remember what a magnificent achievement this truly was. Beekeeper Amos Ives Root, of Medina, gave his eyewitness account of one of the first flights at Huffman Prairie to *Scientific American* and other publications, but it was so unbelievable that it was never printed. Root later published his prophetic article, titled "What God Hath Wrought," in his own magazine, *The Gleanings in Bee Culture.*

The machine is held until ready to start by a sort of trap to be sprung when all is ready; then with a tremendous flapping and snapping of the four-cylinder engine, the huge machine springs aloft. When it first turned that circle, and came near the starting point, I was right in front of it; and I said then, and I believe still, it was ... the grandest sight of my life. Imagine a locomotive that has left its track and is climbing up in the air right toward you — a locomotive without any wheels, we will say, but with white wings instead ... coming right toward you with a tremendous flap of its propellers, and you will have something like what I saw ... These two brothers have probably not even a faint glimpse of what their discovery is going to bring to the children of men.

In his 1996 book, *Grand Eccentrics*, MARK BERNSTEIN points out: "Wilbur and Orville Wright are still underestimated; there still lingers the notion the Wrights were only the luckiest or most determined in a flurry of turn-of-the-century would-be flyers, and, therefore, the first to cross the line. It would be fairer to say that, previous to Wilbur and Orville, no one in flight had done anything fundamentally right; following the Wrights, no one in flight did anything fundamentally differently. Mankind had sought wings for centuries; the Wrights provided those wings in less than five years, for about one thousand dollars, working part-time."

Chicken Alouette in Puff Pastry

An elegant entrée

Yield: 6 servings

1	(17¼ ounce) package frozen puff pastry sheets, thawed	½	teaspoon salt
1	(4 ounce) container garlic-and-spice Alouette cheese	⅛	teaspoon freshly ground black pepper
6	boneless, skinless chicken breasts	1	egg, beaten
		1	tablespoon water
			Kale leaves for garnish (optional)

🕐 *Pastry "bundles" can be completely assembled, covered and refrigerated up to 2 hours ahead.*

- Preheat oven to 400 degrees.

- Unfold pastry sheets. On a lightly floured surface, roll each sheet into a 12x14-inch rectangle.

- Cut 1 sheet into four 7x6-inch rectangles; cut second sheet into two 7x6-inch rectangles and one 12x7-inch rectangle. Set large rectangle aside. Shape small rectangles into ovals by trimming corners.

- Spread cheese evenly over ovals.

- Sprinkle chicken with salt and pepper; place in the center of each oval. Lightly moisten edges of ovals with water. Fold top and bottom edges over chicken, then fold opposite sides together and press to seal. Place bundle, seam side down, on a lightly greased baking sheet.

- Cut remaining pastry into twenty-four ½-inch strips. With the palm of your hand, roll each strip into a twist. Braid two twists together, forming a pastry rope. Center one rope horizontally and one vertically across each bundle, tucking ends under and trimming away excess.

- Combine egg and water; brush over bundles.

- Bake 25 minutes or until golden. Serve on kale leaves.

Menu: *After starting the meal with French Mushroom Soup (page 105), serve this lovely dish with mesclun and Red Wine Vinaigrette (page 98), Provençal Roasted Tomatoes (page 166) and steamed green beans. Make Chocolate Pâté (page 258) for dessert.*

🍷 *Chardonnay, White Burgundy, Red Zinfandel*

I made this chicken recipe for a dinner party of 12 people that I didn't know. My oven would not stay at temperature and I had to keep turning it back on. It took three times as long, but no one knew the difference, and by the time dinner was served, we all were good friends!

—Carol Dickerson

Chicken in Pastry Squares

Simple recipe with an elegant appearance

Yield: 4 servings

4	ounces cream cheese, softened	1	tablespoon chopped pimiento (optional)
2	tablespoons butter, softened		
2	cups cubed or slivered cooked chicken	1-2	teaspoons chopped green onion
¼	teaspoon salt	1	(4 ounce) can water chestnuts, coarsely chopped
⅛	teaspoon freshly ground black pepper	1	(8 ounce) container refrigerated crescent rolls
2-3	tablespoons milk	¾	cup crushed croutons
		2	tablespoons butter, melted

🕐 *Cook and cube chicken up to 1 day ahead. Make entire chicken mix up to 8 hours ahead; place it in crescent rolls just before cooking.*

🍳 Preheat oven to 350 degrees.

🍳 Blend cream cheese and 2 tablespoons softened butter until smooth. Add chicken, salt, pepper, milk, pimiento, onion, and water chestnuts.

🍳 Separate crescent dough into 4 rectangles. Firmly press perforations to seal.

🍳 Divide chicken mixture evenly and place in center of each rectangle. Pull 4 corners of each rectangle to center above chicken mixture; twist slightly. Spread corners and pinch to seal; there may be small openings. Place on a baking sheet.

🍳 Brush tops of squares with 2 tablespoons melted butter. Sprinkle with crouton crumbs.

🍳 Bake 20 to 25 minutes, or until golden brown.

Menu: *Try pairing this dish with Blueberry, Orange and Cherry Salad (page 132) for a delightful luncheon. Make Blackberry Mini-Tarts (page 271) for dessert.*

🍷 *Sauvignon Blanc, Chardonnay*

Howard Solganik's Chicken 2x3x4 ⭐

Yield: 4 to 6 servings

Double Crust Pastry

3	cups flour	4	eggs
	Dash of salt	2	tablespoons lemon juice
2	sticks unsalted butter		

Chicken

2	whole chickens	1½	cups diced, unpeeled new potatoes
2	pounds carrots		
1	bunch celery	1	(10 ounce) package frozen peas
	Fresh parsley	3	tablespoons flour
1	stick unsalted butter	1	cup milk
3	lemons, sliced		Salt and freshly ground black pepper to taste
	Tarragon		
8	medium onions, chopped		Thyme to taste
1	pound fresh mushrooms, sliced		Dash of Tabasco sauce or to taste
1	clove garlic, crushed	1	egg yolk

- To prepare pastry, combine flour and salt in a bowl. Cut in butter until mixture crumbs are pea-sized. Mix in eggs and lemon juice. Refrigerate until ready to roll out and fill. When ready to use, roll out dough into 2 pastry circles. Line a 9-inch pie plate with 1 circle. Reserve other for top crust.

- Remove breasts from chickens. Split each breast in half and wrap separately in foil with some chopped carrot, celery, parsley, butter, lemon slices, and tarragon in each packet. Refrigerate until ready to bake at 350 degrees for about 45 minutes. Cook remaining chicken with 1 chopped onion, 1 carrot and 1 celery stalk in boiling water until tender. Cool and remove meat from bones, discarding skin and fat, reserving broth.

- Preheat oven to 450 degrees.

- To prepare pie filling, sauté 1 cup minced onion, 1 cup sliced mushroom and garlic until softened. Remove from pan and set aside.

- In same pan, mix potatoes and 2 cups of reserved broth. Add 1 cup peas, 1½ cups chopped carrot and 1½ cups chopped celery. Simmer until vegetables are tender. Add to mushroom mixture and set aside.

- In same pan, melt 3 tablespoons butter. Blend in 3 tablespoons flour; cook 1 minute. Gradually stir in 1 cup reserved broth, milk, salt, pepper, thyme, and Tabasco sauce. Cook until thickened.

- Drain vegetables, draining liquid back into reserved broth. Use this broth to make a soup, along with any other remaining ingredients.

- Combine drained vegetables, sauce and some of chicken; mix well. Pour into prepared pastry crust. Place second crust on top. Make a hole in top of crust for steam to escape. Decorate top of crust with pastry scraps. Brush crust with egg yolk.

- Bake 15 minutes. Reduce heat to 350 degrees; bake 35 minutes, or until browned.

Menu: *Serve with a green salad and Mama's Rolls (page 81).*

🍷 *Chardonnay, White Burgundy, Red Zinfandel*

Shortly after I moved back to Dayton, having spent the previous 10 years in Washington, D.C., I entered a cooking contest with the "PM Magazine" television show. I remember the contest was judged at Overbey's Emporium, down in the old Arcade. I am happy to say that I won. The recipe, which I created, was called Chicken 2x3x4.

—Howard Solganik, Owner

Wrapsody Restaurant and Solganik Catering

Judith Ann's Apricot Chicken

So easy and tasty!

Yield: 4 servings

4	boneless, skinless chicken breasts, cut into strips	2	beef bouillon cubes
3	tablespoons flour	1	large onion, chopped
1	tablespoon curry powder	1	cup water
2	teaspoons salt	1	cup apricot preserves
¼	cup vegetable oil	2	tablespoons lemon juice
1	tablespoon sugar	2	tablespoons soy sauce

Cut chicken into pieces and coat with flour mixture.

Preheat oven to 350 degrees.

Shake chicken in a mixture of flour, curry and salt.

Brown chicken in vegetable oil in a skillet. Place chicken in a baking dish, reserving drippings in skillet. Add sugar, beef cubes, onion, water, preserves, lemon juice, and soy sauce to skillet. Heat to a boil, crushing beef cubes. Pour mixture over chicken.

Bake 1 hour.

Menu: *Accompany the chicken with white rice, Green Beans with Toasted Pecans and Blue Cheese (page 156) and sautéed mushrooms.*

Chardonnay, White Burgundy, Red Zinfandel

Ever wonder what happened to the famous first glider? Kitty Hawk, North Carolina Postmaster, Bill Tate, who had housed the Wright brothers until they set up camp, took it apart and gave the sateen wing covering to his wife, who made new dresses for their two little girls.

Poulet Sauté Provençal

French country cooking at its simplest

Yield: 4 servings

1	(3½ pound) chicken, cut into serving pieces	1	tablespoon finely chopped fresh rosemary
	Salt and freshly ground black pepper to taste	2	cloves garlic, crushed
		2	tablespoons minced shallots
2	tablespoons olive oil	½	cup dry white wine
1	tablespoon butter	¾	cup chicken broth
		1	tablespoon butter

Ⓖ Season chicken with salt and pepper.

Ⓖ Heat olive oil and 1 tablespoon butter in a heavy skillet large enough to hold all the chicken pieces in 1 layer. When hot, add chicken, skin-side down. Cook over medium heat for 10 minutes, or until golden brown on 1 side. Turn chicken and add rosemary and garlic. Cook 10 minutes.

Ⓖ Pour half the fat out of the skillet. Add shallots and cook briefly. Add wine and broth, stirring to dissolve the brown particles on the bottom and sides of skillet. Cook 10 minutes longer.

Ⓖ Remove chicken to a dish and keep warm. Continue to cook sauce until reduced to ¾ cup. Add 1 tablespoon butter. Return chicken to skillet along with any juices that accumulated on the dish. Bring to a boil and serve immediately.

Menu: *Create a rustic menu with roasted potatoes, Provençal Roasted Tomatoes (page 166) and mesclun with Red Wine Vinaigrette (page 98). Finish the meal with Raspberry Pear Tart (page 271).*

Ⓨ *French Rose, Red Zinfandel, Red Bordeaux*

I am a surgeon. The first Thanksgiving that I cooked a turkey, I had to call my mother to find out how to get the neck and gizzards out of the turkey cavity. She said just reach in and pull them out with your hand. I could not fathom reaching into a body cavity with my bare hands! I had no surgical gloves in my kitchen, so I improvised and used hot dog tongs to grab the neck and gizzards out of the turkey! Yuck!

—Deanna Chapman

Nonna Zucco's Polenta and Pollo ✩

Yield: 4 servings

Pollo (Chicken)

2	cloves garlic, minced		Salt and freshly ground black pepper to taste
1	medium onion, quartered and thinly sliced	1	(28 ounce) can tomato puree
2-3	tablespoons extra virgin olive oil	¼	cup cold water
4-6	boneless chicken breasts	½	teaspoon crushed basil (optional)

Polenta

3	cups water	2	cups yellow cornmeal
1	tablespoon salt	1	cup cold water

❀ To make chicken, sauté garlic and onion in oil in a skillet for about 5 minutes on medium heat.

❀ Meanwhile, wash and pat dry chicken. Season chicken with salt and pepper, if desired, and add to skillet. Cook, turning frequently, until golden brown.

❀ Add tomato puree, water and basil to skillet. Bring to a boil. Reduce heat to low. Cover and simmer, stirring frequently, for about 45 minutes, or until chicken is tender. Serve immediately with polenta. Use sauce in skillet for polenta "gravy."

❀ To make polenta, bring 3 cups of water and salt to a boil.

❀ Meanwhile, mix cornmeal with 1 cup cold water. Stir until smooth. Use a wooden spoon or wire whisk to stir cornmeal mixture into boiling water. Cook, stirring constantly to prevent lumps from forming and to prevent burning, over medium heat for 5 to 10 minutes, or until polenta thickens and begins to boil (like a pudding). Transfer to a dish and shape and smooth polenta with a wooden spoon like meatloaf. Keep warm until ready to serve.

❀ To serve, slice polenta into 1-inch thick slices with a string or a sharp knife. Place slices on a serving plate and spoon polenta "gravy" on top. Serve with pollo.

Menu: *Serve with Zucchini Casserole (page 168) or Zucchini Imperial (page 168).*

🍷 *Chianti*

Jerk Chicken

Yield: 6 to 8 servings

2	cups finely chopped green onion	1	tablespoon English-style dry mustard
2	Scotch bonnet or habanero chiles, seeded and minced	2	cloves garlic
1	tablespoon Scotch bonnet pepper sauce (try Peppa-Po sauce)	1	tablespoon salt
		2	teaspoons sugar
		1½	teaspoons crumbled dried thyme
2	tablespoons soy sauce	1	teaspoon cinnamon
2	tablespoons fresh lime juice	5	pounds chicken parts, wing tips discarded (or use boneless chicken breasts)
5	teaspoons allspice		

Mix marinade and marinate chicken in plastic bags up to 2 days ahead. Or, freeze in the bags, then thaw and proceed with recipe.

- To make the marinade, combine all ingredients except chicken in a food processor or blender; puree.
- Divide chicken into 2 large plastic bags. Spoon marinade over chicken, coating well. Seal bags, pressing out excess air. Marinate chicken in refrigerator, turning bags several times, for at least 24 hours, or up to 2 days.
- When ready to cook, oil and preheat grill.
- Grill chicken, covered, for 10 to 12 minutes on each side, or until cooked through. Cook in batches if necessary.

Note: *Remember to wear rubber gloves (or use zip-top bags as "gloves") when chopping chile peppers.*

Menu: *Enjoy this chicken with Sweet Potato Salad with Rosemary-Honey Vinaigrette (page 141).*

Red Zinfandel

"Orville Wright dropped out of kindergarten on the fourth day of class. He neglected to inform his mother that he had given up on formal education. He continued, as before, to leave home each morning, to return home each noon and speak brightly of the day's activities. Actually, he was playing at the home of a friend, with an eye on the clock. His mother did not learn of her son's truancy until several weeks had passed, when she went to school to see how he was faring. Orville, unabashed, returned to class."

From *Grand Eccentrics*, by Mark Bernstein

Mexican Chicken Kiev

They'll keep coming back for more

Yield: 6 to 8 servings

8	boneless, skinless chicken breasts
1	(7 ounce) can diced green chiles
4	ounces Monterey Jack cheese, cut into 8 strips
½	cup fine dry bread crumbs
½	cup Parmesan cheese

1	teaspoon chili powder
¼	teaspoon ground cumin
½	teaspoon salt
¼	teaspoon freshly ground black pepper
6	tablespoons butter, melted

Dish must be assembled at least 4 hours, or up to 24 hours, before baking.

⚬ Pound chicken to ¼-inch thick. Place 2 tablespoons chiles and 1 strip Monterey Jack cheese in the center of chicken. Roll up and tuck ends under.

⚬ Combine bread crumbs, Parmesan cheese, chili powder, cumin, salt and pepper in a bowl. Dip chicken in melted butter, then roll in bread crumb mixture. Place chicken, seam-side down, in a 9x13-inch baking dish. Drizzle with remaining melted butter.

⚬ Cover and chill 4 hours, or overnight.

⚬ When ready to cook, preheat oven to 400 degrees.

⚬ Bake 20 minutes.

Note: *For an extra "kick," use Pepper-Jack cheese. Best if made a day ahead of time and chilled overnight.*

Menu: *Pair this dish with Cilantro Cole Slaw (page 126), and white rice tossed with olive oil, lime juice, salt and pepper.*

🍷 *Red Zinfandel, Merlot*

The Wright Brothers made more than 100 flights on Huffman Prairie perfecting the Flyer III, which became the world's first practical airplane. It could take off and land under complete control. By late 1905, it could bank turn, fly circles, fly figure 8's and stay aloft for more than 30 minutes.

Pollo Asado

Tasty Mexican-style barbecued chicken

Yield: 4 servings

1	(6 ounce) can unsweetened pineapple juice (¾ cup)
2	tablespoons lime juice
1	tablespoon vinegar
2	large cloves garlic, crushed and minced
1	teaspoon salt

½	teaspoon crumbled dried oregano
¼	teaspoon mild chili powder
⅛	teaspoon freshly ground black pepper
1	tablespoon vegetable oil
1	(3½ to 4 pound) chicken, cut into pieces

🕐 *Plan to mix marinade and marinate chicken 1 day ahead.*

6   To make marinade, combine all ingredients except chicken in a small bowl.

6   Place chicken in a shallow glass baking dish. Add marinade, turning chicken to coat. Cover and refrigerate overnight. Turn chicken at least once while marinating. Bring chicken to room temperature before cooking.

6   When ready to cook, preheat grill to medium-hot.

6   Drain chicken, reserving marinade for basting. Grill 25 to 45 minutes, or until juices run clear. Cooking time varies depending upon size of chicken pieces and heat of grill. Turn chicken every 10 minutes. After turning, baste with reserved marinade. Do not overcook or skin will become charred.

Note: *This is a great chicken recipe to use in other Mexican dishes; i.e., burritos, tacos, fajitas, quesadillas.*

Menu: *Offer the chicken with Mexicana Rice (page 161) and a green salad.*

🍷 *Red Zinfandel*

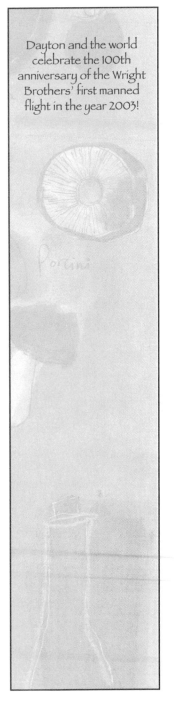

Dayton and the world celebrate the 100th anniversary of the Wright Brothers' first manned flight in the year 2003!

Porcini

Holly's Chicken Enchiladas

You can't go wrong with this wonderful dish

Yield: 8 servings

1	(16 ounce) container sour cream, divided
1	(7 ounce) can diced green chiles
4	large green onions, chopped
½	cup chopped fresh cilantro
1½	teaspoons ground cumin
2	cups diced cooked chicken
1	cup shredded sharp cheddar cheese

	Salt and freshly ground black pepper to taste
8	(8 inch) flour tortillas
1	(8 ounce) package cream cheese, cut lengthwise into 8 strips
3	cups mild picante sauce
1	cup grated sharp cheddar cheese

🕐 *Enchiladas can be assembled up to 3 hours ahead. Chill until ready to cook.*

❻ Preheat oven to 350 degrees.

❻ Combine 1¾ cups sour cream, chiles, onion, cilantro, and cumin in a large bowl. Mix in chicken and 1 cup cheddar cheese. Season with salt and pepper.

❻ Spread a generous ½ cup of filling down the center of each tortilla. Top filling with a strip of cream cheese. Roll up each tortilla, enclosing filling. Arrange enchiladas, seam-side down, in a greased, 9x13-inch baking dish.

❻ Pour picante sauce over enchiladas.

❻ Bake, covered, for about 45 minutes, or until sauce bubbles and enchiladas are heated through. Uncover and sprinkle with 1 cup cheddar cheese. Bake 5 minutes, or until cheese melts. Top enchiladas with remaining sour cream.

Menu: *Serve after Jane's Famous Gazpacho (page 107) with Black Bean, Corn and Avocado Salad (page 143). End with a Brownie Torte (page 265).*

🍷 *Red Spanish, Chilean Red, Red Zinfandel*

A predecessor of the Dayton Air Show, the International Air Races were held in Dayton in October 1924. This event attracted 100,000 spectators!

Summer Lime Chicken Breasts

The lime juice and cilantro are very refreshing!

Yield: 6 servings

6	boneless, skinless chicken breasts	2	tablespoons minced fresh cilantro or parsley
⅓	cup olive oil	½	teaspoon freshly ground black pepper
	Juice of 3 limes		Minced fresh cilantro or parsley for garnish
4	cloves garlic, minced		

🕐 *Plan to prepare recipe at least 1 hour before grilling. Marinade can be made up to 1 day ahead. Chicken can be trimmed and flattened early in the day, and marinated up to 4 hours before grilling.*

🍳 Trim fat and middle tendon from chicken. Pound between wax paper to flatten.

🍳 Combine olive oil, lime juice, garlic, cilantro, and pepper in a large zip-top bag. Add chicken and seal bag. Turn bag to coat chicken; marinate in refrigerator for at least 1 hour. Turn bag occasionally while marinating.

🍳 When ready to cook, preheat grill.

🍳 Grill chicken for 2 minutes on each side, or until done. Remove to a serving platter; garnish with extra cilantro or parsley.

🍳 Alternatively, chicken may be baked on a greased baking sheet at 350 degrees for 30 minutes.

Note: *Sliced leftovers are a great topping for salads.*

Menu: *Serve after Tomato, Garlic, Cilantro Salsa (page 99) and chips. Brazilian Black Beans (page 150) and Peperonata (page 158) are lovely sides.*

🍷 *Chardonnay, White Burgundy*

We rarely had turkey for Thanksgiving in my Chinese family, but Peking duck instead. Patience was the key ingredient to making Peking duck. Dad spent all day checking and basting the duck hanging in the oven so the skin would be crispy and the meat tender. When the duck was done, Dad would carve the skin off and we'd eagerly wrap slices up in pancakes with scallions and hoisin sauce. The leftover duck meat and bones would be used to make duck stew. Nothing went to waste!

—Irene Pang Wong

The Best Chicken Parmesan

Serve with plenty of Parmesan cheese

Yield: 4 servings

Simple Tomato Sauce with Basil and Garlic

2	medium cloves garlic, minced	¼	teaspoon dried oregano
¼	cup extra virgin olive oil	¼	teaspoon sugar
1	(28 ounce) can crushed tomatoes		Salt and freshly ground black
½	teaspoon dried basil		pepper to taste

Chicken Parmesan

1	egg	4	(4 to 5 ounce) trimmed chicken
	Salt and freshly ground black		breasts, pounded to ¼-inch
	pepper		thick
½-1	cup dry bread crumbs	¼	cup olive oil
	(we prefer Panko)	¾	cup shredded mozzarella cheese
8	ounces dry spaghetti or linguine	¼	cup Parmesan cheese, plus extra
			for passing

⏲ *Sauce can be made up to 3 days ahead.*

- In a large saucepan or Dutch oven, heat garlic and oil over medium-high heat until garlic starts to sizzle. Stir in tomatoes, basil, oregano, sugar, salt, and pepper. Bring to a simmer; cook 10 to 12 minutes, or until sauce thickens and flavors meld. Cover and keep warm.

- Beat egg with a heaping ¼ teaspoon of salt in a shallow dish. Combine bread crumbs, a heaping ¼ teaspoon salt and pepper in a separate shallow dish.

- Cook spaghetti in a large pot of boiling water with 2 teaspoons salt until al dente. Drain just before serving.

- Preheat broiler.

- Working with one at a time, dip both sides of each chicken cutlet into egg, then dredge in bread crumb mixture. Set cutlets on a large wire rack set over a jelly-roll pan.

- Heat oil in a 12-inch skillet over medium-high heat. Add cutlets; sauté 5 to 6 minutes, or until golden brown on each side.

- Wash and dry wire racks to remove any egg residue; return to jelly-roll pan. Transfer cutlets to wire rack, and top each with equal portions of mozzarella and Parmesan cheeses. Place jelly-roll pan 4 to 5 inches from heat source; broil chicken about 3 minutes, or until cheese melts and is starting to brown.

- Place a cutlet and a portion of drained spaghetti on each individual serving plate. Spoon 2 or 3 tablespoons sauce over each cutlet. Add sauce to spaghetti as desired. Serve immediately with extra Parmesan cheese on the side.

Note: *Try to find "Panko," the Japanese bread crumbs. They are light, crispy and wonderful! Also, our favorite canned tomatoes are the Muir Glen brand.*

Menu: *Start with an Artichoke and Hearts of Palm Salad (page 121). Offer steamed broccoli or green beans with the dish.*

 Chianti, Barolo, Brunello

Tex Mex Chicken 'N Rice Casserole

A great casserole recipe for large groups

Yield: 12 servings

1	cup chopped onion
2	tablespoons margarine, butter or olive oil
1	(7 ounce) package chicken rice and vermicelli mix
1	cup dry long grain rice
2	(14½ ounce) cans chicken broth
2½	cups water
4	cups chopped cooked chicken or turkey
4	medium tomatoes, chopped

1	(4 ounce) can diced green chiles, drained
2	tablespoons snipped fresh basil, or 2 teaspoons dried
1	tablespoon chili powder
1	teaspoon cumin seed, crushed, or ¼ teaspoon ground cumin
⅛-¼	teaspoon freshly ground black pepper
1	cup shredded cheddar cheese

🕐 *Casserole can be made up to 12 hours ahead and then reheated.*

🌀 In a 3-quart saucepan, sauté onion in margarine until tender. Stir in rice mix with seasoning packet, and dry long grain rice. Cook and stir 2 minutes. Stir in broth and water; bring to a boil. Reduce heat and cover. Simmer 20 minutes; liquid will not be fully absorbed.

🌀 Preheat oven to 425 degrees.

🌀 Transfer rice mixture to a very large mixing bowl. Stir in chicken, tomatoes, chiles, basil, chili powder, cumin, and black pepper. Transfer to a 3-quart casserole dish.

🌀 Bake, covered, for 20 minutes. Uncover and sprinkle with cheese. Bake 5 minutes longer.

Menu: *Serve with Southwestern Baked Beans (page 149), and a big green salad with black olives and artichoke hearts.*

🍷 *Chardonnay, Merlot*

Visit Dayton's Aviation Trail—historical sites that tell of man's conquest of the air.

The Wright Cycle Company

Carillon Historical Park

Kettering-Moraine Museum

Wright B Flyer

Hawthorn Hill

Woodland Cemetery and Arboretum

United States Air Force Museum and the National Aviation Hall of Fame

Wright Brothers Memorial

Huffman Prairie Flying Field

Wright State University

WACO Museum and Aviation Learning Center

Chicken Tetrazzini ❋ 🚲

This classic makes a comeback

Yield: 8 servings

Casserole

4	whole chicken breasts	2	tablespoons sherry
1	onion, chopped	¾	pound very thin spaghetti, broken into thirds
1	cup sliced fresh mushrooms		
2	tablespoons butter	2	cups Veloute Sauce

Veloute Sauce

4	tablespoons butter, melted	2	cups chicken broth
6	tablespoons flour	½	cup heavy cream
½	teaspoon salt	1	cup Romano or Parmesan cheese
½	teaspoon paprika	4	dashes paprika

🕐 *May be frozen up to 3 months before baking. Thaw and heat according to directions.*

⑥ Preheat oven to 350 degrees.

⑥ Put chicken in foil with onion. Bake 30 minutes or until tender. Cool and tear chicken into tiny pieces; reserve onion.

⑥ Sauté mushrooms in butter. Season with sherry and set aside.

⑥ Cook spaghetti according to package directions; drain.

⑥ To make sauce, melt butter in a medium saucepan over low heat. Stir in flour, salt and paprika. Cook and stir until a smooth paste forms. Slowly stir in broth until well-mixed. Cook over medium heat until sauce thickens to a heavy cream consistency. Remove from heat. Stir in cream a little at a time, stopping before sauce becomes too thin.

⑥ Place drained spaghetti in a shallow, 3-quart baking dish. Spoon half of sauce over the top. Arrange chicken, mushrooms with sherry, and reserved onion on spaghetti. Top with remaining sauce. Sprinkle cheese on top. Add paprika for color.

⑥ Bake at 400 degrees for 20 minutes.

Menu: *Just add a green salad with Red Wine Vinaigrette (page 98).*

🍷 *Chardonnay, Red Zinfandel*

A big market-house opened in Dayton in 1845. At that time, a person could buy eggs for 2 cents a dozen, butter for 4 cents a pound, and chickens for 50 cents a dozen (but you had to kill and clean them yourself).

Warm Chicken and Vegetables Wrapped in Flatbread

A winner from one of Dayton's favorite grocers, Dorothy Lane Market

Yield: 8 sandwiches

4	cloves garlic, crushed	1	large tomato, seeded and diced
	Freshly ground black pepper	4	large mushrooms
4	small boneless, skinless chicken breasts	2	medium carrots, julienned
2	sweet onions, sliced ½-inch thick	1	(8 ounce) jar roasted red peppers, thinly sliced
	Kosher salt	1	(14 ounce) can hearts of palm, drained and thinly sliced
¼	cup balsamic vinegar		
1	tablespoon ground cumin	8	lavash-style flatbreads, or large tortillas
2	cloves garlic, minced		
	Salt and freshly ground black pepper to taste	16	sprigs fresh cilantro

🕐 *Grill chicken beforehand. Make marinade a day ahead.*

◎ Combine 4 cloves garlic and pepper; rub over chicken. Grill chicken and onion slices until done. Separate onion into rings. Season with salt as desired. Thinly slice chicken across the grain on the bias.

◎ To make the marinade, combine vinegar, cumin, 2 cloves garlic, and salt and pepper in a bowl.

◎ Add tomato, mushrooms, carrots, red pepper and hearts of palm to marinade. Mix gently. Add cooked onion to marinade; toss to mix.

◎ To assemble, cut each flatbread into a 6x12-inch rectangle. Divide vegetables among rectangles, placing them along one side. Arrange chicken on vegetables. Top with cilantro. Roll lavash tightly to form a roll. Slice off the ends.

Note: *Pitas also work well.*

Menu: *Serve with Spring Island Couscous Salad (page 136) for a nice casual lunch or dinner.*

🍷 *Chianti*

Recently, I planned a luncheon for some friends. I planned to make salads the night before so I wouldn't have to do it in the morning, but I did not plan on having two neighbors ask me to watch their children for "just an hour." The kids finally left and I got my own kids to bed. By this time it was close to 9:00. Earlier, I had put too much in the garbage disposal and it broke. I started on the chicken salad and my husband started fixing the disposal. At about the exact point that I had measured all of my ingredients and put them in the bowl, my husband's hand slipped, and he sprayed all the garbage disposal slime straight into the bowl of "almost" chicken salad! Neither of us said a word. He dumped the entire bowl of ingredients into the sink and I slowly started over.

—Kellie Rhodes

Turkey and Wild Rice Casserole

Excellent recipe to use with Thanksgiving leftovers!

Yield: 8 servings

1	large onion, sliced
2	medium zucchini, sliced
½	cup sliced celery
8	ounces fresh mushrooms, sliced
4	tablespoons butter or margarine
4	cups coarsely chopped cooked turkey
2	cups sliced carrot
1⅓	cups turkey broth
1	(10¾ ounce) can condensed cream of celery soup
1	(10¾ ounce) can condensed cream of chicken soup
¼	teaspoon thyme
¼	teaspoon marjoram
1	(6 ounce) package long grain and wild rice mix, prepared as directed on package
¼	cup chopped fresh parsley for garnish

🕐 *Turkey can be cooked up to 3 days ahead. Onions, zucchini and celery can be sautéed 1 day ahead. Entire casserole can be baked up to 8 hours ahead, then reheated.*

6 Preheat oven to 350 degrees.

6 Sauté onion, zucchini, celery, and mushrooms in butter until almost tender. Transfer to a 3-quart casserole dish. Add turkey; mix to combine. Add carrot, broth, undiluted soups, thyme, marjoram, and prepared rice. Mix lightly.

6 Bake, covered, for about 1 hour. Sprinkle with parsley to garnish.

Menu: *Serve with Watercress Salad with Cranberries and Pecans (page 128).*

🍷 *Chardonnay, Red Zinfandel*

A wonderful Japanese family lived next door to my parents. We enjoyed Japanese food in their home, and loved teaching them to make gravy at Thanksgiving and Buckeyes at Christmas.

One year, our Japanese friends drove to Dayton to join us for Thanksgiving. Just before the turkey was served, our Japanese friend told us that his wife would prepare something in the kitchen. She unboxed all the ingredients to assemble sushi—delicious morsels of crab, rice, avocado, and cucumbers all rolled up in seaweed. Everyone helped roll the sushi, and we ate so much that we had to postpone the turkey for three hours until we were hungry again!

We loved having these wonderful people as part of our family! I often remember this picture—my father, my husband's father, and our Japanese friend all snoozing in the family room—it was a symbol of love and food both shared!

—Cynthia Klinck, Director Washington-Centerville Public Library

Juicy Marinated Turkey Breast

An oven bag is the secret to this amazing recipe

Yield: 6 to 8 servings

1	oven bag	2	tablespoons salt
1	(5 to 7 pound) turkey breast	2	tablespoons freshly ground black pepper
2	tablespoons chopped fresh parsley	1	cup apple cider vinegar
¼	cup vegetable oil		

Recipe must be prepared 5 hours before serving. Turkey can be cooked 2 to 3 days ahead and served at room temperature, or in salads or sandwiches.

- Preheat oven to 300 degrees.
- Prepare oven bag for cooking as directed on package.
- Place turkey breast in bag and place in a shallow roasting pan.
- Combine parsley, oil, salt, pepper, and vinegar; pour over turkey breast. Seal bag.
- Bake 4 to 5 hours, or until browned and done. Serve hot with pan drippings.

Menu: *For a special comfort-food meal, accompany the turkey with Whipped Potatoes Paprika (page 160) and Green Beans with Toasted Pecans and Blue Cheese (page 156).*

Red Zinfandel, Chianti

Combining technology and showmanship, the annual United States Air and Trade Show has been drawing record crowds for more than 25 years, entertaining visitors with precision flying, daredevil acts and lots of hot dogs!

Southwestern Tenderloin of Turkey Breast

Yield: 4 servings

1	(3 pound) turkey tenderloin	2	tablespoons minced garlic
¼	cup finely chopped green onion	1	teaspoon chili powder
2	tablespoons fresh lime juice	¾	teaspoon hot pepper sauce
2	tablespoons tequila	½	teaspoon dried oregano
1	tablespoon plus 1 teaspoon olive oil	½	teaspoon ground cumin

🕐 *Make marinade the day before. Turkey can also be marinated up to 24 hours ahead.*

6 Combine all ingredients and refrigerate. Marinate 1 hour or overnight.

6 Grill turkey, using indirect method, for 8 minutes per side, or until meat is no longer pink in the center.

Note: *The indirect method of grilling is as follows: light only one side of grill; on opposite side, under the grill (but on top of the coals) place a foil pan to catch drippings. Place meat on the side with the pan, put grill lid down and cook.*

Menu: *Accompany the turkey with Zesty Corn and Red Pepper Salad (page 142) and Southwestern Baked Beans (page 149).*

🍷 *Red Zinfandel, Chianti*

Aunt Kate only made caramel popcorn for special celebrations. One Thanksgiving Eve, she brought it to our house in a brown paper grocery bag. Mom put the popcorn in the oven to stay fresh and to hide it from the kids. The next morning, Mom was up at dawn to put the Thanksgiving turkey in the oven. She forgot the popcorn when she preheated the oven. The house filled with smoke. I cried because the popcorn was ruined. To this day, I always check the oven before preheating. I guess I am looking for the popcorn!

—Margaret Brown

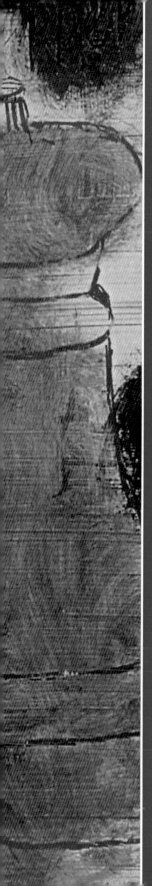

Specialties of the House

MEATS

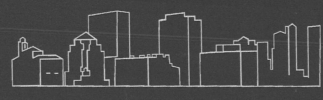

DAYTON BUSINESSES

SPECIALTIES OF THE HOUSE

Did you know that Dayton is the nation's number one 90-minute air market? Fifty-five percent of the U.S. population and 56 percent of the nation's income can be reached within 90 minutes by air. Put together with a highway system that ranks in the nation's top 10 for accessibility, practically the entire nation can be blanketed with one-day deliveries.

In a world where moving goods fast is of the topmost importance, Dayton continues to be at the forefront, taking advantage of its strategic location to create a great place to do business. Over 25,000 firms are located in Dayton, offering an endless array of employment opportunities.

Here are a few of the nationally recognized companies that found their start in Dayton: NCR Corporation, Technology Solutions / Mead Corporation, Paper Products / Esther Price, Candy Makers / Mike-Sells, Potato Chip Producers / Huffy, Bicycle Manufacturer / The Iams Company, Pet Food Producers / LEXIS-NEXIS, Electronic Information Resource / Reynolds and Reynolds, Information Management and Computer Forms / Standard Register, Document Management Systems and Services

Regardless of what the future holds, our diverse industrial base and strong entrepreneurial spirit guarantees Dayton a bright future.

The DOWNTOWN DAYTON PARTNERSHIP points out that Dayton is the region's job center: "From Fortune 500 companies like Reynolds & Reynolds and the Mead Corporation, to hundreds of small professional firms and "mom and pop" retail stores, downtown Dayton is the largest job center in the region, boasting more than 1,000 businesses and nearly 30,000 employees who work downtown every day."

Shadow Mountain Tenderloin

A striking entrée glamorous enough for the most sophisticated palate

Yield: 16 servings

Spinach Stuffing

1¼	pounds fresh spinach, stemmed	2	eggs, beaten
2	tablespoons butter	1	teaspoon fennel seeds
8	ounces fresh mushrooms, chopped	1	teaspoon dried sage
1½	cups shredded Swiss cheese		Salt and freshly ground black pepper to taste

Tenderloin

1	(8 pound) whole beef tenderloin, trimmed of visible fat	1½	teaspoons coarsely ground black pepper
6-8	cloves garlic, minced	½	cup beef broth
1½	teaspoons fennel seeds	½	cup Madeira or dry sherry

🕐 *Stuffing may be made and refrigerated up to 1 day ahead.*

⚬ Rinse spinach, drain briefly and place in a large skillet. Cover and cook over medium heat for about 3 minutes, or until spinach wilts. Uncover, cool and coarsely chop. Squeeze out excess water.

⚬ Using same skillet, melt butter over medium-high heat. Add mushrooms; cook and stir until mushrooms are limp and liquid evaporates. Remove from heat. Stir in spinach, cheese, egg, fennel seeds, sage, salt, and pepper.

⚬ To prepare tenderloin, preheat oven to 500 degrees.

⚬ Cut a lengthwise slash in the tenderloin to within ½ inch of each end and the opposite side, forming a pocket. Spoon spinach filling evenly into pocket; pat in firmly. Sew up tenderloin using a large embroidery needle and a strong thread or dental floss, making stitches ½-inch apart.

⚬ Blend together garlic, fennel seeds and pepper. Rub mixture over outside of beef.

⚬ Place beef in oven and immediately reduce heat to 350 degrees. Roast 18 minutes per pound for medium-rare, or to an internal temperature of 135 to 140 degrees. Let stand for 10 minutes.

⚬ While meat is standing, pour pan drippings into a 3-quart saucepan. Add broth and Madeira. Bring to a boil over high heat and cook until reduced to ½ cup. Serve sauce with meat.

Note: *This recipe can be halved by using a smaller tenderloin and adjusting the stuffing ingredients accordingly.*

Menu: *We suggest serving Make-Ahead Caesar Salad (page 125), Potato Polpettes (page 161) and Baked Vidalias with Sage (page 158) with the tenderloin.*

🍷 *Cabernet Sauvignon, Merlot*

At good dinner parties: conversation flourishes; friendships are forged or reinforced; and good food and drink can be appreciated, and discussed. Between six and eight guests are enough to encourage social intercourse in numerous configurations, but not so many that conversation turns to din. Select friends you think will genuinely enjoy each other, whether or not they've ever met. Invitations (written are preferable, but the phone is an acceptable alternative) should go out two to three weeks in advance; for a party on or near a major holiday, send invitations at least a month ahead of time.

Blackened Filet
with Fresh Mango Salsa

A perfect entrée for a summer dinner party

Yield: 4 servings

Fresh Mango Salsa

1	large mango, chopped	1	cup loosely packed chopped fresh cilantro
1	medium red onion, chopped	¼	cup raspberry vinegar
1	small cucumber, peeled, seeded and diced	½	teaspoon salt
3	green onions, chopped	¼	teaspoon freshly ground black pepper
6	cloves garlic, minced		
1	jalapeño pepper, seeded and chopped		

Filet

4	filet mignon	Blackening spice (we prefer Paul Prudhomme's brand)
2	tablespoons olive oil	

Ⓖ Combine all salsa ingredients in a medium bowl. Mix well and chill.

Ⓖ Rub each filet with oil; generously and evenly sprinkle with blackening spice on all sides.

Ⓖ Place a skillet over high heat for 10 minutes. Add filets to skillet; sear over high heat until bottom forms a crust. Turn and repeat on other side.

Ⓖ Place each filet in the center of individual serving plates. Garnish generously with salsa.

Note: *Can easily be doubled.*

Menu: *Serve with Brazilian Black Beans (page 150), and rice sprinkled with cilantro and green onions. Finish with ice cream, Rich Caramel Sauce (page 282) and blackberries.*

Ⓨ *Red Zinfandel, Cabernet Sauvignon*

Strip Steak with Rosemary Red Wine Sauce

Loaded with flavor!

Yield: 4 servings

4	(1 inch thick) boneless strip steaks (3 pounds total)	1	clove garlic, finely chopped
½	teaspoon salt	1½	cups dry red wine
1	tablespoon cracked black pepper	1	cup canned condensed beef broth
3	tablespoons olive oil	½	teaspoon dark brown sugar
¼	cup chopped onion	1	tablespoon chopped fresh rosemary
1	tablespoon chopped fresh rosemary	1	clove garlic, finely chopped

- Season steaks with salt. Press pepper into surface.

- Heat oil in a large heavy skillet over high heat. Add steaks. Reduce heat to medium and cook, turning once, 4 minutes per side for rare, 6 minutes for medium-rare or 8 minutes for well-done. Remove to a warm platter and keep warm.

- Add onion to skillet; cook and stir 2 minutes, or until browned. Add 1 tablespoon rosemary and 1 clove garlic; cook and stir 20 seconds. Add wine and bring to a boil over high heat. Boil vigorously 2 minutes.

- Add broth, sugar and meat juices that have collected on platter. Boil 10 minutes, or until liquid is reduced to about 1 cup. Add 1 tablespoon rosemary and 1 clove garlic. Pour sauce over steaks and serve.

Menu: *For a memorable meal, start with Tomato, Bacon and Basil Crostini (page 43) and a green salad. Offer mashed potatoes and Mushrooms with Basil Cream (page 155) with the steak. Finish with Amaretto Irish Cream Cheesecake (page 262).*

Cabernet Sauvignon

The Boston Drygoods Store, which would become Elder-Beerman Stores Corporation, was the first department store in Dayton to have an elevator, escalator and drinking fountains.

Flank Steak 🚲

A classic grill recipe

Yield: 4 servings

1	small onion, chopped	½	teaspoon ground ginger
⅓	cup olive oil	2	(1½ pound) flank steaks, well-
⅓	cup sherry		scored on both sides
⅓	cup soy sauce		

🕐 *Marinade can be prepared up to 1 day ahead. Steak must marinate 2 hours before cooking.*

6 Sauté onion in oil in a skillet until transparent. Stir in sherry and soy sauce; simmer 5 minutes. Remove from heat, stir in ginger and cool.

6 Add flank steaks to cooled mixture, cover and marinate in refrigerator for 2 hours.

6 When ready to cook, preheat broiler or grill.

6 Broil steaks, or grill over very hot coals, for 3 minutes per side for rare, 4 minutes per side for medium. To serve, cut into thin slices on the diagonal.

Menu: *To make a simple meal with this steak, add Spring Island Couscous Salad (page 136), and sliced ripe tomatoes drizzled with olive oil.*

🍷 *Cabernet Sauvignon*

Ridgewood Avenue Brisket ❄

Hearty one-dish family meal

Yield: 4 servings

2½	pounds beef brisket	1	envelope onion soup mix
2	tablespoons olive oil	1	(12 ounce) can Coke
1	(12 ounce) bottle chili sauce		

🕐 *If desired, can use a crockpot. After searing meat, cut into quarters and place in crockpot. Combine remaining ingredients but reduce Coke by half. Pour over brisket and cook on low 8 hours.*

6 Preheat oven to 325 degrees.

6 Sear beef in oil over high heat for 3 minutes on each side.

6 Combine chili sauce, soup mix and Coke in a 9x13-inch baking dish. Mix well. Add beef and cover with foil.

6 Bake 3½ to 4 hours.

Note: *Add quartered red skin potatoes and baby carrots during last 1½ hours of cooking for a complete meal.*

Menu: *Just add a salad for a great weeknight meal.*

🍷 *Cabernet Sauvignon, Red Zinfandel*

Sidebar

Suggested cooking temperatures:

180° F Whole poultry

170° F Poultry breast, well-done meats

165° F Stuffed meats and reheated leftovers

160° F Meats-medium, eggs, pork, ground meats

145° F Meats-rare, beef steaks, roasts, veal, lamb

140° F Holding temperature for hot foods

To determine doneness of meat by touch, L'Auberge recommends you follow these guidelines:

Rare: Feels soft, gives to pressure, but not as soft as raw meat.

Medium: Feels moderately firm and resilient, springs back readily when pressed.

Well done: Feels firm, does not give to pressure.

Always let meat rest after removing it from the heat. This is essential so that the juices will retreat back into the flesh.

Thai Lemon Beef

Impressive and colorful, but easy enough for a weeknight family meal

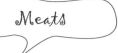

Meats

Yield: 4 servings

1	(1 inch thick) boneless beef top round steak	1	tablespoon vegetable oil
⅓	cup soy sauce	⅓	pound snow peas
¼	cup lemon juice	4	green onions, cut into 2-inch pieces
¼	cup water	4	carrots, julienned
2-3	teaspoons dried red pepper flakes	2	teaspoons cornstarch
4	cloves garlic, minced		Hot cooked Oriental noodles or rice

Marinade can be made 1 day ahead. Steak must marinate at least 1 hour, and up to 8 hours, ahead.

- Cut steak across the grain into ⅛-inch-thick strips and place in a medium bowl.
- Combine soy sauce, lemon juice, water, pepper flakes, and garlic. Pour half of mixture over steak; reserve remaining half. Cover steak and marinate in refrigerator for 1 to 8 hours.
- When ready to cook, drain steak, discarding marinade.
- Stir-fry steak in oil in 2 batches, using a large skillet or wok over medium heat for 1 minute, or until outside of beef is no longer pink. Remove from skillet. Add snow peas, onion and carrot to skillet; stir-fry 3 minutes, or until crisp-tender.
- Whisk cornstarch into reserved soy sauce mixture. Stir into vegetables until thickened. Add steak and stir-fry until heated. Serve over noodles or rice.

Menu: *Finish this one-dish meal with Mrs. Huffman's Legendary Lemon Soufflé (page 255).*

Cabernet Sauvignon, Pinot Noir

In 1942, NCR set up daycare for working mothers and self-defense programs for women working on production lines.

Nancy's Green Pepper Steak ❄

A satisfying family meal

Yield: 4 servings

¼ cup olive oil	2 large green bell peppers, julienned
1 tablespoon Worcestershire sauce	
2 tablespoons soy sauce	1 medium onion, sliced
2 cloves garlic, minced	2 stalks celery, chopped
½ teaspoon ground ginger	4 Roma tomatoes, quartered
1 teaspoon meat tenderizer (optional)	1 (10½ ounce) can mushrooms in gravy
1 pound beef round steak	2 teaspoons cornstarch (optional)
	Hot cooked white rice

🕐 *Steak must be marinated 2 hours, or up to 24 hours, ahead.*

ⓖ Combine oil, Worcestershire sauce, soy sauce, garlic, ginger, and meat tenderizer in a plastic zip-top bag. Add steak; marinate in refrigerator 2 hours or overnight.

ⓖ When ready to cook, add steak and marinade to a large pot; brown over medium-high heat for about 3 minutes. Add bell pepper, onion and celery; cook 10 minutes. Stir in tomato and mushrooms in gravy. Reduce heat to medium-low, cover pot and cook 1 hour.

ⓖ Stir in cornstarch to thicken. Serve over rice.

Note: *A great dish to take to a new mom.*

Menu: *Make a comforting meal with this dish, a green salad and some Moist Oatmeal Cookies (page 276).*

🍷 *Red Zinfandel, Cabernet Sauvignon*

More than one-third of all Japanese investment (Honda, Fujitech and others) in Ohio has taken place within a 50-mile radius of Dayton/ Montgomery County.

Westerly Pot Roast

A most inviting meal on a cold, dreary day!

Yield: 6 servings

1	(3 pound) beef chuck roast
	Flour for dredging
1	stick margarine or butter
2	(28 ounce) cans stewed Italian tomatoes
2	medium onions, quartered
8	ounces fresh mushrooms, sliced
1	bunch celery, cut into 2-inch pieces

4	cloves garlic, minced
1	teaspoon Worcestershire sauce
1	teaspoon salt
¼	teaspoon freshly ground black pepper
1	teaspoon dried thyme
1	teaspoon dried basil
3-4	carrots, cut into 2-inch pieces
2	pounds potatoes, quartered

Can be cooked in a crockpot on low all day. Brown meat before adding to crockpot. Add carrots and potatoes for last hour of cooking time.

- Lightly dredge beef in flour. Melt margarine in a large pot and brown beef on all sides.
- Add tomatoes, onions, mushrooms, celery, garlic, Worcestershire sauce, salt, pepper, thyme, and basil to pot.
- Simmer about 2 hours, or until meat is tender.
- Add carrots and potatoes; cook until tender.

Menu: *Overnight Focaccia (page 80) is the perfect bread to soak up extra sauce. Serve a green salad and end the meal with Provisions' Peanut Butter Cookies (page 281).*

Cabernet Sauvignon, Merlot, Red Zinfandel

Meats

A local horseradish salesman, Loren Berry, invented the Yellow Pages directory in the early 1900s.

Pot O' Gold Dinner

A St. Patrick's Day favorite

Yield: 6 servings

1	(2 to 2½ pound) corned beef brisket (see Cook's Note)	2	medium red onions, cut into wedges
1	teaspoon whole black peppercorns	10-12	new potatoes (1 pound), halved or quartered
2	bay leaves	1	(1 pound) head cabbage, cut into 6 wedges
3	medium carrots, quartered lengthwise	2	tablespoons snipped fresh dill
2	medium parsnips, peeled and cut into chunks		Assorted mustards

Can be cooked in a crockpot on low all day. Add vegetables for last hour of cooking time.

Trim fat from beef. Place beef in a 4- to 6-quart pot. Add juices and spices from package of beef. Add enough water to cover meat. Add peppercorns and bay leaves; bring to a boil. Reduce heat and cover. Simmer about 2 hours, or until meat is almost tender.

Add carrots, parsnips and onions to pot and bring to a boil. Reduce heat and cover. Simmer 10 minutes. Add potatoes and cabbage to pot. Cover and cook about 20 minutes, or until vegetables and meat are tender. Discard bay leaves.

Remove meat from pot and thinly slice across the grain. Place meat and vegetables on a serving platter. Sprinkle with dill and serve with assorted mustards.

Note: *If your brisket comes with a spice packet, add it and omit the peppercorns and bay leaves.*

Menu: *Add purchased Irish soda bread and some hearty ale to round out the meal. For dessert, serve Amaretto Irish Cream Cheesecake (page 262).*

Cabernet Sauvignon, Merlot, Red Zinfandel

"Very well," he said. "I am going into the cash register business—and I will make a success of it."

—John H. Patterson in 1884, after learning that the National Mfg. Co. (to which James Ritty had sold his cash register business in 1883) was for sale.

When John H. Patterson bought the cash register business in 1884, it had only 13 employees. Although a man of formidable vision, he undoubtedly could not have anticipated today's worldwide employment of approximately 33,000 men and women, and a range of machines that can interpret documents at lightening speed, perform arithmetic calculations in a billionth of a second, and print out completed business reports faster than the eye can read.

Rosa's Stuffed Peppers

Rosa is a real Italian grandmother and an amazing cook

Yield: 4 to 6 servings

1	pound ground beef
1	large onion, diced
3-4	cloves garlic, sliced
1	small yellow squash, diced
1	(14½ ounce) can diced tomatoes with juice
2-4	chopped cherry peppers with juice
½	cup Parmesan cheese
½	cup bread crumbs
1-2	eggs, beaten

2	tablespoons chopped fresh parsley
2	tablespoons chopped fresh basil
	Salt and freshly ground black pepper to taste
1	(8 ounce) can tomato sauce
6	large Hungarian or banana peppers, halved lengthwise and seeded
	Olive oil

⚙ Preheat oven to 300 degrees.

⚙ Brown beef in a skillet; drain fat. Add onion and garlic to skillet; sauté until softened. Add squash, tomatoes and cherry peppers. Cook until squash is softened.

⚙ Add cheese, crumbs, egg, parsley, basil, salt, and pepper; mix until mixture is the consistency of meatloaf.

⚙ Pour all but ½ cup of tomato sauce into a 9x13-inch glass baking dish. Place Hungarian peppers, cut-side up, in dish; sprinkle with salt and drizzle with olive oil.

⚙ Spoon beef stuffing into peppers and drizzle with remaining ½ cup tomato sauce. Cover with foil.

⚙ Bake 1 hour. Uncover and increase heat to 350 degrees. Bake 30 minutes longer, or until browned.

Note: *Any long, light green, mild-flavored pepper will work.*

Menu: *Serve the peppers over rice. Add a simple green salad with tomatoes to the meal, if desired.*

🍷 *Pinot Noir, Merlot*

Employment at NCR skyrocketed from 8,000 before the war to 20,000 in 1945. Included were 600 Navy Waves, who worked at Sugar Camp to assemble code-breaking machines. These Enigma Machines later cracked German secrets.

Grandma Walcott's Famous Cabbage Rolls

The best cabbage rolls you'll ever taste…Grandma Walcott makes them by the hundreds!

Yield: 8 to 10 servings

2	cups dry white rice	½	teaspoon freshly ground black pepper
1	small onion, diced		
1	green bell pepper, finely chopped	2	teaspoons chicken base dissolved in ¼ cup water
2	stalks celery, finely chopped	2	heads cabbage, cored
2	tablespoons butter	1	pork rib bone or pork chop (for flavor)
2¼	pounds ground chuck		
1	egg, beaten		Salt to taste
1	teaspoon salt	2	(11½ ounce) cans vegetable juice

🕐 *Rice may be cooked up to 2 days ahead and refrigerated.*

Ⓒ Preheat oven to 350 degrees.

Ⓒ Cook rice according to package directions.

Ⓒ Meanwhile, sauté onion, pepper and celery in butter for 10 minutes, or until softened.

Ⓒ In a large mixing bowl, combine cooked rice, sautéed vegetables, ground chuck, egg, salt, pepper, and chicken-base mixture. Mix thoroughly, with your hands if necessary.

Ⓒ Submerge cabbage in a large pot of boiling water. With a large fork or tongs, peel off 1 layer at a time, removing layers when they are translucent; place on a clean dish or paper towels. The leaves cook quickly, so be careful to not overcook. Use outer two-thirds of leaves; discard or save inner third of heads for another use. Trim core from leaves if too thick.

Ⓒ To assemble rolls, place 2 tablespoons or more of meat mixture at the base of each leaf and roll it to the end, tucking in sides so mixture will not fall out. Place pork bone or chop on the bottom of a large ovenproof pot and begin layering rolls, sprinkling each layer with salt. Pour vegetable juice over top layer.

Ⓒ Cover and bake for 3½ hours.

Note: *This makes about 40 to 45 cabbage rolls.*

Menu: *Serve with Whipped Potatoes Paprika (page 160) and steamed green beans.*

🍷 *Pinot Noir, Merlot*

Presidential Meatloaf ❄

This recipe was submitted by our current Jr. League President, Sue Lipowicz

Yield: 8 servings

1	pound ground beef round	½	cup warm water
½	pound ground pork	1	envelope dry onion soup mix
½	pound ground veal	¼	teaspoon freshly ground black pepper
2	eggs		
1½	cups bread crumbs	2	strips bacon (optional)
¾	cup ketchup	½	cup barbecue sauce
1	teaspoon dry mustard		

🕐 *Can mix together meat mixture up to 1 day ahead. Keep refrigerated. Add 5 to 7 minutes to cooking time.*

🌀 Preheat oven to 350 degrees.

🌀 Combine beef, pork, veal, eggs, bread crumbs, ketchup, mustard, water, soup mix, and pepper in a large mixing bowl. Mix thoroughly. Place into a loaf pan, smoothing into a loaf.

🌀 Lay bacon over loaf and pour barbecue sauce on top.

🌀 Bake 1 hour, 10 minutes.

Note: *You may want to split the recipe into 2 smaller loaf pans and freeze 1 for a night you don't have time to cook!*

Menu: *Whipped Potatoes Paprika (page 160) and Liliana's Fried Cabbage (page 163) are a must with this meatloaf.*

🍷 *Pinot Noir, Merlot*

Wilkie's Bookstore, founded in 1894 in downtown Dayton, is Ohio's oldest independent bookstore.

Veal Saltimbocca ❄

Saltimbocca means "jump into the mouth," and that's what this old-fashioned Italian dish does

Yield: 4 servings

1½ **pounds (8 pieces) thin veal or turkey steaks**	4 **teaspoons chopped fresh sage, or 1½ teaspoons dried**
½ **cup flour**	**Salt to taste**
4 **paper-thin slices prosciutto (about 2 ounces)**	2 **tablespoons unsalted butter**
8 **very thin slices aged provolone cheese (about 5 ounces)**	2 **tablespoons olive oil**
	⅓ **cup dry white wine**

🕐 *Saltimbocca may be assembled early in the day, covered and refrigerated, or frozen for up to 3 months. Return to room temperature before proceeding.*

6   Flatten each steak by placing between 2 sheets of wax paper and pounding with a rolling pin until very thin, but not torn. Dredge steaks in flour.

6   Top 4 steaks each with 1 slice of prosciutto and 2 slices of cheese. Sprinkle with sage. Place remaining steaks on top and press edges together to seal. Season with salt. Cover, and refrigerate or freeze until ready to cook.

6   When ready to cook, return saltimbocca to room temperature. Heat butter and oil in a large skillet. Add veal packages and quickly brown on both sides, about 1½ minutes on each side for veal, and 2½ minutes per side for turkey. Reduce heat to a simmer and stir in wine. Simmer about 30 seconds. Do not overcook or meat will become dry.

Menu: *Accompany the veal with Baked Vidalias with Sage (page 158), Sicilian Carrots (page 152), and some orzo tossed with olive oil and Parmesan cheese.*

🍷 *Brunello, Cabernet Sauvignon, Barolo*

In 1894, John H. Patterson opened the National Cash Register's first sales training school in the "cottage under the elms" near the factory.

Victoria's Veal

Heavenly comfort food!

Yield: 6 to 8 servings

4	tablespoons butter	½	teaspoon nutmeg
4½	pounds veal, shoulder or stew meat, cut into 1-inch cubes	1½	cups chicken broth
		1½	cups water
	Salt and freshly ground black pepper	3	carrots, julienned
		2	leeks, julienned
1	clove garlic, minced	4	tablespoons butter
1	cup chopped onion	8	cups hot cooked rice
2	tablespoons chopped fresh dill	2	tablespoons chopped fresh dill for garnish
½	cup all-purpose flour		

🕐 *Vegetables can be chopped earlier in the day and refrigerated. Rice can also be prepared ahead and reheated in the microwave.*

◎ Preheat oven to 375 degrees.

◎ Melt 4 tablespoons butter in a large Dutch oven. Add veal; sprinkle with salt and pepper. Top with garlic, onion and 2 tablespoons dill. Cook over medium heat, stirring constantly, for 5 minutes, watching carefully to prevent burning. Sprinkle flour and nutmeg over mixture. Add broth and water. Bring to a boil. Remove from heat, cover and bake 1 hour.

◎ Meanwhile, in a skillet over medium heat, sauté carrots and leeks in 4 tablespoons butter until softened. Add to veal when removed from oven.

◎ Serve veal with a generous portion of rice and garnished with fresh dill.

Menu: *This dish works well with mesclun and Red Wine Vinaigrette (page 98), crusty baguettes, and sautéed mushrooms. Make Warm Chocolate Tarts (page 260) or Caramel Apple Bread Pudding (page 256) for dessert.*

🍷 *Cabernet Sauvignon, Merlot, Red Zinfandel*

Through one state-supported training program, our new U.S. Postal Service Remote Encoding Center was quickly able to hire and develop a force of 800 employees, workers who promptly earned a number two ranking for productivity and accuracy among 55 other similar national centers. Another regional newcomer and one of the country's leading apparel companies, Victoria's Secret, hired over 1,000 area employees to staff its large call center. Suitable location, access to high-quality employees, and an inviting business climate all contributed to the company's decision to locate here.

Holiday Pork Roast

A superb special occasion entrée

Yield: 8 to 10 servings

¼	cup dry mustard	1	cup soy sauce
4	teaspoons dried thyme	2	cloves garlic, minced
1	(8 pound) pork loin roast, boned, rolled and tied	2	(10 ounce) jars currant jelly
1	cup cooking sherry	1	tablespoon soy sauce
2	teaspoons ginger	2	tablespoons cooking sherry

🕐 *Marinade can be made 2 days ahead. Meat must marinate at least 3 hours, and up to 24 hours. Make sauce up to 3 days ahead; refrigerate. Reheat before serving.*

6 Combine mustard and thyme; rub over roast. Place in a glass dish.

6 Combine 1 cup sherry, ginger, 1 cup soy sauce, and garlic; pour over roast. Cover and marinate in refrigerator for 3 hours, or overnight.

6 When ready to cook, preheat oven to 325 degrees.

6 Remove meat from marinade, discarding marinade. Place roast on a rack in a shallow roasting pan.

6 Bake, uncovered, for 4½ hours, or until a meat thermometer reaches at least 160 degrees.

6 Melt jelly in a saucepan. Add 1 tablespoon soy sauce and 2 tablespoons sherry. Stir until smooth and serve on the side.

Menu: *Create a memorable holiday menu…start with Creamed Cheeses with Brandied Cranberries (page 61) and Mushroom Tarts (page 45). At the table, serve Spinach Chutney Salad (page 123), Wild Rice with Carrots and Onions (page 163) and steamed Brussels sprouts with the roast. Finish with Mother's Brandy-Pecan Pudding (page 255).*

🍷 *Red Zinfandel, Cabernet Sauvignon, Pinot Noir*

In 1925, the Davis Sewing Machine Company sold its sewing machine business and changed its name to the Huffman Manufacturing Company. The company began making blowtorches and plumbers' furnaces, later transforming itself into the bicycle-making Huffy Corporation.

Pork with Red Plum Sauce

The sauce makes this one a "keeper"

Yield: 6 to 8 servings

Roast

1   (4 pound) pork loin roast   Onion salt to taste
    Garlic salt to taste

Red Plum Sauce

¾   cup chopped onion   ⅓   cup chili sauce
2   tablespoons butter   ¼   cup soy sauce
1   cup red plum preserves   2   teaspoons prepared mustard
½   cup brown sugar   3   drops hot pepper sauce
2   tablespoons lemon juice

🕐 *The sauce can be prepared up to 1 day ahead and reheated.*

6   Preheat oven to 350 degrees.

6   Sprinkle pork with garlic salt and onion salt. Place on a rack in a 9x13-inch baking pan. Add a small amount of water to cover bottom of pan. Cover pan tightly with foil.

6   Bake 2½ to 3 hours.

6   Meanwhile, prepare the sauce. Sauté onion in butter in a saucepan until softened. Add preserves, sugar, lemon juice, chili sauce, soy sauce, mustard, and pepper sauce. Simmer 15 minutes.

6   When roast is done baking, pour off fat from the baking pan. Pour half the plum sauce over the roast and bake, uncovered, 30 minutes longer, basting often with sauce in pan.

6   Remove roast from oven and let stand 10 minutes before serving. Serve with remaining sauce on the side.

Note: *Be careful not to overcook roast or it will be dry. Use a meat thermometer to test for doneness.*

Menu: *Offer rice alongside the pork, and Asparagus and Portobello Mushrooms with Goat Cheese (page 148).*

🍷 *Red Zinfandel, Merlot*

In 1910, NCR controlled 95 percent of the world's cash register market.

Stuffed Pork Tenderloin with Shallots

Beautiful presentation that tastes as good as it looks

Yield: 6 to 8 servings

2	(12 ounce) pork tenderloins	1	(10 ounce) bag fresh spinach
	Salt and freshly ground black pepper	3	heaping tablespoons bread crumbs
9	ounces thinly sliced pancetta or de-rinded bacon	1	teaspoon chopped fresh thyme
		2	tablespoons olive oil
1	pound shallots, peeled	1¾	cups white port
4	cloves garlic	1	tablespoon fresh thyme sprigs

🕐 *Pork may be stuffed up to 1 day ahead. Cover and refrigerate.*

6 Make a lengthwise cut along the long side of each tenderloin, not cutting through to the other side, so that each tenderloin can be unfolded like a book. Flatten each tenderloin with a rolling pin. Season inside of tenderloins with salt and pepper.

6 Chop 3 slices of pancetta, 2 shallots and 1 clove garlic. Heat the chopped pancetta in a skillet until the fat runs, then add chopped shallots and garlic. Cook gently for about 8 minutes.

6 Stir spinach into skillet and cover. Cook briskly until spinach wilts; uncover and continue to cook briskly to evaporate moisture. Stir in bread crumbs and 1 teaspoon chopped thyme. Season well with salt and pepper. Cool.

6 Spread mixture over inside of tenderloins. Fold tenderloins back together to form 2 rolls. Wrap remaining pancetta around rolls and tie with string.

6 Preheat oven to 375 degrees.

6 Heat olive oil in the same skillet. Add remaining whole shallots and cook over medium heat until brown. Remove from skillet and set aside. Add tenderloins to skillet and brown on all sides. Pour port into skillet and simmer for a few minutes. Add 1 tablespoon thyme sprigs, remaining garlic cloves and browned shallots to skillet. Transfer entire skillet contents to a baking dish.

6 Bake 40 to 50 minutes, basting once or twice. Slice pork and serve with shallots on the side.

Note: *You may substitute a 16-ounce can of pearl onions, drained, for the shallots.*

Menu: *Serve the pork with Baked Bread Casserole with Wild Mushrooms and Onions (page 159) and a salad of mixed greens. Southern Sweet Potato Soufflé (page 165) also works well with this dish.*

🍷 *Red Zinfandel, Pinot Noir, Merlot*

Sesame-Garlic Grilled Pork Tenderloin ❄

Everyone will rave about this tenderloin!

Yield: 4 servings

4	tablespoons soy sauce	4	cloves garlic, minced
2	tablespoons sesame oil	2	tablespoons sesame seeds, lightly toasted
2	tablespoons brown sugar		
½	teaspoon honey	4	green onions, sliced
1	tablespoon dry sherry	1½	pounds pork tenderloin

Pork must marinate in a plastic zip-top bag 8 to 12 hours. Or, you may freeze the meat in the marinade up to 3 months.

- Combine all ingredients except pork in a plastic zip-top bag. Add pork and marinate in refrigerator overnight.

- When ready to cook, preheat grill.

- Grill pork over medium-hot coals for 20 minutes, or until a meat thermometer reads at least 160 degrees.

- Remove pork from grill. Let stand 5 minutes before cutting into medallions.

Note: *When preparing this dish, double it and put 1 tenderloin in the freezer for an easy meal at a later time. If you can't grill it, the tenderloin may be roasted in a shallow pan at 400 degrees for 30 minutes. Use a meat thermometer to check for doneness.*

Menu: *Make Almond Orange Garden Salad (page 130), Silky Asian Noodles (page 187), and Asparagus with Chinese Vinaigrette (page 149) or steamed broccoli to complement the pork.*

Red Zinfandel, Cabernet Sauvignon, Pinot Noir

In the body, garlic works to lower the "bad" LDL cholesterol, while increasing the level of HDL or "good" cholesterol. Garlic also lowers triglyceride levels and thins the blood, which helps prevent blockages that can lead to stroke or heart attack.

Rosemary Pork Tenderloin

This recipe originally appeared in the "It's Simple" column by Ann Heller of the Dayton Daily News

Yield: 4 servings

1½	pounds pork tenderloin	2	teaspoons minced fresh rosemary
1	teaspoon coarse salt	2	teaspoons olive oil
2	small cloves garlic, minced		Freshly ground black pepper

🕐 *Garlic/rosemary paste can be made up to 8 hours ahead.*

🌿 Preheat oven to 450 degrees.

🌿 Fold the thin tip of the tenderloin under; secure with a tie or skewer so pork cooks evenly. Place pork on a foil-lined broiling pan.

🌿 In a small bowl, mash the salt and garlic into a paste with the back of a spoon. Blend in rosemary and oil. Rub the paste into the meat; sprinkle with pepper.

🌿 Roast 20 minutes, or until a meat thermometer reads 155 degrees. Remove from oven and let stand, lightly covered with foil, for 10 minutes. The internal temperature will rise to 160 degrees. Slice and serve with pan juices.

Note: *Use an instant read thermometer to eliminate guesswork.*

Menu: *With the pork, serve Potato Polpettes (page 161), Sicilian Carrots (page 152) or Peperonata (page 158), and a green salad.*

🍷 *Red Zinfandel, Cabernet Sauvignon, Pinot Noir*

About 150 years ago, a priest purchased 140 acres from a farmer, paying for the land with a Saint Peter's pendant. After changing hands a time or two, the land eventually became the site of the University of Dayton.

Curried Pork Chops
with Blackberry Sauce

Easy, but packed with flavor

Yield: 4 servings

4	(7 ounce) pork chops	1¼	cups blackberry jam or jelly
	Salt and freshly ground black pepper to taste	6	fresh sage leaves, chopped
	Mild curry paste	1	tablespoon lemon juice

- Preheat broiler.
- Season pork chops with salt and pepper. Coat 1 side of the chops with curry paste. Place chops, paste-side down, in a baking dish and coat tops with curry paste.
- Broil chops 3 to 4 inches from heat source for 4 to 7 minutes on each side.
- Combine jam, sage and lemon juice in a small saucepan; heat over medium heat. Drizzle over each chop.

Note: *Amount of paste used depends on your personal taste. You may want to taste the paste first to determine how much you will use.*

Menu: *Offer Baked Vidalias with Sage (page 158), and Rice Pilaf (page 162) with the chops.*

Red Zinfandel, Merlot

In 1955, Dayton's old Callahan Bank Building got a new name—the Gem City Savings Building—after being bought by Gem City. The clock atop the Callahan Building was later moved to crown the Reynolds and Reynolds building, which can be seen from Interstate 75.

Old Faithful Pork Chop Casserole

Lives up to its name — always a family favorite

Yield: 4 servings

4	medium-sized pork chops, with or without bone	1	medium onion, sliced
1	cup dry white rice		Salt and freshly ground black pepper to taste
1	yellow bell pepper, cut into rings	2	cups canned beef broth
1	green bell pepper, cut into rings	¼	teaspoon dried basil
2	tomatoes, sliced	¼	teaspoon dried thyme

🕐 *Can brown chops and assemble casserole (minus the broth) up to 1 day ahead.*

❻ Preheat oven to 350 degrees.

❻ Brown pork chops in a skillet.

❻ Meanwhile, place rice in the bottom of a large casserole dish that has been sprayed with cooking spray. Place browned chops on rice. Top each chop with slices of bell peppers, tomato and onion. Season with salt and pepper between layers of vegetables. Pour broth over entire casserole; sprinkle with basil and thyme.

❻ Bake, covered, for 1 hour.

Note: *A nice one-dish meal to take to a new mom or elderly neighbor.*

Menu: *Serve a green salad with Nana's French Dressing (page 98) to complete this meal. Make the Brownie Torte (page 265) for dessert.*

🍷 *Merlot, Pinot Noir, Red Zinfandel*

This recipe is from my mom, who made it a lot while I was growing up. If she were going out of town, she would assemble it (minus the broth) and put it in the fridge for my Dad to make one night while she was gone. He'd take it out of the fridge and pour the broth over it, cook it, and feel like a hero presenting us with something other than fish sticks!

—Margot Varley

Pork and Sauerkraut

A traditional New Year's Day meal for many Daytonians

Yield: 6 to 8 servings

3-4	potatoes, quartered lengthwise	1	cup dry white wine
2-3	carrots, cut into ½-inch pieces	1	teaspoon instant chicken bouillon
½	cup chopped onion		
3	juniper berries, crushed	⅛	teaspoon ground cloves
1	bay leaf	⅛	teaspoon freshly ground black pepper
1	(2 to 3 pound) pork roast		
2	green apples, quartered	1	tablespoon caraway seeds (optional)
2	(32 ounce) jars sauerkraut		
½	cup water		

🕐 *You must cook this dish at least 4 hours in your crockpot.*

⟲ Combine potato, carrot, onion, juniper berry, and bay leaf in a crockpot. Place pork on top. Add apple and sauerkraut.

⟲ Combine water, wine, bouillon, cloves, black pepper, and caraway seeds; pour into crockpot. Cover.

⟲ Set on low heat and cook 10 to 12 hours, or on high for 4½ to 5 hours. Discard bay leaf before serving.

Note: *Look for juniper berries in the spice section of your market.*

Menu: *To round out the meal, offer Spinach Chutney Salad (page 123) with this dish. For a fine ending, serve Great-Grandmother's Pound Cake (page 269) with vanilla ice cream and Rich Caramel Sauce (page 282).*

🍷 *Pinot Noir, Merlot, Red Zinfandel*

When NCR was a "young" company, they fully believed in "welfare Capitalism." There were always group exercises, mid-morning malted milk, umbrellas on rainy days, lunchtime speakers, and "owl" classes in the evening.

Devin's Best Baby Back Ribs

Devin's mom discovered this recipe while planning his fourth birthday party — the ribs stole the show!

Yield: 6 to 8 servings

Ribs

2	(12 ounce) cans cola	2	tablespoons hot pepper sauce
2	(12 ounce) cans beer	1	tablespoon freshly ground black pepper
6	cloves garlic, crushed		
10	bay leaves	1	tablespoon liquid smoke
2	cups sliced onion	¼	cup sugar
½	cup soy sauce	6	pounds baby back ribs, cut into 6-inch sections
½	cup salt		

Sauce

¾	cup ketchup	1	tablespoon liquid smoke
¼	cup chili sauce	3	tablespoons molasses
1	tablespoon Worcestershire sauce	1	tablespoon chili powder
2	tablespoons orange juice	½	cup diced onion

Sauce can be prepared up to 3 days ahead. Ingredients for ribs can be assembled up to 24 hours ahead, with the exception of the beer, cola and ribs.

- Combine all ingredients for ribs in a large stock pot. If necessary, add enough water to cover ribs. Bring to a boil. Reduce heat, cover and simmer for about 1 hour.

- Meanwhile, combine sauce ingredients in a saucepan. Cook over low heat for 30 to 40 minutes, stirring occasionally.

- Preheat grill to medium heat.

- Remove ribs from pot and place on a large platter. Brush sauce on ribs to coat both sides. Reserve remaining sauce to serve with ribs.

- Grill ribs for 3 to 4 minutes per side. Serve immediately.

Note: *Six pounds of ribs will yield about twelve (6 inch) sections.*

Menu: *Enjoy these tasty ribs with Heavenly Cornbread (page 82), Southwestern Baked Beans (page 149) and Here Comes the Sun Salad (page 127).*

 Beer

Easter Lamb

A very special spring entrée

Yield: 6 to 8 servings

1	(6 to 7 pound) leg of lamb, boned	1	clove garlic, finely minced
	Salt and freshly ground black pepper	1½	cups soft fresh bread crumbs
2	tablespoons butter	¼	cup finely chopped fresh parsley
½	cup chopped onion	½	teaspoon dried thyme
2	tablespoons finely chopped green onion	1	egg, beaten
		1	bay leaf

- Preheat oven to 400 degrees.

- Place lamb, boned-side up, on a flat surface. Sprinkle with salt and pepper.

- Melt butter in a large, heavy skillet. Add onion, green onion and garlic; sauté until translucent. Remove from heat. Add bread crumbs, parsley, thyme, and egg. Mix well; season with salt and pepper.

- Spoon mixture into boned cavity of the leg. Roll leg and tie together with butcher's string. Place in a baking pan; sprinkle with salt and pepper. Add bay leaf to pan.

- Place pan in oven and immediately reduce heat to 350 degrees. Bake 3½ to 4½ hours, about 35 minutes per pound, or until done. Baste with pan juices while baking.

- When done, transfer lamb to a serving platter and slice. Discard bay leaf and drain off fat from pan. Strain remaining juices over lamb, or make into a gravy.

Note: *Have your butcher trim any extra fat from outer side of the leg.*

Cabernet Sauvignon, Merlot

In 1884, Marianists bought land from John H. Patterson to establish St. Mary's Institute, which is now the University of Dayton. Patterson sold the land for $6,750 to obtain the necessary capital to build his National Cash Register factory.

Mango Lamb Chops

This recipe comes from a Dorothy Lane Market cooking class taught by Dottie Overman

Yield: 4 to 6 servings

¾	cup mango chutney	3	tablespoons apricot nectar
1½	tablespoons red wine vinegar	¼	teaspoon dried red pepper
2	teaspoons chopped fresh		flakes
	rosemary		Salt to taste
1	tablespoon oil	6	(1 inch thick) lamb chops

🕐 *Marinade may be made up to 1 day ahead.*

🌀 Combine all ingredients except lamb chops in a bowl. Spread some of mixture over both sides of each lamb chop, reserving remaining mixture to use as a dipping sauce. Marinate lamb chops 15 minutes.

🌀 When ready to cook, gently scrape off most of marinade.

🌀 To grill, cook about 4 minutes on each side.

🌀 To pan fry, heat a nonstick skillet over medium heat. Sauté chops 4 minutes on first side, 2 minutes on the other, or until browned on both sides.

🌀 Serve with reserved dipping sauce.

Note: *Mango chutney is available in most grocery stores.*

Menu: *Serve these chops alongside Lemon Rice with Pine Nuts (page 162) and Asparagus and Portobello Mushrooms with Goat Cheese (page 148). Make Shortcakes with Strawberries and Whipped Cream (page 264) for dessert.*

🍷 *Cabernet Sauvignon, Red Zinfandel*

The Barney mansion was built in 1890 by Eugene Judson Barney, who headed the Barney & Smith Co. Built for his wife, Belle, and their four children, the home had 27 rooms and 40,000 square feet. The Barney Mansion was one of the most exquisite houses ever built in Dayton. Interiors featured lavish paneling of rare woods, highlighted with pearl, onyx, marble and bronze ornament or inlay, and tooled leather wall coverings. There were etched Tiffany glass windows. The house was demolished in April 1969 to make room for a parking lot.

Rike's Famous Sloppy Joes ✳

A Dayton favorite

Yield: 6 to 8 servings

1	pound ground beef chuck	2	teaspoons dry mustard
1	large sweet onion, chopped		Salt to taste
1	green bell pepper, chopped	¾	cup ketchup
1	tablespoon vinegar	¾	cup tomato juice
1	tablespoon sugar		

🕐 *Chop vegetables earlier in the day. Sauce ingredients may be combined in a bowl and kept covered at room temperature until beef has been browned.*

🌀 Brown beef; drain off fat. Add onion and bell pepper to beef; cook until soft. Stir in vinegar, sugar, mustard, salt, ketchup, and tomato juice.

🌀 Simmer 20 to 30 minutes, or until sauce is thick and dark in color. Serve on warm buns.

Menu: *For a crowd, serve Mike-Sell's Potato Chips, Grandma Ruby's Garlic Sweet Pickles (page 101) and your favorite coleslaw with the sandwiches. Make a Century-Style Chocolate Sheet Cake (page 267) for dessert.*

Cajun Hamburgers

A welcome twist on the humble hamburger!

Yield: 6 to 8 servings

2	pounds ground beef	1	teaspoon paprika
1	green bell pepper, minced	1	teaspoon Cajun seasoning
½	cup chopped green onion		Dried red pepper flakes to taste
3	cloves garlic, minced		Salt to taste
2	teaspoons ground cumin		Sliced tomatoes and sour cream
2	teaspoons oregano		for toppings
1	teaspoon thyme		

🕐 *Patties may be assembled up to 8 hours ahead. Cover and refrigerate.*

🌀 Combine beef, bell pepper, onion, and garlic in a mixing bowl. Blend in cumin, oregano, thyme, paprika, Cajun seasoning, pepper flakes, and salt. Shape into patties.

🌀 Grill patties to desired doneness. Place on toasted buns and top with tomato slices and sour cream.

Menu: *Serve with corn on the cob, green salad and Fresh Peach Crisp (page 275).*

🍷 *Red Zinfandel*

This was a favorite sandwich served on the mezzanine of Rike's Department Store. Many of us enjoyed this sandwich for a quick lunch when we were teenagers in the 1940s and '50s. Later, when the recipe became available, we were able to serve it to our families.

—Natalie Bettcher

The backyard barbecue is perhaps the easiest and most comfortable way we have of entertaining, and for that reason might well serve as a model for entertaining of all types. "Come on over for burgers!" we say casually, remembering (at least for the moment) that the elementary urge to welcome guests and feed them well is at the heart of entertaining.

BBQ Beef Sandwiches ❄

Great for a tailgate or Super Bowl party

Yield: 16 to 20 servings

1	(4 pound) beef brisket	⅛	teaspoon freshly ground black pepper
1	envelope dry onion soup mix		
2	cups ketchup	½	teaspoon dried oregano
2	teaspoons horseradish	½	teaspoon celery salt
1	(12 ounce) bottle beer	2	cups of your favorite barbecue sauce
1	tablespoon Worcestershire sauce		
		½	cup brown sugar
½	teaspoon garlic salt	1	pound BBQ shredded pork

🕐 *This dish benefits from being made 1 day in advance. Using the crockpot makes it even easier. Refrigerate, then reheat and serve.*

⑥ Preheat oven to 300 degrees.

⑥ Place beef in a Dutch oven (or crockpot). Add soup mix, ketchup, horse-radish, beer, Worcestershire sauce, garlic salt, pepper, oregano, and celery salt.

⑥ Bake, covered, for 4 hours; or cook on low in a crockpot for 8 hours. Cool slightly and shred meat.

⑥ Combine shredded beef, barbecue sauce, brown sugar and shredded pork. Heat and serve on warm buns.

Note: *The BBQ shredded pork can be found in the frozen meat section — ask your grocer if you can't locate it.*

Menu: *Offer Southwestern Baked Beans (page 149), and corn on the cob or Phyl's Layered Salad (page 146) with the sandwiches.*

🍷 *Merlot, Red Zinfandel*

Apparently, John H. Patterson was no different from other parents in realizing the romance between teenagers and telephones! Patterson had a telephone installed in the first floor of his gatehouse. He promptly had it removed when his son, Fred, and his friends, took advantage of his largesse by making numerous long-distance calls.

Warm Pastrami Panino

Wrap these in foil for your next picnic

Yield: 4 to 6 servings

⅓ cup chopped fresh basil

2 tablespoons olive oil

1 tablespoon balsamic vinegar or white wine vinegar

1 (8 ounce) or ½ (16 ounce) loaf unsliced crusty bread

6 ounces thinly sliced mozzarella cheese

4-6 ounces thinly sliced best-quality pastrami

2 plum tomatoes, thinly sliced lengthwise

⅛ teaspoon cracked black pepper

◎ Preheat broiler.

◎ Combine basil, oil and vinegar in a small bowl.

◎ Slice bread in half lengthwise and hollow out inside of bottom half, leaving a ½-inch thick shell. Layer half of the cheese, all of the pastrami and the tomatoes on the bread shell. Top with basil mixture and sprinkle with pepper. Top with remaining cheese.

◎ Place on the unheated rack of a broiler pan. Broil 3 to 4 inches from heat source for 2 to 3 minutes, or until cheese melts. Top with bread top.

◎ To serve, cut crosswise into 4 to 6 pieces.

Note: *It's important to use a high-quality crusty loaf. In Dayton, we recommend Dorothy Lane Market's Classic Italian loaf.*

Menu: *Pack your picnic basket with this sub, Greek Peasant Salad (page 124) and/or Pasta Salad with Grilled Zucchini and Olives (page 134).*

🍷 *Chianti, Merlot*

Meats

Sandwich suggestions:

Grilled German sausage, sautéed onions, mustard, and melted cheese in a sandwich roll

Baked ham, Cheddar cheese, honey mustard, and tomatoes on whole grain bread

Roast beef, dill-horseradish mayonnaise and watercress on French bread

Roast beef, herb and garlic cheese, and sliced green pepper on pumpernickel bread

Baked ham, cream cheese mixed with fruit chutney, and butter lettuce

Salami, sliced green peppers and cream cheese on rye bread

Roast pork, apple slices and Cheddar cheese broiled open-face on whole-grain bread

Italian Sausage and Pepper Heroes

A satisfying sandwich

Yield: 8 servings

8	fresh Italian sausages
1	green bell pepper, julienned
1	red bell pepper, julienned
1	yellow bell pepper, julienned
1	large onion, sliced
2	cloves garlic, minced
¼	cup olive oil
½	teaspoon salt
¼	teaspoon freshly ground black pepper
1	cup tomato sauce
8	fresh hot dog or hoagie buns
2	cups shredded mozzarella cheese (optional)

Veggies can be sliced, cooked and refrigerated up to 2 days ahead.

6 Preheat oven to 350 degrees.

6 Place sausages in a 9x13-inch baking dish and add 1 inch of water. Bake 1 hour, turning halfway through cooking for even browning.

6 Meanwhile, sauté bell peppers, onion and garlic in oil over medium heat for about 30 minutes, or until peppers are tender. Add salt and black pepper.

6 When sausages are done, pour off water; add sautéed vegetables to dish. Add tomato sauce and mix thoroughly. Bake 20 minutes, or until heated through.

6 Serve on warm buns with cheese sprinkled on top of sausage.

Note: *Use high-quality Italian sausage — fresh from the butcher.*

Menu: *Serve with Greek Peasant Salad (page 124) for a great family meal. Finish with a Brownie Torte (page 265).*

 Chianti

Brockman's Brew Brats

Ideal for cookouts

Yield: 16 servings

2	large Vidalia onions, sliced, or more to taste	16	large bratwurst or Mettwurst, or a combination
8	(12 ounce) cans beer	16	fresh hot dog or hoagie buns
1½	sticks butter		Spicy brown mustard

🕐 *The brats must simmer at least 1 hour, and up to 3 hours.*

- Place onion in a large stock pot or crockpot. Add beer and butter. Bring to a boil, then reduce heat to a simmer.

- Meanwhile, grill brats until they split slightly. Remove from grill and allow to stand 30 minutes. Add cooled bratwurst to beer mixture. Simmer 1 to 3 hours.

- Keep brats in pot until serving to prevent them from shriveling up. Serve on buns with the mustard. Top with cooked onions.

Note: *For best results, use fresh bratwurst from a butcher (we like the East Dayton German Sausage Company), and high-quality buns fresh from the bakery (we suggest you order them from Evans Bakery in Old North Dayton).*

Menu: *Stop by the deli for sauerkraut and German potato salad before serving these fabulous brats.*

🍷 *Beer works best!*

This recipe comes from Brock Anderson, owner of our local Miller Beer Distributor, Bonbright. The brats have been served countless times at company functions. They pair especially well with beer!

Ham and Cheese Tailgate Sandwiches

A snap to make and a major crowd-pleaser!

Yield: 8 servings

1½ sticks butter, softened	1 medium sweet onion, diced
3 tablespoons mustard	8 sandwich buns
½ teaspoon poppy seeds	1 pound shaved ham (we prefer honey ham)
1 tablespoon Worcestershire sauce	½ pound shaved Swiss cheese

The "spread mixture" can be made the night before and refrigerated. Allow 2 hours to come to room temperature before spreading on buns. Also, sandwiches can be assembled up to 12 hours ahead. Heat according to instructions.

⚬ Preheat oven to 400 degrees.

⚬ Combine butter, mustard, poppy seeds, Worcestershire sauce and onion. Spread mixture on inside of buns. Add layers of ham and cheese. Wrap each sandwich in foil. Refrigerate until ready to bake.

⚬ Bake 10 to 15 minutes and serve.

Note: *These sandwiches, wrapped in foil, will keep warm in an insulated cooler for 2 hours, thus making them perfect for tailgates and picnics!*

Menu: *Make Grandma Ruby's Garlic Sweet Pickles (page 101) and Marinated New Red Potato Salad (page 140) to go with the sandwiches.*

Beer

A Peace of Cake

DESSERTS

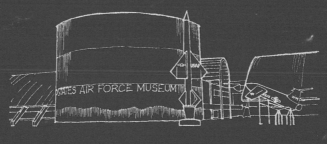

DAYTON PEACE ACCORDS

A PEACE OF CAKE

For three weeks in November 1995, the Hope Hotel at Wright-Patterson Air Force Base was the site of negotiations among Balkan leaders Franjo Tudjman, Slobodan Milosevic, and Alija Izetbegovic. Chosen by President Bill Clinton, Wright-Patterson provided the ideal environment for the feuding leaders. On November 21, the three presidents signed the Dayton Peace Accords, which ended 43 months of war and signaled the start of the long road toward peace. At the fourth anniversary of the Accords signing, the song "Day One" was performed.

A child walks down to the water / Draws a circle in the sand / Wave comes and takes it away / Out from under his hand / The child learns a lesson / He can use later on / Anything worth doing / Takes a good while to get done / We're building a circle, right here right now / Half a million people, ten thousand miles around / We've only just started, but you can feel it growing strong / Two cities showing the world how to get along

THIS COULD TAKE A LIFETIME / A HUNDRED TRIPS ROUND THE SUN / IF IT TAKES A LIFETIME / LET THIS BE DAY ONE

Crossing the ocean on a runaway tide / Harmony in motion, cannot be denied / Every mother's daughter, every father's son / Giving all they have to give till the work is done

MAKE IT LAST A LIFETIME / A HUNDRED TRIPS ROUND THE SUN / KEEP IT YOUNG FOREVER / JUST LIKE ON DAY ONE   "Day One," © 2000 James Rounds

"Everywhere I've been, in Bosnia, in Croatia, the thing that amazes people the most is that the people in Dayton really do care about their problems. We're not just celebrating an anniversary, we're celebrating a relationship." MIKE TURNER, DAYTON MAYOR

Mrs. Huffman's Legendary Lemon Soufflé

Fabulous make-ahead dessert for a luncheon or special party

Yield: 8 servings

1	envelope (1 tablespoon) unsweetened gelatin	1	scant cup sugar
¼	cup cold water	⅓	cup lemon juice
3	eggs, separated		Zest of 1 lemon
		2	cups heavy cream, or less to taste

🕐 *Dessert must be chilled for several hours before serving.*

- Soak gelatin in cold water in a glass bowl. Place bowl in a pan of hot water and heat until mixture turns to liquid.

- Beat egg yolks until light-colored. Gradually add sugar. Continue beating while adding lemon juice and zest. Stir in gelatin mixture. Allow to cool until mixture starts to thicken.

- Beat egg whites until stiff. In a separate bowl, beat cream until stiff. Fold egg whites and cream into lemon mixture. Place in a serving bowl or in individual serving bowls. Cover with plastic wrap and chill several hours.

Note: *Top just before serving with lemon peel rolled in sugar; or serve in bowls with fresh raspberries and/or a small amount of raspberry puree, and a mint leaf.*

Mother's Brandy-Pecan Pudding

A truly old-fashioned pudding with a crunchy top and a rich sugar custard underneath

Yield: 8 servings

5	eggs	3	tablespoons brandy
1	cup sugar	1½	teaspoons vanilla
1⅓	cups light corn syrup	1	cup chopped pecans
5	tablespoons butter, melted		Rich vanilla ice cream

- Preheat oven to 350 degrees.

- Beat together eggs, sugar, corn syrup, butter, brandy, and vanilla in a mixing bowl until thoroughly mixed. Stir in pecans. Pour into a greased 8-inch square pan.

- Bake 40 minutes, or until just set. Cool on a rack until barely warm. Spoon into dessert dishes and add scoops of ice cream.

Note: *Do not cook until hard — should be texture of pudding.*

The Huffman family often referred to exceptionally good food as "doglicious." This originated from a brand of dog food known as Kasco. Road signs in the 1950s would extol the virtues of Kasco and end the message with "It's doglicious!" This expression now is used by the grandchildren... and somehow it is meant to be a compliment... and is actually received as such!

—Tony Huffman

The National Aviation Hall of Fame was founded in 1962 and is located at the United States Air Force Museum. The NAHF honors those who have contributed to America's rich legacy of aviation achievement, celebrating American ingenuity and individual acts of great vision, persistence, skill and courage. Some famous Ohioans included in the Hall are astronauts, John Glenn and Neil Armstrong, and of course, Orville and Wilbur Wright.

Caramel Apple Bread Pudding

The ultimate dessert for the autumn season

Yield: 10 to 12 servings

Pudding
1	cup milk
1	(18 ounce) container caramel dip (we prefer Marzetti's brand)
½	cup sugar
3	eggs
1	tablespoon vanilla
1	teaspoon cinnamon
½	teaspoon nutmeg
6-8	cups French bread, torn into 1-inch pieces
2	cups milk
4	medium apples, peeled and sliced ¼-inch thick
1	cup pecans or walnuts
½	cup dried cranberries or raisins (optional)

Cinnamon Whipped Cream
1	(8 ounce) container heavy cream
¼	cup sugar, very fine works best
1	teaspoon cinnamon
1	teaspoon vanilla

Tear bread into pieces up to 1 day ahead.

Preheat oven to 350 degrees.

To make pudding, whisk together 1 cup milk, half the container of caramel dip, sugar, eggs, vanilla, cinnamon, and nutmeg.

Soak bread briefly in 2 cups milk. Fold caramel mixture and apple slices into soaked bread. Pour mixture into a greased 9x13-inch casserole dish. Sprinkle with pecans and cranberries. Dot with remaining caramel dip.

Place dish on a baking sheet and bake 1 hour. Serve with Cinnamon Whipped Cream.

To make cream, whip cream until soft peaks form. Combine sugar and cinnamon; slowly add mixture to cream. Mix in vanilla. Continue to beat until thickened to desired consistency.

Menu: *Serve after roasted pork and other autumn fare.*

Mocha Latte Decadence ❄

The name describes it perfectly

Yield: 8 to 10 servings

Crust and First Layer

24	Oreo cookies, crushed	½	gallon coffee ice cream
5	tablespoons butter, melted		

Filling

2	tablespoons butter, melted		Dash of salt
3	ounces unsweetened chocolate	1	(12 ounce) can evaporated milk
½	cup sugar	½	teaspoon vanilla

Topping

1½	cups heavy cream		Sliced almonds, lightly toasted,
1½	ounces Kahlúa		for garnish
	Powdered sugar to taste		Grated chocolate for garnish

🕐 *This recipe is done in stages, requiring it to be made at least 1 day, or up to 2 weeks, ahead. However, prepare topping just before serving.*

☙ To make crust, mix together crushed cookies and butter; press into a 9x13-inch pan. Chill at least 30 minutes.

☙ Meanwhile, soften ice cream. Spread over chilled crust. Freeze at least 12 hours.

☙ Combine all filling ingredients, except vanilla, in a saucepan. Bring to a boil. Reduce heat; stir until mixture thickens. Remove from heat and stir in vanilla. Cool, then refrigerate at least 2 hours. Spread chilled filling over ice cream layer. Return to freezer for at least 6 hours.

☙ To prepare topping, beat together cream, Kahlúa and powdered sugar with an electric mixer until soft peaks form. Spread over filling and garnish with almonds and chocolate.

During the Dayton Peace Talks, the atmosphere at the Hope Hotel—named after Bob Hope—was of pure business. This was to be no vacation. The Balkan leaders were given identical accommodations-identical suites, identical furniture, even identically colored towels. This sent the message to the three leaders that they enjoyed equal status, but that they bore equal responsibility to resolve their differences.

Chocolate Pâté ❄

Easy, elegant and freezes beautifully

Yield: 8 to 10 servings, 1½ cups sauce

Pâté

15	ounces semisweet chocolate
1	cup heavy cream
4	tablespoons unsalted butter
4	egg yolks

¾	cup powdered sugar
6	tablespoons dark rum
	Sweetened whipped cream for garnish

Raspberry Sauce

2	(10 ounce) packages frozen raspberries in syrup, thawed
¼	cup sugar

2-3	tablespoons Grand Marnier liqueur

🕐 *Pâté must be made 1 day ahead; may be frozen up to 2 weeks. Raspberry sauce may be made up to 2 days ahead and refrigerated, or frozen up to 2 months.*

- Grease a 4-cup loaf pan. Place wax paper in pan, leaving a small overhang. Grease sides and bottom of paper lining. Set aside.

- Melt chocolate with cream and butter in the top of a double boiler over simmering water. Beat with a wire whisk until mixture is smooth and glossy. Remove from heat and add yolks, one at a time, beating well after each addition. Whisk in powdered sugar until smooth. Mix in rum. Pour mixture into prepared pan and cover with plastic wrap. Freeze overnight.

- When ready to serve, remove pâté by gently loosening wax paper from pan. If it sticks, set pan in hot water for a few seconds. Invert pâté onto a serving plate and remove wax paper. Using a hot knife, cut pâté into ⅓- to ½-inch slices.

- To make raspberry sauce, drain 1 package of raspberries, discarding juice. Reserve juice when draining second package of berries. Puree all berries, reserved juice, sugar, and liqueur in a food processor or blender. Strain puree to remove seeds. Chill until ready to use.

- To serve, place a slice of pâté in a pool of raspberry sauce on each plate. Top with a generous dollop of whipped cream.

Do you know where the Marvel comic book hero The Hulk's alter ego was born? Bruce Banner was born at our own Wright-Patterson Air Force Base. His father was an Air Force officer.

Frozen Tropical Gingersnap Cake ❄

Colorful and uniquely flavorful

Yield: 8 servings

Cake

1¼	cups crushed gingersnaps (about 25 cookies)	14	(2 inch) gingersnap cookies	
4	tablespoons butter or margarine, melted	1	pint mango sorbet	
1	pint vanilla ice cream, softened	½	cup shredded coconut, toasted, for garnish	

Salsa

2	kiwi fruit, peeled and chopped	2	tablespoons fresh lime juice	
1	papaya, peeled, seeded and chopped	1	tablespoon honey	
1	cup chopped fresh strawberries	1	teaspoon lime zest	

🕐 *Pie needs to be prepared at least 5 hours prior to serving. Can be frozen up to 5 days if well-covered.*

❻ Combine gingersnap crumbs and butter in a medium bowl; blend well. Press mixture into the bottom and ½ inch up the sides of a 9-inch springform pan. Freeze 10 minutes.

❻ Spoon ice cream over crust, pressing firmly with the back of a spoon to level surface. Arrange whole gingersnaps on top and cover. Freeze 1 hour, or until firm.

❻ Soften sorbet in refrigerator for 30 minutes. Spoon over gingersnaps and press firmly with the back of a spoon to level and smooth surface. Cover and freeze 3 hours. Remove cake from pan; place on a serving plate. Cover and freeze until serving time.

❻ Stir together salsa ingredients in a medium bowl.

❻ To serve, cut cake into wedges. Top each serving with salsa and garnish with coconut.

The United States Air Force Museum, located at Wright Patterson Air Force Base, is the oldest and largest military aviation museum in the world. Adjacent to the Museum is the Memorial Park. Statuary memorials, plaques, trees, and benches dedicated to Air Force-associated individuals and units adorn this 9-acre park.

Warm Chocolate Tarts ❄

Very rich and easy to make

Yield: 6 servings

4	ounces bittersweet or semisweet chocolate	1½	tablespoons unsweetened cocoa
3½	ounces unsweetened chocolate	¾	teaspoon baking powder
1¼	sticks unsalted butter	3	eggs
½	cup plus 2 tablespoons sugar		Vanilla ice cream (optional)
½	cup plus 2 tablespoons flour		Fresh berries (optional)

🕐 *Tarts must be made and frozen at least 3 hours ahead. They also may be frozen up to 2 weeks ahead.*

6 Melt chocolates and butter in a double boiler set over simmering water. Stir in sugar until dissolved.

6 Scrape mixture into a mixing bowl. Add flour, cocoa, baking powder, and eggs. Beat 7 to 8 minutes, or until mixture thickens to almost a mousse consistency.

6 Divide mixture among six (1 cup) greased soufflé dishes or ramekins. Cover with foil and freeze for at least 3 hours.

6 When ready to serve, preheat oven to 375 degrees.

6 Remove foil and bake 11 to 13 minutes, or until edges set and center is moist and shiny. Bake 1 minute longer; do not overbake.

6 Cool 10 minutes before inverting onto dessert plates. Serve with vanilla ice cream and fresh berries.

Bananas Caribbean

Delicious and festive

Yield: 4 servings

1	tablespoon butter	2	bananas, sliced lengthwise
½	cup brown sugar		Brandy
3	tablespoons banana liqueur		Vanilla ice cream

6 Melt butter with sugar in a skillet. Mix in liqueur. Add bananas.

6 Warm brandy and pour over bananas. Light with a match. Serve over vanilla ice cream.

Note: *This dessert comes together quickly!*

Wright-Patterson Air Force Base is one of the nation's most important military installations, and Ohio's largest single-site employer. This installation is headquarters for the foremost research and development center in the U.S. Air Force. The transfer of technology from military to civilian uses is an important part of the relationship between Wright-Patterson and the Greater Dayton Region. Together, WPAFB and the larger community share the best and brightest minds in aerospace technology, providing everything from materials technology to artificial intelligence, nuclear engineering to electro-optics, and engineering physics to aeronautical research.

Try these simple fruit desserts: honeydew drizzled with honey, blueberries drizzled with lemon cream, or pineapple chunks dressed with Kirsch and lemon zest.

Chocolate Caramel Pecan Cheesecake

A chocolate dessert to die for!

Yield: 12 servings

Crust

2	cups crushed vanilla wafers	6	tablespoons margarine, melted

Caramel Filling

1	(14 ounce) package caramels	1	cup chopped pecans
¼	cup milk		

Cheesecake Filling

2	(8 ounce) packages cream cheese, softened	2	eggs
½	cup sugar	4	(1 ounce) squares semisweet chocolate, melted and slightly cooled
1	teaspoon vanilla		

🕐 *Crust can be baked up to 1 day ahead, or frozen up to 1 month. Caramels can be unwrapped ahead of time and kept in a zip-top bag. Cheesecake must be made at least 4 hours, and up to 3 days, ahead. Keep covered and refrigerated.*

⚬ Preheat oven to 325 degrees.

⚬ To make crust, mix wafer crumbs and margarine; press into the bottom and 1½ inches up the sides of a 9-inch springform pan. Bake 10 minutes.

⚬ For caramel filling, place caramels and milk in a microwave-safe bowl. Microwave on high for 4 to 5 minutes, or until melted, stirring every minute. Pour over crust and sprinkle with pecans.

⚬ To prepare cheesecake filling, beat cream cheese, sugar and vanilla with an electric mixer at medium speed until well-blended. Add eggs, one at a time, mixing on low speed after each addition until just blended. Blend in chocolate. Pour mixture over pecans.

⚬ Bake 45 to 50 minutes, or until center is almost set. Remove from oven.

⚬ Run a knife or metal spatula around the rim of pan to loosen cake. Cool before removing from pan. Refrigerate 4 hours or overnight.

Use your microwave oven when a recipe calls for you to melt chocolate. It gives great results and is truly faster than the traditional method. Place ½ pound of chocolate in a glass bowl or measuring cup. Melt uncovered at 50-percent power for 3 to 4 minutes; stir after 2 minutes.

Amaretto Irish Cream Cheesecake ❋

Very rich and elegant

Yield: 12 servings

Crust
1¾ cups crushed sugar cookies	4 tablespoons butter, melted
½ cup chopped almonds	1½ teaspoons amaretto liqueur

Filling
3 (8 ounce) packages cream cheese, softened	⅓ cup heavy cream
	¼ cup amaretto liqueur
1 cup plus 2 tablespoons sugar	¼ cup Irish cream liqueur
4 eggs	

Topping
1½ cups sour cream	½ teaspoon amaretto liqueur
1 tablespoon sugar	¼ cup sliced almonds
½ teaspoon vanilla	

🕐 *Crust can be made up to 1 day ahead, or frozen up to 1 month. Cheesecake can be made up to 3 days ahead, covered and refrigerated.*

6 Preheat oven to 350 degrees.

6 Mix together crust ingredients; press into a 10-inch springform pan that has been sprayed with nonstick cooking spray. Bake 10 minutes; cool.

6 To make filling, beat cream cheese. Add sugar and mix well. Add eggs, cream and liqueurs; mix well. Pour over cooled crust. Bake 30 minutes. Turn off oven, leaving cheesecake in oven for 45 minutes before removing to cool.

6 When cheesecake has cooled, preheat oven to 500 degrees.

6 To make topping, combine sour cream, sugar, vanilla, and amaretto. Spoon over cheesecake. Sprinkle almonds around edge.

6 Bake 5 minutes. Cool and refrigerate until ready to serve.

Note: *If you can find them, use Voortman's Tea Ring Sugar Cookies for crust.*

Cheesecake-Filled Strawberries:

Whip 8 ounces of room temperature cream cheese on medium speed for 2 to 3 minutes until slightly fluffy. Add 1 teaspoon pure vanilla extract and 2 tablespoons confectioners' sugar. Trim bottom of 12 strawberries so that each stands upright. Use a melon baller to scoop out stems and tops. Fill pastry bag fitted with a ½-inch star tip with cream cheese mixture. Pipe into strawberries until cream cheese brims over the top. Top each berry with a mint leaf.

Pecan Torte

Delightful!

Yield: 14 to 16 servings

4	eggs, separated
2	cups granulated sugar, divided
1	cup Ritz cracker crumbs
1	cup chopped pecans

1	teaspoon vanilla
2	cups heavy cream
¼	cup powdered sugar
1	teaspoon vanilla

🕐 *This torte needs to be refrigerated 6 to 8 hours before serving.*

◌ Preheat oven to 350 degrees.

◌ Beat egg whites in a medium bowl until stiff. Gradually add 1 cup granulated sugar.

◌ In a separate bowl, beat yolks. Gradually beat in remaining 1 cup granulated sugar. Fold egg white mixture into yolk mixture. Add crumbs, pecans and 1 teaspoon vanilla. Carefully stir until well-blended. Spoon into 2 greased and paper-lined 8- or 9-inch cake pans.

◌ Bake 35 minutes. Cool and turn out of pans, removing paper.

◌ To make icing, whip cream until soft peaks form. Add powdered sugar and 1 teaspoon vanilla. Whip to stiff peaks.

◌ To assemble, place 1 torte layer on a serving plate. Cover this with half of icing and place second layer on top. Cover cake with remaining icing. Refrigerate 6 to 8 hours to absorb cream. Don't worry if the torte crumbles, the icing will "glue" it all together.

Rum Cake ❄

Yield: 12 to 16 servings

Cake

½	cup chopped pecans
1	(18¼ ounce) box yellow butter cake mix
1	(3 ounce) package instant vanilla pudding

½	cup light rum
½	cup vegetable oil
½	cup water
4	eggs

Glaze

1	stick butter
¼	cup water

1	cup sugar
¼	cup light rum

🕐 *Can be made up to 3 days ahead, or frozen up to 3 months.*

◌ Preheat oven to 350 degrees.

◌ Sprinkle pecans in the bottom of a greased and floured Bundt pan.

◌ Combine cake mix, pudding, rum, oil, water, and eggs; pour into pan.

◌ Bake 1 hour.

◌ Meanwhile, prepare glaze. Combine glaze ingredients in a saucepan and bring to a boil. Cook 2 to 5 minutes.

◌ Pour glaze over cake as soon as cake is removed from oven. Cool cake in pan.

My friends insisted I submit this recipe. It is my oldest and most-beloved!

—Marty Ebeling

My husband says this cake is one of the reasons he married me!

—Susan Watkins

Shortcakes with Strawberries and Whipped Cream

A delicious spring sensation!

Yield: 6 servings

Topping

1	pint strawberries, crushed with a potato masher	2	pints strawberries, quartered
		6	tablespoons sugar

Shortcakes

2	cups all-purpose flour	1	egg, beaten
½	teaspoon salt	½	cup plus 1 tablespoon half-and-half
1	tablespoon baking powder		
3	tablespoons sugar	1	egg white, lightly beaten
1	stick unsalted butter, frozen	2	tablespoons sugar

Whipped Cream

1	cup heavy cream, chilled	1	teaspoon vanilla
1	tablespoon sugar		

🕐 *Hull strawberries and refrigerate up to 1 day ahead. Topping ingredients can be mixed together up to 2 hours ahead. Unbaked biscuit rounds can be covered and refrigerated up to 2 hours before baking.*

- For topping, mix crushed and quartered berries with sugar in a medium bowl. Set aside.

- To make shortcakes, adjust oven rack to lower middle position. Preheat oven to 425 degrees.

- Combine flour, salt, baking powder, and 3 tablespoons sugar in a medium bowl. Coarsely grate butter into dry ingredients. Toss to coat butter. Use a pastry blender or fork to finish cutting in butter.

- Combine egg and half-and-half; pour into flour mixture. Toss with a fork until large clumps form. Turn mixture onto a floured surface and lightly knead until mixture sticks together.

- Pat dough into a 9x6-inch rectangle, ¾-inch thick. Using a floured 2¾-inch biscuit cutter, cut 6 dough rounds. Place rounds 1 inch apart on a small baking sheet. Brush top of rounds with egg white and sprinkle with 2 tablespoons sugar. At this point, rounds can be covered and refrigerated up to 2 hours before baking.

- Bake rounds 12 to 14 minutes, or until golden brown. Place baking sheet on wire rack and cool about 10 minutes.

- Meanwhile, prepare whipped cream by chilling a nonreactive, deep, 1- to 1½-quart bowl and electric mixer beaters in the freezer for at least 20 minutes.

- Combine cream, sugar and vanilla in chilled bowl. Beat on low speed until small bubbles form. Increase speed to medium and continue to beat until beaters leave a trail. Increase speed to high and beat until cream is smooth, thick and nearly doubled in volume. If necessary, finish beating by hand to adjust consistency. Use immediately, or place in a fine sieve or strainer over a measuring cup and refrigerate up to 8 hours.

⚘ Split each cake crosswise by gently pulling apart with hands. Spoon topping over cake bottoms and add a dollop of whipped cream to each. Place top of cakes over cream and serve.

Menu: *Serve after spring menus, such as Mango Lamb Chops (page 248), steamed asparagus and Lemon Rice with Pine Nuts (page 162).*

Brownie Torte ❄

Rich and chocolaty

Yield: 8 servings

Torte

1	stick butter	3	eggs
½	cup light corn syrup	1	teaspoon vanilla
1	cup semisweet chocolate chips	1	cup all-purpose flour
½	cup sugar	1	cup chopped pecans

Chocolate Glaze

½	cup semisweet chocolate chips	1	tablespoon light corn syrup
2	tablespoons butter	1	teaspoon vanilla

🕐 *Cake must chill in refrigerator before serving. Can also be made ahead and frozen up to 3 months.*

⚘ Preheat oven to 350 degrees.

⚘ To make torte, melt butter with corn syrup in a saucepan. Stir in chocolate chips until melted. Remove from heat. Add sugar and eggs. Stir until well-blended. Stir in vanilla, flour and pecans. Use a whisk if needed to smooth out batter. Pour batter into a greased and floured 9-inch cake pan.

⚘ Bake 30 minutes, or until the center springs back when touched.

⚘ Cool in pan 10 minutes. Invert onto a cooling rack. When completely cooled, invert onto a serving dish so torte is upright.

⚘ To make glaze, combine chocolate chips, butter and corn syrup in a saucepan. Stir over low heat until chocolate melts. Remove from heat and stir in vanilla.

⚘ Frost top and sides of torte with glaze. Chill torte until glaze sets.

Note: *The glaze cannot be made ahead of time. If desired, top with whipped cream and chocolate shavings. For a romantic Valentine's Day dessert, use a heart-shaped cookie cutter to cut out a heart-shaped mini-torte; sprinkle with powdered sugar. Serve with strawberry sorbet that has been molded in another heart-shaped cookie cutter (soften sorbet, spoon into cookie cutter on a flat plate, freeze) and drizzled with chocolate syrup. Add a strawberry for a garnish.*

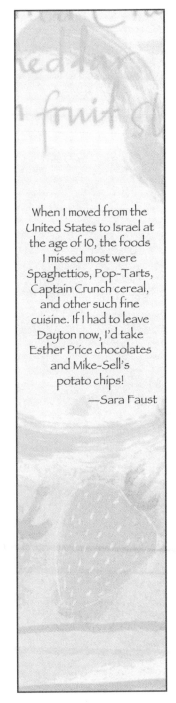

When I moved from the United States to Israel at the age of 10, the foods I missed most were Spaghettios, Pop-Tarts, Captain Crunch cereal, and other such fine cuisine. If I had to leave Dayton now, I'd take Esther Price chocolates and Mike-Sell's potato chips!

—Sara Faust

Grandma Mo's Amazing Almond Sheet Cake

This very special cake has been adored for years

Yield: 20 servings

Cake

2	sticks butter	½	cup sour cream
1	cup water	1	teaspoon almond extract
2	cups all-purpose flour	1	teaspoon salt
2	cups sugar	1	teaspoon baking soda
2	eggs, beaten		

Frosting

1	stick butter	½	teaspoon almond extract
¼	cup milk	1-1½	cups sliced almonds, lightly
4	cups powdered sugar		toasted

🕐 *This cake is better if made at least 1 day ahead.*

6　Preheat oven to 375 degrees.

6　To make cake, bring butter and water to a boil in a large saucepan. Remove from heat; stir in flour, sugar, egg, sour cream, almond extract, salt, and baking soda. Mix until smooth. Pour into a greased or parchment paper-lined 10x15-inch jelly-roll pan.

6　Bake 20 to 22 minutes, or until cake is golden brown and a toothpick inserted in the center comes out clean. Cool 20 minutes or until warm.

6　Meanwhile, prepare frosting. Combine butter and milk in a saucepan over medium-low heat. Bring to a boil. Remove from heat; add powdered sugar and almond extract. Mix well.

6　Spread frosting over warm cake. Sprinkle with almonds.

Note: *If you'd like to serve this cake on a platter rather than in a jelly-roll pan, be sure to line the pan with parchment paper for easy removal of cake.*

White chocolate is cocoa butter with sugar and milk, but has no chocolate liqueur!

Century-Style Chocolate Sheet Cake ❄

A tester could have sworn she was eating the cake from the Old Century Bar in downtown Dayton!

Yield: 20 servings

Cake

2	sticks butter	1	teaspoon baking soda
1	cup water	1	teaspoon salt
2	tablespoons cocoa	2	eggs, lightly beaten
2	cups flour	½	cup buttermilk
2	cups sugar		

Icing

1	stick butter		Pinch of salt
6	tablespoons milk	1	teaspoon vanilla
¼	cup cocoa	½-1	cup chopped pecans
1	(1 pound) package powdered sugar		

🕐 *Can be made ahead and frozen up to 3 months.*

6 Preheat oven to 375 degrees.

6 Combine butter, water and cocoa in a saucepan. Bring to a boil; immediately remove from heat. Stir in flour, sugar, baking soda, and salt. Mix thoroughly. Add eggs and buttermilk; stir. Pour into a jelly-roll pan.

6 Bake 22 minutes.

6 Meanwhile, prepare icing. Melt butter in a saucepan. Mix in milk, cocoa, powdered sugar, salt, and vanilla.

6 Pour icing over cake while still hot. Spread icing evenly and sprinkle with pecans.

Many years ago, downtown Dayton's Century Bar was owned by one of my great relatives. My grandmother's sister loved to spend the entire day in the kitchen preparing meals for family get-togethers. One day, the Century Bar was in desperate need of a cook, so they called Aunt Mimi. Aunt Mimi jumped right into the kitchen and began preparing orders. Being a perfectionist and a gourmet cook, she took way too long on each order. Quickly the orders began to pile up and customers became angry. The waiters tried to hurry her up, so anytime they brought more orders to her, she would start throwing pots, pans and anything else she could grab at them. With the bar being so small, the pots and pans would land out in the restaurant where all the customers could see. Aunt Mimi never worked at the bar again.

—Kellie Rhodes

Mimi's Carrot Cake

Sweet, moist and delicious

Yield: 12 servings

Gravity-defying frosting turns ordinary cake into a spooky, spiky dessert. Make a devil's food cake, then frost with Betty Crocker's Fluffy Homestyle Frosting, a mix version of meringue-like, seven-minute frosting. Once the cake is iced, use a spoon to add more dollops of frosting, pulling the back of the spoon away from the cake as the icing is released and twisting the ends into spikes. Make frosting spikes all over the top and sides of the cake. (You'll use a lot to get the effect—you may want to use two boxes of frosting. But don't try this if the weather is humid!)

Cake

1¼	cups canola oil	2	teaspoons baking powder
1	cup brown sugar	2	teaspoons cinnamon
1	cup granulated sugar	3	cups packed shredded carrot
4	eggs	1	(8½ ounce) can crushed
1	cup all-purpose flour		pineapple, drained
1	cup less 2 tablespoons whole	½	cup shredded coconut
	wheat flour	½	cup chopped walnuts (optional)
1	teaspoon salt	½	cup raisins
2	teaspoons baking soda		

Lemon Cream Cheese Frosting

1	(8 ounce) package cream cheese, softened	2	cups powdered sugar
		1½	teaspoons vanilla
4	tablespoons butter, softened	1	tablespoon lemon zest

🕐 *This cake may be made up to 3 days ahead and kept covered.*

6 Preheat oven to 350 degrees.

6 Blend oil and sugars together in a mixing bowl. Beat in eggs, one at a time.

6 In a separate bowl, sift together flours, salt, baking soda, baking powder, and cinnamon.

6 Add dry ingredients to egg mixture. Fold in carrot, pineapple, coconut, walnuts, and raisins. Pour batter into 2 greased 9-inch cake pans.

6 Bake 35 to 40 minutes. Cool.

6 To make frosting, blend cream cheese and butter. Add sugar, vanilla and zest; mix thoroughly. Spread frosting over cooled cake.

Note: *Buy shredded carrot to save time.*

Great-Grandmother's Pound Cake ❄

These cakes were sold by "great-grandmother" for $5.00 each — in the 50's!

Yield: 16 servings

2	sticks butter	1	cup milk
1	stick margarine	2	teaspoons vanilla
3	cups sugar	½	teaspoon salt
5	eggs	½	teaspoon baking powder
3	cups flour		

🕐 *This cake is better if made up to 2 days ahead. Cake can also be frozen up to 3 months.*

6 Preheat oven to 350 degrees.

6 Cream butter, margarine and sugar until smooth. Beat in eggs, one at a time. Add flour, alternating with milk, combining well after each addition. Pour into a greased and floured angel food cake pan or Bundt pan.

6 Bake 1 hour, 15 minutes to 1 hour, 30 minutes, or until a toothpick inserted in the center comes out clean.

Best Easy Chocolate Bundt Cake ❄

A quick dessert to make for a crowd

Yield: 10 to 12 servings

1	(18¼ ounce) box devil's food cake mix	½	cup water
		½	cup oil
1	(3 ounce) package instant chocolate pudding	1	cup sour cream
		1	cup chocolate chips
4	eggs		Powdered sugar for garnish

🕐 *Cake may be made up to 1 day ahead and kept covered. Cake may be frozen up to 1 month.*

6 Preheat oven to 350 degrees.

6 Combine cake mix, pudding, eggs, water, oil, and sour cream in a bowl. Beat 4 minutes. Stir in chocolate chips. Pour into a generously greased and floured Bundt pan.

6 Bake 50 minutes, or until a toothpick inserted in the center comes out clean. Cool and sprinkle with powdered sugar.

Use a bit of dry cake mix to flour your cake pan instead of actual flour—it will prevent the white mess on the outside of your cake!

The fragrant oils in lemon zest give a distinctive aroma and flavor to foods. Make some lemon sugar to keep on hand for use in baking recipes that call for sugar, to sprinkle over sugar cookies, or to add to hot tea for a delicious lemony treat. Lemon Sugar: Use a citrus zester to remove the zest from 3 lemons. Roughly chop zest and transfer to food processor fitted with the blade attachment. Add 1 cup sugar to zest, and pulse until zest has been finely ground, about 3 minutes. Transfer mixture to medium bowl. Add 1 cup sugar and toss until evenly mixed. Spread lemon sugar on baking pan and let sit at room temperature until dry, about 1 hour. Store in airtight container up to 1 month.

Almond Fruit Tart

This recipe is delicious, gorgeous and easy to make

Yield: 8 to 10 servings

Crust

1	stick butter	½	teaspoon almond extract
½	cup sugar	1½	cups flour
1	egg yolk	½	cup sliced almonds, toasted
1	teaspoon vanilla		

Filling and Topping

1	(8 ounce) package cream cheese, softened		Fresh fruit, such as strawberry slices, kiwi slices, blueberries, or pineapple chunks
2	tablespoons sugar		
2	tablespoons amaretto liqueur, or ½ teaspoon almond extract	¼	cup apricot jam
		1	tablespoon water
1	teaspoon vanilla	¼	cup sliced almonds, toasted

🕐 *Recipe requires an 11-inch tart pan. Tart shell can be made and frozen up to 3 months ahead. Tart can be made up to 8 hours ahead and kept covered at room temperature.*

❻ Preheat oven to 375 degrees.

❻ Cream butter and sugar in a bowl. Beat in egg yolk, vanilla and almond extract. Mix in flour and almonds to form a dough. Press into an 11-inch tart pan. Prick shell and bake 10 minutes, or until golden. Cool.

❻ To make filling, beat cream cheese and sugar. Blend in amaretto and vanilla. Spread in cooled crust. Chill until firm.

❻ Place fruit on filling in a decorative arrangement.

❻ Whisk jam and water over medium heat until jam melts. Boil 30 seconds. Cool slightly and brush over fruit. Sprinkle with almonds.

Raspberry Pear Tart

A scoop of vanilla ice cream on the side will make this recipe even more delicious

Yield: 6 servings

1 sheet puff pastry dough	⅓ cup sugar
1 (16 ounce) can pears, drained and sliced	1 teaspoon vanilla
1 cup heavy cream	¼ teaspoon cinnamon
2 eggs, beaten	6 ounces fresh raspberries

❦ Preheat oven to 350 degrees.

❦ Press pastry dough into a pie plate and trim edges. Bake 10 minutes, or until lightly browned.

❦ Arrange pear slices in a circular pattern in the crust.

❦ Combine cream, egg, sugar, vanilla, and cinnamon; pour over pears. Scatter raspberries over top.

❦ Bake 40 to 45 minutes. If necessary, place foil around tart crust to keep edges from browning before filling is set.

Raspberries are delicious when sprinkled with balsamic vinegar and sugar.

Blackberry Mini-Tarts

Great for a brunch, shower or dessert buffet

Yield: 20 tarts

1 (15 ounce) package refrigerated pie crusts	1 (3 ounce) package cream cheese, softened
⅓ cup water	2 tablespoons butter or margarine, softened
½ cup granulated sugar	
2 tablespoons cornstarch	1 teaspoon vanilla
2 tablespoons butter or margarine	1 cup powdered sugar
1 pint fresh blackberries	

❦ Preheat oven to 350 degrees.

❦ Unfold pie crusts. Press out fold lines with a rolling pin on a lightly floured surface. Use a 2½-inch, star-shaped cutter to cut out shapes; fit into lightly greased miniature-muffin pans.

❦ Bake 7 minutes, or until golden. Remove from pans and cool on wire racks.

❦ Bring water, granulated sugar, cornstarch, 2 tablespoons butter, and blackberries to a boil in a heavy saucepan over medium heat. Boil, stirring constantly, for 1 minute. Remove from heat and set aside.

❦ In a separate bowl, stir together cream cheese, 2 tablespoons butter, vanilla, and powdered sugar.

❦ Spoon blackberry mixture into tart shells. Pipe or dollop cream cheese mixture on top. Sprinkle with extra powdered sugar, if desired.

Berry, berry good—top blackberry sorbet and blackberry frozen yogurt with fresh blackberries!

Lemon Blueberry Pie

A delightful taste of summer

Yield: 8 servings

6	eggs, lightly beaten	1	(9 inch) pie crust, baked
1	cup sugar	3	cups fresh blueberries
1	stick butter or margarine	⅓	cup sugar
⅓	cup fresh lemon juice	¼	cup orange juice
2	teaspoons lemon zest	1	tablespoon cornstarch

Pie crust must be baked prior to assembling the pie. Also, pie must be made ahead and chilled for 4 to 6 hours.

⬡ Combine egg, 1 cup sugar, butter, lemon juice, and zest in a saucepan. Cook, stirring constantly, over medium-high heat for about 20 minutes, or until thickened. Remove from heat and cool 20 minutes, stirring occasionally. Pour into baked pie crust.

⬡ In a saucepan, toss blueberries and ⅓ cup sugar together.

⬡ Mix orange juice and cornstarch in a small bowl. Add orange juice mixture to blueberries in saucepan; bring to a boil over medium heat. Cook, stirring gently, 8 to 10 minutes, or until thickened. Cook 2 minutes longer.

⬡ Cool 15 minutes, stirring occasionally. Spoon blueberry mixture over lemon layer. Chill 4 to 6 hours, or until set.

Brown Bag Apple Pie 🚲

One of the most requested recipes from our first cookbook!

Yield: 8 servings

½	cup sugar	1	(9 inch) pie crust, unbaked
2	tablespoons flour	1	stick butter, melted
¾	teaspoon cinnamon	½	cup sugar
6-7	medium baking apples, peeled and sliced	½	cup flour

⬡ Preheat oven to 400 degrees.

⬡ Mix ½ cup sugar, 2 tablespoons flour and cinnamon together. Toss mixture with apple slices. Heap sugared slices into pie crust.

⬡ Combine butter, ½ cup sugar and ½ cup flour to make a thin paste. Spread paste evenly over apple slices. Place pie in a brown paper bag and close securely with paper clips or staples.

⬡ Bake in the center of the oven for 1 hour, taking care that the bag does not touch any other surface in the oven. When done, cut away bag.

To remove lemon zest without a lemon zester, grate lemon peel from the lemon with a box-style cheese grater covered with plastic wrap. The plastic will keep the lemon zest from sticking to the grater, making it easier to remove, measure and use.

To blind-bake a pie shell, cover the bottom with a sheet of aluminum foil and top with dry beans; bake for 10 to 20 minutes. Remove beans and foil, and continue to bake as directed. The beans will keep the empty bottom of the pie crust flat; removing them allows the crust to brown. Save the beans to use again next time, but do not try to cook and eat them.

Apple Pie with Walnut Streusel

This pie is one of the best you'll ever taste

Yield: 8 to 10 servings

Pastry Dough
1½ cups all-purpose flour
2 tablespoons granulated sugar
¾ teaspoon salt

1¼ sticks unsalted butter, cold
4-6 tablespoons ice water

Topping
4 tablespoons unsalted butter, softened
¼ cup brown sugar
¼ cup all-purpose flour

½ cup coarsely chopped walnuts
2 tablespoons milk
1 tablespoon granulated sugar

Filling
4 pounds (about 8 medium) apples, combination of Granny Smith, Golden Delicious and Empire, peeled and cut into ½-inch wedges
½ cup brown sugar

¼ cup granulated sugar
2 tablespoons all-purpose flour
1 tablespoon fresh lemon juice
¾ teaspoon cinnamon
Ice cream (optional)

You may make pie pastry up to 1 day ahead, cover and refrigerate; or freeze for up to 3 months. Pie may be baked earlier in the day and served at room temperature.

- To make pastry dough, combine flour, sugar, salt, and butter with a pastry blender in a large bowl or food processor until mixture resembles coarse meal. Add 2 tablespoons water; toss with a fork or pulse in processor until incorporated. Add enough of remaining water, 1 tablespoon at a time, tossing or pulsing to incorporate, until mixture begins to form a dough. Knead dough on a floured surface for 3 or 4 strokes. Form dough into a ball and flatten to a 1-inch thick disk. Wrap in plastic and chill 30 minutes.

- Meanwhile, prepare topping by blending butter, sugar and flour in a small bowl with your fingertips until smooth. Blend in nuts. Cover and chill.

- For filling, toss all ingredients together until apple slices are coated.

- When ready to assemble pie, preheat oven to 350 degrees.

- Roll out dough, on a lightly floured surface, into a 15-inch round (about ⅛-inch thick) and fold into quarters for easy handling. Unfold dough in a 10-inch, deep dish (1½-quart) pie plate, easing to fit and letting dough overhang rim.

- Spoon filling into pastry crust and fold overhanging dough over filling, leaving center uncovered.

- Bake in middle of oven for 1 hour. Remove from oven. Pie will not be completely cooked.

- Crumble topping over center of pie, breaking up any large chunks. Brush crust with milk and sprinkle with 1 tablespoon sugar. Bake in middle of oven for another 30 minutes, or until crust is golden and filling is bubbling. Cool on a wire rack. Serve warm or at room temperature with ice cream.

Every Thanksgiving since I can remember, I've watched the Macy's parade on television. When I was growing up it was "nuts!" My mom gave my sister and me what seemed like a wheelbarrow full of nuts to crack for her pies. We spent hours cracking and shelling pecans and walnuts. Of course, the reward was the scrumptious taste of those pies!

—Stephanie Geehan

Rum Pie

An elegant blend of flavors

Yield: 2 pies, 16 servings

Crust

2	cups graham cracker crumbs	1	stick butter, melted
3	tablespoons sugar		Grated bittersweet chocolate for
1	teaspoon cinnamon		topping

Filling

6	egg yolks	½	cup cold water
1	cup sugar	2	cups heavy cream
1	tablespoon gelatin	⅓-½	cup rum

🕐 *Must make at least 3 hours ahead.*

- Preheat oven to 350 degrees.
- Combine all crust ingredients. Press onto the bottom and sides of two (9 inch) pie pans. Bake 15 minutes. Cool.
- Combine egg yolks and sugar in a bowl. Beat until light-colored.
- In a saucepan, dissolve gelatin in water. Bring to a boil; pour into egg mixture, beating briskly. Cool, but do not allow to get too stiff.
- Whip cream until stiff. Fold whipped cream into egg mixture. Stir in rum.
- Pour into cooled crusts. Refrigerate pies until set. Sprinkle chocolate over top just before serving.

Mixed Berry Crumble

Great summer dessert that's incredibly easy

Yield: 6 servings

1	cup blueberries	¼	teaspoon cinnamon
1	cup raspberries	1	cup flour
1	cup blackberries	1	stick butter, softened
5-6	tablespoons sugar	6	tablespoons sugar
	Juice of 1 lemon	½	teaspoon salt

🕐 *Bake the crumble earlier in the day. If you'd like to serve it warm, just pop it back in a 300 degree oven for 10 to 15 minutes.*

- Preheat oven to 350 degrees.
- Combine all berries in a greased 8-inch square baking dish. Add 5 to 6 tablespoons sugar, lemon juice and cinnamon; stir to coat berries.
- Mix together flour, butter, 6 tablespoons sugar, and salt with a fork or your fingertips until crumbly. Sprinkle over berries.
- Bake 30 to 40 minutes. Delicious served alone or over a scoop of vanilla ice cream.

Note: *Crumble works equally well when made with all blueberries.*

Fresh Peach Crisp

Sweet and refreshing, this recipe found its way to us from a Minnesota roadside peach stand

Yield: 12 servings

Crisp

5-6	cups peeled and sliced peaches (about 6 large)	1	cup dry quick-cooking oats
1	tablespoon sugar	1	cup brown sugar
1½	cups flour	1	teaspoon cinnamon
		1½	sticks margarine, melted

Vanilla Crème Fraîche

1	(8 ounce) container crème fraîche or sour cream	½	vanilla bean, split lengthwise
		4½	teaspoons sugar

🕐 *Dry ingredients can be combined up to 1 day ahead and kept covered.*

- Preheat oven to 350 degrees.
- Place peach slices in an ungreased 9x13-inch baking pan. Sprinkle with sugar.
- Combine flour, oats, brown sugar, and cinnamon in a mixing bowl. Add margarine and mix well. Spoon evenly over fruit.
- Bake 40 to 50 minutes. Serve warm with Vanilla Crème Fraîche or ice cream.
- To make Vanilla Crème Fraîche, place crème fraîche in a medium bowl. Add seeds from vanilla bean. Stir in sugar. Cover and refrigerate 1 hour, or up to 3 days. Serve with fresh fruit or fruit desserts.

For a yummy treat, splash fresh peaches and blackberries with champagne!

Hawthorn Hill Coconut Macaroons 🚲

A favorite any time of year

Yield: 2½ dozen cookies

½	cup egg whites (about 4 whites), room-temperature	2½	cups granulated coconut
1	cup sugar	1	teaspoon vanilla

- Preheat oven to 325 degrees.
- Beat egg whites with an electric mixer until stiff peaks form. Gradually add sugar while beating at medium speed. Gently fold in coconut by hand. Fold in vanilla carefully.
- Drop by tablespoonfuls onto a nonstick baking sheet, or a regular baking sheet covered with parchment or brown wrapping paper.
- Bake for about 18 minutes, or until light gold in color. Cool slightly before removing from pan with a stiff spatula.

Note: *If using flaked coconut, process in a food processor or blender until granulated.*

These cookies were always served to the elementary school children who were Christmas carolers at Hawthorn Hill, home of Orville and Wilbur Wright, in the 1950s. Ruth Deddens, editor of Discover Dayton, obtained the recipe from the Wrights.

Brown Sugar Pecan Shortbread Cookies ❄

Melt in your mouth!

Yield: 4 dozen (1 inch) cookies

2	cups flour	2	sticks unsalted butter, softened
1	cup pecan pieces	½	cup dark brown sugar
	Pinch of salt		

🕐 *Must make dough at least 3 hours, or up to 24 hours, ahead. Baked cookies may be frozen up to 3 months.*

ⓖ Grind flour, pecans and salt to a fine powder in a food processor.

ⓖ Cream butter and sugar until smooth. Add flour mixture and mix. Wrap with plastic and refrigerate at least 3 hours.

ⓖ When ready to bake, preheat oven to 300 degrees. Line a baking sheet with parchment paper.

ⓖ Roll dough to ¼-inch thick on a floured surface. Cut with cookie cutters and place on prepared baking sheet.

ⓖ Bake 20 to 25 minutes.

Note: *An alternative to grinding dry ingredients in a food processor would be to grind pecans in a coffee grinder or a blender, then mix thoroughly with flour and salt.*

Moist Oatmeal Cookies

Wonderfully delicious!

Yield: 4 dozen cookies

1	cup shortening	1	teaspoon salt
1	cup brown sugar	1	teaspoon baking soda
1	cup granulated sugar	1½	cups flour
2	eggs, beaten	3	cups dry oatmeal
1	teaspoon vanilla	1	cup raisins

ⓖ Preheat oven to 350 degrees.

ⓖ In a large mixing bowl, cream together shortening and sugars. Mix in egg and vanilla.

ⓖ In a separate bowl, combine salt, baking soda, flour, and oatmeal.

ⓖ Soak raisins in warm water for 5 minutes; drain.

ⓖ Mix dry ingredients into creamed mixture. Add drained raisins and gently combine. Form dough into rolls on wax paper. Refrigerate 1 hour.

ⓖ Slice and place on baking sheets. Bake 10 minutes.

Note: *Do not overcook cookies or they will lose their moist quality. They may appear to not be completely done, but they are.*

Store brown sugar in an airtight container or zip-top plastic bag to keep it from drying out. To soften brown sugar that has hardened, place it in an airtight container with a slice of apple; remove the apple after the sugar softens. Or, microwave it on high for a few seconds.

These are my absolute favorite cookies. When I was growing up, my mom made them especially for me. Sometimes I even requested these cookies instead of a birthday cake!

—Alicia Dixon

Walnut Butter Cookies

Yield: 4 dozen cookies

2	cups all-purpose flour	1	egg
½	teaspoon salt	¾	cup chopped walnuts, toasted
2	sticks unsalted butter, softened		Powdered sugar
½	cup light brown sugar		

🕐 *Dough can be prepared ahead and refrigerated up to 2 days, or frozen up to 2 weeks, before being sliced and baked. Cookies can be baked 3 days ahead, then stored in an airtight container.*

6 Sift flour and salt into a medium bowl.

6 Using an electric mixer, beat butter and brown sugar together in a large bowl until light and fluffy. Beat in egg. Beat in flour mixture until well-blended. Stir in walnuts.

6 Turn dough out onto a lightly floured surface. Divide dough in half. Roll each half into an 8x1½-inch log. Wrap each log in wax paper; freeze 30 minutes or until firm, or refrigerate up to 2 days.

6 When ready to bake, preheat oven to 350 degrees.

6 Cut logs crosswise into ⅓-inch-thick rounds. Place rounds 1 inch apart on 2 ungreased baking sheets.

6 Bake about 15 minutes, or until cookies are light gold around edges. Transfer cookies to racks and cool 10 minutes.

6 Place powdered sugar in a shallow dish. Turn cookies in sugar to coat completely. Cool on racks.

Gingersnaps ❄

Kids like to help with this recipe!

Yield: 4 dozen cookies

¾	cup shortening	2	teaspoons baking soda
1	cup sugar plus extra for dipping cookies	¼	teaspoon salt
		1	teaspoon cinnamon
¼	cup molasses	1	teaspoon ground cloves
1	egg	1	teaspoon ground ginger
2	cups flour		

🕐 *Baked cookies may be frozen up to 3 months.*

6 Preheat oven to 375 degrees.

6 Cream shortening and sugar. Add molasses and egg; beat thoroughly.

6 Sift together flour, baking soda, salt, cinnamon, cloves, and ginger. Add dry ingredients to creamed mixture and mix well.

6 Using a teaspoon to measure out dough, roll into small balls. Dip balls into granulated sugar and place 2 inches apart on a baking sheet.

6 Bake 5 to 8 minutes.

The IMAX Theatre at the United States Air Force Museum gives audiences an incredible emotional experience. Its sophisticated motion picture system carries viewers on an amazing journey, from early flight to present-day, high-speed acrobatics.

This is wonderful "comfort food." I usually make the dough, and the kids love rolling it into balls and dipping them in the sugar. I think they eat the unbaked cookies when I am not looking! I always end up with fewer cookies than I should.

—Karleen Materne

Granny's Iced Shortbread Cookies ❄ 🚲

Freeze a batch for the holidays

Yield: 4 dozen cookies

Shortbread

4	sticks butter, softened (no substitutes)	1	cup superfine sugar
		3¼	cups flour

Butter Icing

1	stick butter, softened	2-3	teaspoons half-and-half, or enough to reach spreading consistency
1	(1 pound) package powdered sugar		
1	teaspoon almond extract		

🕐 *Baked cookies may be frozen up to 2 months.*

6 Preheat oven to 225 degrees.

6 Beat butter until light and fluffy. Gradually beat in sugar and flour.

6 Knead dough on a generously floured, cloth-covered surface. Roll dough to ¼-inch thick using a floured, cloth-covered rolling pin. Dip cookie cutters in flour and cut out dough. Place on a lightly greased baking sheet.

6 Bake for about 1 hour, or until edges become beige. Cool before icing and decorating.

6 Meanwhile, mix all icing ingredients until smooth. Spread over cooled cookies. Decorate as desired. Store in an airtight container.

Coconut Macadamia Cookies ❄

Your soon-to-be favorite cookie of all time!

Yield: 3 dozen cookies

½	cup granulated sugar	1	cup dry quick-cooking oats
½	cup light brown sugar	½	cup flaked coconut
1	stick butter or margarine, softened	½	teaspoon baking soda
		¼	teaspoon salt
1	egg	1	cup coarsely chopped
1	teaspoon vanilla		macadamia nuts
1¼	cups all-purpose flour		

🕐 *Baked cookies may be frozen up to 3 months.*

6 Preheat oven to 350 degrees.

6 Beat sugars, butter, egg, and vanilla with an electric mixer on medium speed until fluffy.

6 Combine flour, oats, coconut, baking soda, salt, and nuts in a bowl. Add half of dry ingredients at a time to sugar mixture, beating at low speed until blended.

6 Drop dough by heaping teaspoonfuls 2 inches apart onto lightly greased baking sheets.

6 Bake 7 to 10 minutes, or until edges are golden brown. Cool 1 minute on baking sheets before transferring to wire racks to cool.

Note: *Try to find a nut store (in Dayton, try Dayton Nut Co.) for the macadamias. The price will be much more reasonable.*

Best Chocolate Chip Cookies ❄

If these cookies are kept sealed, they will stay soft and chewy

Yield: 5 dozen small cookies

2	sticks butter, softened	2	eggs, or ½ cup egg substitute
¼	cup sugar	2¼	cups flour
¾	cup light brown sugar	1	teaspoon baking soda
1	(1.7 ounce) package instant vanilla pudding	1	(12 ounce) package chocolate chips
1	teaspoon vanilla	1	cup chopped pecans (optional)

🕐 *Baked cookies can be frozen up to 3 months.*

6 Preheat oven to 375 degrees.

6 Cream butter, sugars, pudding, and vanilla in a large bowl. Beat in eggs. Add flour, mixing baking soda into last cup of flour. Mix in chocolate chips and pecans. Drop by large or small spoonfuls onto a baking sheet.

6 Bake 7 to 10 minutes, or until light golden brown. Cool 1 minute before removing from baking sheet.

Line cookie sheets with parchment paper. Cookies will slide off easily and clean-up will be a snap.

Keep toasted or chopped nuts in the freezer to have on hand for recipes, or to use as garnishes for ice cream or salads.

Double Chocolate Walnut Biscotti ❄

Delicious with coffee or tea

Yield: about 30 biscotti

2	cups all-purpose flour	1	cup granulated sugar
½	cup unsweetened cocoa	2	eggs
1	teaspoon baking soda	1	cup chopped walnuts
1	teaspoon salt	¾	cup semisweet chocolate chips
6	tablespoons unsalted butter, softened	1	tablespoon powdered sugar

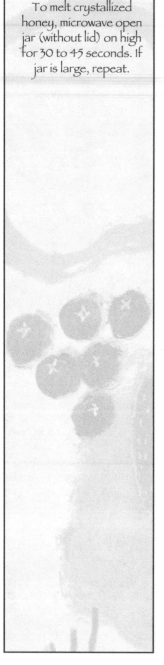

To melt crystallized honey, microwave open jar (without lid) on high for 30 to 45 seconds. If jar is large, repeat.

🕐 *Biscotti can be kept in an airtight container for 1 week, or frozen up to 1 month.*

- Preheat oven to 350 degrees.

- Mix together flour, cocoa, baking soda, and salt in a bowl.

- In a separate bowl, beat together butter and granulated sugar with an electric mixer until light and fluffy. Add eggs and beat until well-combined. Stir in dry ingredients to form a stiff dough. Mix in walnuts and chocolate chips.

- Using floured hands, form dough into 2 slightly flattened logs, each 12 inches long and 2 inches wide, on a greased and floured baking sheet. Sprinkle logs with powdered sugar.

- Bake 35 minutes, or until slightly firm to the touch. Cool on baking sheets 5 minutes.

- On a cutting board, cut biscotti diagonally into ¾-inch thick slices. Arrange biscotti, cut sides down, on baking sheet and bake 10 minutes, or until crisp. Cool on wire racks.

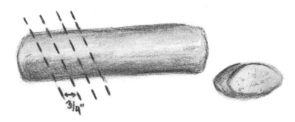

3/4"

Provisions' Peanut Butter Cookies

Big, old-fashioned cookies

Yield: 4 dozen cookies

3	cups all-purpose flour	2	teaspoons vanilla
1	teaspoon baking powder	1	cup light brown sugar
1	teaspoon salt	1	cup granulated sugar
2	sticks unsalted butter, softened	2	eggs
1	cup creamy or chunky peanut butter (do not use old-fashioned style or freshly ground)		

- Preheat oven to 350 degrees. Line 2 baking sheets with parchment paper.

- Mix flour, baking powder and salt in a medium bowl.

- Beat butter, peanut butter and vanilla with an electric mixer in a large bowl until well-blended. Beat in both sugars. Scrape down the sides of the bowl. Stir in half of the dry ingredients. Add eggs, one at a time, stirring well after each addition. Mix in remaining dry ingredients.

- For each cookie, roll 1 heaping tablespoon of dough into a 1¾-inch ball. Arrange dough balls 2½ inches apart on prepared baking sheets. Flatten balls using a fork, making a crosshatch design on top.

- Bake cookies 14 minutes, or until dry on top and golden brown on bottom. Cool cookies on baking sheet 5 minutes. Use a metal spatula to transfer cookies to racks and cool completely.

Note: *Make sure you follow the directions for rolling the dough to get the right size cookie.*

Mocha Truffles

Easy to prepare and they melt in your mouth!

Yield: about 5½ dozen candies

2	(12 ounce) packages semisweet chocolate chips	2	teaspoons water
1	(8 ounce) package cream cheese, softened	1	pound dark chocolate confectionery coating
3	tablespoons instant coffee granules		White confectionery coating (optional)

- *Can be frozen for several months before dipping in chocolate. Thaw in refrigerator before dipping.*

- Melt chocolate chips in a microwave or double boiler. Add cream cheese, coffee and water. Mix well. Chill 1 hour, or until firm enough to shape. Shape into 1-inch balls and place on a wax paper-lined baking sheet. Chill 1 to 2 hours, or until firm.

- Melt chocolate coating in a microwave or double boiler. Dip chilled balls in chocolate coating and return to wax paper to harden. If desired, melt white coating and drizzle over truffles. Serve in foil miniature candy cups.

This recipe is from Provisions, a sandwich shop in Nantucket. My friends and I have started a tradition of going for a long weekend every year, and we always stop at Provisions for a sandwich, Cape Cod Chips and these cookies!

—Lisa Hoffman

My mother always said, "It's a shame to turn on the oven for just one thing!" So, she would whip up a batch of cookies or baked apples "in case company drops by." They invariably did!

—Sara Faust

Raspberry Coconut Squares

Yield: 35 (2½ inch) squares

Crust

15 (2½x5 inch) graham crackers, finely ground, or 2 cups packaged graham cracker crumbs	1 cup sugar
	1 stick margarine or unsalted butter, cold and cut into small pieces
1½ cups all-purpose flour	2 eggs, lightly beaten

Filling

1 (12 ounce) jar seedless raspberry jam (about 1 cup)	2 eggs
1 stick unsalted butter, softened	2 (7 ounce) packages sweetened flaked coconut (about 4 cups)
1 cup sugar	

🕐 *Squares must chill at least 1 hour before serving.*

⚬ Preheat oven to 350 degrees.

⚬ Combine cracker crumbs, flour and sugar in a large bowl. Add margarine pieces and blend with your fingertips until mixture resembles coarse meal. Add egg; toss with a fork to blend. Press mixture evenly into a lightly greased 17x12-inch jelly-roll pan.

⚬ For filling, spread jam evenly over crust.

⚬ Beat butter briefly with an electric mixer in a large bowl. Add sugar; beat until light and fluffy. Add eggs, one at a time, beating well after each addition. Add coconut and beat until combined.

⚬ Drop coconut mixture by small spoonfuls over jam and spread carefully until evenly covered.

⚬ Bake in middle of oven for 20 minutes, or until golden brown. Cool on a rack. Chill at least 1 hour before cutting.

Rich Caramel Sauce

Drizzle over ice cream, apple tarts and cakes

Yield: 2 cups

1¼ cups sugar	3 tablespoons unsalted butter, softened and cut into pieces
½ cup water	
1½ cups heavy cream, heated	

⚬ Combine sugar and water in a deep, heavy saucepan. Cook over medium heat 15 to 20 minutes, or until mixture turns golden brown. Watch carefully after 10 minutes to prevent burning.

⚬ Remove from heat. Wearing oven mitts on both hands, immediately add cream, stirring with a long-handled wooden spoon until smooth. Add butter and allow to melt, then stir to combine thoroughly. Strain through a fine mesh strainer into a glass bowl.

Sidebar:

For a quick dessert using fresh raspberries, pile 3 cups fresh berries in a baking dish. Spoon on ½ cup sour cream mixed with 2 tablespoons of brown sugar and 1 tablespoon of raspberry liqueur. Chill for 1 hour; sprinkle with more brown sugar and broil 1 minute, or until the sauce bubbles.

Before measuring honey, peanut butter or corn syrup, spray the measuring spoon or cup with vegetable cooking spray. This will allow for easy clean-up.

Classic Pumpkin Bars

Perfect for fall tailgates and hayrides

Yield: 24 bars

Bars

2	cups all-purpose flour	1	(15 ounce) can pumpkin
2	teaspoons baking powder	1⅔	cups granulated sugar
2	teaspoons cinnamon	1	cup vegetable oil
1	teaspoon baking soda	¾	cup chopped pecans
¼	teaspoon salt	24	pecan halves for garnish
4	eggs		

Frosting

1	(3 ounce) package cream cheese, softened	1	teaspoon vanilla
		2	cups sifted powdered sugar
4	tablespoons butter, softened		

🕐 *Bars may be made up to 2 days ahead and kept in an airtight container.*

☙ Preheat oven to 350 degrees.

☙ Sift together flour, baking powder, cinnamon, baking soda, and salt in a medium bowl.

☙ In a large mixing bowl, beat eggs, pumpkin, sugar, and oil. Add dry ingredients and beat until well-combined. Stir in chopped pecans. Spread batter into an ungreased 15x10-inch jelly-roll pan.

☙ Bake 25 to 30 minutes, or until a toothpick inserted in the center comes out clean. Cool on a wire rack.

☙ To make frosting, beat cream cheese, butter and vanilla until fluffy. Gradually add powdered sugar and beat until smooth.

☙ Spread frosting over cooled bars. Cut into squares and garnish top of each bar with a pecan half.

Ever wonder what happened to the "aliens" who supposedly crash-landed in Roswell, New Mexico? Wright Patterson Air Force Base is the home of building 18F, often claimed to be the elusive "Hangar 18," where the "aliens" were purported to have been brought in 1947. A presidential candidate in 1992, Kip Lee from California, even claimed that extraterrestrials, "short, stout beings," were still being held prisoner here and would be released if he was elected president!

Chocolate-Covered Caramels ❄

These will disappear fast!

Yield: about 100 (1 inch) caramels

1	(14 ounce) can sweetened condensed milk		2	(14 ounce) packages chocolate candy melts (we suggest Wilton), or about 2 pounds melting chocolate
1	cup granulated sugar			
1	cup brown sugar			Pecan halves (optional)
1	cup corn syrup			
3	sticks butter			

🕐 *Caramels will keep up to 2 weeks at room temperature, or frozen up to 3 months.*

🌀 Combine milk, sugars, corn syrup, and butter in a saucepan. Cook 25 minutes, or until mixture turns tan in color. Pour into a greased 9x13-inch baking pan. Cool, then refrigerate until completely cooled.

🌀 Remove pan from refrigerator and cut into 1-inch squares, a few at a time.

🌀 Melt chocolate. Dip caramel squares into chocolate one at a time; place on wax paper until chocolate hardens. If desired, place 1 pecan half gently on the top of the caramel before chocolate hardens. Store in an airtight container.

Note: *You may want to make some with the pecans and some without, depending on how many nut lovers you'll be serving.*

Frosted Pecans ❄

Great idea for a hostess gift

1	pound pecan halves		1	cup sugar
1	stick butter			Dash of salt
2	egg whites		1	teaspoon cinnamon (optional)

🕐 *Can be made and frozen up to 3 months.*

🌀 Preheat oven to 325 degrees.

🌀 Toast pecans in oven until lightly browned.

🌀 Melt butter in a shallow, glass baking dish.

🌀 Beat egg whites, sugar, salt, and cinnamon until stiff peaks form. Fold in pecans. Stir mixture into butter.

🌀 Bake 30 to 45 minutes, stirring every 10 minutes, or until all the butter is absorbed.

At Christmas time, I am reminded of watching Mom and Mamadear (my paternal grandmother) make this amazing candy called cream candy. It smelled of warm butter and cream as it cooked, and melted in your mouth when it was finished. It was pulled between two people (like taffy) until it turned light in color and became impossible to stretch. I loved watching them work in my grandmother's small kitchen. There was always a trick to it... it couldn't be raining, it had to be cold outside, it had to be cooked to just the right temperature, it was poured on a huge marble slab to cool before pulling, it had to be pulled just long enough, etc. My job in the process was to wrap the cut candy in small wax-paper squares when it was done. As an adult, I have never made this candy in my own home, but rather in my mother's kitchen, and never without her.

—Liz Cline

Ohio Buckeyes ❄

A traditional Ohio favorite that is sure to please everyone!

Yield: 6 dozen candies

1	(18 ounce) jar creamy peanut butter	1	(12 ounce) package semisweet chocolate chips
1	stick margarine, softened	3	tablespoons paraffin wax
1	(1 pound) package powdered sugar		

- Combine peanut butter, margarine and sugar. Form into smooth 1-inch balls. Chill.

- Melt chocolate chips and wax together in the top of a double boiler. Using a toothpick, dip all but the very top of the balls into the chocolate mixture. Drop onto wax paper and allow to harden. Refrigerate.

Note: *Can melt chocolate in microwave rather than double boiler.*

Chocolate Almond Toffee Bark

A tasty treat perfect for holiday gifts and entertaining

Yield: about 36 pieces

3	cups sliced almonds (10 ounces)	½	teaspoon vanilla
1	stick unsalted butter, softened	¼	teaspoon salt
1½	cups sugar	6	ounces fine-quality bittersweet chocolate, chopped
⅓	cup water		
1	tablespoon fresh lemon juice		

Can be made up to 1 week ahead. Keep layered between sheets of wax paper in an airtight container at cool room temperature or chilled.

- Preheat oven to 350 degrees.

- Spread almonds evenly over a large baking pan. Toast in middle of oven, stirring halfway through, for 10 minutes, or until golden.

- In a 3-quart heavy saucepan, bring butter, sugar, water, lemon juice, vanilla, and salt to a boil over medium heat, stirring with a wooden spoon. Boil mixture without stirring, swirling pan occasionally, for 12 minutes, or until deep gold.

- Remove pan from heat and stir in two-thirds of almonds. Immediately pour mixture onto a large greased baking sheet. Spread into a thin layer. Carefully transfer baking sheet to a rack to cool.

- Melt chocolate in a double boiler, stirring until smooth. Pour chocolate over cooled toffee; spread evenly. Sprinkle remaining almonds over the top. Chill, uncovered, for 1 hour or until firm. Break into 2-inch pieces.

Peppermint Crunch Bark

Very pretty and festive for the holiday season

Yield: 18 to 24 pieces

17	ounces good-quality white chocolate, finely chopped	7	ounces bittersweet or semisweet chocolate, chopped
30	red and white peppermint disk candies, coarsely chopped	6	tablespoons heavy cream
		¾	teaspoon peppermint extract

🕐 *Can be made 2 weeks ahead of time and chilled in an airtight container.*

Turn a large baking sheet upside down. Cover securely with foil and mark a 12x9-inch rectangle on the foil.

Stir white chocolate in a metal bowl, set over a saucepan of barely simmering water, until melted. Pour ⅔ cup of melted chocolate onto foil and spread to fill rectangle. Sprinkle with ¼ cup of crushed candy. Chill about 15 minutes, or until set.

Stir bittersweet chocolate, cream and extract in a saucepan over medium-low heat until melted and smooth. Cool 5 minutes, or until barely lukewarm. Pour entire mixture over white chocolate rectangle, quickly spreading to cover rectangle. Refrigerate about 25 minutes, or until very cold and firm.

Rewarm remaining white chocolate and spread quickly over bittersweet chocolate layer. Sprinkle with remaining crushed candy. Chill about 20 minutes, or until firm.

Transfer foil with bark onto a work surface. Cut crosswise into 2-inch-wide strips. Cut each strip into 3 sections and each section diagonally into 2 triangles.

Hot Fudge Sauce

Wonderful topping for ice cream!

Yield: about 1½ cups

2	squares bittersweet chocolate	1	scant cup sugar
6	tablespoons margarine or butter	1	(5 ounce) can evaporated milk

🕐 *Sauce can be made up to 8 hours ahead. Reheat very slowly on stovetop and serve.*

Melt chocolate and butter in a skillet over low heat. Add sugar and milk, whisking to keep the sauce smooth. Do not let sauce get too hot. Pour over ice cream or other desserts.

During the Dayton Peace Talks, Wright-Patterson AFB was sealed from the media, and the three Balkan Presidents were not invited to speak publicly. Security was so tight that some called the conference "a boot camp run by the Americans" and complained that "life is really, really boring."

Dark-chocolate-dipped dried apricots contrast orange with near-black for a sophisticated sweet. Melt chocolate chips in a bowl over simmering water, but don't let the bowl touch the water. Once the chocolate is melted, turn off the heat (but keep the bowl over the hot water), dip apricots in halfway, then lay them on sheets of wax paper to dry. When dry, remove from paper and store in an airtight container.

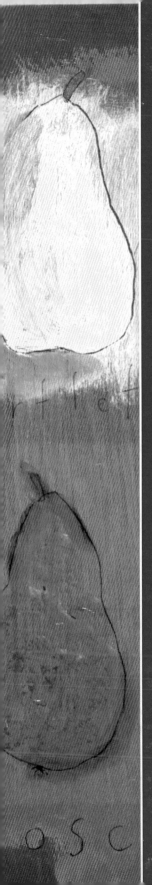

A Few of Our Favorite Things

FOOD FOR KIDS

OUR FAVORITE THINGS

Encouraging inspiration and creativity, the Muse Machine is an established extracurricular presence in 158 Miami Valley elementary, middle and high schools. Founded by former Daytonian, Suzy Bassani, the mission of the Muse Machine is "to enhance the lives of young people by providing them with opportunities to experience and value the arts." Once on the cutting edge, the private, nonprofit agency has matured into a national model for incorporating arts into day-to-day education. It was recognized by The Kennedy Center Performing Arts publication as a model Arts in Education program.

Of course, Dayton has even more to offer its younger citizens. Carillon Historical Park and the Kettering Family Education Center celebrate the history of invention, transportation and pioneer life in Dayton and the Miami Valley. In addition, the K12 Gallery for Young People offers Saturday workshops, after-school art enrichment classes, art camps, and community outreach programs. K12 founder Jerri Stanard explains, "It's a way for kids to learn fine-arts skills and meet people from different backgrounds...whether inner city, suburban or rural. Everybody can be friends and learn about art in the process.'

Other popular kid destinations include the Boonshoft Museum of Discovery, the U.S. Air Force Museum and IMAX Theater, the Aullwood Audubon Center and Farm, Dayton Art Institute's Experiencenter, Sunwatch Indian Village...the list goes on. Let your children be your guide, and find your own favorite places to adventure.

OSCAR BOONSHOFT recently had the opportunity to observe children experiencing the renovated Boonshoft Museum of Discovery. He was thrilled with the results: "You take a look at the kids' faces, and it's phenomenal. Especially in the laboratory areas where they can get explanations of the scientific principles they see demonstrated. It's bound to generate a curiosity about science and the way things work, and that's what's important."

Eggs in Fried Bread

Healthy breakfast for kids of all ages

Yield: 2 servings

2   slices whole wheat toast   2   eggs
     Butter

◔ Cut a hole about 2 inches in diameter in the center of each slice of bread. Butter bread on both sides and pan-fry gently until brown on both sides. Crack an egg into each hole, cover the pan and cook until eggs are set.

Monkey Bread

Fun treat for breakfast

Yield: 10 to 12 servings

1 cup brown sugar	1 stick butter, melted
3 tablespoons cinnamon	1 cup granulated sugar
4 (7½ ounce) tubes buttermilk biscuit dough	

◔ Preheat oven to 350 degrees.

◔ Combine brown sugar and cinnamon in a bowl.

◔ Quarter each biscuit and roll in cinnamon sugar mixture. Place sugared biscuits in an ungreased Bundt pan.

◔ Stir together butter and granulated sugar; pour over biscuits.

◔ Bake 40 minutes. Cool 10 minutes before inverting pan onto a serving plate.

Warm and Wonderful Grapefruit

A different way to serve grapefruit

Yield: 4 servings

2	grapefruit, halved	2	tablespoons brown sugar
2	tablespoons unsalted butter, melted		

- Preheat broiler.
- Leaving sections in grapefruit rind, cut sections from membrane and seed.
- Pour butter over grapefruit and sprinkle with sugar. Place, cut side up, on a baking tray.
- Broil 5 minutes, or until butter and sugar begin to bubble. Serve warm.

The beautiful Cox Arboretum consists of 160 acres of cultivated gardens and mature woodlands. Fifteen garden areas display plant materials, including the nationally recognized Edible Landscape Garden. In the past, children have enjoyed the butterfly house, giant bug sculptures and other changing exhibits.

Jelly-Topped Peanut Butter Muffins

Wonderful after-school snack

Yield: 12 servings

1½	cups all-purpose flour	¾	cup chunky peanut butter
½	cup cornmeal	2	tablespoons honey
3	tablespoons sugar	2	large eggs
2	teaspoons baking powder	1	cup milk
½	teaspoon salt	¼	cup grape or other flavor jelly

Dry ingredients may be mixed together the night before to save time.

- Preheat oven to 375 degrees.
- Combine flour, cornmeal, sugar, baking powder, and salt in a large mixing bowl. Make a well in the center of mixture.
- Mix together peanut butter and honey. Stir in eggs and milk. Add mixture to dry ingredients, stirring just until moistened.
- Spoon into a greased muffin pan, filling each cup three-fourths full. Place 1 teaspoon jelly in center of each.
- Bake 20 minutes or until golden. Remove from pan immediately and cool on a wire rack. Serve with additional jelly, if desired.

A friend of my mom used to make peanut butter and jelly sandwiches, then put them in the freezer while we played. After about an hour, she would take them out of the freezer, cut the crust off and cut the sandwiches into squares. They were thawed just enough for us to eat and not make a mess. The freezing helped to keep the sandwiches together. I do this at home for my kids now and I smile in remembrance of her.

—Margie Harrell

Grandma Mac's Cinnamon Toast 🚲

Keep a bowl of this in the refrigerator for a special treat on cold winter mornings

Yield: enough for 1 loaf of bread

1	stick butter, softened	Dash of salt (optional)
1	cup light brown sugar	Desired number of bread slices,
2	teaspoons half-and-half or milk (optional)	lightly toasted (we prefer whole wheat)
½	teaspoon cinnamon, or to taste	

🕐 *Spread can be made up to 2 weeks ahead and kept in refrigerator.*

- Preheat broiler.
- Cream butter and brown sugar in a small mixing bowl until light and fluffy. Beat in half-and-half, cinnamon and salt.
- Spread mixture on toasted bread.
- Place bread on a baking sheet; broil briefly until mixture bubbles. (Watch carefully, as bread will burn quickly.)
- Cool slightly on a wire rack. Cut bread into triangles and serve warm for breakfast toast.
- Cover and refrigerate remaining mixture for future use.

Note: *Recipe can easily be multiplied for crowds. Great accompaniment to oatmeal.*

Cheesy Oven Fries

Make plenty!

Yield: 4 to 6 servings

⅓	cup Parmesan cheese	3	medium potatoes, each cut into 8 wedges
¾	teaspoon salt		
¼	teaspoon garlic powder	3	tablespoons butter or margarine, melted
¾	teaspoon paprika		

- Preheat oven to 375 degrees.
- Combine cheese, salt, garlic powder, and paprika in a bowl.
- Dip potato wedges in butter; arrange in a single layer on a lightly greased 10x15-inch jelly-roll pan. Sprinkle cheese mixture over potatoes.
- Bake 40 minutes, or until potatoes are tender and browned.

Easy Fresh Fruit Jam

Great to make with the kids after a visit to the fruit farm

Yield: 2½ cups

1	pound prepared fruit (see chart)	2	tablespoons fresh lemon juice
1	cup (minimum) sugar (see chart)		

🕐 *Fruit may be sliced earlier in the day. Jam will keep, covered, in the refrigerator for up to 2 weeks.*

🌀 Set a small bowl over a large bowl of ice water; set aside.

🌀 In a 10- or 12-inch skillet, bring fruit, sugar and juice to a boil over medium-high heat, stirring occasionally. Reduce to medium heat; cook and stir, skimming foam as necessary, until mixture begins to thicken slightly.

🌀 Spoon ½ teaspoon fruit mixture into bowl over ice water. Allow to set 30 seconds. Tip bowl 45 degrees to one side; jam should be a soft gel consistency that moves slightly. If mixture is liquid and runs to side of bowl, return skillet to heat; cook and stir 1 to 2 minutes longer. Repeat test.

🌀 Cool to room temperature before serving.

Strawberries: thinly sliced, use 1 cup (minimum) sugar, cook about 5 minutes

Apricots: peeled and very thinly sliced, use 1 cup (minimum) sugar, cook about 5 minutes

Plums: very thinly sliced, use 1 cup plus 2 tablespoons (minimum) sugar, cook 8 to 9 minutes

Peaches/Nectarines: peeled and very thinly sliced, use 1¼ cups (minimum) sugar, cook 8 to 9 minutes

Wegerzyn Horticultural Center, on the banks of the Stillwater River, is a 60-acre horticultural educational center comprised of a horticulture library; the lovely Stillwater Gardens, which includes children's, rose, Federal, English, and Victorian gardens; and a 350-foot boardwalk meandering though a mature lowland forest.

Kids are more interested in healthy food when they are part of the process. Take them to the supermarket and encourage each child to pick out a new fruit or vegetable in the produce section. Talk about the various colors, sizes, shapes, and textures. Try star fruits, kiwi and artichokes. You may be surprised by what your children love!

Sticky Sweet Carrots

A little sweetness goes a long way

Yield: 6 servings

1	(1 pound) bag baby carrots	⅛	teaspoon cayenne pepper
2	tablespoons butter or margarine	½	cup orange marmalade

🌀 Cook carrots in a large saucepan of boiling salted water for 10 to 15 minutes, or until crisp-tender. Drain.

🌀 Add butter, cayenne pepper and marmalade. Mix well. Keep warm over low heat until ready to serve.

Note: *Omit the cayenne pepper if your children prefer less spicy foods.*

Veggie Bites

They'll love their vegetables with this recipe

Yield: 4 servings

1	tablespoon margarine or butter, melted	2	cups fresh vegetables (broccoli florets, cauliflower florets, ¼-inch carrot slices, ½-inch zucchini slices, ½-inch bell pepper strips)
1	egg		
2	teaspoons water		
½	cup all-purpose flour	4	tablespoons margarine or butter, melted
½	teaspoon salt		Parmesan cheese (optional)

Vegetables may be sliced 1 day ahead.

- Preheat oven to 450 degrees. Brush bottom of a 9x13-inch baking pan with 1 tablespoon margarine.
- Beat egg and water in a shallow dish. Combine flour and salt in another shallow dish.
- Dip about a fourth of vegetables in egg mixture. Remove 1 piece at a time with a slotted spoon or fork; roll in flour mixture to coat. Place in pan. Repeat with remaining vegetables. Pour melted margarine carefully over each vegetable in pan.
- Bake, uncovered, for 10 to 12 minutes, or until vegetables are crisp-tender and golden brown. Turn once while baking.
- Sprinkle lightly with Parmesan cheese.

Note: *Be sure to use fresh vegetables.*

Crazy Quesadillas

A wonderful way to introduce your child to Mexican food

Yield: 4 servings

½	cup refried beans	⅔	cup shredded Colby-Jack cheese
4	(6 to 8 inch) flour tortillas		Salsa (optional)

- Spread beans on two tortillas. Sprinkle cheese over beans and top with remaining two tortillas.
- Cook one at a time in a skillet, cheese side up, over medium heat for about 3 minutes, or until cheese starts to melt. Turn and cook 2 minutes longer.
- Cut each quesadilla into 6 triangles. Serve with salsa.

Note: *You may substitute fat-free refried beans. Kids can help assemble quesadillas.*

Kids

How to make tomato juice:
Squeeze the juice in the jar. Drop the tomatoes in. Let them sit there for 20 or 60 days. Then the tomatoes will disappear and it will turn into red juice.

—Weston Davis, 4 years old

SunWatch Indian Village recreates the Fort Ancient Native Americans' way of life. More than 800 years ago, the Fort Ancient tribe settled along the banks of the Great Miami River and created an elaborate wooden counterpart to England's Stonehenge. Posts placed in the middle of their village told, in nature's words, of the passing of time. SunWatch Summerfest and other celebrations bring Native American storytelling and music to festival-goers.

Hash Brown Potato Casserole ❄

Children always ask for more

Yield: 8 servings

1	(2 pound) package frozen hash browns	1	(10¾ ounce) can condensed cream of chicken soup
½	cup chopped onion	1	teaspoon salt
4	tablespoons margarine, melted	½	cup sour cream
1	(10 ounce) package shredded cheddar cheese	½	cup bread crumbs
		4	tablespoons margarine, melted

🕐 *Bake earlier in the day and then reheat, or freeze up to 3 months before baking. Thaw and bake as directed.*

6 Preheat oven to 350 degrees.

6 Combine hash browns, onion, 4 tablespoons margarine, cheese, soup, salt, and sour cream; place in a well-greased 9x13-inch casserole dish.

6 Sprinkle crumbs on top. Drizzle with 4 tablespoons margarine.

6 Bake 1 hour, 10 minutes.

Tin Foil Hamburgers

A great "make-ahead meal" for kids

Yield: 12 servings

1	pound ground chuck		Dash of chili powder
1	medium onion, chopped	2	tablespoons sweet pickle relish
1	(8 ounce) package sharp cheddar cheese, cut into ½-inch cubes	¼	cup mustard
	Dash of salt	⅓	cup mayonnaise
	Dash of freshly ground black pepper	12	hamburger buns

🕐 *Hamburgers may be completely assembled, wrapped and refrigerated up to 3 days ahead; or, freeze up to 2 months. Thaw and bake as directed.*

6 Preheat oven to 300 degrees.

6 Brown meat and drain off fat. Add onion; cook until softened. Stir in cheese until melted. Mix in salt, black pepper, and chili powder. Cool.

6 Add relish, mustard and mayonnaise. Mix well.

6 Spoon mixture onto buns and wrap individually in foil.

6 Bake 20 to 25 minutes, or until heated through.

While having a "cooking experience" with a class of three-year-olds, I learned that milk comes from the grocery store that gets it from a truck that comes from a farm that has a cow. I also learned that eggs come from the grocery store that gets them from a factory that gets them from a farm out of a nest....I'm sure the chicken fits in there somewhere!

Later, while pouring milk for lunch, we reviewed this information. As an extension of this lesson I asked where they thought the hamburgers came from that we were eating that day. There was a unanimous response from all the children....
"McDonalds." Logically concluding this lesson, one little boy spoke up and said, "Then bananas must come from monkeys and apes!"

—Molly Hegman, preschool teacher

6 6 6

Kid Fun:

Climb on the giant wooden truck, rocket ship, train, and pirate ship at Windmill Farm.

Monster Cookies

Enough dough to make lots of monster-sized cookies

Kids

Yield: 150 cookies

2	sticks butter or margarine, softened	1½	teaspoons light or dark corn syrup
1	pound brown sugar	1½	pounds peanut butter
2	cups granulated sugar	9	cups quick cooking oats
6	eggs	1½	cups chocolate chips
1½	teaspoons vanilla	1½	cups M&M plain candies
4	teaspoons baking soda		

๑ Preheat oven to 350 degrees.

๑ Cream butter and sugars thoroughly. Add eggs and vanilla; beat well.

๑ Add remaining ingredients in order listed, mixing well after each addition.

๑ Drop by tablespoons onto a greased baking sheet.

๑ Bake 5 to 8 minutes.

I remember making these as a young girl at a birthday party. We found the recipe in our mothers' "Charity League" cookbook. I think we ate more dough than cookies!

—Amy Miller

Wild West Wagon Train Supper

Kids will come running for this favorite meal

Yield: 4 large servings

4	cups dry wagon wheel (rotelle) pasta	1½	teaspoons chili powder, or to taste
	Oil for sautéing	½	teaspoon garlic powder
1	cup chopped onion	1	(16 ounce) jar mild salsa
1	pound extra-lean ground beef	1	(11 ounce) can condensed cheddar cheese soup

🕐 *Wagon wheel noodles can be cooked ahead of time. Meat can be browned ahead of time and kept in the freezer until ready to use.*

๑ Cook pasta in 2½ quarts of unsalted boiling water for 7 minutes; drain.

๑ Meanwhile, heat oil in an extra-deep, 12-inch nonstick skillet over medium heat. Add onion and sauté 2 minutes, or until onion starts to soften. Add beef; increase heat to high. Stir in chili powder and garlic powder. Cook, stirring to break up meat, for 5 to 6 minutes, or until meat is browned and crumbled.

๑ Add salsa and soup to meat mixture. Stir well to combine. Add hot pasta and stir until noodles are coated with sauce. Serve immediately.

Kid Fun:

Check out "Museum Mondays" at the Dayton Art Institute. It is a unique program for preschoolers and adults that combines art-making, stories, and gallery hunts.

Crunch Top Tuna ❉

The cheddar cheese soup gives a great flavor to this tuna casserole

Yield: 6 servings

2	cups medium noodles	1	(9 ounce) can tuna, drained
1	(11 ounce) can condensed cheddar cheese soup	1	(8 ounce) can peas or diced carrots, drained
½	cup milk	2	handfuls potato chips, crushed

🕐 *Casserole may be made earlier in the day and reheated. Or bake, cool and freeze up to 3 months.*

⊘ Preheat oven to 350 degrees.

⊘ Cook noodles in boiling salted water for 5 minutes. Drain; rinse with cold water.

⊘ Combine soup and milk in a 2-quart casserole dish. Add tuna and peas; stir well. Mix in drained noodles. Sprinkle potato chips over top.

⊘ Bake 50 minutes.

Note: *This is a great dish for kids to make, with some help from an adult.*

Caramel Popcorn

Yummy snack for Friday night movies

Yield: 16 cups

4	quarts fresh popped popcorn	½	cup corn syrup
1	cup roasted peanuts (optional)	½	teaspoon salt
1	cup brown sugar	½	teaspoon vanilla
1	stick butter	½	teaspoon baking soda

🕐 *The caramel popcorn may be made up to 2 days ahead.*

⊘ Preheat oven to 250 degrees.

⊘ Place popcorn in a greased, large, shallow roasting pan. Sprinkle peanuts over popcorn.

⊘ In a heavy saucepan, combine sugar, butter, corn syrup, and salt. Stir over medium heat until boiling. Continue boiling without stirring for 5 minutes.

⊘ Remove from heat. Stir in vanilla and baking soda. Pour over popcorn. Mix until well-coated.

⊘ Bake for 1 hour, stirring several times. Cool.

⊘ Break apart and store in a tightly sealed container.

Wright Cycle Co. Shop is a designated National Historic Landmark and one of four stops in the proposed Dayton Aviation Heritage National Historical Park. Here, in the late 1800s, Orville and Wilbur Wright conceived the ideas that gave birth to powered flight.

The Miamisburg Mound is the best known, but least understood, prehistoric Indian remnant in Ohio. It measures 65 feet in height and 877 feet in circumference, and is the largest conical earthwork of its kind on Ohio. 116 steps are built into the surface. Archaeologist believe the mound is the work of the Adena Indians, who arrived about 1000 B.C. They were the first Indians in the region to domesticate plant foods, such as sunflowers and pumpkins.

Honest-to-Goodness
Soft Pretzels 🖋 ❄

Let's do the twist!

Yield: 16 pretzels

1 tablespoon canola oil	½ cup flour
1 pound store-bought dough for bread or rolls	Salt (optional)

6 Preheat oven to 450 degrees.

6 Brush baking tray with oil. Cut dough into 16 balls. Using lightly floured hands, roll or stretch each ball into a 12-inch "snake." If dough stiffens, let it stand for about 10 minutes and then continue.

6 Form dough "snake" into a pretzel twist, or invent your own design. Pinch ends together tightly so shapes stay together while cooking. Let dough stand for 5 minutes.

6 Gently drop pretzel dough into a pot of boiling water. Cook 1 minute, then promptly remove using a slotted spoon. Place pretzels on a baking tray.

6 Lightly spray with water to help make pretzels crisp. Sprinkle with salt.

6 Bake 8 minutes. Turn pretzels and spray with water. Bake 7 minutes longer. Cool 5 to 10 minutes before serving.

Note: *This recipe calls for salt, or you could use colored sprinkles for a rainbow effect.*

Kids

Kid Fun:

Visit Young's Dairy Farm in Yellow Springs. See cows and other animals, feed goats, climb old tractors, and best of all, eat ice cream!

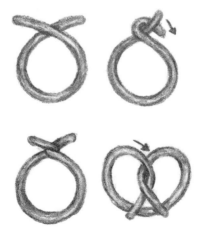

Strawberry Sparklers

A mouthwatering treat for the whole family

Yield: 4 to 6 servings

4 ounces cream cheese, softened	Colored sugar
2 teaspoons powdered sugar	Strawberries, washed and
4 teaspoons milk	patted dry
½ teaspoon vanilla	

- In a mixing bowl, combine cream cheese, powdered sugar, milk, and vanilla until smooth and creamy.
- Pour colored sugar into a shallow dish.
- To serve, allow guests to dip strawberries by their stems into cream cheese mixture, then roll in colored sugar.

Note: *You can make your own colored sugar by mixing 2 drops of food coloring into ¼ cup sugar. Add more milk if needed to get the right consistency.*

Chocolate Pudding Cake

It's magic!

Yield: 4 servings

½ cup all-purpose flour	2 tablespoons vegetable oil
¼ cup sugar	1 teaspoon vanilla
1 tablespoon unsweetened cocoa powder	½ cup sugar
¾ teaspoon baking powder	2 tablespoons unsweetened cocoa powder
¼ teaspoon salt	¾ cup boiling water
¼ cup milk	Whipped cream (optional)

- Preheat oven to 350 degrees.
- Combine flour, ¼ cup sugar, 1 tablespoon cocoa powder, baking powder, and salt in a medium mixing bowl. Stir until well-mixed.
- Add milk, oil and vanilla to dry ingredients. Stir until a smooth batter forms. Pour into an ungreased 1-quart casserole dish.
- Combine ½ cup sugar and 2 tablespoons cocoa powder in a small mixing bowl. Gradually stir in boiling water. Pour evenly over batter.
- Bake about 30 minutes, or until a toothpick comes out clean. Cool on a wire rack for 20 to 30 minutes. Serve with whipped cream.

Note: *We recommend doubling the recipe for a family. This is a fun recipe. After baking, the pudding is on the bottom and the cake is on top!*

People Puppy Chow

Quick, easy and delicious

Yield: 15 to 20 servings

1	stick margarine	1	(12 ounce) box Crispix cereal
1	(12 ounce) package milk chocolate chips	1	(16 ounce) package powdered sugar
1	cup peanut butter		

🕐 *Puppy Chow can be made up to 3 days ahead. Cover tightly.*

- In a saucepan, melt together margarine, chocolate chips and peanut butter over low heat, stirring constantly.
- Place cereal in a large bowl. Pour chocolate mixture over cereal and toss lightly until evenly coated.
- Pour sugar into an 8 gallon trash bag. Add cereal mixture and shake well to coat.

Aunt Vi's
Chocolate Peanut Butter Bites ❄

Loved by generations of "Aunt Vi's" family

Yield: 50 or more bites

1	cup sugar	1	(12 ounce) package semisweet chocolate chips
1	cup light corn syrup	2	(11 ounce) packages butterscotch chips
1½	cups crunchy peanut butter		
6	cups Rice Krispies cereal		

🕐 *May be made up to 3 months ahead and frozen.*

- Combine sugar and corn syrup in a saucepan. Bring to a boil. Remove from heat; immediately stir in peanut butter and cereal. Mix well.
- Pat mixture into an ungreased 10x15-inch jelly-roll pan.
- Melt chocolate and butterscotch chips together in the top of a double boiler. Spread over cereal mixture.
- Chill 15 to 20 minutes. Cut into bite-sized squares or triangles.

After Elsie Mead spent a short time in the hospital, she realized that sick children were being given the same treatment as adults. With the help of the Junior League of Dayton, she made it her goal to provide a hospital just for children, where they could be given the special attention that they required. The JLD took the project to heart, and funnelled most of their efforts and funds into the project. They established a beautiful Junior League shop on First Street, and all the proceeds went to the Children's Hospital. The store was a huge success, and the number one registry for every bride and new mother. The Little Exchange on Park Avenue continues this wonderful fundraiser for the Children's Medical Center.

👣 👣 👣

In 1940, Steele High School closed. It's majestic bronzed lion statue, which was imported from Italy, now sits on the Dayton Art Institute grounds.

Pumpkin Mousse

Plenty of stirring and measuring for kids to do.

Yield: 4 to 6 servings

1½	cups milk	¼	teaspoon cinnamon
½	cup canned pumpkin	⅛	teaspoon ground ginger
1	(3 ounce) package instant vanilla	⅛	teaspoon ground cloves
	pudding mix	1½	cups whipped topping
½	teaspoon ground nutmeg		

○ Stir together milk and pumpkin in a mixing bowl.

○ Add pudding, nutmeg, cinnamon, ginger, and cloves. Whisk until thickened.

○ Fold in whipped topping and chill.

Rosie's Chocolate Toffee Grahams

An EASY treat!

Yield: 12 to 14 servings

1	(1 pound) package graham crackers	1	(12 ounce) package chocolate chips
2	sticks butter	½	cup sliced almonds, toasted (optional)
1	cup brown sugar		

⊙ *Almonds (if using) may be toasted up to 3 days ahead.*

○ Preheat oven to 400 degrees.

○ Line a jelly-roll pan with foil. Break grahams into individual sections. Line pan, edge to edge, with cracker sections.

○ Combine butter and sugar in a small saucepan. Bring to a boil. Reduce heat and simmer 3 minutes. Immediately pour mixture over crackers.

○ Bake 5 minutes.

○ Remove from oven and sprinkle chocolate chips over crackers. As they melt, spread chocolate. Sprinkle almonds over chocolate.

○ Cool completely before breaking into pieces.

African Elephant Ears

Fun to make and fun to eat!

Yield: 1 serving

1	teaspoon butter	1	teaspoon brown sugar
1	flour tortilla		Cinnamon

- Melt butter in a skillet. Add tortilla; fry lightly on each side.
- Sprinkle with sugar and cinnamon.

Flower Cookies

These beautiful blossoms have a sweet surprise inside

Yield: 12 cookies

Cookies

1	stick butter, softened	12	bite-sized Milky Way bars, unwrapped
¼	cup brown sugar		
1	cup flour	12	wooden craft sticks

Decorations

15	large marshmallows	1	tube yellow icing
1	tube icing, any color	12	(7 inch) strips green ribbon

- Cookie "pops" can be made up to 2 days before decorating.

- Preheat oven to 325 degrees.
- Cream butter and sugar in a mixing bowl. Stir in flour. Form dough into a ball. If dough is sticky, stir in more flour, 1 tablespoon at a time.
- Insert a wooden craft stick into the side of each candy bar.
- Place a tablespoon of dough in the palm of your hand. Flatten into a disk. Place a candy bar on a stick in the center of dough and wrap the dough completely around the candy. Repeat with remaining candy. Place cookie pops on a foil-lined baking sheet. Flatten each pop slightly.
- Bake 18 to 20 minutes, or until edges are golden. If cookies split open while baking, gently press edges together while cooling. Cool completely before decorating.
- To decorate, use scissors to snip each marshmallow into 4 round slices.
- Cover the face of each cookie with colored icing. Carefully press 5 marshmallow slices into the frosting to look like flower petals. Fill the center with a dab of yellow icing.
- Tie ribbon to craft sticks to look like leave

Note: *To simplify this recipe, eliminate candy bar filling and use refrigerated sugar cookie dough.*

Kid Fun:
Have you ever been on an Elephant? Take a ride on one at Harveysburg's Renaissance Festival.

How can little kids help in the kitchen?

Three to five year olds can tear lettuce, sort foods by color and shape, sprinkle toppings on pizza, stir mixtures, and pour from a small pitcher.

Five to seven year olds can toast bread in the toaster, crack an egg, mix or shake salad dressing, spread butter on bread, and measure ingredients.

Kids

Crunch Crowned Brownies

Brownies with a splash of color and a dash of crunch!

Yield: 12 to 15 brownies

1	(21 to 23 ounce) package fudge brownie mix	4	tablespoons margarine, melted
1	cup chopped nuts	1	teaspoon cinnamon
⅔	cup quick cooking oats	1	(10 ounce) package M&M plain candies
½	cup light brown sugar		

- Preheat oven to 350 degrees.
- Prepare brownie mix according to package directions for cake-like brownies. Spread batter into a greased 9x13-inch baking pan.
- Combine nuts, oats, sugar, margarine, and cinnamon. Mix well.
- Stir candies into nut mixture and sprinkle over batter.
- Bake 40 to 45 minutes.

Kid Fun:

Go to a Dayton Dragons baseball game and give Heater a hug.

How can bigger kids help in the kitchen?

Seven to ten year olds can read recipes, broil in a toaster oven (with supervision), cut foods with a table knife, grate cheese, and use a blender.

Children older than ten can begin to do most anything in the kitchen with strict supervision.

Make cooking fun and they will remember it for a lifetime!

Delicious Dirt

No messy hands after playing in this dirt!

Yield: 30 servings

1	(20 ounce) package Oreo cookies	3½	cups milk
1	(8 ounce) package cream cheese, softened	1	(12 ounce) container frozen nondairy whipped topping
4	tablespoons butter or margarine		Gummy worms candy (optional)
1	cup powdered sugar		Decorative flower pot (optional)
2	(3 ounce) packages instant vanilla or chocolate pudding		

Crush Oreo cookies up to 2 days ahead.

- Place cookies in a zip-top bag and crush into dirt-like crumbs with a rolling pin.
- In a bowl, mix cream cheese, butter and sugar.
- Combine pudding, milk and whipped topping in a separate bowl. Fold in cream cheese mixture.
- Fill flower pot with pudding mixture. Top with cookie crumbs and gummy worms.
- Serve on paper plates. If desired, you may layer dessert in individual plastic cups and serve.
- Garnish flower pot or cups with fake flowers for a realistic touch!

Homemade Preschool Ice Cream

Making your very own ice cream is always a special treat!

Yield: 1 serving

1	cup milk	6	tablespoons salt
¼	cup sugar		Ice cubes
2	teaspoons vanilla		Zip-top bags

6 Fill a small zip-top bag with milk, sugar and vanilla. Seal tightly.

6 Place small bag in a large zip-top bag. Add salt and ice cubes to large bag. Seal tightly.

6 Squeeze and gently shake bag for 5 to 10 minutes.

Note: *Place the bag in the freezer. Remove after 20 to 25 minutes, or when ice cream is ready.*

Kids

Stuff a miniature marshmallow in the bottom of a sugar cone to prevent ice cream drips.

Hard-Boiled Egg Mice

Kids will smile right back at these little guys!

Yield: 2 egg mice

1	egg	2	fresh chives
1	black olive	1	tiny wedge Swiss cheese
1	radish		

6 Place egg in a small saucepan and cover with cold water. Bring to a boil over high heat. Boil 1 minute, then turn off heat and cover saucepan. Let egg sit in hot water for 12 minutes. Remove from water and let cool.

6 Peel egg; cut in half lengthwise. Place cut-side down on a plate.

6 Cut 2 thin slices of radish. Cut each slice into 2 semicircles. Cut slits in egg for ears and insert radish slices.

6 Cut little circles out of the olive for eyes. Cut slits in egg and insert olive eyes.

6 Lay each egg half on top of a chive for a tail. Garnish with Swiss cheese.

Note: *Use this recipe to teach your child how to boil eggs. Use an egg timer and decorate a dish for presentation.*

Have fun getting clean with Shaving Cream Bath Paint! Squirt shaving cream into each section of a muffin tin. Add food coloring and mix. Be sure to test first, especially on grout, and rinse immediately after bath.

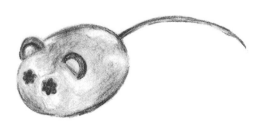

Peter Cauliflower Tail

Kids will enjoy dipping veggies in this bunny bowl

Yield: 3 cups dip

Hummus Dip

6	tablespoons tahini
6	tablespoons fresh lemon juice
6	tablespoons olive oil

4	cloves garlic, crushed
2	(14 ounce) cans chickpeas, drained

Bunny Bowl

1	(4 inch) roll
3	raisins
6	chives
1	small loaf French bread, halved vertically
1	(8 inch) loaf round bread, unsliced

1	medium cauliflower floret
	Raw vegetables, such as baby carrots, celery sticks and radishes
	Toothpicks

🕐 *Make hummus dip up to 3 days ahead. Store in refrigerator.*

❦ To make dip, combine ingredients in a food processor. Process until smooth. If necessary, add water, 1 tablespoon at a time, to the mixture until creamy.

❦ To make the bunny bowl, use the roll to make the bunny's face. For the bunny's eyes and nose, make slits in the roll and insert raisins. For whiskers, poke holes with a toothpick and insert chives. For ears, secure the cut ends of the French bread to the top of the roll with toothpicks.

❦ To make the body of the bunny, cut and scoop out a 3-inch hole in the top of the round bread. Fill with hummus dip. Attach cauliflower floret for a tail. Surround bunny with raw vegetables.

Note: *You may substitute any vegetable dip for the hummus.*

To make sidewalk chalk, mix 1 part plaster of paris, 1 part water and Tempera paint. Pour into small paper cups. Let dry overnight. Peel away paper to expose the chalk.

Spooky Ghost Cookies

Boo! These friendly ghosts will be a yearly favorite

Yield: 32 cookies

9   (2 ounce) vanilla candy coating squares

1   (1 pound) package peanut butter sandwich cookies

1   (4¼ ounce) tube black or brown icing

- Place 6 candy coating squares in a microwave-safe bowl. Microwave on high for 1 to 2 minutes or until melted, stirring once.
- Dip cookies in coating, allowing excess to drip. Place on wax paper and let stand until firm.
- Place remaining 3 squares of candy coating in bowl. Microwave on high for 1 minute, stirring once.
- Dip cookies again in coating, allowing excess to drip. Place on wax paper and let stand until firm.
- Pipe icing eyes and a mouth on each cookie to resemble a ghost.

Note: *We recommend Nabisco Nutter Butter cookies.*

Monster Mouths

This dessert will make your kids smile

Yield: 35 servings

5   medium-size Red Delicious apples, cored

¼   cup orange juice

1   cup creamy peanut butter

1   (10½ ounce) package miniature marshmallows

- Cut each apple into 14 wedges. Brush each wedge with orange juice.
- Spread 1 side of each wedge evenly with peanut butter.
- Press 4 marshmallows into peanut butter on half of the wedges. Top with remaining wedges, peanut-butter-side down.

Make Witches' Wagons. Cut celery into 2-inch pieces. Spread with peanut butter and dot with candy corn or gummy creatures. For wheels, slice carrots into thin coins and secure with toothpicks to the celery. Healthy snack, plus kids love it.

Or create mini Jack O' Lanterns. Draw faces on oranges; cut off the top and scoop out pulp. Pour in orange gelatin that's not quite set. Add Red Hots, candy corn and/or chocolate chips. Chill until set. (Put the oranges in muffin tins to keep them steady while they chill.)

Try these other Halloween party ideas:

Hand Jive. Put a maraschino cherry in each finger of a clear plastic glove. Fill the glove with water and put in the freezer. When frozen, float the ice hand in a bowl of red punch. Or fill clear gloves with popcorn, using candy corn for fingernails. Tie the end with ribbon or skinny black licorice.

Witches' Hats

A small-tip tube of icing makes it easy

Yield: 32 cookies

1   (4¼ ounce) tube orange or red decorating icing
1   (11½ ounce) package fudge-striped shortbread cookies

½   (13 ounce) package milk chocolate kisses, unwrapped (32)

🕑 *Work in an assembly line. It goes much quicker than completing one at a time.*

🌀 Pipe a small line of icing around the center of each cookie.

🌀 Press a chocolate kiss on icing.

🌀 Pipe icing band and bow around base of each kiss.

Easy ideas for Halloween parties:

An Apple a Day: Start with caramel apples, made from kits. Let kids create their own monsters by adding marshmallow eyes, for instance, or licorice legs and arms. (If needed, use icing to make the stuff stick to the apple.)

Corny: Substitute candy corn for chocolate chips in cookies. Or add a big bunch of candy corn and pumpkins to Rice Krispies Treats.

Hot Stuff: Put Red Hots in hot apple cider to add a burst of cinnamon and an eerie red color!

Kid Fun:

See the animals at the Boonshoft Museum of Discovery and learn about local wildlife.

Dracula's Eyes

Don't serve these right before bed!

Yield: 20 eyeballs

½   cup peanut butter
3   tablespoons butter, softened
1   cup sifted powdered sugar
4   ounces vanilla candy coating

20   M&M plain candies
      Red and black decorating gel icing

🌀 Mix together peanut butter and butter in a mixing bowl. Gradually stir in powdered sugar. Shape into 1-inch balls and place on wax paper. Let stand 20 minutes or until dry.

🌀 Melt candy coating in a small saucepan over low heat. Dip balls, one at a time, into coating. Let excess drip off and place on wax paper. Immediately press an M&M into the center of each ball. Let stand until coating is firm.

🌀 Add a dot of black gel to the center of each M&M for a pupil. Drizzle red gel onto balls for bloodshot eyes.

Gingerbread Cookies ❄

Your home will be filled with the wonderful holiday scent of gingerbread

Kids

Yield: 3½ to 4 dozen cookies

Cookies

2	cups sugar	8	cups all-purpose flour
1	cup vegetable shortening	1½	teaspoons ground ginger
1	cup light molasses	1	teaspoon cinnamon
2	egg yolks, room temperature	1	teaspoon allspice
2	teaspoons baking soda	¾	teaspoon salt
1	cup hot water		

Frosting

2	egg whites	½	teaspoon light corn syrup
2½	cups sugar	1	teaspoon vanilla extract
½	cup water		

🕐 *Begin recipe at least 2 hours ahead of baking time.*

ⓖ Preheat oven to 350 degrees.

ⓖ Combine sugar, shortening, molasses, and egg yolks.

ⓖ Mix baking soda and hot water together in a separate bowl. Stir until dissolved. Add to molasses mixture.

ⓖ Mix in flour, ginger, cinnamon, allspice, and salt. Cover and refrigerate at least 2 hours, or until firm.

ⓖ Roll dough ¼-inch thick on a floured board.

ⓖ For friendship rings, cut dough with a floured scalloped circular cutter. Poke a hole in the center of each. Place cookies about 1 inch apart on a lightly greased baking sheet.

ⓖ For gingerbread friends, cut with a floured gingerbread boy cutter. To make gingerbread girls, collect dough scraps and attach to form a skirt and hair. Poke holes in tops with a straw to provide hanger holes, if desired. Place on a lightly greased baking sheet about 2 inches apart.

ⓖ Bake 10 to 12 minutes or until edges brown. Cool on pan for 1 minute. Transfer to a wire rack to cool completely.

ⓖ To prepare frosting, beat egg whites to form soft peaks.

ⓖ In a saucepan, combine sugar, water and syrup. Bring to a boil; cook and stir until sugar dissolves. Pour slowly at first, then faster, over egg whites, beating constantly until thick.

ⓖ Add vanilla and beat until almost cool. When spread, frosting should look glossy, not dull.

ⓖ Frost cooled cookies and decorate with raisins, currants or sprinkles, or pipe flowerets around rings. Store in an airtight container. Thread ribbon or fishing line through holes to hang as ornaments.

Sometimes it's okay to play with your food...make Edible Peanut Butter Clay! Mix 4 tablespoons peanut butter, 1 tablespoon honey, 1 tablespoon wheat germ, and 2½ tablespoons powdered milk. Mix. Sculpt. Eat!

Easy Homemade "Gingerbread" House

Using graham crackers makes this house as much fun to assemble as it is to decorate!

Yield: 1 house

Frosting

2	eggs, separated	
4	cups powdered sugar	**Empty squeeze bottle**

House

6 graham cracker squares, honey or chocolate

1 half-pint milk carton, rinsed, dried and stapled shut

Decorations and Scenery

Candy canes
Hard candy sticks
Hard candy mints
M&M plain candies
M&M mini baking bits
Sour gummy strings
Gumdrops

Orange-slice candy
Spearmint-leaf candy
Sandwich cookies
Red licorice laces, vines and bits
Sugar cones
Mini pretzel twists
Shredded coconut

🕐 *Clean milk container and staple shut. Collect all decorating items before starting.*

🌀 To make frosting, beat egg whites in a mixing bowl until peaks form.

🌀 Mix in 3 cups powdered sugar. Slowly beat in more sugar until frosting is thick, but will still squeeze through a squeeze bottle (an empty ketchup bottle works well). Spoon frosting into bottle.

🌀 To assemble house, trim 4 cracker squares as needed to fit the sides of the milk carton. (Nibbling is an easy way to trim them!) Squeeze a layer of frosting on one side of crackers and press frosting side of crackers onto sides of carton.

🌀 Squeeze a thick layer of frosting onto 1 side of remaining 2 crackers. Press frosting side of crackers onto top of carton for the roof.

🌀 Squeeze frosting to fill in the triangle-shaped spaces of the milk carton at the front and back of the roof.

🌀 Squeeze a thick stripe of frosting to fill in each corner of the house. Press licorice or candy sticks into frosting.

🌀 To decorate, use frosting to attach candy to the roof. Add more candy to make a door, chimney, windows, and bushes. Let the house dry overnight.

🌀 To make a tree, slice about 12 spearmint-leaf candies in half so that each candy gives you 2 thin leaves.

🌀 Turn a sugar cone upside down. Cover the entire cone with frosting. Starting at the bottom, press a row of leaves into the frosting. Add more rows of leaves, overlapping the rows as you move up the cone.

🌀 Make smaller trees by using only part of the cone.

🌀 Arrange finished house and trees on a piece of cardboard large enough to hold them. Use frosting to attach house and trees to the cardboard.

6   To make a fence, attach mini pretzel twists to the cardboard with dots of frosting. To make a sidewalk, squeeze a path with frosting. Press M&M's into the path.

6   Sprinkle coconut over the whole scene to look like snow.

Sugar Plum Fairy Wands

Every fairy princess will want one of these delicious wands

Yield: 6 stars

4	cups large marshmallows
4	tablespoons butter or margarine
4	(2 ounce) squares vanilla candy coating
6	cups Rice Krispies cereal

6	(12x⅜ inch) wooden dowels
	Melted vanilla candy coating, assorted candies, multicolored edible glitter, and thin satin ribbon for decoration

⏲ *Plan to begin recipe at least 1 hour before decorating. Stars can be made up to 2 days ahead.*

6   Microwave marshmallows, butter and candy coating in a 6-quart microwave-safe bowl on high for 3 to 3½ minutes, or until melted, stirring once after 2 minutes. Stir in cereal. Press into a lightly greased 10x15-inch jelly-roll pan.

6   Place an 8-inch star-shaped cutter on warm mixture; cut with a knife around edges of cutter. Remove trimmings and press together into the same thickness. Repeat procedure, cutting stars and reshaping remaining mixture. Cool stars on a wire rack for at least 1 hour.

6   Insert a dowel into each star between 2 points. Decorate as desired, tying ribbons around dowels.

Make Soap Crayons. Add 1 cup of mild powdered laundry soap (such as Ivory Snow) to bowl. Add drops of food coloring. Slowly add water by the teaspoon until the soap is liquid. Stir well. Pour into ice cube trays and set in a sunny, dry spot for a few days. Allow to harden. Great for writing on sinks or bathtubs.

Marshmallow Candy Snowman

Sweet treat that's a piece of cake to make!

Yield: 1 snowman

1	wedge angel food cake	1	piece black licorice, snipped into tiny pieces
3-4	tablespoons whipped cream or topping	1	piece fruit roll-up
5	pretzel sticks	2	gumdrops
3	large marshmallows	2	pieces red or black licorice

6 Lay cake wedge flat on a serving plate. Spoon whipped cream over wedge for snow.

6 Push 2 pretzel sticks through a stack of 3 marshmallows to create a snowman's body. Stick 2 more pretzel sticks into the sides of the middle marshmallow to form arms. Press in licorice pieces for facial features and buttons.

6 Use a fruit roll-up to make a scarf and gumdrops for a hat.

6 Make skis out of red or black licorice. Place skis on top of snow on cake. Use final pretzel stick to anchor snowman to skis.

Homemade Finger Paint

Tiny fingers will love this paint

Yield: 2½ cups — plenty to divide into 4 to 5 colors

⅓	cup cornstarch	2	cups cold water
3	tablespoons sugar		Food coloring

6 Combine cornstarch, sugar and water in a 1-quart saucepan.

6 Cook and stir over medium heat about 5 minutes, or until thickened. Remove from heat.

6 Divide the mixture into separate cups or containers. Tint individual cups with different colors of food coloring. Stir several times until cool. Store in an airtight container.

Note: *The paint works best if you use it the same day it is made. Great activity for learning to mix colors; i.e., red + blue = purple.*

Kid Fun:
At Carriage Hill Farm, experience rural life from the 1800s, as recreated on this working historical farm.

Kid Fun:
Gather together buckets, paintbrushes, rollers, etc. Fill the buckets with water and let kids "paint" the driveway, sidewalks, even the house!

Rudolph the Red-Nosed Reindeer Sandwiches

Sing Rudolph the Red-Nosed Reindeer while making these adorable sandwiches

Yield: 1 sandwich

Peanut butter	1 maraschino cherry or red M&M
Jelly (optional)	2 raisins
1 slice bread	6 pretzel sticks

- Spread peanut butter and jelly on bread. Cut in half diagonally. Place the 2 pieces together with peanut butter and jelly to the inside. Lay sandwich on a plate with cut side toward top of plate.
- Place cherry on the bottom point to make a nose. Add raisins for eyes and pretzel sticks for antlers.

Papier Mache

Perfect outside summer activity

2 cups cold water	Newspaper cut into 1x15-inch
1½-1¾ cups all-purpose flour	strips

- Whisk water and flour in a large bowl until smooth. Mixture should be the same thickness as heavy cream.
- Coat a mold with one layer of newspaper strips that have been dipped in water.
- Dip more strips in flour mixture and lay over first layer of strips. Repeat until mold is well-coated.
- Let stand until dry and hard. Paint as desired.

Note: *Molded clay or an inflated balloon makes a good mold.*

Kid Fun:

Have some indoor fun. Make tents by covering tables and chairs with old sheets or blankets. To complete the camping theme, spread a blanket on the floor and have an indoor picnic.

It takes patience, praise and setting a good example to help young children learn how to behave properly at mealtime. As early as age 3 or 4, they can begin to learn the basics: arriving at the table with clean hands; chewing with their mouths closed; sharing news of the day; listening to the conversation without interrupting others; and using napkins and utensils. As kids get older, they gradually learn the more subtle rules adults observe. Children under 7 should be given permission to be excused from the table once they're finished eating. It's expecting a lot for them to sit still if the meal goes on for too long.

Kool-Aid Playdough

Save some money and let your kids be creative and happy

Yield: 3 cups

2½ cups flour	1 package unsweetened drink
½ cup salt	mix, such as Kool Aid
1 tablespoon powdered alum, or	2 cups water
cream of tartar	2 tablespoons vegetable oil

๏ Mix together flour, salt, alum, and drink mix. Set aside.

๏ In a medium saucepan, bring water and oil to a boil. Remove from heat and pour over flour mixture.

๏ Stir until well-mixed, then knead dough to a smooth consistency.

๏ Store in an airtight container or a zip-top bag.

Gunk

This will "wow" you as much as it does your kids

Yield: 3 cups (1 glob of gunk)

1 cup water	1⅓ cups warm water
1 cup white glue	4 teaspoons Borax
2 tablespoons non-toxic paint or a	
few drops food coloring	

๏ Combine 1 cup water, glue and paint.

๏ In a separate container, mix 1⅓ cups warm water and Borax.

๏ Pour glue mixture into Borax mixture. Do not mix! Lift resulting solid mass out of liquid and knead.

๏ Store in an airtight container.

Note: *Keep this one off the carpeting!*

Giant Bubble Liquid

Bubbles are always a favorite!

Yield: 5¾ cups

5 cups water (distilled works best)	2 tablespoons glycerin
½ cup Joy or Dawn liquid dish	
soap	

๏ Slowly add water to soap.

๏ Gently mix in glycerin.

Note: *Glycerin is available in pharmacies.*

Kid Fun:
Go to Carillon Park for a ride on a miniature train.

In 1825, people came from miles around to see the first full circus to visit Dayton. The circus pitched its tent in the barnyard of Reid's Inn.

One of the most exciting events in my life happened in 1911, when Uncle Orv took me, my sister and my cousin up for a flight. We were the first children in the U.S. to fly!
—Ivonette Wright Miller

Children's Birthday Party Ideas

❀ ❀ ❀

THE GREAT OUTDOORS PARTY

Ages: 3 to 10 *(change activities according to age of the children)*

Menu:

Pigs in a Blanket
Vegetables and Dip
People Puppy Chow (page 297)
Delicious Dirt (page 300)

Decorations:

- Hang pictures of birds and other animals from the overhead light fixtures.
- Make different footprints of animals and put them around the party room.
- Cut out trees and shrubs from large pieces of paper to hang on the walls.
- Decorate the table with potting moss.

Favors:

- Put each child's name on an empty flower pot with a glue pen.
- Fill the empty flower pots with such party favors as animal stickers, animal coloring books, animal crackers, zoo discount coupons, small potted plants, or children's gardening tools.

Games and Activities:

1. Make bird feeders.
    - Take pinecones and tie a string around the top, dip the edges in peanut butter and then dip in birdseed.
    - You can also use empty milk or cream cartons instead of pinecones. First, cut openings on the opposite sides of a clean carton and coat with non-toxic paint. Then glue Popsicle stick shingles onto the roof. For the perch, poke holes just under the openings and slip a stick through the holes. Fill the bottom with birdseed.
2. Make food chains to hang on trees by stringing popcorn, dried fruit, raisins, and cranberries.
3. Make sunprints.
    - Purchase paper that is sensitive to light from a local museum or camera shop.
    - Place flowers and leaves on the paper and set in the sunlight. The outline will show up on the paper.
4. Decorate small flower pots and plant a seed or small plant inside.
5. Send the children on a scavenger hunt in the yard to search for natural objects such as rocks, leaves, moss, etc.

A Beach Party

Ages: 4 to 10 (change activities according to age of the children)

Menu:

Serve the food on Frisbees® instead of paper plates.

Sandwiches/Pizza

Strawberry Sparklers (page 296) (Let the children do their own.)

Hash Brown Potato Casserole (page 292)

Aunt Vi's Chocolate Peanut Butter Bites (page 297)

Decorations:

- Cover the table with fish net, plastic fish, and crêpe paper the color of seaweed.
- Use a large fish bowl for the centerpiece. Fill it with shells or other beach items.
- Ask the children to wear their swimsuits and bring beach towels to sit on.
- Place beach balls and other blow-up beach toys around the house or have them outside in the yard.

Favors:

Use fish nets, onion bags or small beach buckets for goodie bags. Fill them with "Go Fish" cards, fish-shaped jelly candy, saltwater taffy, Frisbees®, sunglasses, or waterguns. Let the children take home their Frisbee® plates.

Games and Activities:

1. Make paper and pasta lei.
   - Paint pieces of uncooked ziti and let them dry.
   - Cut out bunches of three-petaled flowers from colored crêpe paper sheets.
   - Tie a knot at one end of a three-foot piece of string and thread the other end through the eye of a large sewing needle.
   - Sew through the centers of a dozen or so flowers and ziti. When finished, tie a knot at the end and tie the ends of the string together.
2. Decorate sunglasses or picture frames with seashells, paint, or paint markers. You can also glue on plastic fish.
3. Make tissue-paper fish. Trace two large fish on paper. Have the children decorate their fish with stickers or markers. Glue the sides of the fish together and stuff with tissue paper.
4. Jump-rope splash. Have the children hold a full glass of water while they jump rope and see who can spill the least amount of water.

THE MYSTERY PARTY
Ages: 7 to 10

Menu:
Hamburgers
Carrot and Celery Sticks with Tasha's Dip (page 62)
Chips and Pretzels
Crunch Crowned Brownies (page 300) or Cupcakes

Decorations:
- Decorate a red paper tablecloth with cutouts of large black footprints or question marks.
- Fill a large jar with candy. When the children arrive, have them guess how many pieces of candy are in the jar. At the end of the party, the child whose guess is closest wins the jar of candy.
- Decorate cupcakes spelling out certain messages that are mixed up. Have the children guess the mystery message.

Favors:
Decorate paper bags with question marks and fill with disguises, flashlights, magnifying glasses, cards, or magic tricks.

Activities:
1. Play a mystery game.
   - Place children in small groups and give them coded messages that will lead them throughout the house or yard, and eventually to a treasure chest.
   - For your treasure chest, decorate a shoe box with black paper and gold marker trim, and fill it with goodies. Be sure to allow each team to find its own treasure chest.
2. Gift wrap everyday objects and pass them around a circle. Let the children guess what they are.
3. Write coded messages stating something about each child present at the party. Have the group decipher which child each message describes.
4. Have a helper go into another room and use everyday items to make noises, one at a time. Let the children guess which item is making each noise.

Special Thanks

The Junior League of Dayton, Ohio, Inc. respectfully thanks the following businesses that so generously donated products and services for the production of Causing A Stir. *We are deeply indebted to you for all of your financial support, creativity and enthusiasm for this project.*

❦ ❦ ❦

Catherine Sherk

duo communications, inc.
For designing the beautiful cover and recipe section dividers.

❦ ❦ ❦

Dayton Daily News

For their support and advertising space.

❦ ❦ ❦

National City Bank

For their financial advice and support.

❦ ❦ ❦

Carrie Scarff

Five Rivers MetroPark
For providing the section divider art of RiverScape.

❦ ❦ ❦

Kevin Maxwell

Ikon Office Solutions
For the donation of a lease on a copier.

❦ ❦ ❦

Jim Varley

Champion Paper Company
For the countless reams of paper.

❦ ❦ ❦

Thomas Hartzell

Deck the Walls
Specialists in art, custom framing and design.

Special Friends

*The Junior League of Dayton, Ohio, Inc. gratefully thanks the
many friends who, by their participation, have made possible
this cookbook. We are grateful for your expertise, counsel,
support, creativity, and generous donations.*

6 6 6

Keith & Pam Browning
Vins Extraordinaire
For the wonderful wine suggestions and information on wines.

6 6 6

Ruth Deddens & Linda Snyder
Our supportive sustainers for sharing their wealth
of wisdom from our first cookbook, *Discover Dayton*.

6 6 6

Melanie Dymek
For the creative recipe page illustrations.

6 6 6

Scott Grimes
For his artistic support of the recipe section dividers.

To Our Cookbook Committee Families:
*Our heartfelt thanks and love goes to our wonderful
families for all of their endless sacrifices, constant support, and
encouragement for this seemingly never-ending project.*

JLD Cookbook Contributors

The Junior League of Dayton, Ohio, Inc. fondly thanks our members, families and friends who contributed recipes and food memories to our book. To the many members and friends who hosted Testing Parties and tested recipes, our sincere gratitude for your time, money, advice, and discerning tastes, ensuring that our recipes are fabulous. It is our sincere hope that no one has been overlooked.

Tricia Ackerman
Lisa Aidt
Carol Allen
Kim Allen
Will Allen
Madonna Allread
Nancy Alway
H. Brockman Anderson, Jr.
H. Brockman Anderson, III
Heather Anderson
Margy Anderson
Debbie Anglin
Laura Arber
Harriet Argue
Linda Augustine
Leslie Baas
Linda Baker
Patti Ballard
Lori Barhorst
Sarah Barlage
Marilyn Barnwall
Angie Barth
Abe Basset
Helen Bates
Chris Bausman
Denise Bay
Jill Bayley
Ann Becker
Gayle Becker
Nikki Behr
Paige Benedict
Kara Bernsen
Sherri Besselman
Moira Betts
Natalie Bettcher
Gretchen Beust
Terry Bevis
Bob Bickel
Pam Bickel
Molly Bishop
Patti Blessing
Martha Alice Boatner
Tracy Bockhorst
Debbie Bolmida
Kathy Boomershine
Susan Bradley
Maria Brennan
Sherri Bricker

Patty Bringman
Yvonne Brinkman
Corinne Broad
Anita Brothers
Diana Brown
Karin Brown
Margaret Brown
Kaki Browner
Olive Brubaker
Marnie Whaley Buckel
Pat Campbell
Leslie Carson
Carol Cartwright
Ann Casebere
Marilyn Casebere
Diane Castro
Caroline Chamberlain
Deanna Chapman
Lestrita Chappell
Patricia Christensen
Holly Clark
Pam Clark
Liz Cline
Lynn Collins
Stephanie Collins
Erin Conaghan
Laura Conley
Dante Connell
Judy Cook
Jane Corbly
Becky Coughlin
Patricia Cox
Beth Coy
Carrie Craig
Joanne Cronin
Marian Crawford
Suzanne Crooke
Molly Cross
Tara Crowl
Gail Cumming
Annabelle Cummings
Jim Cushing
Carol Creager
Barbara Crutchfield
Jan Culver
Tracy Danehy
Lisa Darnell
Stephen Darnell

Jill Farley Davis
Phyllis C. Davis
Amy Deal
Jennifer Dehner
Barb Deitenmayer
Valerie Deluca
Wendy Derieux
Carol Dickerson
Mary Dietz
Carole Ann Disher
Julie Dill
Alicia Dixon
Cherie Dixon
Kimberly Komro Donnelly
Heidi Donnelly
Mary Lynn Dorow
Leslie Douglas
Alison Duchene
Joan Dudley
Michael R. Duff
Ann Dunham
Susan Dziubek
Marty Ebeling
Rose Eckerle
Bobbie Eckstein
Pattie Edmonson
Sally Kindrick Ekkens
Thressa Ekkens
Debra Elliot
Mindy Ellis
Amy Emanuel
Laura Ensbrenner
Helene Erhart
Carolyn Spring Ettinger
Deborah Evans
Kristin Evans
Karen Hurley Evans
Sally Ten Eyck
Barb Farley
Sara Faust
Sara Feldmiller
Laurie Fink
Sally W. Fisher
Kyra Fleming
Janelle Forbes
Jerry Ford
Judy Ford
Valerie Fortin

Theresa Franklin
Laurie Franz
Susan Freeh
Liz Fultz
Jane Gamble
Oscar Gamble
Gloria Gardner
Beth Garey
Cindy Garner
Maureen Geehan
Sean Geehan
Stephanie Geehan
Elizabeth Georgin
Victoria Ghilaga
Denise Gibbs
Colleen Gilardi
Kim Gilbert
Christine Moore Goad
Rachel Ekkens Goad
Shirley Goad
Robin Golden
Diana Grabeman
Laura Gruhl
Gigi Guillen
Sandy Gutermuth
Paula Guttenberg
Alana Haberman
Denise Hale
Linda Hallinan
Shannon Hallinan
Dana K. Halverson
Ardith P. Hamilton
Margie Harrell
Kerry Harlan
Kelly Harrison
Connie Harstel
Cathleen Hart
James D. Harvey
Sherry Mills Hayes
Rachel Hernandez
Patti Highfill
Nora Hillard
Susan Hodapp
Lisa Hoffman
Ann Hohne
Isaac Hollon
Emily DuChene Holt
Nancy Horlacher
Vicki Howard
Kim Howell
Milly Hubler
Dawn Huff
Pokey Huffman
Shawna Huffman
Tony Huffman
Ann Hughes
Kelly Huntington
Linda Hurt
Jane Huson

Beverly Hyman
Mimi Ilg
Amy Ingram
Sandy Ingberg
Rebecca Cress Ingebo
Jean Ireland
Martha Jacobs
Tracy Janess
Debbie Janis
Macy Janney
Natalie Jaycox
Susan Jenkins
Christian Jennings
Dawn Johnson
Hilary Johnson
Linda Johnson
Amale Joseph
Colleen Joss
Jennifer Kane
Sharon Karcher
Sonnie Kasch
Susan Kathol
Susan Kavanaugh
Kristina Kean
Jane Key
Jenny Kinsey
Barbara Kleet
Jo Kleinhenz
Jack Koepke
Rebecca Koesters
Kristen Konnerth
Francie Kowal
Suzanne Kreusch
Sherry Kroger
Jan Kurdin
Nicole Kussman
Cate Laden
Sherry Lambert
Sally Lanz
Ann LaPrise
Tracy Laughlin
Jean Laughner
Jody Lee
Clara Legeay
Faye Leist
Deborah LiBrandi
Lisa Lieberman
Kim Lindley
Susan Maguire Lipowicz
Linda Little
Jean Lochner
Kevin Lowden
Kathy Lutz
Barbara Macaulay
Joan Macaulay
Teri Macaulay
Stacy Mach
Evelyn M. Mackenzie

Mary Jo Maffie
Wendolyn Magato
Moni McGill Malacos
Linda Maloney
Kathleen Marshall
Debra Martin
Diana Martin
Judy Martini
Trina Maschino
Karleen Materne
Stephanie Maxwell
Lee McCormick
Regina McCurdy
Marianne McFall
Kristine McGee
Carrie McHenry
Carla McKelvey
JoAnn McKelvey
Amy McMillan
Sheryl McMillan
Carolyn Medford
Karen Blair Medford
Linda Meily
Georgia Mergler
Joe Mergler
Gerry Meyer
Allyson Miller
Caroline Elizabeth Miller
Chrissie Miller
Jane Miller
Linda Miller
Pam Miller
Vail Miller
Denise Molen
Martha Moody
Susan Mooney
Melanie Moore
Pat Moore
Sandy Moore
Pam Morrow
Amy Mount
Melanie Mousaian
Dana Muckerheide
Lisa Mullen
Loreen Murray
Leslie Nagel
Holly Nielsen
Kristin Marie Oberheu
Kathy O'Neill
Mary Ellen Oomens
Maxine Orr
Dottie Ostermueller
Ellie Otto
Missy Pask
Jennifer Patterson
Lisa Paul
Joanna Penry
Polly Petricola

Suzanne Petrusch
Kari Pfarrer
Marsha Pfeiffer
Diane R. Philips
Jennifer Pickard
Stephanie Pitcock
Carol Pohl
Michele Potts
Paula Powers
Sharon Probst
Leslie Prondzinski
Debbie Proud
Betty Pupko
Paige Purmort
Lucinda Ragland
Beth Rank
Chris Rankin
Jennie Ravlin
Cindy Raymond
Sue Rehorst
Christine Reilly
Jim Reilly
Lynn Ret
Angela C. Retzios
Kellie Rhodes
Pam Ridings
Sally H. Riffle
Joann Ringer
Sally Rintoul
Gerry Anne Rocco
Nancy Rose
Anne Ross
Andrea Roth
Susan Rudd
Kristen Russ
Rita Ryan
Marylou Salmon
Glenda Salyer
Ellen Samuels
Kim Saylor
Linda Scaia
Erin Scanlon
Cindy Scarff
Molly Schellin
Lori Scherger
Christine Schmitt
Bev Schneider
C.J. Schoeff
Laura Wood Schofield
Carole Schram
Helen Shackelton
Cindy Shafer
Martha Shaker
Karen Shaner
Joni Sherk
Kirsten Sherk
Maridel Sherk
Jan Sherman
Jan Shie

Lori Simms
Carolyn Shockey
Jackie Shultz
Lisa Sickinger
Binford Sievers
Sheilah Johnson Silvio
Mary Pat Simmons
Sharon Sisco
Terri Sisco
Cindy Sisto
Amy Skardon
Becky Slanker
Judy Slanker
Linda Smalley
Audrey Smith
Jacinda Santon Smith
Julie Smith
Tina Smith
Karla Snead
Linda Snyder
Christie Sodler
Karen Solarek
Karen Sollars
Michelle Sollars
Diane Sommer
Lori Sowder
Julie Sparks
Sharon Sprowl
Mary Staley
Martha Steinkamp
Dorothy Stoermer
Judy Wade Stoermer
Michelle Storgion
Kathy Strickler
Tammy Struder
Peggy Stutzman
Kelly Tangeman
Julie Taylor
Martha Taylor
Nancy Orr Taylor
Sallie Taylor
Julie Teeters
Lisa Theado
Melinda Thesing
Kate Thiel
Melodie Thiel
Joey Thiele
Phyllis Thompson
Vicki Thompson
Laura Thurston
Joanne Totleben
Amy Townley
Judi Tracy
David Treese
Molly Treese
Virginia Treese
Catherine Tsatalis
Michelle Turner
Vallery Tzagournis

Kelly Uhl
Kim Ulowetz
Amy Uttermohlen
Cindy Uttermohlen
Margot Varley
Nancy Varley
Ellen Vaughn
Nicci Vickroy
Gwen Voiles
Michelle Vollmar
Jane Wachna
Patty Wachna
Bill Wade
Jacque Wade
Jeanne Wade
Jim Wade
Kim Wade
Leigh Bradley Wade
Abby Wagner
Cynthia Wagner
Maureen Wagner
Jennie Walcott
Julie Walker
Sharon Rushing Walter
Kathleen Walworth
Susan Watkins
Jana Watson
Pam Watson
Ragan Watson
Jill Weisblatt
Chip Wenz
Debbie Wenz
Sondra Whaley
Betsy Whitney
Cathy Wiley
Danielle M. Williams
JoAnn Williams
Susan Teach Williams
Sue Seifert Williams
R. C. Willie
Jane Winch
Julie Beyer Winch
Karen Wolters
Irene Pang Wong
Kristin Dehner Woodward
Peirce F. Woodward
Stacey Yarger
Joyce Young
Katrina Young
Linda Young
Irene Valen Zalants
Carolyn Zangri
Maureen Walsh Zavakos
Amy Zebney
Kathleen Zehenney
Tonya Zengel
Kathy Zimmer
Nanci Zink
Nikki Zippilli

Resources

The Junior League of Dayton, Ohio, Inc. sincerely thanks the following sources and individuals for their contributions to the many varied components of our text. Your willingness to share food tips, fond memories and engaging stories about Dayton make reading the cookbook a true pleasure!

Business News
American City Business Journals

Dayton, Ohio Chamber of Commerce

Cooking the Wright Way
Melba Hunt
Kettering-Moraine Museum
1998

Dayton Daily News
Cox Ohio Publishing

Dayton: The Cradle of Creativity
Dale Huffman and Andy Snow
Towery Publishing
1998

Emily Post's Entertaining
Harper Collins

Fifty Treasures
of the Dayton Art Institute
Published to commemorate
the DAI 50th Anniversary
Dayton Art Institute
1969

For the Love of Dayton
Theresa Zumwald
Dayton Daily News
1996

The Grand Eccentrics
Mark Bernstein
Orange Frazer Press
1996

Oakwood: The Far Hills
Bruce W. Ronald and Virginia Ronald
Sponsored by the Oakwood Historical Society
Reflections Press
1983

Sports in Dayton:
A Bicentennial Retrospective
Ritter Collett
Landfall Press
1996

Mark Adams
Suzy Bassani
Abe J. Bassett
Bill Bombeck
Cheryl Brandewie
Bill Castro
Jaci Clark
Ritter Collett
Peter Danis
Tim Davis

Dax Dunbar
Linda Mercuri Fischbach
Roger Glass
Jay Haverstick
Molly Hegman
Ann Heller
Laura Frock Hinders
Elizabeth Upham Howell
Allison Janney
Mike Kelly

Cynthia Klinck
Mark Light
Dennis McCarthy
Alex Mohaikhi
Terry Morris
Alex Nyerges
Peggy Post
Oliver Purnell
Kevin M. Rochlitz
James Rounds

Anne Kearney Sand
Nanci Schaefer
Howard Solganik
D.L. Stewart
Jane Thomas
Ming Tsai
Rob Urbanowicz
Lisa Wagner
Edin Dino Zonic

Index

320

ᴳ

LIGHT AND HEALTHY

❝ M ❞

MANGOES

MUSHROOMS

❝ N ❞

NUTS

            ◦◦ 𝒬 ◦◦

❀ R ❀

RASPBERRIES

RICE

❦

SALAD DRESSINGS

SALADS

SANDWICHES

SEAFOOD

SOUPS

SPINACH

SQUASH *(also see Zucchini)*

STRAWBERRIES

SWEET POTATOES

ᴼᴼ 𝒯 ᴼᴼ

Junior League of Dayton, Ohio, Inc.
26 Brown Street
Dayton, Ohio 45402
Phone: (937)222-5541
Fax: (937)222-8646
E-mail: jldohio@earthlink.net
Or order through our Website: jldohio.com

Name: _____

Address: _____

City: _____ State: _____ Zip: _____

    Number of copies _____ @ $22.95 per copy _____

    Sales tax @ $ 1.49 per copy _____

    Shipping and handling @ $ 4.50 per copy _____

    Total: $ _____

❏ Check enclosed (payable to the Junior League of Dayton-Cookbook)

❏ Visa Card _____ ; _____ ; _____
      (card number)   (expiration date)   (signature)

❏ MasterCard _____ ; _____ ; _____
      (card number)   (expiration date)   (signature)

- -

Junior League of Dayton, Ohio, Inc.
26 Brown Street
Dayton, Ohio 45402
Phone: (937)222-5541
Fax: (937)222-8646
E-mail: jldohio@earthlink.net
Or order through our Website: jldohio.com

Name: _____

Address: _____

City: _____ State: _____ Zip: _____

    Number of copies _____ @ $22.95 per copy _____

    Sales tax @ $ 1.49 per copy _____

    Shipping and handling @ $ 4.50 per copy _____

    Total: $ _____

❏ Check enclosed (payable to the Junior League of Dayton-Cookbook)

❏ Visa Card _____ ; _____ ; _____
      (card number)   (expiration date)   (signature)

❏ MasterCard _____ ; _____ ; _____
      (card number)   (expiration date)   (signature)